"*The Coaching Kaleidoscope* provides a terrific overview of the most recent ideas in leadership development and coaching. In this book, scholars and practitioners, recognized authorities and rising stars in leadership thought, paint a colourful and multifaceted picture of how clinical perspective can help not only transform individuals and teams, but also create better places to work. Impressive in the range of techniques and cases discussed, solid in its theoretical underpinnings, and yet accessible, this book will guide you through the journey of becoming a more effective coach and a more reflective leader."

> —**Natalia Karelaia**, *Assistant Professor of Decision Sciences, INSEAD*

"*The Coaching Kaleidoscope* brings together the reflections of different practitioners as a way to promote learning and help executives discover their 'inner journey'. Manfred Kets de Vries takes the 'clinical perspective' one step further in establishing a coaching culture in organizations, taking the reader where they have not been before."

> —**Jean-Claude Noël**, *Adjunct Clinical Professor of Management &*
> *IGLC Programme Director, INSEAD, former Group COO, Christie's*

"Drawing on years of experience in leadership coaching Professor Kets de Vries, and his team of brilliant co-authors and contributors, invite us to move beyond the focus on coaching for just a lucky few in a management team. To make an organization vital, innovative, and the best place to work, organizations need to create a coaching culture. By allowing employees to share a conversation, an organization will create an environment in which knowledge is shared, employees' voices are heard, and where employees are engaged and empowered."

> —**Svetlana N. Khapova**, *Associate Professor of Career Studies & Director of*
> *Doctoral Education, VU University Amsterdam, The Netherlands*

THE COACHING KALEIDOSCOPE

Insights from the inside

Manfred Kets de Vries

Clinical Professor of Leadership Development and the Raoul de Vitry d'Avaucourt Chaired Professor of Leadership Development, INSEAD Global Leadership Centre, France

Laura Guillén

Assistant Professor, European School of Management and Technology, Germany

Konstantin Korotov

Associate Professor, European School of Management and Technology, Germany

Elizabeth Florent-Treacy

Associate Director, Research, INSEAD Global Leadership Centre, France

First published 2010 by
PALGRAVE MACMILLAN

Palgrave Macmillan in the UK is an imprint of Macmillan Publishers Limited,
registered in England, company number 785998, of Houndmills, Basingstoke,
Hampshire RG21 6XS.

Palgrave Macmillan in the US is a division of St Martin's Press LLC,
175 Fifth Avenue, New York, NY 10010.

Palgrave Macmillan is the global academic imprint of the above companies
and has companies and representatives throughout the world.

Palgrave® and Macmillan® are registered trademarks in the United States,
the United Kingdom, Europe and other countries

ISBN 978–0–230–23998–2

This book is printed on paper suitable for recycling and made from fully
managed and sustained forest sources. Logging, pulping and manufacturing
processes are expected to conform to the environmental regulations of the
country of origin.

A catalogue record for this book is available from the British Library.

A catalog record for this book is available from the Library of Congress.

10   9   8   7   6   5   4   3   2   1
19   18   17   16   15   14   13   12   11   10

Printed and bound in Great Britain by
CPI Antony Rowe, Chippenham and Eastbourne

CONTENTS

CONTENTS

PART THREE: CREATING BETTER PLACES TO WORK

LIST OF FIGURES AND TABLES

Figures

Tables

LIST OF CONTRIBUTORS

EDITORS

Manfred F. R. Kets de Vries brings a different view to the much-studied subjects of leadership and the dynamics of individual and organizational change. Bringing to bear his knowledge and experience of economics (Econ. Drs., University of Amsterdam), management (ITP, MBA, and DBA, Harvard Business School), and psychoanalysis (Canadian Psychoanalytic Society and the International Psychoanalytic Association), Kets de Vries scrutinizes the interface between international management, psychoanalysis, psychotherapy, and dynamic psychiatry. His specific areas of interest are leadership, career dynamics, executive stress, entrepreneurship, family business, succession planning, cross-cultural management, team building, coaching, and the dynamics of corporate transformation and change.

A clinical professor of leadership development, he holds the Raoul de Vitry d'Avaucourt Chair of Leadership Development at INSEAD, France and Singapore. He is also the Distinguished Professor of Leadership at ESMT, European School of Management and Technology in Berlin, Germany, and Director of the Centre for Leadership and Development Research. He is the director of INSEAD's Global Leadership Centre. In addition, he is program director of INSEAD's top management program, "The Challenge of Leadership: Developing Your Emotional Intelligence," and "Consulting and Coaching for Change (and has received INSEAD's distinguished teacher award five times). He has also held professorships at McGill University, the Ecole des Hautes Etudes Commerciales, Montreal, and the Harvard Business School, and he has lectured at management institutions around the world.

Kets de Vries is the author, co-author, or editor of more than 30 books, including *The Neurotic Organization, The Leadership Mystique, The Leader on the Couch*, and *Sex, Money, Happiness and Death*. In addition, Kets de Vries has published over 300 scientific papers as chapters in books and as articles. He has also written approximately a hundred case studies, including seven that received the Best Case of the Year award.

Laura Guillén is Assistant Professor at ESMT, European School of Management and Technology in Berlin, Germany as of September, 2010. Prior to joining ESMT, she was the recipient of a Marie Curie Intra-European Fellowship for postdoctoral studies within the 7th European Community Framework Programme, from the European

Commission (2008–2010), during which she conducted research at INSEAD. She is member of the Research Center for Leadership at ESADE and the Research Group on Survey Research and Applied Statistic of the European Social Survey. Her research interests are emotional intelligence, leadership development, identity change, coaching, and social science methods. Her research has appeared in *Personality and Individual Differences, Journal of Management Development* and other outlets. She received her PhD from ESADE (Barcelona, Spain) on organizational studies (specialization on organizational behavior). She holds an undergraduate and MBA degree in Business Administration from ESADE and has studied Psychology (UNED, Madrid, Spain).

Konstantin Korotov is Associate Professor at ESMT, European School of Management and Technology in Berlin, Germany, and a senior researcher fellow and executive coach with the INSEAD Global Leadership Centre in Fontainebleau, France. In addition to his academic work, he has over 15 years of practical leadership development experience in Europe, North and South America, and Asia.

Konstantin received his PhD in Management (Organizational Behavior) at INSEAD. Konstantin currently conducts research on leadership development, leadership coaching, and executive education. He has authored, co-authored, or edited numerous books, articles, columns, and special issues of journals on the subjects of leadership, careers, and executive education. As an expert on leadership and management in Russia and post-Soviet economies, Konstantin also conducts research on leadership styles of business elite and emerging leaders in the region.

Elizabeth Florent-Treacy, INSEAD Global Leadership Centre Associate Director, Research, has conducted research in the following areas: global leadership; global organizations; corporate culture in European and global organizations; American, French and Russian business practices; family business issues (governance, succession, strategy); entrepreneurial leadership; cross-cultural management; women and global leadership; cultural aspects of mergers and acquisitions; transformational leadership; expatriate executives and families; and the psychodynamics of leadership. She also coaches in the areas of leadership development and family business. She holds degrees in Sociology (BA), Organization Development (MA), and a Diploma in Clinical Organizational Psychology (INSEAD, magna cum laude). In the areas of leadership development and family business, Elizabeth has written over 20 case studies, six of which won top case writing awards. She has co-authored or authored 25 articles, working papers, and book chapters, and co-authored five books on leadership and family business topics. She has also contributed to the design of four 360-degree leadership development survey instruments.

CONTRIBUTING AUTHORS

Andreas Bernhardt is program director and executive coach at ESMT (Berlin, Germany), a founding member of ESMT's Center for Leadership Development

Research, and has about 20 years of practical leadership development and coaching experience. He has designed and delivered executive programs for many international companies, and teaches and coaches in the areas of Organizational Behavior and Leadership in MBA, Executive MBA, and company-specific executive programs. His research and consulting interests focus on leadership development, executive coaching, and leading and coaching teams in tough times. Andreas Bernhardt studied Clinical and Organizational Psychology, Management and Organizational Behavior; he holds a Masters degree in Psychology; and is an alumnus of INSEAD's executive program, "Consulting and Coaching for Change."

Richard E. Boyatzis is Professor, Departments of Organizational Behavior, Psychology, and Cognitive Science at Case Western Reserve University, and holds the H. R. Horvitz Chair in Family Business. He is also an Adjunct Professor at ESADE. While at Case, he was Department Chair of Organizational Behavior from 1996–2004 and Associate Dean of Executive Education from 1994–1999. He has won special awards at Case for research, two awards for teaching, and two awards for service.

His research interests include leadership and developing emotional intelligence, lifelong learning, competency and outcome assessment. He is the author of more than 150 articles and books. His books include *The Competent Manager*; the international best-seller, *Primal Leadership* with Daniel Goleman and Annie McKee; *Resonant Leadership*, with Annie McKee; and *Becoming a Resonant Leader*, with Annie McKee and Fran Johnston. Professor Boyatzis has a PhD and MA in Social Psychology from Harvard University and a BS in Aeronautics and Astronautics from MIT.

Randel S. Carlock is the Berghmans Lhoist Chaired Professor in Entrepreneurial Leadership and the founding director of the Wendel International Center for Family Enterprise at INSEAD (Europe and Asia). Previously he was the first Opus Professor of Family Enterprise and founder of the family business center at the University of St. Thomas in Minneapolis, MN (USA). Carlock has an MA in education and training (1976), an MBA in strategic management (1983), and a PhD (1991), all from the University of Minnesota. He has also completed a postgraduate certification in family and marriage therapy at the Institute of Psychiatry, King's College, University of London (1998) and a certificate in psychodynamic counseling at Birkbeck College, University of London (1999). He was awarded a Certificate in Family Business Advising with Fellow Status (2001) by The Family Firm Institute, Boston, MA (USA).

He is the author or co-author of several books, articles, book chapters, videos, and case studies including *Family Business on the Couch: A Psychological Perspective* (with Manfred Kets de Vries and Elizabeth Florent-Treacy) and *Strategic Planning for the Family Business* (with John L. Ward). He has over 25 years' experience serving as an executive with a global family business and as CEO and chairman of his own NASDAQ-listed corporation.

Alicia Cheak is a research associate with IGLC, working mainly on the development of a new executive coaching instrument, The Organizational Culture Audit. Prior to this, she was at INSEAD's Center for Advanced Learning Technologies, developing a set of simulation-based learning experiences addressing collaboration challenges in different educational and business contexts. Her research interests include problem solving, knowledge mapping, performance-based assessments, collaborative learning, technology-based learning (e.g. Web 2.0, emergent communities), virtual communities, and simulation-based learning. She holds a BA in English and Psychology, and an MA in Education from the University of California, Los Angeles.

Vincent H. Dominé is Managing Partner of Dominé & Partners, a leadership consulting firm that he founded in Switzerland in 1989, and co-founder of the International Coaching Faculty, a global coaching network. He is also a program director and executive coach at the INSEAD Global Leadership Centre, where he conducts group coaching interventions and leadership development seminars for some of the world's leading organizations. His area of expertise lies at the intersection of organizational culture and leadership, with a particular emphasis on cross-cultural issues, innovation, and entrepreneurship. A graduate of INSEAD's Consulting and Coaching for Change Program, where he earned a degree in clinical organizational psychology, Vincent also holds a degree in business administration.

Francesc Granja developed his professional career in the marketing arena working as a marketing manager in multinational companies and as a freelance strategic marketing consultant. He started his coaching practice in 2002. He is a member of CoachU, CoachVille, ASESCO (Coaching Spanish Association). He is secretary of AEPCO (Spanish Association of Onthologic Coaching Professionals). Currently, he collaborates at ESADE Business School as an assistant facilitator and coach for MBA students in a leadership development program. He holds an MBA from ESADE, Barcelona, Spain.

Christoph H. Loch is the GlaxoSmithKline Chaired Professor of Corporate Innovation and Professor of Technology and Operations Management at INSEAD. He also serves as the director of INSEAD's Israel research center. His research revolves around the management of R&D and the product innovation process, strategy execution, project management under high uncertainty, and the emotional aspects of motivating professional R&D employees.

Professor Loch served as dean of INSEAD's PhD program from 2006–2009, was department editor of *Management Science* from 2004 through 2008, and he continues to serve as associate editor for *Management Science* and *Manufacturing & Service Operations Management* (M&SOM). He also serves on the editorial board of the *Journal of Engineering and Technology Management* (JETM) and *Research Technology Management*. He has written over 40 articles in the leading journals in technology and operations management, and he has co-authored four books on management quality in manufacturing, on portfolio management in R&D, and on managing highly novel projects. He teaches MBA courses and executive seminars at INSEAD, consults European corporations on technology management, and serves on the supervisory board of an educational software start-up company.

Professor Loch holds a PhD in business from the Graduate School of Business at Stanford University, an MBA from the University of Tennessee in Knoxville, and a Diplom-Wirtschaftsingenieur degree from the Darmstadt Institute of Technology in Germany. Prior to joining INSEAD, he worked as a consultant for McKinsey & Company in their San Francisco and Munich offices.

Katty Marmenout is Assistant Professor of Management at EM Lyon Business School. She holds an MBA from Brussels University and PhD in Organizational Behavior from McGill University. Katty acquired extensive professional experience in change management consulting with KPMG and CGEY. She was a visiting doctoral student at Chicago GSB and Kellogg School of Management, and a research assistant at the University of Geneva. Katty has taught organizational behavior and change management at the University of Geneva, Leicester University, and Dubai School of Government. Before joining EM Lyon Business School, Katty was a research fellow at INSEAD in Abu Dhabi, where she has worked on various research projects related to women-focused leadership in the Middle East and delivered workshops on work-life balance and self-leadership. Her cross-cultural experience, living in Europe, the Middle East, and Northern America, has made her particularly sensitive to issues of collaboration, coping with uncertainty and adapting to change.

Jacki Nicholas is a founding partner with the Air Institute and is dedicated to strengthening the authentic leadership capability of individuals, teams, and organizations across Asia Pacific and beyond. Her 20-year corporate career has spanned corporate finance, management consulting, and human capital development, working with organizations such as Deloitte Ross Tohmatsu, Coopers & Lybrand, the Hay Group and Deutsche Bank. In her consulting practice, she designs and delivers executive programs in international leadership, change, and high-performance teams, and provides executive coaching on both a one-on-one and small group basis. Her clients are typically C-suite and senior executives in Fortune 500 companies from diverse industries. Jacki is a certified executive coach and has coached regularly with the INSEAD Global Leadership Centre (IGLC) since 2004. She is adjunct faculty for the Lee Kong Chian School of Business at the Singapore Management University.

Murray Palevsky is an executive coach at the INSEAD Global Leadership Centre with an extensive business and entrepreneurial background. He has 25 years of first hand business experience as a senior executive, entrepreneur, and CEO of a major construction business in Canada. Murray is a graduate of

Brandeis University and holds an MBA from McGill University. He has received psychoanalytic training in Montreal and is a graduate of the Coaching and Consulting for Change program (INSEAD, magna cum laude). Murray has developed a unique approach to coaching using a music focused intervention technique. Murray is a member of the International Coaching Federation (ICF).

Katherine Twaddell is a certified executive coach and principal with Apeiron Consulting, based in Singapore. In her practice she draws from her extensive international background in the global financial services, media, and retail sectors to coach many well respected corporate leaders from across a broad range of businesses, as well as several of Asia's most successful entrepreneurs. Since 2006, Katherine has coached regularly with the INSEAD Global Leadership Centre. Katherine's career started on Wall Street, as an analyst focusing on the insurance sector. She joined the financial media industry where she worked with organizations such as Institutional Investor, CNN, and Fortune magazine. Katherine then moved to Asia and founded her own successful business, and was a finalist in Singapore's Woman Entrepreneur of the Year 2001. Katherine holds a BA in English Literature from New York University and a postgraduate certificate in executive coaching from the University of Derby. She is a regular participant in the SI program at the CG Jung Institute in Zurich. Katherine is a member of the International Coaching Federation and the European Mentoring and Coaching Council.

Graham Ward is a partner of the Kets de Vries Institute and a leadership consultant. A financier by profession, he spent 16 years at Goldman Sachs, the majority of which co-leading a European business. He specializes in C-suite leadership interventions, leadership coaching, and group dynamics with multinationals globally. He is currently based in Scandinavia.

PREFACE

In 2007, we published *Coach and Couch: The Psychology of Making Better Leaders* to address the increasing demand for understanding how coaching can be used in organizations. We provided a psychodynamic/systemic framework for coaching interventions for leadership development, coupled with practical applications of this approach by numerous INSEAD Global Leadership Centre (IGLC) faculty, researchers, and coaches, who have worked with thousands of executives in programs and leadership modules at INSEAD. Our focus was to provide leaders with interventions that go beyond transferring tools and techniques. Our goal was to create more reflective and self-aware leaders with the purpose of generating great places to work.

The Coaching Kaleidoscope is the successor to that earlier book. In it, we go deeper into what actually happens in the processes of human transformation triggered by coaching interventions. The aim is to create more reflective people whom we hope will, in turn, create better organizations. These authentizotic* organizations have a set of metavalues that give employees a sense of purpose and self-determination. They are places where people feel competent, experience a sense of belonging, believe that they can have an impact on the organization, and where they derive meaning and enjoyment from their work. Organizations with authentizotic cultures are an anchor for health and psychological well-being in the workplace. People are pleased and proud to work in such exceptionally creative, dynamic, and productive environments.

The group coaching methodology was originally developed by Manfred Kets de Vries, and is used at IGLC and by the Center for Leadership Development Research (CLDR) at ESMT, Berlin. It is the basis for many of the theoretical assumptions developed in the chapters in this book, in which we share the research methodologies and intervention and change techniques used in the development and education of executive coaches. We aim to contribute to a better understanding of how organizations can enhance the impact of coaching to create best places to work. The chapters are written by a number of academics and leadership coaches who take diverse perspectives relevant to leadership development: academic investigation, pedagogical mastery, consulting experience, and practitioner expertise. The authors draw on their research experience, observations,

*A term derived by Manfred Kets de Vries from the Greek *authenteekos*, meaning "authentic," and *zoteekos*, meaning "vital to life."

trial-and-error experimentations, and real-life implementations of leadership development processes in business schools and companies.

IGLC was set up in 2003 by Manfred Kets de Vries and his associates to meet the need for research-based global executive leadership development programs with a practical, applied orientation. The vision of IGLC is to help executives create results-driven, sustainable organizations by putting people first, creating a work environment in which people feel competent, effective, and able to "stretch." As the knowledge organization becomes the twenty-first century paradigm, IGLC programs provide the tools for top executives to reflect on their own strengths and weaknesses as an essential step in the process of creating high-performance teams and sustainable, effective organizations that are great places to work. The successful expansion of the IGLC coaching and teaching methodology to programs at ESMT and other educational institutions testifies to its generalizability beyond one particular business school—while interventions in many different companies confirm its generalizability from educational to organizational environments.

KNOWLEDGE BASE AND DATA COLLECTION

IGLC brings together faculty and thought leaders on leadership from around the world with the objective of studying leadership practices in public and private organizations. The center's research focuses on exemplary leadership in high-performance organizations, dysfunctional leadership practices, and leadership development approaches. IGLC researchers work collaboratively with faculty and professionals from other institutions that share the underlying quest for helping executives to become more effective and to create more viable organizations. This book is a joint project with the Center for Leadership Development Research (CLDR) at ESMT.

Every year IGLC and CLDR faculty, researchers, and coaches work with thousands of executives in various programs and leadership modules at INSEAD and ESMT. Faculty from other innovative business schools with a strong emphasis on leadership development in countries all over the world, as well as the participating executives themselves, contribute to our knowledge base—an ongoing process by which IGLC programs and tools are continually tuned to the most recent and cutting-edge management practices and academic findings. The content of our leadership development programs is updated on a regular basis and new questions for investigation are generated.

In putting this book together, we have involved academics who conduct research, teach, and consult; leadership development coaches; change consultants; and executives who are familiar with the IGLC methods for reflecting about leadership development opportunities and challenges. We have included people who have experienced IGLC methods in the process of their developmental journeys. We also invited people from various academic orientations to give us an opportunity to look beyond what we already know and do. They have put their heads together, dug into their research and practice notes, analyzed data from inquiry projects, and shared their personal experiences in individual chapters.

INTENDED AUDIENCE

The purpose of this book is to share relevant research findings and practical methods with academics, executives, leadership coaches, and consultants working with organizational leaders who are faced with the daily task of setting and meeting their own and their followers' expectations for achievement. The book responds to strong calls to explore how the "magic" of coaching works, what coaches actually do, and how their clients respond.

It is also intended for executives concerned with maximizing their own potential as leaders of organizations; leaders in charge of succession planning in their companies; human resources, organizational development and training professionals interested in effective and efficient leadership development efforts; leadership development consultants and executive coaches; faculty who teach leadership courses; academics doing research on leadership and coaching topics; and MBA students and graduate students in the fields of organizational behavior, HR, OD, entrepreneurship, and strategy. In addition, the leadership group coaching intervention technique has proved to be extremely helpful for individuals working in family businesses, organizations that are prime examples of the applicability of systemic and psychodynamic orientations.

BOOK OUTLINE

Introduction: Holistic organizational coaching

Manfred F. R. Kets de Vries and Alicia Cheak

We begin with an examination of various forms of holistic coaching intervention—individual, team, and organizational. Conceptual models describe the process of transformational change, and the chapter ends with observations about what it means to be a reflective practitioner. We also describe what we mean by "best places to work."

PART ONE: SETTING THE STAGE

Chapter 1   The proof of the pudding: An integrative, psychodynamic approach to evaluating a leadership development program

Manfred F. R. Kets de Vries, Elizabeth Florent-Treacy, Laura Guillén, and Konstantin Korotov

Methodological issues are a serious inhibitor for assessing leadership development. In this chapter we describe intrinsic evaluation components that cannot and should not be dissociated from the program dynamic itself. Additionally, we identify ways to continually verify that teaching and coaching pedagogies are in sync with participants' needs.

Chapter 2   Bringing the clinical paradigm into executive education programs: Fantasies, anxieties and hopes

Konstantin Korotov

Building on the results of research on executive education and the practice of designing and delivering executive development programs, as well as his experience of consulting to organizations, program directors, and faculty in business schools, Konstantin Korotov identifies typical anxieties and fantasies associated with the introduction of such methods as 360-degree instruments, psychodynamically oriented group coaching, individual and peer coaching, case-in-point, and the like.

Chapter 3   Are you feeling mad, sad, bad, or glad?

Manfred F. R. Kets de Vries

This chapter takes the theme of countertransference beyond the couch and explores how consultants or coaches can use themselves as a source of information when dealing with their clients, or interpreting what the client is trying to transmit to them. Manfred Kets de Vries suggests what coaches and consultants need to pay attention to when listening to their clients, and explores dysfunctional communication patterns.

PART TWO: CREATING REFLECTIVE PRACTITIONERS

Chapter 4   Case studies of self-awareness and change

Elizabeth Florent-Treacy

Elizabeth Florent-Treacy uses a conceptual interpretation approach to examine the written narratives of 28 participants' experiences in one lengthy executive leadership development program, shedding light on the way they explore and experiment with new working identities in the leadership development identity laboratory. Her study reveals that group psychotherapy can be adapted to create an identity laboratory experience for executives, and that the process of writing can be a critical success factor in executives' passage through it.

Chapter 5 Something from nothing: The use of transitional space and how group coaching changes people

Graham Ward

Coaching is prevalent in many organizations, but while individuals typically receive coaching in the traditional dyadic form, groups are generally formed only for training purposes. Coaching executives in groups is an efficient and potent way for executives to transform. Drawing on conceptualizations from psychoanalytic psychology and group dynamics, Graham Ward presents a model that practitioners at educational establishments and within organizations can deploy with sustainable results.

Chapter 6 A coach tells a story of change

Vincent H. Dominé

In this chapter, a participant in a leadership development-focused executive education program is interviewed by the executive coach who facilitated her group coaching sessions. The executive shares the phases of the development she went through, from the pain and confusion of the initial stages of behavior change to a positive outcome and ultimate internalization of new ways of acting. Her story is rich in anecdotes and metaphors, and it is captured visually by the very expressive drawings she made during the process.

Chapter 7 360-degree group coaching from the inside out

Murray Palevsky

In this chapter, a coachee gives his personal insights and impressions of the 360-degree group coaching experience. Murray Palevsky's account includes several case-oriented anecdotes and narratives related to the coaching process and the synergies provided by group coaching. This personal account fleshes out the descriptions of group coaching sessions and 360-degree feedback instruments provided in earlier chapters.

Chapter 8 Is there anybody in there?

Francesc Granja

Starting from the moment when he made his choice of university, Francesc Granja highlights the key moments of his professional career until his realization that not only would he would like to be a leadership coach but that, surprisingly, he had always been one. Granja describes the learning and discoveries he made during his coaching training courses following this personal revelation. He describes a deeply intimate journey, an open diary linking personal references and emotions to various coaching theories and approaches.

Chapter 9   Becoming a better coach: A story of transition

Andreas Bernhardt and Konstantin Korotov

This chapter is based on a case study of a professional psychologist and consultant, involved in executive coaching in organizational and academic settings, who learns how to become a better coach by deepening his understanding of his own inner theater. The story of the coach's development is paralleled by his experience of serving his clients better and discovering new opportunities for using self as an instrument for helping others. The chapter also touches on the important issue of professional development and personal growth for people professionally involved in developing better leaders and creating better organizations.

PART THREE: CREATING BETTER PLACES TO WORK

Chapter 10   Imagining better places to work: Individual-organizational interfaces and coaching practices

Laura Guillén

The objective of this chapter is not to offer a recipe for creating better places to work but to illustrate real attempts made by organizations to do so. Laura Guillén considers various ways of making the workplace more attractive and reviews the mechanisms that affect the creation and sustainability of a healthy culture in an organization. She explores the relationship between organizational culture, leadership, and socialization practices, and highlights the need for coaches and HR professionals to align coaching agendas with organizational realities.

Chapter 11   Coaching teams for sustainable, desired change

Richard E. Boyatzis

Team development, like any sustained, desired change, is a multilevel phenomenon. Helping or coaching a team requires an understanding of how teams develop from a multilevel complexity perspective. Effective teams and their leaders use emotional and social intelligence to make it all happen; they also need to develop emotional and social intelligence in the teams. In this chapter, Richard Boyatzis describes Intentional Change Theory, an integrated, multilevel theory of sustained, desired change, and applies it to team development.

Chapter 12   Connecting the science of management systems with the clinical paradigm

Christoph Loch

Christoph Loch addresses where and how management science and clinical psychology can be fruitfully combined, and the potential benefits of doing so. He begins with a brief overview of some fundamental themes in management discipline, introduces the clinical paradigm, and outlines how the two approaches can complement each other. He indicates how the marriage of these two approaches will contribute to more realistic and lasting change interventions.

Chapter 13   Failure in family business coaching

Randel Carlock and Elizabeth Florent-Treacy

The authors draw on their deep experience of family business to tell a cautionary tale, highlighting the pitfalls of hubris that can lessen the effectiveness of a coach in a family business context. They position the case story within a wider framework that examines the causes and lessons to be learned from failure, with a reminder that all coaches should be prepared for failure—and also concerned for their own well-being.

Chapter 14   Coaching for work-life balance

Katty Marmenout

In this chapter, Katty Marmenout presents recent advances in work-life balance research and argues that organizations can benefit by embracing the view of work-life balance as harmony and fit, rather than equality. As individuals face life transitions, priorities shift between domains and the alignment of workplace realities with individual priorities requires a proactive approach. Organizations can diffuse work-life balance coaching practices aiming to increase effectiveness and satisfaction, allowing employees to reach that much-sought-after sense of harmony.

**Chapter 15 Cultural diversity in global leadership—group
executive coaching in Asia**

Jacki Nicholas and Katherine Twaddell

Some interesting observations emerge from this chapter, written by two executive coaches who have worked together in Asia for many years. Jacki Nicholas and Katherine Twaddell build on their experience and survey data to identify and comment on the critical success factors of group executive coaching in Asia. The chapter offers readers coordinates from which to begin to chart their own group coaching journey.

Conclusion: Turning the coaching kaleidoscope

Manfred F. R. Kets de Vries, Elizabeth Florent-Treacy, Konstantin Korotov, and Laura Guillén

The final chapter takes us beyond the "leader on the couch" to apply lessons learned. We discuss how we can create best places to work by creating coaching cultures that diffuse throughout the entire organization and explore some of the levers used to create effective, humane, and sustainable organizations. We comment on how to establish the foundation to help executives embark on transformational journeys and how to extend transformational energy beyond individuals to create better places to work.

ACKNOWLEDGMENTS

This book resulted from the contributions from a myriad of people who generously shared their insights and stretched their imaginations to help us describe how people change and how others can accompany this fascinating process. We listened to executives in our executive education programs, to professional coaches and colleagues at IGLC, to coaches-to-be and their stories about their journeys, to coachees' experiences and their hopes and anxieties, to change consultants and to academics who gave us the opportunity to look beyond what we already knew. Their generous willingness to share their experiences and reflections has enabled us to capture a kaleidoscopic view of the coaching profession.

We gratefully acknowledge the chapter authors, each of whom brings a different angle and colored the book in very distinct and personal ways. We would also like to thank our IGLC and ESMT colleagues, and in particular Silke Bequet who has assisted to perfection many coaches and coaches-to-be at INSEAD. We are grateful also for the generous institutional support of INSEAD and ESMT. We would also like to thank Sally Simmons, of Cambridge Editorial, and Kate Kirk, for editing the manuscript.

MANFRED KETS DE VRIES
LAURA GUILLÉN
KONSTANTIN KOROTOV
ELIZABETH FLORENT-TREACY

Fontainebleau, February 2010

INTRODUCTION: HOLISTIC ORGANIZATIONAL COACHING

MANFRED F. R. KETS DE VRIES
AND ALICIA CHEAK

We live in an age of permanent, unrelenting change. The traditional business organization of the past has all but disappeared, and for many people, the resulting uncertainty triggers fear, anxiety, distress, and resistance. The pressure on executives and their employees to deal quickly and frequently with the paradoxes that are inherent to organizational life has increased dramatically. But for those who can adapt, change also opens up new opportunities for growth and development. A rapidly changing environment may encourage people to seek creative opportunities as a survival strategy, and those who do so will thrive in this brave new world. No wonder both organizations and individual executives are looking for methods and tools that can help them stay competitive and able to reinvent themselves.

If organizations are to remain competitive in this age of change, they need to be able to adapt and respond to changing realities, to understand the changing needs of their various stakeholders. In addition, it will be imperative to develop, manage, and retain talent. Above all, they must be guided by imaginative, empathetic, and adaptive leadership. To grasp the opportunities and lessen the anxieties that accompany change processes, these leaders must possess not only an astute understanding of how to analyze complex organizational processes but also have collaborative, problem solving, and influencing skills. They must be able to grasp the intricacies of the company's value chain, and have the ability to deal with inefficiencies. However, they cannot do this alone. They must recognize the interdependencies with other stakeholders in the organization. Only through inclusion can they create organizations that motivate and empower employees to perform at peak capacity.[1] Making this happen is not easy. Many obstacles will be encountered on the way. A lot of courage will be required to overcome resistance to change, their own and that of the organizational members.

It is rare for an individual to possess these various skills naturally. There are not many supermen or superwomen about. Instead, leadership studies show that the most successful organizations are not led by one, powerful, charismatic leader, but are the product of *distributive, collective, and complementary* leadership. Leadership qualities are not the properties of a few people at the top of the organization. On the contrary, these highly successful organizations utilize the leadership talent present throughout an organization[2]. Today, we live in an age of "post-heroic" leadership. In the highly complex, diverse, and global organizations of the twenty-first century, there is little room for the "great man" theories of leadership of the past. No one is talented enough to go it alone. Today's successful organizational leadership is characterized by highly effective teams of people who embark together on an exciting journey.

One of the critical tasks on the path of executive development is learning to bring together talented individuals who possess a constellation of skills and competencies that allows them to be highly productive teams. A second critical task is to maintain the teams' constant drive and willingness to learn and develop. The difficulties of embarking on such an endeavor are often underestimated, however. To build a high performance team takes a lot of effort. The most effective executive teams are those in which individuals' natural leadership styles and strengths are matched to particular roles and challenges, supported by a coaching culture within the organization. Such a culture is characterized by learning, feedback, experimentation, dialogue, developing and testing hypotheses, taking risks, learning to use emotions productively, and sharing knowledge. We refer to this type of corporate cultures as coaching cultures. But such coaching cultures are not easy to accomplish because they involve changes to the organizational system at both macro and micro levels. Creating and sustaining more inclusive corporate cultures requires a high degree of openness, trust, and adaptability on the part of all the people in an organization. Fortunately, leadership coaching can be a catalyst for the creation of such work environments.

LEADERSHIP COACHING

Leadership coaching implies a specific type of intervention that can be carried out strategically with individuals, teams, or an entire organization.[3] Its aim is to direct a person or group of people toward a specific, mutually determined goal, accelerating progress by providing focus and awareness. It is about helping the people who are being coached to reach a fuller potential; to help them actualize their strengths and minimize their weaknesses. In addition, as a holistic process, leadership coaching can also result in more effective, healthier, and better organizations, which have been termed "authentizotic," a term coined from the Greek meaning "authentic" and "vital to life."[4] When executives are able to work together to find more creative ways of dealing with their professional environment and one another; when people feel empowered to experiment and improve themselves and the organization; and when knowledge is shared in a supportive way, a positive kind of contagion infects the organization, spreading hope and enthusiasm as a coaching culture replaces a former toxic one. Conducted properly, leadership coaching can be very dynamic, contributing to creativity, innovation, and even reinvention in organizations.

COACHING FOR CHANGE AT MICRO AND MACRO LEVELS

When coaching is an element of an organization's leadership development plan, the visible business outcomes are long-term improvements in individual and organizational effectiveness, indicated by profit increase or cost-containment, or both. To enable these changes, a psychodynamic/systemic perspective becomes a sine qua non. To affect this level of change and transformation, a leadership coach experienced in moving easily between micro and macro levels can contribute significantly to the success of a change process in the short term and the creation of a self-sustaining coaching culture in the long term.

Change at the micro level can be the starting point in an individual's reinvention process, contributing to higher satisfaction at work and at home, greater productivity,[5] lower stress levels, less frustration, and increased self-esteem and satisfaction with life. Such coaching may focus on key competencies, including how-to techniques, skill development, and the attainment of stretch goals.[6] In contrast to mere performance and skills coaching, leadership coaching is concerned with emotional intelligence, the ability to bring meaning to people's work, and developing a more effective leadership style. Coaching can be an intervention around career transition, focusing on empowering people to make effective career decisions, dealing with career moves or personal growth. At times, coaching may be focused on life issues, helping executives explore what they want, how they might achieve their aspirations, and how to fulfill their needs. It entails dealing with midlife transition, work-life balance, or relationships with significant people in their lives. For clients coached at the micro level, the result is often realignment and congruence between their public and private life: they acquire a greater sense of authenticity, which is then reflected in the way they deal with others around them.[7] At the macro level, leadership coaching can help transform the organization's culture, structures, and patterns of decision-making, contributing to organizational rejuvenation and reinvention.

A long-term culture shift naturally requires a focus on the underlying systemic and psychological dynamics that determine an organizational culture.[8] Here we need to keep in mind that understanding the role that culture plays within an organization is like receiving the key to a secret code. Leadership coaches can guide organizational players in an exploration of aspects of organizational culture that may enhance or stifle creativity, productivity, and human motivation and performance—because if change leaders ignore the micro undercurrents that shape the macro culture, the transformation process will undoubtedly fail. To win the hearts and minds of the culture bearers is not an exercise for the faint of heart, however. It requires great competence on the part of the leadership coach to nurture this process.

THE INSEAD COACHING BRAND

INSEAD's Global Leadership Centre's (IGLC) unique coaching brand focuses on holistic, systemic executive coaching with a psychodynamic orientation, a process by which we help leaders to lead and direct individual and organizational transformation and change and to create a coaching culture within organizations. The approach includes and integrates both the micro and macro focuses (individual leaders in the organizational context) described above and presents some distinguishing features.

A clinical paradigm

One of these is its grounding in the clinical paradigm. Although we have no rigid ideological orientation, we apply ideas from psychoanalysis (in particular object relations theory), psychotherapy, developmental psychology, family systems theory, paradoxical intervention, appreciative inquiry, motivational interviewing, network contagion, behavioral concepts, and cognition to understand the behavior of individuals and teams in organizations.[9] Our willingness to borrow from a variety of intellectual perspectives on human functioning reflects the complexity of the phenomena coaches deal with when working with today's executives, and, more importantly, the intricacy of the issues that the latter encounter in their daily practice. We are far from claiming that a single model or approach can be used fully to understand human beings, dyadic relationships, and complex organizations. Still, through years of practice and research we have remarked the human capacity to learn to see ourselves, people around us, and the world as multidimensional.

The clinical paradigm is an orientation through which participants examine and reflect on their own behavior and are enabled to change some elements of it. The paradigm consists of the following five premises:

What you see isn't necessarily what you get. The world around us is much more complex than it appears from a superficial point of view. Most of what happens is beyond conscious awareness.

We are not rational human beings. Irrational behavior is a common pattern in organizational life, although in fact it has a rationale to it. This rationale is critical in understanding a person's inner theater—the core themes that affect an individual's personality and leadership style. Well-intentioned and well-thought-out plans derail daily in offices around the world because of out-of-awareness influences on behavior. Finding the rationale is rarely easy, however. In corporate life, we often have to be something of an organizational detective to tease out what's going on behind an executive's quirky behavior and attitudes.

We are influenced by our own basic human needs. These needs determine our character and create the tightly interlocked triangle of our mental life (the three points of which are cognition, emotion, and behavior). To influence behavior, both cognition and emotions have to be taken into consideration. Emotions determine many of our actions and emotional intelligence plays a vital role in the leadership equation—bluntly speaking, people who are emotionally intelligent are more likely to be effective as leaders.

We all have a shadow side. Although leaders are often depicted as paragons of virtue, and we speak in glowing terms of the attributes that constitute leadership, all leaders have an out-of-awareness shadow side. Many leaders derail due to blind spots in their personality. None of us is a stranger to defensive processes.

We are products of our past. As the saying goes, the hand that rocks the cradle rules the world. The sum total of all of us is the developmental outcome of our early environment, modified by our genetic endowment. And because of the heavy imprinting that takes place at the earliest stages of life, we tend to repeat certain behavior patterns. Like it or not, there's a continuity between past and present.

Applying the clinical paradigm helps us to tease out the central interpersonal role in which clients consciously and unconsciously cast themselves. It also helps us explore the complementary roles other people adopt in an executive role constellation. It helps us identify self-defeating expectations and negative self-appraisal, as well as outdated perceptions of ourselves—behavior patterns that had a useful function at one point but are now counter-effective.

A Socratic method of leadership coaching

When an organization supports its executives through leadership coaching programs, both the individual and the organization will benefit—if the leadership coach takes into consideration both conscious and out-of-awareness behavior. By encouraging self-awareness and an understanding of the common obstacles of life, coaches help their clients acquire a new lens through which to examine knotty personal and organizational problems. These inner journeys help provide answers to the existential conundrums we all face at times. Whether these dilemmas are conscious or unconscious, leadership coaching can help executives become more successful at managing their day-to-day responsibilities, meeting their goals, recognizing when they find themselves at crossroads, and, most importantly, creating a fulfilling life.

How does this work in practice? At IGLC, we believe leadership coaching is more an art of discovery than a technology of delivery. By its nature, leadership coaching has a Socratic quality; it involves asking a series of questions about a central issue, and trying to find satisfactory answers through dialogue. The use of questions and conversation implies that a leadership coach begins from a position of humility and curiosity, rather than authority and knowledge.

The Socratic coach is a guiding figure, who respects and draws upon the experience and knowledge of the client. While coaching interventions are therapeutic, they are not therapy. Good leadership coaches are aware of—and respect—the (often subtle) boundaries between coaching and psychotherapy, always keeping in mind the guiding philosophy, "Do no harm." Leadership coaches act as a mirror; they help people work out what they want, what they are good at, what they are not so good at, and where and how they can improve. Successful leadership coaches effect transformational change by creating transitional space for their clients—a place where the client can experiment with fresh perspectives without being afraid of failure or criticism—giving them enough trust to be able to deal with "undiscussables." Confronting undiscussables usually opens the way for new, highly productive dialogues and unblocks the decision-making process.

Leadership coaches do not necessarily provide answers to problems. They are not career advisors, consultants, mentors, or trainers, but leadership coaching through inquiry does help individuals understand their own strengths, weaknesses, desires, hopes, and fears. Leadership coaches partner with clients in a thought provoking and creative way that inspires them to explore leadership effectiveness and life satisfaction. Having said that, we need to mention that through professional training and work experience, many leadership coaches develop a catalogue of ideas or suggestions for tackling specific issues that their clients may be dealing with, although the tools and techniques usually come last in coaching interventions. The coach provides support to enhance skills, resources, and creativity of which the client has been only subliminally aware. Improved self-knowledge and a sense of life balance help people prepare for and adapt to change and build commitment to self-development and achievement.

In terms of impact, the Socratic coaching approach expands executives' communication skills and helps them to develop a more authentic leadership style. Effective leadership coaches help executives develop cognitive agility, emotional capacities, motivation, skills, knowledge, and expertise. They support executives as they fine-tune their goals and strategies, challenge and reassess their assumptions, and align followers to the organization's goals. Through a more developed self-awareness, they learn to take into account the impact they have on others. Leadership coaches also encourage executives to be more effective in team and organizational culture management.[10] No one can be good at everything; participants are encouraged to let go of a narcissistic desire for control and create diverse and well-balanced executive teams. Furthermore, leadership coaches help executives understand that career development and lifelong learning are their own responsibility.

Holistic intervention

Another distinguishing feature of our coaching brand is that it is made up of three kinds of intervention process: individual (one-on-one), team (especially with natural working groups), and systemic (or organizational/cultural) coaching.

At the *individual level*, one-on-one coaching allows the client's private self to be explored, heard, honored, and challenged. This offers clients the opportunity to create the space for their vision, explore and set clearly defined goals that support that vision, and evaluate the results. Individual coaching involves skills and performance, style, career, transition, "legacy," life, or "on-boarding" coaching.

At the *team level*, IGLC has been in the vanguard of coaching. We strongly believe that team coaching, as opposed to one-on-one coaching, is ultimately more effective for both individual and organization. We have discovered that coaching in a team setting is more likely to create tipping points for change. Many executives know what needs to be done, but many unconscious forces prevent them from doing so. Group coaching is unsurpassed as a method of uncovering these blocks and providing the impetus for change.

Although we do not discount the benefits of one-on-one coaching—this book provides several examples of its effectiveness under various conditions and with various clients—we nevertheless emphasize that one-on-one coaching is not sufficient to tackle systemic difficulties in organizations. Through team coaching, we help existing teams within an organization arrive at better collaboration and results, with a focus on key organizational challenges and an enhanced level of individual and collective responsibility for the actions and outcomes. Here, the leadership coach's role is to facilitate an improvement in group dynamics, often against a background of open or covert conflict. When leadership coaching is applied to teams (and done effectively), it leads to more egalitarian, trust-based exchanges that transcend traditional hierarchical relationships. The fundamental premise in team coaching is that all members of the team develop a genuine realization that "we're all working for the same company." Furthermore, team coaching not only supports and enables the realization of a team's performance potential but also increases a team's capacity for self-sustained development. When a team operates at full capacity, all members pull their weight and are accountable for their contribution to the team performance.

The ultimate goal, however, is to treat every coaching session—micro or macro—as a part of a *holistic or systemic* intervention, contributing in a small or significant way to transforming the cultural fabric of the entire organization. Organizations that foster a coaching culture demonstrate that they value their people by contributing to their individual development and fulfillment. The objective of taking a systemic coaching approach is to create a culture where all members of the organization are able to engage in candid, respectful, coaching conversations about how they are doing and how they can improve the way they perform. Creating a culture where employees have voice and can make a difference will improve the overall performance of the organization. In our coaching work, we have found that the most successful organizations are those that have coaching principles embedded in their culture and whose executives possess the skills necessary for living those principles.

CONCEPTUAL FRAMEWORKS

People skilled in individual and group coaching are expected to move seamlessly from an individual to a systemic orientation to lead transformation and change. They need to be familiar with various models of individual and organizational change and the models or frameworks, explicit or implicit, within which a particular organization operates. Furthermore, coaches need to be able to tailor any coaching program to the individual organization's unique systems needs. Generic solutions are no longer feasible or acceptable in the marketplace.

Our own methods are quite eclectic. We use various conceptual schemes to help create tipping points, or powerful moments, that lead to change in behavior. Figure I.1 shows the various conceptual models used to facilitate individual and group coaching processes. These schemes include psychodynamic conceptualizations, particularly ideas from object relations theory. This theory is concerned with the relation between individuals and their internalized, as well as external, objects. A basic tenet of object relations theory is that we are driven to form relationships with others and that failure to form successful early relationships leads to later problems.[11] In addition, we use conceptual frameworks from short-term dynamic psychotherapy. These are intervention techniques that help overcome internal resistance to experiencing true feelings about the present and past that have been warded off because they are either too frightening or too painful.[12] Ideas from developmental psychology are also helpful in understanding better the various challenges faced by our clients at different phases of the life cycle.[13]

The challenge of developing effective teams requires leadership coaches to understand the psychology of groups. Deciphering the interaction and interpersonal relationships between members of a group and the ways in which groups

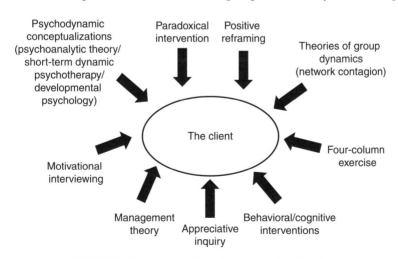

FIGURE I.1 **Group coaching: Conceptual methods**

form, function, and dissolve, is a central concern.[14] To make sense of group dynamics in family owned or controlled businesses, a deep understanding of systems will also be helpful.[15] This kind of systems perspective allows leadership coaches to see how changes in one component of a family system will affect the others, which in turn affects the initial component. Within the boundaries of the system, patterns develop as the behavior of certain participants in the system is caused by and influences the behavior of other members of the system in predictable ways.

Understanding the principles of network contagion will also be a powerful tool for making sense of change processes. Social networks cannot merely be understood in terms of the behavior or psychology of the individuals within them. Networks can also acquire a life of their own. As Christakis and Fowler have shown, we seem to operate under conditions of three degrees of influence. Our actions and moods—whether we are happy or depressed, and why we make certain decisions—will affect our friends, our friends' friends and our friends' friends' friends, which is an important finding when functioning in a group context. Although we prefer to imagine that we have control over our own lives, much of what we do, and even the way we feel, is significantly influenced by those around us—and those around them, and those around them.[16]

Another intervention method we incorporate in our work is motivational interviewing. This is a client-centered, counseling style that elicits behavior change by helping clients to explore and resolve the ambivalence about important decisions. An important factor of motivational interviewing is its nonjudgmental, nonconfrontational, and nonadversarial nature. Using motivational interviewing, we attempt to increase clients' awareness of the potential problems caused, consequences experienced, and risks faced as a result of their behavior. We have learned from experience that even though our clients may have thought about various changes, they are less likely to take steps to change the behavior in question unless they have dealt with the ambivalence associated with the change process. Through motivational interviewing we put the burden on our clients to argue for change.[17]

In situations where we encounter serious resistance, we find paradoxical intervention (or strategic psychotherapy) very helpful. The element of surprise is one of the salient aspects of this form of intervention. We use paradox to change our clients' frame of reference through, for example, prescribing the symptom. By taking this approach—the communication of two apparently contradictory messages—we create new ways of looking at problems.[18]

Another method of encouraging change is the Four-Column Exercise.[19] The four-column exercise helps people understand why certain behaviors do/do not occur due to competing hidden commitments which are held by them, and how those "big assumptions" drive behavior, limiting or blocking personal change and development. The exercise helps elucidate how we subconsciously keep ourselves from reaching our personal and professional change goals, engaging in self-sabotage through competing these commitments. Helped by the exercise clients move from the language of "complaint" to the language of "commitment."

By engaging in such an activity, our clients uncover the big assumptions that hold them back and start the process of moving forward.

Appreciative inquiry and positive reframing[20] are perennially important techniques used to encourage an individual's sense of self-efficacy.[21] Appreciative inquiry can be viewed as a particular way of asking questions and envisioning a future that fosters positive relationships and builds on the basic goodness in an individual, a situation, or an organization. By taking this outlook, the individual and organization's capacity for collaboration and change will improve.

Above all, as in all forms of intervention, as coaches we need to speak the language of our clients to be sure of being understood. Coaches would do well to have a deep understanding of what the practice of management is all about. We have to speak the language of management to be able explain the action steps that need to be taken following the coaching process.

We expect that with the development of coaching as a profession, with deeper analysis of coaching practice and new research, and with the further expansion of the systemic, psychodynamically oriented approach developed at IGLC, there will be further conceptual models and approaches for helping individuals, teams, and organizations to be happier and more effective. We are also constantly open to ideas from other coaching traditions, as well as psychological, leadership, and even hardcore management science research. To assemble this book, we invited academics, executives, and coaches from various academic orientations to give us an opportunity to look beyond what we already know and do. We were guided by the principles of our own coaching brand to create a platform (this book) for reflecting on current coaching practices in which we can be even more effective in helping clients.

DEVELOPING REFLECTIVE PRACTITIONERS

Our aim is to create reflective practitioners and authentizotic organizations. The famous words of the Greek philosopher Epictetus—"We have two ears and one mouth so that we can listen twice as much as we speak"—are as valid today as they were nearly 2000 years ago. Coaches, as well as leaders, need to learn how to use themselves as instruments. In every conversation, the coach and coachee need to ask themselves a series of questions, the most important of which are, "How do I feel listening to this person?" and "What effect does this person have on me?" Concretely, the challenge for leadership coaches is to make their clients more like reflective practitioners—people who have the capacity to reflect and listen.[22]

To be effective in creating reflective practitioners, leadership coaches have to use themselves as a receptive organ for the unconscious signals the coachee is transmitting. They have to learn to look out for transferential and counter-transferential reactions—when they and their client respond to one another on the basis of archaic responses founded on past relationships. This confusion in time and place is common in most interventions. Executives need to realize that behavior that may have been effective at one stage in their life has become obsolete and avoid playing a role that is no longer appropriate.[23]

Leadership coaches should also be wary whenever they feel a strong urge to move into action. The "action trap" can be exactly that, leading us to take some kind of action that we will regret later. Perhaps the best time to hold our tongue is when we feel we must say something or explode. Far too frequently, acting is a substitute for thinking—a refusal to reflect on why we are doing what we are doing.

Once we help people to believe in themselves, they can risk curiosity, wonder, spontaneous delight, or any experience that reveals the human spirit. Although others' ideas will have merit, executives have to practice listening to their own inner voice. If they acquire this ability, they will have a clearer idea of themselves and be better at recognizing what is important to them.

BEST PLACES TO WORK

As we have mentioned, leadership coaching is about more than just helping individuals become more reflective and effective as leaders; it is also a powerful means to propagate the culture necessary to build healthy, authentizotic organizations. Indeed, the interest in high-quality work cultures has resulted in the annual publication of a number of lists on best places to work, notably by *Fortune* magazine, the *Financial Times* and the *Sunday Times*. Being a great workplace does not only benefit employees. Companies at the top of these lists also tend to be very successful businesses, often outperforming their peers with high growth rates, higher numbers of job applicants, low employee turnover, lower absenteeism rates, a higher sense of pride and levels of loyalty, and are more innovative in terms of bringing new products and processes to the market.[24] These companies are also distinguished by high levels of employee trust—in management as well as among themselves—that in turn are associated with higher levels of cooperation among employees and commitment to the company. Not surprisingly, companies who make it to the top of these lists also tend to be great companies to invest in.[25]

According to Jonathan Austin, chief executive of Best Companies Ltd., workplace culture underpins the success of all these top companies. "The best companies to work for are those that want to nurture their staff and reward them with a thriving workplace culture, as well as pay and benefits commensurate with their achievements," he said. "Our survey shows year after year that a happy, engaged workforce is also a productive and profitable one."[26] A great culture is also the glue for creating a high-performance workforce that will successfully execute an organization's strategy.

It appears that trust between managers and employees is the primary defining characteristic of the best workplaces. Beyond keeping employees happy with fairness of promotions and strong benefits packages and perks, a great company is also one that takes its employees' interests to heart by placing a high priority on establishing work-life balance, offering flexible work schedules, the option to telecommute or work from home, paid sabbaticals (especially popular in Europe), individual employee development and competence plans, and formal job training. In general, great places to work are defined by the following values:

Open organizational culture. Top companies distinguish themselves by running the organization on strong values and principles. They have clear corporate objectives to look after their employees and are usually driven by values such as openness, fairness, respect, autonomy, flexibility, and collaboration. An open organizational culture results in a high level of cooperation among employees, high trust levels in management, and an intense commitment to and pride in the company.

Leadership. Integrity and credibility should be played out in an organization's leadership. In the top companies, managers are role models, leading by example and communicating a clear idea of the organization's values, mission, and expectations, as well as the direction in which the company is going. They create a healthy exchange where employees are solicited for their opinions and feedback is acted upon. Credible leaders motivate their workforce and inspire confidence and trust in the organization.

Fairness. Employees will have higher trust in their organization if they believe that their work and the extra effort they put in will be recognized in a fair manner and acknowledged accordingly, in terms of compensation, bonuses, and reward systems.

Challenge, innovation, and creativity. Innovation and creativity are frequently cited as qualities of top companies. Unsurprisingly, many of the top companies are IT companies, whose work is naturally creative.

Continuous learning: Personal and professional growth. In today's work climate, continuous learning and professional growth are important factors for job satisfaction and retention. The best places to work are those that provide a challenging and stimulating environment where employees are kept up-to-date with changes in the industry, given opportunities to advance, and are equipped with the skills to do so.

Work-life balance. Long working hours and overtime are stressful and can be disruptive to family life. An overworked staff can lead to discontent, increased stress, and poor performance. Recognizing this, companies have implemented a number of practices to help employees better achieve a healthy work-life balance. This means offering greater flexibility, for example, by telecommuting, flexible working hours, and even job sharing.

Camaraderie. A sense of friendship and solidarity with one's colleagues fulfills an important social need within the working environment. Camaraderie is important for fostering sociability among employees and encouraging teamwork.

Fun in the workplace. Humor and playfulness are important tools to help relieve stress, improve communication, build camaraderie, promote creative thinking, and increase productivity.[27] To this end, top companies find ways to contribute to the conviviality of the working environment.

In an economic crisis, organizational culture is even more critical for helping companies to buffer shocks. Recent rankings for best places to work show that companies that have made it to the top of the lists and remain there are those driven by strong values, progressive people management policies, and high levels of trust.

TOWARD A COACHING CULTURE

An organization's culture determines its ability to deal successfully with increased competition, globalization, mergers, acquisitions, strategic alliances, the introduction of new technologies, talent management, and diversity issues. If executives do not understand the role that organizational culture plays in these processes, many of their efforts at corporate change will fail. Coaches need to realize that building and maintaining a unique corporate culture can make or break an organization.

Best places to work have organizational cultures that implicate everyone in the process of organizational change: all employees are aligned with the organization's goals and the means to achieve them. Such a coaching culture maximizes the organization's resources, realigns relationships, and drives a focus on long-term strategy. Moreover, in a true coaching culture organization, there are not only systems of formal leadership coaching but the organization's members use coaching behavior as a means of managing, influencing, and communicating with each other. In addition, these organizations go one step further, integrating coaching modules into their leadership development and their general way of doing things. They facilitate the behaviors and practices of continuous learning, the exchange of explicit and tacit knowledge, reciprocal coaching, and self-leadership development.

A coaching culture supports formal communication but also informal exchanges of information and knowledge; individuals feel free to discuss challenges and concerns and to evaluate appropriate actions. When such a culture is in place, it also contributes to a sense of mutual ownership, better networking, more effective leadership practices and higher commitment, creating better results across the organization. Not surprisingly, companies with a successful coaching culture also report significantly reduced staff turnover, increased productivity, and greater job satisfaction.

W. L. Gore & Associates, Inc., a privately held global company with more than 9000 employees (best known for its Gore-Tex fabrics), is recognized for this kind of coaching culture. The company has repeatedly been named among the "100 Best Companies to Work For," in the US by *Fortune* magazine. The company is well known for its ability to unleash creativity and foster teamwork. At Gore, there are no traditional organizational charts, no chains of command, and no specific channels of communication. Gore associates (not employees) communicate directly with each other and are accountable to the fellow members of their multidisciplined teams. In this organization, innovation permeates the company, involving those closest to a project in decision making. Teams are organized around opportunities, a process whereby natural leaders emerge. As might be expected, this unique kind of corporate structure has proved to be a significant contributor to the satisfaction and retention of associates. Gore associates adhere to the four basic guiding principles articulated by the company's founder:

- fairness to each other and everyone with whom they come in contact,
- freedom to encourage, help, and allow other associates to grow in knowledge, skill, and scope of responsibility,
- the ability to make one's own commitments and keep them, and
- consultation with other associates before undertaking actions that could affect the reputation of the company.

Guided by these principles, at Gore, a supportive, coaching culture has been created where people feel free to pursue ideas on their own, communicate with one another, and collaborate out of self-motivation rather than out of a sense of duty. Senior management fosters the notion that by giving people the tools and knowledge, it will bring out the best in everyone. They strongly believe that people are fundamentally motivated to do the right thing. In this company, leaders become leaders by leading. The people in the organization emphasize that to be a leader, people have to recruit followers. They have to attract talent that is willing to work with them.

Companies like Gore are relatively rare. In many instances, a coaching culture is still an ideal to strive for. Such a culture does not appear by itself; it is a product of the efforts of a number of people. As a rule, these are people who have experienced the power of coaching for themselves and their teams, and want to expand the experience to the organization at large. Having become better leaders themselves through coaching, they now want to use a coaching philosophy in their daily organizational and personal lives.

In the chapters that follow, we describe the practice of implementing holistic executive group coaching interventions in business schools and companies. Part 1 presents the model and application of our psychodynamic/systemic approach to leadership coaching and development. Using case studies and personal narratives, Part 2 provides a deeper investigation into what goes on in coaching sessions to create more reflective practitioners, from the perspectives of both participants and coach. Part 3 extends the discourse to the macro level, by discussing the ways in which the creation of coaching cultures can transform organizations into more effective, humane, and sustainable best places to work. We do our best work when we do something that makes us happy. Work can be either fun or a chore—and we prefer fun.

INTRODUCTION

NOTES

1. Kets de Vries, M. F. R. (2001). *The Leadership Mystique*. London: Financial Times/Prentice Hall; Kets de Vries, M. F. R. (2006a). *The Leader on the Couch: A Clinical Approach to Changing People and Organizations*. New York: Wiley; Kets de Vries, M. F. R., Korotov, K. and Florent-Treacy, E. (2007). *Coach and Couch: The Psychology of Making Better Leaders*. New York: Palgrave Macmillan.
2. Kets de Vries, M. F. R. (2006b). "The Eight Roles Executives Play." *Organizational Dynamics*, 36(1): 28–44.
3. Flaherty, J. (2005). *Coaching: Evoking Excellence in Others*. Burlington, MA: Elsevier Butterworth-Heinemann; Kets de Vries, M. F. R. (2005). *Global Executive Leadership Inventory: Facilitator's Guide*. San Francisco: Pfeiffer; Orem, S., Binkert, J., and Clancy, A. (2007). *Appreciative Coaching: A Positive Process for Change*. San Francisco: Jossey-Bass.
4. Global Executive Leadership Inventory: Facilitator's Guide. San Francisco: Pfeiffer; Kets de Vries, M. F. R. (2009). *Sex, Money, Happiness and Death: The Quest for Authenticity*, London: Palgrave Macmillan.
5. Flaherty, J. (2005). *Coaching: Evoking Excellence in Others*. Burlington, MA: Elsevier Butterworth-Heinemann; Hudson, F. M. (1999). *The Handbook of Coaching*. San Francisco: Jossey-Bass. Hunt, J. and Weintraub, J. (2002). *The Coaching Manager: Developing Top Talent in Business*. Thousand Oaks, CA: Sage Publications.
6. Kilberg, R. R. (2000). *Executive Coaching*. Washington, DC: American Psychological Association.
7. Kets de Vries, M. F. R., Korotov, K., and Florent-Treacy, E. (2007). *Coach and Couch: The Psychology of Making Better Leaders*. New York: Palgrave Macmillan.
8. Schein, E. (1985). *Organizational Culture and Leadership*. San Francisco, Jossey-Bass; Schein, E. H. (1992). *Organizational Culture and Leadership*. 2nd edn. San Francisco, CA: Jossey-Bass.
9. Kets de Vries, M. F. R. (2000). "The Clinical Paradigm: Manfred Kets de Vries' Reflections on Organizational Theory: Interview by Erik van de Loo." *Academy of Management Executive & European Management Journal*, 18 (1 February), 2–21; Kets de Vries, M. F. R. (2006a). *The Leader on the Couch: A Clinical Approach to Changing People and Organizations*. New York: Wiley; Christakis, N. A. and Fowler, J. H. (2009). *Connected: The Surprising Power of our Social Networks and how they Shape our Lives*. Boston: Little, Brown and Company.
10. Palmer, S. and A. Whybrow (2007). *Handbook of Coaching Psychology: A Guide for Practitioners*. London: Routledge.
11. Greenberg, J. R. and Mitchell, S. A. (1983). *Object Relations in Psychoanalytic Theory*. Cambridge, MA: Harvard University Press.
12. Mann, J. (1973). *Time Limited Psychotherapy*. Cambridge, MA: Harvard University Press; Malan, D. and Osimo, F. (1992). *Psychodynamics, Training, and Outcome in Brief Psychotherapy*. Oxford: Butterworth Heinemann.
13. Erikson, E. (1993). *Childhood and Society*. New York: Norton; Levinson, D. (1991). *The Seasons of Man's Life*. New York: Ballantine.
14. Bion, W. R. (1991). *Experiences in Groups and Other Papers*. London: Routledge; Yalom, I. D. (1985). *The Theory and Practice of Group Psychotherapy*. New York: Basic Books.
15. Nichols, M. P. and Schwartz, R. C. (2006). *Family Therapy: Concepts and Methods*. 7th edn. Boston: Pearson/Allyn & Bacon.
16. Christakis, N. A. and Fowler, J. H. (2009). *Connected: The Surprising Power of our Social Networks and how they Shape our Lives*. Boston: Little, Brown and Company.
17. Miller, W. R. and S. Rollnick (2002). *Motivational Interviewing*. New York: The Guilford Press.
18. Watzlawick, P., J. Weakland, and Fisch, R. (1974). *Change: Principles of Problem Formation and Problem Resolution*. New York: W. W. Norton.
19. Kegan, R. and Lahey, L. L. (2009). *Immunity to Change: How to Overcome It and Unlock the Potential in Yourself and Your Organization*. Boston: Harvard Business School Press.
20. Cooperrider, D. L. and Whitney, D. (Eds) (2008). *Appreciative Inquiry Handbook: For Leaders of Change*. Brunswick, OH: Crown Custom Publishers.

21. Bandura, A. (1997). *Self-Efficacy: The Exercise of Control*. New York: Freeman.
22. Schon, D. A. (1983). *The Reflective Practitioner: How Professionals Think in Action*. New York: Basic Books.
23. Kohut, H. (1971). *The Analysis of the Self*. New York: International Universities Press; Kets de Vries, M. F. R. (2010). *Reflections on Leadership and Career Development*. London: Wiley.
24. 100 Best Workplaces in Europe, 2008; Working Women Top 100 Companies, 2009; Fortune 100 Best Companies to Work for, 2009. 100 Best Workplaces in Europe report, 2009. Available at: http://www.greatplacetowork-europe.com/gptw/GPTW-Magazine-EU.pdf; Financial Times 100 Best Workplaces in Europe (2008) http://www.ft.com/cms/s/0/5f624db0-2bc2-11dd-9861-000077b07658.html; Fortune 100 Best Companies to Work for (2009) http://money.cnn.com/magazines/fortune/bestcompanies/2009/; Sunday Times 100 Best Companies to Work for (2009) http://business.timesonline.co.uk/tol/business/career_and_jobs/best_100_companies/.
25. Watson, N. (2002). "Happy Companies Make Happy Investments." *Fortune*, 27 May, 162; Joyce, K. E. (2003). "Lessons for Employers from *Fortune*'s 100 Best." *Business Horizons*, 46, 2, March–April, 77–84; Fulmer, I. S., Gerhart, B. and Scott, K. S. (2003). "Are the 100 Best Better? An Empirical Investigation of the Relationship Between Being a 'Great Place to Work' and Firm Performance." *Personnel Psychology*, 56, 965–993.
26. "Awards Recognize the Top Employers." *Times Online*, March 10, 2008.
27. Isaksen, S. G. and Lauer, K. J. (2002). "The Climate for Creativity and Change in Teams." *Creativity and Innovation Management*, 11, 74–85; Sutton, R. I. (2001). "The Weird Rules of Creativity." *Harvard Business Review*, 79, 8, 96–103; Ekvall, G. (1996). "Organizational Climate for Creativity and Innovation." *European Journal of Work and Organizational Psychology*, 5, 105–124.

PART ONE: SETTING THE STAGE

1

THE PROOF OF THE PUDDING: AN INTEGRATIVE, PSYCHODYNAMIC APPROACH TO EVALUATING A LEADERSHIP DEVELOPMENT PROGRAM

MANFRED F. R. KETS DE VRIES, ELIZABETH FLORENT-TREACY, LAURA GUILLÉN, AND KONSTANTIN KOROTOV

The demand for leadership development in organizations is increasing exponentially.[1] Whether provided internally or externally through business school courses, a diploma earned in a leadership development program is no longer simply the goal of losers, has-beens, or brilliant but eccentric managers, it is something that most young and mid-career executives want to have on their resume. Even senior executives find that participating in such programs can help them cap their career with a move to a CEO or board position, deal with knotty problems, create a legacy, or simply explore, with a group of like-minded peers, the difficulties of being alone at the top.

But leadership development programs are still in the honeymoon phase, and many have not stood the test of time, let alone any other empirical outcome measure. Our experience in designing and teaching leadership programs shows that participants tend to rate them highly—a phenomenon arguably related to the fact that, to a certain extent, the participants who attend our programs are self- and pre-selected, and are predisposed to seeing a positive outcome. They are often top performers before the course even begins, and are in a feel-good state when the evaluation forms are filled in at the end of the course, having been listened to, and having vicariously experienced and learned from other participants' existential dilemmas.

The honeymoon effect is even more noticeable in leadership development programs that include leadership coaching practices. Evaluation forms completed immediately after a coaching module show that participants are extremely positive about their experience and optimistic about its long-term outcome. They make comments like: "This was a difficult experience, but truly life-changing"; "The coaching module helped me understand my own behavior and that of others in a new and challenging way"; "I have learned skills here that I will use to create a coaching culture in my organization"; "I know now what corporate transformation really implies"; "I have learned how to build a team that really works."* From a

---

*Comments taken from standard evaluation forms completed after IGLC programs or coaching modules.

quantitative point of view, their evaluation of the coaching and the program as a whole is similarly positive. For example, out of a total possible score of 5, our coaching modules received an average score of 4.6 in the time period 2007–2009.

Although affect is undeniably a factor that influences long-term behavioral change,[2] anecdotal measurement of outcome satisfaction is no proxy for significant indicators of real change. Even if we momentarily set aside the meta-question "Were the changes caused by the program that is being evaluated?" two broad and difficult questions face evaluators of leadership development programs.[3] *What* changes have occurred, in terms of dimension, increase or decrease, magnitude of change, and *where* (individual, team, or organizational level)?

Methodological issues make it very difficult to assess the effectiveness of leadership development programs.[4] To measure the effectiveness of a program accurately under ideal conditions, a control group with no leadership development input should be compared to the study group; both should be tested and retested over time, using the same instruments and observers; everyone should answer with complete honesty and full self-awareness to avoid desirability bias; and the whole exercise should take place in a quasi-vacuum, with no discernable extenuating circumstances in the organizational environment during the time of the study.

We are well aware of the constraints facing such studies and have struggled, like many others, to design an evaluation method that takes these factors into account. Unfortunately, we have found that busy executives do not want to participate in control groups, since they see no value to themselves in exchange for their time. Furthermore, organizations are constantly evolving; and the executives who have attended a leadership development program and are willing to participate in an evaluation study are, most likely, already highly invested in the leadership process, and therefore can be predicted to report correlated improvement in leadership competencies over time. On the other hand, participants who feel they gained little or no new skills or knowledge in the program will not be very interested in participating in a follow-up study.

However, research is beginning to demonstrate that leadership development interventions, and in particular coaching, can be effective.[5] In one study[6] executives who completed a leadership development program followed by coaching showed increased productivity, and additional evidence demonstrated that the gain was significantly greater when a leadership coaching activity was included in the development program than when it was not. Many of our own leadership development programs include leadership coaching models, so we are particularly interested in evaluating leadership development programs that include coaching—this model is very high-contact, and therefore is provided at a high tuition fee that must be justified.

The rationale of this chapter is to explore possibilities for evaluation through describing one of our leadership development programs, the Challenge of Leadership (COL), which has been taught and directed by Manfred Kets de Vries for the past 19 years. We believe that the COL program contains intrinsic evaluation components that cannot and should not be disassociated from the program dynamic itself, and we have identified ways to continually verify that our teaching and coaching pedagogies are in sync with the participants' needs.

We refer to the COL program as a *leadership development intervention*. In this program, we use specific methodologies to create a *transitional space* in which participants can identify and enable desired behavioral change.[7] The pedagogies used in COL programs are designed to match the personal expectations of the participants, which are to increase self-awareness, overcome personal blind spots, acquire better people-management skills, acquire a more sophisticated repertoire of leadership behaviors, become more adept at complex problem solving in their respective organizations, and, not least, arrive at a better quality of life. The intervention techniques include socially guided methods—such as 360-degree feedback instruments, leadership coaching, role play, storytelling, vicarious learning, mirroring, positive reframing, stressing self-efficacy, and network contagion—techniques that by definition require active participation to shape not only what executives do but also who they are and how they interpret what they do.[8] Participants are encouraged to learn and are helped to acquire new skills and insights that will positively affect the way they behave at work and in their private life.[9]

In this chapter, we explore how the framework for a leadership development program can provide a framework for evaluation. We discuss how the COL program structure and objectives reflect how such programs can be adapted to support the assessment of leadership development programs. We describe the theoretical foundations of the leadership development intervention: the clinical paradigm, some of our proprietary 360-degree feedback instruments, the live case study approach, and group coaching methodologies. We end by suggesting directions for future research and sharing a few final thoughts.

THE PROGRAM FRAMEWORK AS A FRAMEWORK FOR EVALUATION

When considering ways to evaluate the COL program, we speculated that the dimensions of leadership distilled from the grounded theory research upon which the program is based would provide a domain of outcomes to be considered. We believed we could make use of existing measurements to evaluate progress and outcome, including pre-program interviews and essays; a mid-program feedback process using 360-degree instruments specifically designed for the program being measured; and an ongoing process of testing new behaviors, further moderated by feedback through presentation of live case studies by each participant.

It was also apparent that, if evaluation only took place at a fixed point at the end of the program, it was neither very useful as a means continually to improve individual elements of the program design, nor could it indicate precisely what change occurred, or when. We felt that evaluation needed to be embedded in the teaching methodologies and tools used throughout the COL program. Given the well tested, stable, and smooth functioning of the program components, we theorized that the underlying teaching philosophy, feedback instrument design and use, and coaching practices unique to the COL program could be reframed as an internally integrated, collaborative method for evaluating the programs' outcomes longitudinally.

The crucial embedded components of COL that permit longitudinal evaluation of the program in this way are (1) the participants' expected outcomes of the COL program; (2) the theoretical framework of a clinical orientation to leadership development; (3) the IGLC 360-degree feedback questionnaires that form the basis for defining the leadership dimensions the program targets; and, finally (4) the methodological focus on live case studies and group coaching.

Thus more generally, a framework that embeds assessment should include the following:

- clearly defined expected outcomes;
- a theoretical leadership framework that is coherent with the organizational context;
- carefully selected leadership dimension(s) as program targets; and
- the identification and selection of the appropriate pedagogical tools.

THE EXPECTED OUTCOMES OF THE PROGRAM

Evaluating leadership development programs can be complicated by the fact that frequently, the ultimate outcome or objectives are not set out clearly beforehand.[10] Measuring outcome at, or after, the end of a program becomes a very difficult exercise if the objectives have not been built into the original program design. Vague expectations lead to ambiguous results. What are the participants and/or organization trying to gain by taking a particular program? Answering this question prior to any intervention facilitates not only program design but also program assessment. The *purpose* of the intervention program is a key variable in the selection of practices for a specific program.

The outcome and objectives of the COL program are introduced from the moment future participants first consider it. As they flip through the COL brochure or visit the web site, they soon realize that this is not a typical leadership development program. Although they may not be familiar with the concepts, it becomes apparent that this particular program takes a double-pronged approach, focusing on both cognition and affect to create behavior change. They read:

> *Act, think, react, rethink.* The COL program aims to improve senior executives' understanding of how human behavior (their own and that of others) affects the functioning of their organization. By focusing on conscious and unconscious behavior, as well as rational and irrational action, it helps executives manage both irrational and dysfunctional processes in their companies. It accompanies them in an exploration of their personal leadership style and addresses ways of dealing with processes that fall outside recommended models.

6

As they read, they are introduced to the overarching objective of the program: that they will become reflective practitioners, making them better equipped to moderate their own actions, behavior, feelings, emotions and drives, and to understand these processes in others.[11]

The most curious and courageous among them will pursue the matter and fill out an in-depth application, answering essay questions designed to help them explore their readiness for change. Sample questions include What is the hardest decision you have ever taken? What do you like best/least about your life? What are you deeply passionate about? If you could have an entirely different life, what would you want to be or do?

Once the future participants have submitted their essays, each candidate has private interviews with one of the two faculty members. The purpose of the interviews is to assess the psychological readiness of the potential participant. The interview becomes a semi-structured exchange between the individual and the faculty member (both faculty members teaching this program are trained therapists/psychoanalysts as well as business school professors), during which they discuss the candidate's strengths and weaknesses, and fears, fantasies, and desires regarding the future of his or her career. They often bring concerns about family members into the conversation as well. The admission process becomes an important preparatory stage for further discovery, reflection, and experimentation, so that the learning starts before the actual beginning of the course.[12]

The essays and entry interviews provide qualitative data in terms of a baseline record of participants' leadership accomplishments, as well as a record of the areas in which they believe they need to develop their leadership skills. The interviews are triangulated, as the two professors discuss their impressions of each candidate before the program begins. Key factors in the discussion are the degree of psychological readiness, personal strength (the ability to tolerate the anxieties that emerge in such a program), whether they have an observing ego (the ability to oscillate between "going from the dance floor to the balcony"), and their capacity to draw connections between past and future events.

The right theoretical framework

The essential concept underlying the COL program is the application of a clinical paradigm to the study of human beings in organizations, and we draw on several key concepts. Participants are introduced to and experience theories of group processes and dynamics. Since the focus of the program remains very much on the world of work—in this systemic approach, both the micro (the individual) and the macro (the organization) are considered to be equally important—theories of organizational behavior are integrated and explored. But the clinical lens allows participants to dig deeper, to seek out and understand the ambiguities inherent to change,[13] and to work together to create an action plan for change, in a cognitive behavioral approach. Most critically, it introduces participants to psychodynamic conceptualizations, such as psychoanalytic theory, systems theory, and short-term dynamic psychotherapy. It also uses concepts of network contagion.[14]

Using the clinical paradigm as a lens to look at the world is a way to understand better "under the surface" behavior.[15] The clinical paradigm can be described metaphorically as a way to explore a person's inner theater—the scripts that determine a person's behavior and actions.[16] We all have our own rich tragicomedy playing out on an inner stage, with key actors representing the people we have loved, hated, feared, or admired. Some of them are associated with painful experiences, others with great joy. These unconscious associations are more than just a private screening of secret events, however, because they affect not only a person's real-life loves, friendships, and artistic expressions (in other words, how we reconcile our need for affiliation and exploration) but also provide the source of behavior patterns that affect a person's leadership style. And these behavioral patterns are not only rehearsed in relationships with one's boss, colleagues, or subordinates but may affect the organizational culture as a whole, becoming a subtle force influencing how insiders and outsiders act in relation to the organization.[17]

By exploring these themes in a leadership development program, we can tease out important keys to understanding a person's behavior and relationship patterns. We can draw parallels between past relationships and current behavior, and explore how a person might be using behavioral responses learned in the past—in interactions with those key, inner actors—to deal with situations in the present. Thus the clinical perspective enables individuals to evaluate their own behavior better, and helps them decide what is no longer working for them. Armed with this greater self-insight, they are more likely to embark on a journey of personal change.

In the COL program, executives explore not only manifest issues but also what lies beneath the surface, and use what they discover there to become more effective leaders. Our integrative, systemic, clinical perspective helps leaders understand the hidden dynamics associated with individual perception, motivation, leadership styles, interpersonal relationships, team behavior, collusive situations, social defenses, corporate culture, and the extent to which individuals, groups and teams, organizations, and even societies can be prisoners of their past. We want our participants to be open to the idea that they can be detectives, deciphering their organizations' internal and social dynamics, and becoming aware of the various unconscious and invisible psychodynamic processes and structures that influence the behavior of individuals, dyads, and groups in organizations. And most importantly, we want them to understand that organizational life is like a mirror, and what they see reflected in the organization, they must examine inside themselves. Although they do not leave our programs believing themselves to be trained psychotherapists, our participants are better equipped emotionally to bring a greater dose of realism to organizational interventions. It makes sense to them that in-depth approaches to organizational interventions have a greater chance of addressing the deeply entrenched causes of individual and organizational problems.

Leadership programs have been described as having a therapeutic quality, although they are not therapy.[18] The aim of our programs is not a temporary high but lasting transformation and change. To make this happen, we teach participants self-analytic activities so they can eventually engage in organizational interventions on their own, facilitating the creation of a coaching culture that potentially includes people at every level of the organization.

The leitmotif of our work is to help people rethink their answers to the following questions: "Is the typical executive really a stable, logically minded human being?" "Is management really just a series of predictable tasks performed by rational executives and stakeholders?" And we pay attention to the out-of-awareness processes that raise the most difficult questions of all: "How aware am I of the reasons behind my *own* behavior?" "How does *my* behavior affect those around me?" "How can I *change* my behavior?" The faculty makes it very clear in the intake interview that if participants are looking to become a transformational leader in one easy lesson, they are at the wrong address and should look elsewhere. If, however, they want to learn more about their own behavior and how this behavior affects others, help can be provided. And paradoxically, by working on themselves, they can have a major effect on others, making transformational activities a reality.

Targeting carefully selected leadership dimensions

Many of the executives who attend our programs are global leaders. They are either working for a global or transnational organization with at least one subsidiary outside of the home country, or they are in organizations that focus on domestic markets but are very attuned to the global context in which their competitors operate. The participants are also typically top organizational executives—group CEOs, CEOs of divisions, board directors, and the like.

In designing programs and teaching tools appropriate for this executive level, we had to answer some fundamental research questions: What do such leaders have to do to be effective? What roles do they play? What—if anything—distinguishes an effective leader from an effective (global) leader? By what criteria should excellence be judged? Our process of exploration—as always, informed by the clinical paradigm—was both heuristic and hermeneutic. We conducted a large number of consultations and research projects in global organizations. Data were collected and themes were interpreted in an iterative way to arrive at a set of working hypotheses about global leadership practices, in a process known as grounded theory. In other words, while engaged in the process of hypothesis formulation, we delineated connections, patterns, and themes, at the individual and organizational level, and continuously modified our hypotheses. Through this ethnographic and clinical orientation, ideas were developed and thick descriptions emerged.[19]

The constructs that emerged from this research were content-analyzed by five faculty members working independently of one another, and then grouped in terms of themes relevant to leadership. Inspection of the groupings revealed a very high level of agreement among faculty members. The constructs of the inventory were derived through triangulation of the data in-group discussions.

Decades of research on the effects of psychotherapy,[20] self-help programs,[21] training programs,[22] and education[23] have shown that people can change their behaviors, motivations, and self-perception. But most of the studies focus on a single characteristic. To address this gap, and based on our research, we designed a set of three 360-degree instruments, the Personality Audit (PA), the Leadership Archetypes Questionnaire (LAQ), and the Global Executive Leadership Inventory (GELI), which would complement each other and provide insights not only about behaviors and character attributes, but also about a person's inner theater. In our experience, a side-by-side comparison of the results from these instruments often helps participants to understand how personality traits affect leadership styles, which in turn helps them to initiate change in manifest actions and behaviors.

Personality traits as measured as individual constitutional factors by the PA can be understood as a set of potentials that the individual may or may not activate in daily situations. But personality may not be sufficient to understand why individuals differ in performance or in choosing activities within organizational contexts. The next step is to grasp the constellations of character traits that help to interpret observational phenomena and understanding individual behavior. These constellations of behaviors are called archetypes, as measured by the LAQ. These archetypes are closely linked to the specific organizational context in which individuals operate and in which a specific behavior is produced. The outcome supports the GELI, which deals with the identification of effective behaviors that may have a strong explanatory power over performance.

In designing the PA, LAQ, and GELI, we paid particular attention to the fact that our participants have very diverse worldviews and cultural values. We had a specific set of criteria, setting parameters for both the instruments and the feedback process for which they would be used. The instruments were designed by a multicultural team, with items written so they would be clear to nonnative English-speaking participants. They had to have culture face validity and be culturally relevant. The instruments were tested and validated on a mixed culture group, and, following psychometric validation, have been used in all our programs.

To date, our instruments have been used by over 50,000 people from around the world, so that we have accrued experience, predictability, and stability over time. We have also created an archival database to collect and aggregate the data generated. (Identifying information is stripped from the data immediately after a program ends, with one exception: if participants agree in writing to a follow-up study, their names remain linked with their responses until the end of the study.) This database is accessible through a web site, allowing researchers to analyze the data in different ways, for example, by age, gender, nationality, or position. Participants' scores are converted into percentile rankings derived from the data, allowing them to compare their own leadership behaviors to all the other top executives in our database. With this data, we can recalculate norms and standard deviations for specific geographical regions, translate and test new target language versions, and with participants' permission, use it for test-retest longitudinal studies.

The Personality Audit (PA) [24]

To be effective leaders, executives must understand the reasons why they do what they do.[25] They need to study their motivation from the inside to truly understand what is happening on the outside. This requires taking into consideration their relational world, paying attention to the forces of human development, and considering their emotional management. This approach creates a more three-dimensional appreciation of human behavior and helps executives obtain greater access to, and understanding of, their emotional lives.

To help participants in the COL and other leadership development programs to gain insights about facets of their personality that may come into play in the workplace, we developed the 360-degree Personality Audit (PA). By providing insight about the ways in which conscious/observable and unconscious/invisible processes influence behavior, the PA supports a better understanding of interpersonal relationships, recurring conflict patterns, and the meaning of one's actions and experiences. What distinguishes the PA in particular is that it facilitates a comparison between executives' behavior in the world of work, and in their private life.

The PA is designed to provide an assessment of seven of the major personality dimensions important in human functioning. The seven dimensions of the instrument—derived from basic aspects of personality—can help people understand the complexities of personality functioning. These dimensions, when assessed by the test-taker and others, provide a glimpse of the executive's inner world. Each of the seven dimensions of personality assessed in the PA has two anchor points. The dimensions are: high–low self-esteem, trustful–vigilant, conscientious–laissez-faire, assertive–self-effacing, extroverted–introverted, high-spirited–low-spirited, and adventurous–prudent.

The Leadership Archetypes Questionnaire (LAQ) [26]

We designed the Leadership Archetype Questionnaire (LAQ) as a survey instrument to facilitate discussions about the concept and creation of effective teams. We focus on the idea that no single leader can be perfect in all dimensions. It is important to be able to recognize individual strengths and weaknesses in order to form well-balanced executive role constellations. It is also important to keep in mind that different phases in the organizational lifecycle will often require different kinds of leadership skills.[27] To help participants grasp these concepts, we introduce them to the idea of leadership archetypes.

Personality theorists recognize that certain constellations of character traits—archetypes—recur on a regular basis. A leadership archetype characterizes the way leaders deal with people and situations in an organizational context. These archetypes represent prototypes for ideas, a template for interpreting observed phenomena and understanding behavior. The eight leadership archetypes included in the LAQ are: strategist, change-catalyst, transactor, builder, innovator, processor, coach, and communicator.

The LAQ helps leaders understand the way they deal with people and situations in an organizational context, identify situations in which a particular leadership style could be most effective, and think about what it is like to work with people who demonstrate certain dominant behaviors. It also helps them determine the best roles for each team member, the best way to manage and work for people with certain dominant characteristics, which combination of styles works well, and which to avoid. Finally, it can help leaders create teams of executives best suited to particular challenges, for example, merger integration, new product development, or transition periods.

Global Executive Leadership Inventory (GELI) [28]

Analysis of leadership practices in various types of organizations and countries confirmed our belief that the most effective leaders simultaneously fulfill two roles: the first is charismatic and the second "architectural."[29] The first involves *envisioning, empowering* and *energizing*—behaviors that direct, inspire, and motivate followers. The second involves *designing and aligning* organizational structures and processes. The most successful leaders appeared to be extremely talented at fulfilling the charismatic and architectural roles, or at creating top executive teams that complemented their own shortcomings in either of these areas.[30]

These two roles consist of a number of sub-roles. In fact, we determined that the world-class executives in our study focus on 12 main tasks, which we conceptualized as dimensions: visioning, empowering, energizing, designing and aligning, rewarding and giving feedback, team-building, outside stakeholder orientation, global mindset, tenacity, emotional intelligence, life balance, and resilience to stress.

Building on our research studies on the dimensions of excellent leadership, we designed a proprietary 360-degree survey instrument with a clinical perspective, the Global Executive Life Inventory (GELI), specifically for use in our leadership development programs. In addition, in our exploratory interviews with potential participants, we discovered that emotional intelligence, resilience to stress, and life balance are little-explored, yet critical themes that emerge in discussions with executives about their concerns. An important objective in developing the GELI, therefore, was to combine an exploration of these essential dimensions in one 360-degree questionnaire.

360-DEGREE INSTRUMENTS AS EVALUATION TOOLS

Use of 360-degree instruments brings an element of ongoing evaluation to leadership development programs. Participants judge the face validity of the instruments' dimensions and their applicability to their own specific leadership situations. In addition, when instruments are used in coaching interventions, they comprise part of the joint sense-making process, and involve individual participants and their peers, faculty, and coaches. Discussion of 360-degree results in the context of a program immediately provides signals about how the concepts apply to daily life. Moreover, when executives from different organizations and countries converge in their opinion about the importance of a particular dimension for leadership success, a kind of spontaneous triangulation occurs, involving the program-learning community at large (participants, faculty, and coaches).

The appropriate pedagogical focus

Transformational programs work well in a modular format. A modular structure[31] gives the learner a chance to tie the educational environment to the working experience. This structure makes it possible to create a safe environment for "pausing," allowing reflection and experimentation outside the pressures of daily life, which permits individual change and development to ferment and emerge. This in turn encourages individuals to experiment with new ways of behaving in their daily life (private and personal), then to come back in subsequent modules and report to the group on their experiences in a context of mutual reflection. The faculty refers to this as the "shame, guilt, and hope" approach. Many people have "dreams"—good intentions of leading life differently—but with no action, nothing happens, hence shame. In the class setting, participants make public declarations of intent regarding what they want to change, leading to a sense of obligation and, given the public nature of their declarations, anticipation of guilt if they fail to deliver. The understanding and encouragement of the group leads all to hope that change is indeed possible.

The COL program consists of four one-week intensive modules. The first three modules are spread over six months; the final module follows half a year later to assess if participants' good intentions have been internalized. It becomes a built-in alumni session. In the first module, participants are introduced to the clinical paradigm through lecture and discussion sessions that show the links between the inner theater of the individual, and the culture and strategy of the organization. References are made to life cycle and developmental issues. Simultaneously, participants are invited to plunge into the difficult work of exploring themselves and dealing with unfinished business.

Given the psychoanalytic background of the two faculty members, by its very nature COL establishes participatory processes, and sets trust-building as a key primary goal. The two faculty members model multilateral self-awareness, empathy, and the use of the self as a responsive instrument.[32] To create a pause, there is an emphasis on learning and practicing executive leadership coaching. Through a virtuous cycle of reflection (supported by a live case study approach, group coaching, and vicarious learning), action (testing new behaviors in the workplace) is created, implemented, evaluated, accepted, and if all goes well, internalized.[33]

The clinical paradigm offers a tremendous opportunity for faculty members to use the leaders' own behavior as real-life case studies, with the added advantage that individual case studies are sure to be of interest to the executive concerned. In each module, participants take the "hot seat": each tells his or her "live case study" to the group. In a context of safe, *transitional space*,[34] participants bare their souls (as far as they wish to go), describing fears, doubts, and hopes around salient issues in both their personal and professional life. They share their PA, LAQ, and GELI 360-degree feedback results with the members of a small study group (and, at times, the whole group). When that happens, the other members of the group respond, challenging their fellow participants to explore possible options and potential outcomes. Each participant listens, then with the help of the group and the faculty members, identifies an action plan, with several key points to be tested in real-life situations between modules. All participants report back in the next module whether or not they feel satisfied with progress made, and the feedback loop begins again. In an appreciative inquiry approach, the participant's world is reframed not as a problem to be solved but a mystery to be explored.[35]

For example, one executive began by telling the group that he was wondering if he should be in the running for the CEO position in his organization. Currently a senior executive in the organization, he was very effective, but taking the number one position seemed very frightening to him. The discussion with his peers in COL was enlightening. He told them that, as the son of the headmaster of the school he attended as a teenager, he had learned always to operate under the radar. Being an extremely talented student, he was often singled out by his father. Growing up as the focus of what he perceived as negative attention, he had always felt that it was less risky to be second best. This behavior pattern, which was associated with many confusing emotions, had continued into his adult life. Listening to the comments from the group after his live case study presentation, he became more aware of the relationship between his past and present behavior, and the anxiety he associated with standing out. This gave him the motivation to stop holding himself back and join the race for the CEO position. He continued to report back to the group over the next few modules as he tested his new impressions and action plan in his work setting. As this example illustrates, involving the group in a participant's leadership development is an important social process that supports introspection and change. It helps to create safe environments for "pausing" and experimentation, and group pressure can provide a tipping point that pushes participants into taking the action steps needed.

Beyond live cases, another significant opportunity for group involvement is group coaching. To create the "pause" that leads participants to experiment with change, leadership development programs should contain at least some form of leadership coaching. Typically, leadership coaching is a one-on-one experience, rather than a group process. However, some professionals familiar with both kinds of intervention argue that executive development and leadership coaching are more effective when carried out in a group setting than one-on-one. Coaching in a group setting offers access to the minds, hearts, and experiences of several individuals. In a group where trust has been well established, a supportive, collective approach facilitates constructive conflict resolution, stronger commitment to personal and professional development, and greater accountability. Group coaching also makes it more likely that a tipping point will be created, whereby the person finds the courage to embark on a process of transformation. Another advantage to group coaching is that it allows participants to practice their own coaching and peer coaching skills, and continue to help one another learn through follow-up peer coaching.[36] In addition, group coaching goes beyond one-on-one relationships, but addresses the socio-dynamics of organizational life (with all its underlying conflicts). Coaching sessions also serve as opportunities to provide immediate feedback to the faculty about important issues in participants' lives or careers that are not explicitly raised through the program.

In sum, the pedagogical focus described above becomes what has been described as a responsive evaluation in which "all stakeholder groups . . . provide on-going feedback through periodic surveys and emergent oral check-ins to help modify intervention activities, increase alignment, and foster desired outcomes."[37] Even more importantly, the *process* becomes *practice*, as over time participants begin to consciously integrate a more reflective behavior into their daily life. This newly learned behavior has proved to be stable over time for many participants, as evidenced by the fact that most of the cohorts continue to meet regularly as a group, years after their program has ended.

Figure 1.1 illustrates the key elements of the program. First, participants embark on what they expect to be a journey of self-discovery (an awareness that

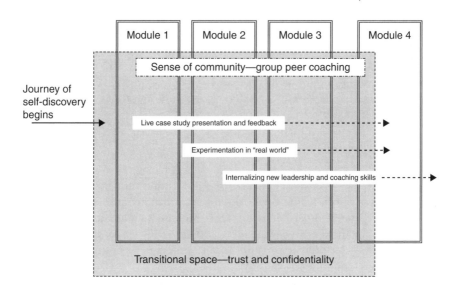

FIGURE 1.1 **A schematic outline of the COL program**

15

begins prior to the program, during the baseline interviews). Next, a transitional space is created; then, as participants become familiar with the transitional space, a feedback loop of narrative, experimentation, and peer coaching is established. Finally, new skills are consolidated and internalized through the interplay of action in the "real world" and reflection during the module.

DIRECTIONS FOR FUTURE RESEARCH

Leadership has traditionally been conceptualized at the individual level, focusing more on the leader than on the social dimension.[38] There is an increasing awareness of the relevance of leader and leadership development in many areas, including facilitating organizational change, developing new business, increasing competition, increasing collaboration across the organization, and facing the challenges posed by globalization.[39] Leadership development at group and organizational levels is encouraged. Leadership development programs trigger the developmental process if they are well designed. But how change is maintained in the long-term needs to be further explored in the literature.

Management and leadership theories and development practices emerge and make sense in a specific time and place, linked to personal issues concerning identity.[40] If we are to truly understand these interventions, they should be constructed within the boundaries of personal experience and identity. More research into leadership development programs that consider the evolution of individual and social identity are needed to understand how training accompanies and reinforces the natural adult development process.

The pedagogies used in leadership interventions cannot simply be cut-and-pasted from one collective to another. They must be in sync with the particular needs of participants. Thus, the different objectives, methods, and learning impacts for novice, intermediate, and senior managers need to be clearly conceptualized. In addition, the evaluation components outlined here should be tested in other leadership development programs—not by applying our methodology per se but through a careful and creative program design that is relevant to the specific pedagogical objectives of those programs.

FINAL THOUGHTS

Our assessment practices are embedded and integrated into the rhythm of the work and lives of the participants who attend our programs, at multiple levels, and with multiple participant perspectives.[41] Our program design matches Symonette's description of mainstreaming evaluation, whereby "the process spotlights and clarifies the intimate interconnections among program visioning, development, implementation, and ongoing improvement."[42]

We describe our leadership development program as the beginning of a journey, and we propose that for this type of program, an integrated collaborative approach to evaluation is logical and appropriate. Our assessment practices—including baseline entry interviews, 360-degree testing, action planning, experimentation, and most significantly, live case study presentations and feedback loops—are embedded and integrated into the rhythm of the work and lives of the participants who attend our programs.

To use another kind of metaphor, we can think of the participants in our leadership development program as captains of sailing vessels. Their destination, a far off, unexplored land, is set. But they know—or at least, they quickly learn—that they cannot sail there in a straight, predetermined line. The unpredictable whims of winds and currents require a constant reevaluation of actions and directions. Compasses are read, depth soundings are taken, the weather report is consulted, and the day's route is adjusted accordingly. At times the ship may be forced to tack in a direction that appears to set it far off course, or allow itself to be propelled by trade winds that add thousands of miles to the journey. If the ship finally arrives safely at port, it is a result of small and constant evaluations of direction and speed.

We believe that the integrative method of evaluation we have outlined in this chapter provides this kind of constant measuring and adjusting—on the part of the faculty as well as participants—and allows individuals to progress in the direction they wish to take when they enter the program. The fact that the COL participants are in the program together for one year, and often remain in contact with each other for years after their program ends, strengthens the validity of the internally integrated evaluation approach.

NOTES

1. Mintzberg, H. (2004). *Managers Not MBAs: A Hard Look at the Soft Practice of Managing and Management Development*. San Francisco: Berrett-Koehler Publishers, Inc.
2. Malan, D. and Osimo, F. (1992). *Psychodynamics, Training, and Outcome in Brief Psychotherapy*. Oxford: Butterworth Heinemann and McCullough.
3. Craig, S. B. and Hannum, K. M. (2007). "Experimental and Quasi-Experimental Evaluations." In K. M. Hannum, J. W. Martineau, and C. Reinelt (Eds) *The Handbook of Leadership Development Evaluation*. San Francisco, CA: Jossey-Bass.
4. Yorks, L., Beechler, S., and Ciporen, R. (2007). "Enhancing the Impact of an Open-Enrollment Executive Program Through Assessment." *Academy of Management Learning and Education*, 6(3), 310–320.
5. Dubouloy, M. (2004). "The Transitional Space and Self-Recovery: A Psychoanalytical Approach to High-Potential Managers' Training." *Human Relations*, 57(4), 467–496; Boyatzis, R. E., Smith, M., and Blaize, N. (2006). "Developing Sustainable Leaders Through Coaching and Compassion." *Academy of Management Journal on Learning and Education*, 5(1), 8–24.
6. Smither, J., London, M., Flautt, R., Vargas, Y., and Kucine, I. (2003). "Can Working with an Executive Coach Improve Multisource Feedback Ratings Over Time? A Quasi-Experimental Field Study." *Personnel Psychology*, 56, 23–44.
7. Kets de Vries, M. F. R. and Korotov, K. (2007). "The Clinical Paradigm: A Primer for Personal Change." In Kets de Vries, Korotov, and Florent-Treacy (Eds) *Coach and Couch: The Psychology of Making Better Leaders*. London: Palgrave Macmillan.
8. Wenger, E. (1998). *Communities of Practice: Learning, Meaning and Identity*. Cambridge: Cambridge University Press.

9. Korotov, K. (2005). "Identity Laboratories." INSEAD PhD Dissertation. Fontainebleau, France: INSEAD.
10. Craig, S. B. and Hannum, K. M. (2007). "Experimental and Quasi-Experimental Evaluations." In K. M. Hannum, J. W. Martineau, and C. Reinelt (Eds) *The Handbook of Leadership Development Evaluation*. San Francisco, CA: Jossey-Bass; Kets de Vries, M. F. R. and Korotov, K. (2007). "Creating Transformational Executive Education Programs." *Academy of Management Learning and Education*, 6:3, 375–387; Mintzberg, H. (2004). *Managers Not MBAs: A Hard Look at the Soft Practice of Managing and Management Development*. San Francisco: Berrett-Koehler Publishers, Inc.
11. Schön, D. A. (1983). *The Reflective Practitioner*. New York: Basic Books.
12. Korotov, K. (2005). "Identity Laboratories." INSEAD PhD Dissertation. Fontainebleau, France: INSEAD.
13. Miller, W. and Rollnick, S. (2002). *Motivational Interviewing: Preparing People for Change* (2nd edn). New York: Guilford Press.
14. Christakis, N. A. and Fowler, J. H. (2009). *Connected: The Surprising Power of Our Social Networks and How They Shape Our Lives*. Boston: Little, Brown and Company.
15. Kets de Vries, M. F. R. (2006a). *The Leader on the Couch*. London: Wiley; Kets de Vries, M. F. R. (2006b). *The Leadership Mystique*. London: FT Prentice Hall.
16. McDougal, J. (1985). *Theaters of the Mind: Illusion and Truth on the Psychoanalytic Stage*. New York: Basic Books.
17. Kets de Vries, M. F. R. and Miller, D. (1984). *The Neurotic Organization*. San Francisco: Jossey-Bass.
18. Kets de Vries, M. F. R., Korotov, K., and Florent-Treacy, E., (Eds) (2007). *Coach and Couch: The Psychology of Making Better Leaders*. London: Palgrave Macmillan.
19. Glaser, B. (1992). *Basics of Grounded Theory Analysis*. Mill Valley, CA: Sociology Press; Strauss, A. (1987). *Qualitative Analysis for Social Scientists*. Cambridge, England: Cambridge University Press; Charmaz, K. (2006). *Constructing Grounded Theory: A Practical Guide Through Qualitative Analysis*. Thousand Oaks, CA: Sage Publications.
20. Hubble, M. A., Duncan, B. L., and Miller, S. D. (Eds) (1999). *The Heart and Soul of Change: What Works in Therapy*. Washington, DC: American Psychological Association.
21. Kanfer, F. H. and Goldstein, A. P. (1991). *Helping People Change: A Textbook of Methods*. New York: Pergamon Press.
22. Morrow, C. C., Jarrett, Q., and Rupinski, M. T. (1997). "An Investigation of the Effect and Economic Utility of Corporate-Wide Training." *Personnel Psychology*, 50(1), 91–117.
23. Pascarella, E. T. and Terenzini, P. T. (1991). *How College Affects Students: Findings and Insights from Twenty Years of Research*. San Francisco, CA: Jossey-Bass; Winter, D. G., McClelland, D. C., and Stewart, A. J. (1981). *A New Case for the Liberal Arts*. San Francisco, CA: Jossey-Bass.
24. For a complete discussion of the Personality Audit see Kets de Vries, M. F. R. (2005). *Personality Audit: Participant Guide*. Fontainebleau: INSEAD Global Leadership Center; Kets de Vries, M. F. R. (2005). *Personality Audit: Facilitator Guide*. Fontainebleau: INSEAD Global Leadership Center; Kets de Vries, M. F. R, Vrignaud, P., Korotov, K., and Florent-Treacy, E. (2006). "The Development of The Personality Audit: A Psychodynamic Multiple Feedback Assessment Instrument." *International Journal of Human Resource Management*, 17(5), 898–917.
25. Daudelin, M. W. (1996). "Learning from Experience Through Reflection." *Organizational Dynamics*, 24(3), 36–48; Schön, D. A. (1983). *The Reflective Practitioner*. New York: Basic Books.
26. For a complete discussion of the Leadership Archetype Questionnaire see Kets de Vries, M. F. R. (2006). *Leadership Archetype Questionnaire: Participant Guide*. Fontainebleau: INSEAD Global Leadership Center; Kets de Vries, M. F. R. (2006). *Leadership Archetype Questionnaire: Facilitator Guide*. Fontainebleau: INSEAD Global Leadership Center; Kets De Vries, M. F. R., Vrignaud, P., Agrawal, A., and Florent-Treacy, E., "Development and Application of the Leadership Archetype Questionnaire." *International Journal of Human Resource Management*, Fall 2010.
27. Lord, R. G. and Hall, R. J. (2005). "Identity, Deep Structure and the Development of Leadership Skill." *Leadership Quarterly*, 16, 591–615; Mumford, M. D., Marks, M. A.,

Shane Connelly, M., Zaccaro, S. J., and Reiter-Palmon, R. (2000). "Development of Leadership Skills: Experience and Timing." *Leadership Quarterly*, 11(1), 87–114; Charan, R., Drotter, S. J., and Noel, J. (2001). *The Leadership Pipeline*. San Francisco: Jossey-Bass.

28. For a full report of the psychometric design and testing of the GELI, see Kets de Vries, M. F. R., Vrignaud, P., and Florent-Treacy, E. (2004). "The Global Leadership Life Inventory: Development and Psychometric Properties of a 360° Instrument." *International Journal of Human Resource Management*, 15:3, 475–492.

29. Kets de Vries, M. F. R. (2006a). *The Leader on the Couch*. London: Wiley; Heifetz, R. A. and Laurie, D. L. (1997). "The Work of Leadership." *Harvard Business Review*, 75(1), 124–134; Kotter, J. P. (1990). *A Force for Change: How Leadership Differs from Management*. New York: Free Press/Collier Macmillan.

30. Kets de Vries, M. F. R. (2006a). *The Leader on the Couch*. London: Wiley.

31. Mintzberg, H. (2004). *Managers Not MBAs: A Hard Look at the Soft Practice of Managing and Management Development*. San Francisco: Berrett-Koehler Publishers, Inc.

32. Kets de Vries, M. F. R., Vrignaud, P. Florent-Treacy, E., and Korotov, K. (2007). "INSEAD Global Leadership Center—360-Degree feedback Instruments: An Overview." *INSEAD Working Paper* 2007/01/EFE; Kets de Vries, M. F. R. (2007). "Are you Feeling Mad, Bad, Sad, or Glad?" *INSEAD Working Paper* 2007/09/EFE.

33. Korotov, K. (2005). "Identity Laboratories." INSEAD PhD Dissertation. Fontainebleau, France: INSEAD.

34. Schrage, M. (1999). *Serious Play: How the World's Best Companies Simulate to Innovate*. Boston, MA: Harvard Business School Press; Dubouloy, M. (2004). "The Transitional Space and Self-Recovery: A Psychoanalytical Approach to High-Potential Managers' Training." *Human Relations*, 57(4), 467–496; Korotov, K. (2005). "Identity Laboratories." INSEAD PhD Dissertation. Fontainebleau, France: INSEAD; Kets de Vries, M. F. R. and Korotov, K. (2007). "The Clinical Paradigm: A Primer for Personal Change." In Kets de Vries, Korotov, and Florent-Treacy (Eds) *Coach and Couch: The Psychology of Making Better Leaders*. London: Palgrave Macmillan.

35. Cooperrider, D. and Avital, M. (2004). *Constructive Discourse and Human Organization*. Boston: Elsevier.

36. Korotov, K. (2008). "Peer Coaching in Executive-Education Programmes." *Training & Management Development Methods*, 22 (2), 3.15–3.24.

37. Symonette, H. (2007). "Making Evaluation Work for the Greater Good: Supporting Provocative Possibility and Responsive Praxis in Leadership Development." In K. Hannum, J. Martineau, and C. Reinelt (Eds) *The Handbook of Leadership Development Evaluation*. San Francisco: Jossey-Bass Business & Management Series, and Center for Creative Leadership, 2007 (p. 121).

38. Day, D. V. (2001). "Leadership Development: A Review in Context." *Leadership Quarterly*, 11(4), 581–613; Avolio, B. J., Sosik, J. J., Jung, D. I. and Berson, Y. (2003). "Leadership Models, Methods and Applications." In D. K. Freedheim, I. B. Weiner, W. F. Velicer, J. A. Schinka, and R. M. Lerner (Eds) *Handbook of Psychology*. Hoboken, NJ: Wiley & Sons.

39. Bolt, J. F. (2005). *The Future of Executive Development*. New York: Executive Development Associates, Inc.

40. Pittaway, L., Rivera, O., and Murphy, A. (2005). "Social Identity and Leadership in the Basque Region: A Study of Leadership Development Programmes." *Journal of Leadership and Organizational Studies*, 11(3), 17–29.

41. Symonette, H. (2007). "Making Evaluation Work for the Greater Good: Supporting Provocative Possibility and Responsive Praxis in Leadership Development." In K. Hannum, J. Martineau, and C. Reinelt (Eds) *The Handbook of Leadership Development Evaluation*. San Francisco: Jossey-Bass Business & Management Series, and Center for Creative Leadership, 2007.

42. Symonette, H. (2007). "Making Evaluation Work for the Greater Good: Supporting Provocative Possibility and Responsive Praxis in Leadership Development." In K. Hannum, J. Martineau, and C. Reinelt (Eds) *The Handbook of Leadership Development Evaluation*. San Francisco: Jossey-Bass Business & Management Series, and Center for Creative Leadership, 2007, p. 117.

2

BRINGING THE CLINICAL PARADIGM INTO EXECUTIVE EDUCATION PROGRAMS: FANTASIES, ANXIETIES, AND HOPES

KONSTANTIN KOROTOV

In this chapter I discuss the challenges of bringing leadership development approaches based on the clinical paradigm into executive education and development programs in companies and business schools. It builds on the program description in the previous chapter to identify the typical anxieties and fantasies associated with introducing methods such as psychodynamically oriented 360-degree instruments, leadership group coaching, and peer coaching. This chapter is based on research into executive education and the experience of designing and delivering programs, as well as consulting, to organizations, program directors, and faculty in business schools. Understanding the concerns and reservations of decision makers, faculty, and program participants should help designers of developmental programs address them and manage stakeholders' expectations better. The chapter will be a useful resource for academics, educators, coaches, and learning and development professionals involved in designing transformational executive development experiences.

I begin by exploring the connection between executive education and the clinical paradigm, and then go further into deliberations about transformational executive education programs and the place of instruments based on the clinical paradigm in such programs. Next, the challenges of introducing 360-degree feedback, group coaching, and peer coaching to executive development programs are discussed. Each of the challenges is viewed from the standpoints of human resources (HR) and learning and development professionals, participants in executive programs, and, finally, directors of programs, that is, faculty members or the consultants who design courses and bear responsibility for program results. Recommendations for dealing with the challenges, based on the experience gained at INSEAD Global Leadership Center and the ESMT Center for Leadership Development Research, are put forward. The chapter concludes with observations regarding the requirements for faculty members and program staff that work with approaches based on the clinical paradigm.

KONSTANTIN KOROTOV

EXECUTIVE DEVELOPMENT AND THE CLINICAL PARADIGM

Executive development inevitably deals with exploring one's identity, or sense of self, and inner theater. Moving to a new organizational role, or to a deeper under-standing of how to manage and lead people, teams, and organizations more effec-tively, while at the same time maintaining a high level of subjective well-being (or happiness), leads us to think about who we are and why we do what we do, the types of relationships we develop at work and beyond, the dos and don'ts that we accept unquestioningly, and the things that we should let go, stop doing, or even, sometimes, stop thinking about. Development for executives thus involves contemplating change, experimenting with change options, trying something new, and eventually incorporating the changes that work into daily behaviors, attitudes, and their view of self and its presentation to the outside world.

Moving (or hoping to move) toward new levels of executive responsibilities—arguably one of the reasons why people attend executive programs—also demands an understanding of what drives other people, why people cooperate with us (or fail to do so), and how to achieve our objectives by eliciting support and help. A significant part of all executives' job is to help their subordinates progress to new challenges and roles; in other words, leaders not only have to develop themselves but also have to be able to help others develop. As mentioned above, development is about change, about creating new aspects of self, of developing new roles.[1] Undertaking conscientious efforts to change oneself and help others change means we must look for explanations for human behavior and feelings. We need to be better equipped to identify our productive and not-so-productive behaviors, and figure out what may lie behind them. While other chapters in this volume elaborate further on the manager's role in developing other people, for example, those that deal with creating better groups and better organizations, the clinical paradigm suggests that shedding light on our own cognitions, emotions, and behaviors may explain success in helping other people grow and develop.

Clinical paradigm literature suggests that there is an explanation for all types of managerial behaviors, even the most unusual ones. It also states that our actions, hopes, fears, and fantasies, which have an impact on our functioning in leadership roles and beyond, are deeply rooted in our unconscious. As the clinical paradigm tells us, emotions play a critically important role in shaping our identities and behaviors. Indeed, human development, according to the clinical paradigm, is simultaneously an interpersonal and intrapersonal process.[2]

Executive education programs often aim to help participants grasp new oppor-tunities, overcome resistance to change, jettison ineffective behavioral patterns, and develop new approaches to working with other people in their organizations. By their nature, such programs require an extensive exploration of the participant's identity and inner theater. This is particularly important for programs designed for people who have already advanced significantly along the career ladder. These individuals tend to face fewer and fewer well-structured challenges and business issues, and be more deeply involved in managing relationships with others as a critical requirement for achieving organizational success. As executives attending development programs often look for support or a push toward changing their behavior or relationships with important people around them (at work, and, quite often, in private life as well), they expect the program to provide them with guidance and tools on how to make such a change.[3]

TRANSFORMATIONAL EXECUTIVE EDUCATION PROGRAMS

Years of designing and delivering executive education programs in the field of leadership have shown me that organizations often expect the short period of time a person spends in a program to lead to dramatic changes, not only in knowledge and skills but also in attitudes and behaviors. The lists of "wants" that companies expect an executive education program to satisfy often includes making their managers more innovative, more inclusive, more coaching oriented, more prepared to delegate, more open-minded, more resilient, more tenacious, more balanced, and less risk-averse. It is incredibly rare for companies to want their executives to concentrate on a particular set of management theories or even particular types of skills during an education program. In essence, they want some deeper change in the individuals themselves and in the relationships between those individuals and other organizational stakeholders.

Understanding that executive development programs, particularly those designed for current and future organizational leaders, are expected to help people change brings us inevitably to the premises of the clinical paradigm. If a particular behavior is ineffective, it makes sense to try and understand what explains it. If an executive is afraid of taking risks, or suffers from an irrational block when it comes to effective delegation, the reasons may be found somewhere beyond the rational, conscious level. If leaders want to exert influence, they need to acknowledge the emotions, in themselves as well as in others, that support or hinder progress. Last but not least, today's relationship patterns may be based on ingrained responses to important people from the past, and may no longer be as effective as they were before. Failing to recognize transference relationships may prevent executives from developing productive connections with subordinates, peers, or bosses.

To help executives really change, we need to influence them at three levels: cognitive, emotional, and behavioral. Business schools and other executive education providers can manage the first component relatively well. After all, generating and packaging knowledge about the functioning of organizations is their raison d'être. However, as we often hear from participants and faculty, new concepts, ideas, models, and research findings sound very promising in the executive classroom, but seem to be very difficult to implement in the context of organizational life. In essence, what we hear is that the cognitive input is really great and refreshing, but managers do not know how to overcome resistance (their own and that of others) to introducing these new ideas. They intellectualize why these ideas would not work in their particular job, and leave the executive classroom with a nice binder full of great academic papers, a bit more body weight from the copious coffee breaks, heavy lunches, and dinners, and a slight aftertaste of frustration about their organization or themselves.

The problem is that participants often do not even try to implement the ideas or concepts they learned in the classroom, whether they are recommendations about strategic planning, advice on running a team, or suggestions on how to show more assertiveness in relationships with their boss, clients, or suppliers. They are not motivated enough to take up the psychological burden of managing the pain associated with modifying their own behavior. As we have often heard, participants do not find it too difficult to start working hard toward some goal—it is much more difficult for them to convince themselves that the goal is worth working hard toward. In other words, they have not developed an emotional foundation for their desire to change. Involving others (bosses, colleagues, and subordinates) in implementing new ideas learned in an executive development program means taking into account how others view new ideas, and how implementing those new ideas affects their emotional well-being. Learning to recognize and work with one's own emotions as well as those of other people goes beyond the cognitive input of a lecture.

Even a motivated participant with cognitive input and the right motivational foundation to get things done may need guidance and help in developing new behaviors that support the intended goals. Opportunities to experiment with new behaviors, get feedback and advice, and discuss and try out various behavioral alternatives create psychological safety and contribute to the self-efficacy needed to turn the knowledge obtained in an executive program into actionable steps.

Programs designed with the ideas and approaches of the clinical paradigm in mind attempt to combine the cognitive, emotional, and behavioral sides of executive development. Importantly, the clinical paradigm argues for methods that encourage executives to look at developments around themselves through the lens of their own motivational driving forces, relationship patterns, and deeply ingrained beliefs about self and others. Discussion of theoretical models is normally combined with putting a participant into the shoes of an executive who has to make a decision (e.g., in a case study analysis, a participant's life case, or a simulation). Then, through peer coaching, group leadership coaching, or individual executive coaching, participants' current situations are discussed within the context of their own work and life, with the hope that personal "aha!" moments will lead to insights. Encouragement from faculty, coaches, and fellow participants leads to clarification of the emotional need for change. Behavioral experimentation through in-class activities or, ideally, through practice in "real life" between program modules (in the case of a multi-module executive course), provides a basis for becoming more effective in work and life.

Many leader and leadership development methods based on the clinical paradigm are in fact based on ideas and experiments from the field of short-term dynamic psychotherapy and group psychotherapy.[4] These approaches help people acquire insights into their experiences and the role of various life events and encounters from the past in the issues they face today. Executives cannot afford to ignore the fact that issues related to their nonworking life are important influences on their effectiveness at work. Unlike traditional therapy, however, the leader development path is significantly shorter, at least in terms of time. The goals of executive education are naturally different from those of a therapeutic intervention. However, executives very often need to be helped to recognize their talents and strengths, as well as their limiting behaviors and the negative impacts these may have on the task at hand, the people around them, or their own career.[5] This can only be done if an executive development program incorporates a significant number of opportunities for participants to engage in reflection, to experiment with their thoughts by discussing them with other participants and/or program faculty, and to receive feedback in a safe environment. Opportunities for such reflection come from analyzing 360-degree feedback, group coaching sessions, and peer coaching discussions.

Although course feedback forms and follow-up communication with participants indicate that including these elements in executive education is usually highly appreciated afterward, the idea of incorporating such elements generates a lot of anxiety among learning and development professionals, program directors, and faculty at the time. Implementing 360-degree feedback, group coaching sessions, and peer coaching discussions may also meet with a certain level of initial resistance from program participants. In the rest of this chapter, I will look in detail at the concerns that designers of transformational executive development programs need to address when incorporating psychodynamically oriented methods in their courses. I will look at the issues of concern to clients (learning and development or HR professionals), recipients of the service (program participants), and, last but not least, the program directors who are responsible for the overall program quality and budgets.

CHALLENGES OF BRINGING 360-DEGREE FEEDBACK INTO EXECUTIVE EDUCATION PROGRAMS

360-degree feedback is commonly used to personalize the learning in an executive program and to stimulate the process of behavior and identity exploration and experimentation. The results of 360-degree feedback are often used to initiate discussions in groups or during individual coaching sessions. Recent literature on multisource feedback has discussed the potential virtues and vices of the method extensively. In this chapter, I am only talking about using 360-degree feedback for executive development, not for organizational decision-making (e.g., using the results of feedback to determine promotion opportunities or pay increases for a particular manager). The challenges for organizational decision-making have been identified and discussed elsewhere.[6]

Self-awareness, or our ability to be conscious of our own sense of self, emotions, behavior, and impact on others, is based on self-knowledge and an understanding of the congruence between how we see ourselves and how we are perceived by others. The ability to see oneself through the perception of others is seen as an important part of human growth.[7] Giving executive education participants an opportunity to check the congruence of their own view of themselves with that of observers should lead to a desire to reduce discrepancies and adapt to the performance expectations of the organization.[8]

Although HR professionals and most business school faculty accept the value of 360-degree feedback in principle, many are often hesitant when such a tool is suggested as part of an executive development program. This caution may be explained by a number of factors. First of all, quite a few organizations have already experimented with 360-degree feedback, and some have firmly established it as part of HR processes; including the instrument in an executive education program may interfere with the organization's plans to use 360-degree feedback in its normal business cycle. Members of the organization may also object to being asked to undertake a 360-degree assessment more than once a year, whether as recipients of feedback or as observers.

More importantly, however, the effectiveness of the 360-degree method may be viewed with some skepticism. Scholars have noted that individuals who receive feedback sometimes perform worse subsequently than those who do not. They suggest that contextual or individual differences may have an impact on the effectiveness of 360-degree results.[9] When my colleagues and I talk to executives who are concerned about the use of this method in executive programs, we often find that they have been given the results of a previous 360-degree assessment in the form of a colorful brochure full of charts, tables, and graphs, but are then left to figure out what the charts mean by themselves. Moreover, they are left alone with the questions, hopes, disappointments, frustrations, fears, anger, and other reactions that reading a 360-degree feedback report might generate. There is no significant discussion of the results in a trusting environment, which is essential to make sense of the charts and numbers. HR professionals notice, therefore, that the efforts they have invested in administering the tool at best cause irritation. Later in this chapter I discuss the process of making sense of 360-degree results as part of an executive education program. We normally do this in the context of a group leadership coaching session. If no time is scheduled for processing 360-degree results within a program, we recommend not using the methodology at all for that particular course.

HR and learning and development managers are often concerned with the type of 360-degree tools suggested for executive programs. They might question the methodological basis of a questionnaire being offered to their participants, or express concern with the norms being used for possible comparisons. Unfortunately, the most successful managers in many organizations from an objective point of view (e.g., those who have made a significant contribution to the organization's results or those who have made it to a very high level in the organizational hierarchy) are often exempt from taking internal 360-degree assessments. In these cases, there are simply no intra-organizational norms to help in interpreting the results.

The concerns of HR and learning and development professionals, and potential participants, need to be managed. One way to do this is to ensure that the tools used are based on research. They should also offer a solid and convincing norm base for comparison purposes. It is helpful to refer to published questionnaire development research papers, particularly for skeptical participants who might question the validity of the tool in attempting to protect their egos from what they may see as less than positive results. It may be appropriate to use instruments that are designed for global use, and that have norms based on the results of participants from various nations.

When 360-degree tools offer more than a reflection of an executive's behavior, when they look deeper into the driving forces behind the behavior, there is even more potential for anxiety. For example, suggesting the use of the Personality Audit described in Chapter 1 often meets with caution from HR and learning and development managers, who are afraid that their executive program participants might, as one of them put it, "engage in too much self-reflection and find out something about themselves that they'd better not know."

One of the motivations behind this book is to make professionals who are concerned with creating better places to work more aware of the need to develop reflective leaders who are unafraid to search for a better understanding of themselves, and then use their findings to improve their success in leading other people. But designers of executive education programs should remind HR and learning and development professionals that programs do not change people; they create the environments and stimuli for executives to want to change themselves. From this standpoint, 360-degree instruments that help people see where they are doing very well, where change is necessary, and where they may need further help, are among the stimuli for executive transformation.

Having said that, the concerns of HR and learning and development professionals who are a bit skeptical about "too much psychology" in the clinically oriented use of 360-degree instruments should still be taken into account. The roots of their concerns come from the practice (mentioned above) of giving people lots of instruments without supporting them with adequate interpretation, reflection, and action planning. Explaining the premises of the clinical paradigm, showing the link between the inner theater and an executive's effectiveness in a leadership role, and assuring that time and space for reflection will be included in the design of the program normally addresses many of the concerns.

Participants themselves are also very anxious about going through a 360-degree process as part of an executive development course. We often hear that they are worried about how the data from the reports will be used. Apparently, participants need confirmation that the data will only be used for the purposes of their growth and development, and will not go into their personal files. Their next concern is how useful the method is for their own growth and development, since they may not have seen it used effectively. Program participants who have had coaching sessions based on their results, or who have managed to make sense of their reports in a candid and supportive discussion with their boss or an HR professional in the past, usually respond significantly more enthusiastically to an offer to go through 360-degree feedback.

The quality of the results obtained from 360-degree feedback and subsequent analysis and sense-making is directly related to the efforts of the observers providing the feedback. Unfortunately, the challenges and concerns of this group of stakeholders are often underestimated, or even completely ignored. Providing feedback requires time, effort, and courage. First of all, filling out 360-degree questionnaires takes time. If an organization regularly puts a lot of its executives through 360-degree feedback processes, chances are that people have to fill out quite a few feedback forms. Detailed questionnaires, which are usually more informative, may take up to an hour to complete. Secondly, observers very often have to make a judgment about a particular behavior (e.g., is this typical or occasional?), which requires mental effort. Qualitative comments are valuable and often provide fertile ground for subsequent sense-making and discussion. Unfortunately, space for such comments is often found at the end of the questionnaire, and observers may be tired or bored by the time they get to that section. Last but not least, just as the executives are concerned about how the data will be used, respondents are equally concerned about anonymity and potential repercussions if they provide candid views on their boss's or colleagues' behavior. It is no secret that one of the very first instincts of recipients of 360-degree feedback is to try and figure out who gave them which scores or comments. It is not by chance that we discourage participants in every program from trying to figure out who is responsible for the anonymous numbers in their 360-degree report.

A special instance of using 360-degree methodology in leadership development programs based on the clinical paradigm is to offer participants an opportunity to gather short, non-anonymous feedback on what they are doing well, what they should continue doing, what they should stop doing, and what they should start doing. Asking those few questions may add a lot of value to sense-making and subsequent coaching sessions using 360-degree assessment results. With this tool, participants can approach not only those who work with them but also people from other organizations (e.g., clients or providers) or even other parts of their lives (e.g., family members or friends). Although this powerful tool is very simple, getting participants past the fear of asking for feedback may not be so easy. Our experience suggests that the best response rate and comment quality are achieved when participants have had a chance to spend some time in the program environment, to develop trust with other participants and faculty or coaches, and have seen the value of the clinical approach. When executives trust the faculty, they also trust the methodology used in the program. Typically, this is only possible in a longer-term, multi-module program. If the program is short, we normally suggest that participants gather this type of 360-degree feedback during the program by sending an e-mail or a fax with a number of questions about the person's leadership style to their designated respondents, or, if possible, by giving them a phone call and recording the answers themselves.

Furthermore, program directors in business schools and consultancies offering leadership development services are often initially wary about introducing 360-degree feedback into their programs. They are not against the method per se, but rather the costs associated with implementing it correctly. Managing 360-degree data gathering may become an ordeal if the provider is not well equipped to tackle the technology challenges, such as user-friendliness of the interface, potential concerns about data security, data collection, and report generation. Even more importantly, the use of 360-degree feedback in an executive course requires processing and discussion opportunities, which are often done in individual or group coaching sessions. Individual sessions may not always be feasible in a short program, and they are clearly expensive. Group coaching sessions[10] also take a substantial amount of program time, and have significant costs, due to the need to have one coach for every five to six participants.

Obviously, positive post-program results (as a minimum, participants' feedback) often take care of the concerns raised by HR and learning and development professionals and make them more likely to use the methodology in subsequent programs. To obtain those positive results, however, the quality of feedback data is critical. Good quality data are necessary to provide participants with valuable information and opportunities for sense-making that can be tied to the content of the program. Years of experience using 360-degree feedback in open-enrollment and customer-specific leadership development programs have shown us time and again the need to explain the method carefully, as well as how it will be used for the purposes of the program.

In multi-module programs, nothing works better than a presentation by a trusted faculty member or program director in a module preceding the use of 360-degree feedback, where the place this method has in the overall logic of the program can be explained. Discussing executives' possible issues and concerns (including engaging, if necessary, in the pros and cons of taking the instrument again if a similar process was recently employed by the participants' company) contributes positively to participants' enthusiasm and willingness to engage as many observers as they can in the data-generating process.

In our experience with programs where it is not possible to hold such a discussion in a classroom setting, participants get a detailed explanatory letter, a written document, and a technical note or article which clarifies the purpose and practice of using the tool, during the pre-program procedure.[11] Participants are encouraged to send the documents about the 360-degree feedback to all their designated observers, so that the latter understand the purpose of their efforts and are motivated to help. We usually encourage program directors or managers to offer the participant and his or her observers an opportunity to address any issues or concerns that they may have. The fact that the results are to be used for developmental purposes in the context of an executive education program is made particularly salient.

Obtaining and processing feedback based on 360-degree methodology is only one of many building blocks in the clinically oriented development process. One of the outcomes of discussing feedback results is the need to go back to those who provided the feedback, thank them for their effort, get some clarification on any issues that are still unclear, and possibly engage them in working on planned changes. The role of the participant's direct boss is critically important in this regard. Unfortunately, many bosses are not prepared to work with participants on making sense of their results. Bosses are sometimes surprised that their responses to the 360-degree feedback are not anonymous (it does not take too much effort to figure out how your boss evaluates you numerically on most 360-degree instruments, particularly when there is a "Boss" line in the results graph). We have been contacted several times by angry bosses who were unhappy that their assessment of the subordinate could not be blended with those of the recipient's subordinates or colleagues. The fact that the boss is afraid of being recognized as providing particular feedback, coupled with the fact that 360-degree feedback instructions are usually totally clear about whose responses will be protected by anonymity, is an interesting learning outcome: it tells you how much such a boss contributes to creating a great place to work.

These considerations are only relevant if there is dedicated time for making sense of the data obtained in the program, otherwise the 360-degree methodology, as I already mentioned, should not be used. Moreover, our experience suggests that the results obtained through clinically oriented 360-degree feedback are only an introduction to the developmental work that is done through another tool based on the premises of the clinical paradigm, namely leadership coaching.

CHALLENGES OF BRINGING GROUP LEADERSHIP COACHING INTO EXECUTIVE EDUCATION PROGRAMS

Group leadership coaching is a way of personalizing the learning from the executive education program for a particular participant. It is an opportunity for the individual to look at their motivation and behavior, process feedback, gain additional insights through exploring their own narratives, engage in discussions with other people, learn vicariously by listening to other people, ask for the impressions of others, actively stage micro-experiments, and commit to post-program action.

Human resources and learning and development professionals usually respond positively to the inclusion of coaching elements in executive education programs. Their concern is typically about the type of coaches who will be involved in the process. When clinically oriented leadership coaching methods are suggested, and particularly when group coaching is offered, the questions are usually about the coach's ability to overcome participants' natural resistance to opening up in a group setting and their ability to act as a useful resource for other group members. They are also concerned about potential rivalry among participants who come from the same organization. In some, relatively rare, cases there may be an element of envy from HR and learning and development professionals who have developed themselves into internal executive coaches in their own organizations.

My colleagues and I work with the IGLC group coaching methodology described in this book and in *Coach and Couch: The Psychology of Making Better Leaders*.[12] The method has been used in long- and short-term open-enrollment executive programs, executive MBA programs, and courses tailor-made for specific customers. Normally, a coaching day is held after participants have spent some time on the course (in a longer program it may take place in the second or third module, in a short, four-day course on day three). The coaching day is preceded by an in-depth discussion of the role reflection plays in developing leaders, and about what value can be drawn from spending a day with a group of peers and a coach. We normally also distribute the 360-degree feedback reports at the end of the day that precedes coaching. Participants are told how to begin to interpret their reports, and are given a chance to raise any immediate questions with the faculty. We normally provide participants with supporting tools, such as workbooks for the instruments with which they are working.[13] The presence and availability of the faculty and additional resources, such as workbooks, serve as "transitional objects," helping participants overcome their initial reactions to the findings in their reports, and help them to deal with the defensive reactions of dismissing the value of the report and diminishing the expected value of the next day's coaching sessions.

As coaching, and particularly group coaching, is a relatively new phenomenon in the experience of many participants, they tend to be cautious about their expectations of such an intervention. In fact, a frequent reaction *after* the coaching day is for participants to report that they did not expect the day to be so personally valuable. Most anticipate that discussion will stay "on the surface" and are surprised to discover that they reach the real issues that are important to them. The learning value of listening to and questioning other group members is usually a revelation.

One critical issue for participants is their perceived psychological safety in a coaching session. More than 40 years ago, scholars discussed the need to create psychological safety as a precondition for individuals to feel capable of changing.[14] Psychological safety has been defined as "feeling able to show and employ one's self without fear of negative consequences to self-image, status or career."[15] Research on using executive education programs as a laboratory for personal exploration and change suggests that executives are ready to open up when they see that the environment and people within it are not a threat to their subjective or objective well-being. Many executives do not perceive their working environments as a psychologically safe place to explore work-related identities and behaviors.[16] This may explain some of the challenges of bringing coaching (particularly group coaching) into the internal world of organizations. Such coaching may not always provide an environment in which there is no perceived threat to sense of self or career prospects.

An executive education program, particularly a leadership program, is usually seen as a legitimate environment for exploration and experimentation, and for learning from self and others. The reputation of the provider, the faculty involved, and the coaches the program employs increases trust in the procedure and raises the level of perceived safety for the participants. However, participants will still have concerns about how they will feel during the coaching process, how far they will want to go, and how other group members might react to their words and behavior. In a customized, company program, participants are also concerned about the confidentiality of the coaching discussions, and about the possibility that their fellow participants may misuse the information or feelings that they share, since many may be internal competitors. Composing coaching groups that are as diverse as possible (e.g., making sure that people from the same office do not end up in the same group) is one way of mitigating this challenge. Spending time describing what leadership coaching is about and how it can help executives as part of the program is also helpful. Telling the participants that they are in control of choosing what to share and what to keep to themselves is another way of building psychological safety. We have also noticed that simply reiterating the principles of confidentiality at the beginning of the executive program and particular modules within it, and at the start of the coaching process, contributes to perceived safety. Equally important are the anecdotes of faculty or coaches showing how the coaching process had been helpful for them personally. Finally, during the coaching process itself, asking participants if it is all right to raise an issue from, for instance, their 360-degree feedback results, also helps.

An interesting observation is the importance of feeling "normal" for participants in executive education programs. Our research findings and practice observations show that individuals are ready to work on the issues related to their behavior or emotions when they are reassured that it is all right to have such issues to work on. The feeling that it is normal to look into oneself and, if something does not match what a situation requires, decide whether to work on it or change the situation, should be developed throughout the course. By the time participants come to the coaching session, they are much more ready to acknowledge the issues they face and to start working on them. The ability of executives to show their weaknesses is a prerequisite for being able to take a leadership position.[17]

Examples and cases used during teaching in an executive program should underline the value of leaders' self-exploration and learning, their attention to emotions, and attempts to discover the roots of their behaviors or reactions toward other people. Naturally, the issues may vary in depth and complexity, as will the personalities of the participants in a group coaching session. The role of the leadership coach is to avoid opening a Pandora's box of issues during the session and rather to concentrate on something with which participants can really experiment. A coaching session then becomes a good laboratory in which participants can personalize their own learning experience and come up with two or three actionable steps at the end.

We have found it helpful to build the possibility of a follow-up coaching session (in person or by phone) into our executive programs for participants who need to go deeper into their issues or to discuss something that they cannot raise in the group setting. Here we again advocate a multi-module design for executive development programs to facilitate follow-up with a coach and/or program faculty. Despite the natural tendency of companies to cut costs in turbulent times, including budgets dedicated to executive development, organizations cannot stop investing in developing their leaders. Although a multi-module design sounds more expensive, it does not have to be. Some of the work may be shifted to pre-course assignments, blended learning, phone conferences, etc. Follow-up telephone coaching sessions, which involve no travel costs and can be held at a time convenient for individual executives, may be built into the program as well.

It should be noted that program directors who are not familiar with clinically oriented leadership development methods may also be anxious about building a coaching day into the program, or offering such an opportunity to their clients or prospects. First of all, a coaching day increases both the complexity of program management and the costs. Secondly, selecting coaches is another challenge. With a variety of coaching schools and approaches, and with no established quality assurance mechanisms, it may be difficult to decide who is suitable for a coaching assignment. Thirdly, the evaluations that participants give to the provider upon completion of the course, and which serve as a proxy for the success of the overall program (and its director), may be less predictable when there are several coaching groups involved. Program directors may also find it difficult to help coaches prepare adequately for their coaching day, as they may not know what kind of information coaches should be provided with prior to the event. Finally, since the program director cannot observe the coach's performance during the coaching day, obtaining feedback on the quality of the coaching may also be challenging. The only source of information for the program director will be the course evaluations provided by the participants.

One way for program directors to deal with these challenges is to go through a similar program as a participant and learn more about the methodology. Chapter 9 illustrates the importance of putting oneself in participants' shoes, even for experienced professionals. It is also advisable to have a staff member on the team who has been trained in the methodology and who maintains contacts with a network of suitably trained coaches. Such a person can serve as an internal resource to other program directors when it comes to designing coaching elements into executive programs, explaining the method to clients and participants, developing a coaching pool, and briefing and debriefing coaches after their work.

It is important that coaches are able to react to any references to course materials the participants might make, so they should be given an information pack explaining the objectives, content, and logic of the program. It is useful to meet with the coaches the evening before the coaching day and explain any important issues and concerns raised by the participants. Finally, getting coaches together and running a debriefing session on the process and outcomes of the coaching day is good preparation for managing the subsequent parts of the program and dealing with possible deviations from the program flow or participants' expectations.

It is costly to include a group coaching day in the design of a leadership program. Bringing a group of coaches into an executive program involves professional fees, travel and accommodation costs, administrative burdens and other time- and money-consuming aspects. Most coaches are freelancers for a particular provider, and should be integrated into the program delivery team and given the resources they need to prepare properly for the work ahead of them. At the same time, they should apply their skills to understanding the concerns of faculty and program directors and, where necessary, help the latter overcome their natural anxieties about bringing clinically oriented executive development methods into their programs.

CHALLENGES OF INTRODUCING PEER COACHING TO EXECUTIVE EDUCATION PROGRAMS

Peer coaching in executive education programs uses the power of the work and life experiences of fellow participants to help other members of the group clarify their goals, assess the reality of their situation, elaborate available options or alternatives, identify necessary resources and support mechanisms, and, last but not least, commit to action through developing and obtaining peer approval for an action plan and agreeing to a follow-up session with a peer coach as they implement it.

Peer coaching may be suggested either as a follow-up activity after a group leadership coaching day or as a stand-alone activity undertaken once or repeated over several modules. Participants may be assigned a peer coach from the group as part of the group coaching exercise or during the program. The task of peer coaches could be to follow up on the progress coachees make on the action plan and the commitments they made as a result of the coaching day. Peer coaching may also be concerned with in-program development of personalized plans based on class discussions of leadership and management topics. In longer-term programs, peer coaching sessions may be part of the module structure. In shorter programs, they can be included as a post-program follow-up element.

Peer coaching is particularly effective when participants pair up with a partner from a different organization. For company-specific programs or in-house courses, participants may gain particular value from peer coaching interactions with someone from a different part of the organization. Since both coach and coachee will have been through the same emotional experience of working with clinically oriented developmental methods, this arrangement will help participants to overcome the feeling of being "on their own" when it comes to discussing their ideas, hopes, feelings, anxieties, etc.

HR and learning and development professionals are usually supportive of the inclusion of peer coaching in an executive development program. Sometimes, however, they express concerns about potential confusion between the various coaching models that are suggested for use in peer coaching sessions. Recently, many organizations have declared a need to enhance their managers' coaching skills and have begun to offer coaching skills training sessions. With a number of competing providers and competing models for such sessions, HR and learning and development professionals may become concerned that the approach used in executive education will not be in line with the tools offered through in-house training programs.

However, the purpose of using peer coaching in a psychodynamically oriented approach is not mastery of a particular coaching model but rather experimentation with using self as a tool in one's own development and the development of others. We usually explain to HR professionals that, as an outcome of this experience, participants have a greater appreciation of the value of listening, empathizing, and observing their own feelings while another person is talking. We also reassure HR professionals that, if they use a particular coaching algorithm in their internal training, we can incorporate a link between that model and the activities we run in the classroom (provided that we jointly agree on the value of the algorithm used).

Initially, participants may be cautious about working together in a group coaching session. Staging small peer coaching experiments before the group session often helps to ensure that they have a positive reaction to the experience. At times, we even find it useful to let pairs of participants hold relatively unstructured discussions for a short period of time to taste the potential value of listening and being listened to. We then discuss the value of peer coaching with them in more detail, and provide them with additional opportunities for experimentation. However, participants may sometimes need some kind of structure or support to engage in meaningful discussions with one another. We usually start with a short in-class discussion about peer coaching and provide participants with another "transitional object"—a set of slides or a handout about peer coaching.[18]

We have also found it helpful to discuss the psychological burdens of being a leader, as described in the introduction to *Coach and Couch: The Psychology of Making Better Leaders*.[19] When we talk to participants about the loneliness of being at the top, fear of envy, feelings of being constantly under watch, questioning the future, dealing with power addiction, and managing an ever steeper learning curve, we usually see nods of agreement and hear comments illustrating those psychological burdens. We then ask participants what can be done to help them handle such burdens better. Usually several people in the class come up with the idea of having a network of people who would be ready to listen, support, challenge, care, advise, and encourage. Those people should be competent and interested in professional or managerial issues, but at the same time not perceived as a threat to the career or psychological well-being of the executive. After this type of discussion, we then make a link to peer coaching, positioning it as both a possible tool for dealing with executive issues and also as an opportunity to start developing or adding to a network of people who can act as future emotional resources.

We usually encourage participants to share their action plans and commitment letters with a peer coach, and to plan a follow-up peer coaching conversation, in person or by phone, while in the program. In some programs, as mentioned above, we build peer coaching follow-up sessions into the learning process. We also often ask people to reflect on their role as a peer coach, and in doing so we re-emphasize the value of clinically oriented executive development in helping leaders use themselves as powerful tools for sensing emotions, defenses, motivational drivers, and other aspects of people's inner theater.

Program directors may not always be clear how to position peer coaching in their programs. By definition, peer coaching requires time. Program directors may find it difficult to schedule peer coaching sessions when, for instance, they feel pressured to accommodate a particular session by a faculty member. Using varying methods and including peer coaching in the learning process, however, is generally well received by participants. They appreciate the chance to digest new information by exploring their feelings toward the topic and reflecting on the applicability of what has just been learned through a mutual coaching exercise.

Obviously, many other types of the clinically oriented approach may be used in executive education, but the methods discussed above are among those most frequently used, at least in our experience. These methods allow learning to be personalized, and take the learning process from the level of cognitive interest, through personal reactions, to the material being learned and possible behavioral implications. The latter is achieved through the action orientation of clinically oriented approaches. All three methods require some kind of action planning and a commitment to experimenting with new behaviors. They also involve other people as observers and assistants in making personal change. Using clinical methods as part of learning requires participants to make commitments to themselves and others, thus increasing the likelihood that they will attempt to change and have support from others during their journey.

THE CHALLENGE OF HAVING THE RIGHT FACULTY AND PROGRAM DIRECTORS

Applying the clinical paradigm to executive development in organizations and in business schools requires the deep involvement of faculty, program directors, coaches, facilitators, etc. This raises the question of how to find or develop such professionals and make them interested in supporting managers on their developmental journeys. Executives attending leadership development programs benefit greatly not only from the content of the course but also from the processes to which they are exposed.[20] Educators are seen not just as repositories of knowledge about a particular subject but rather as sparring partners, guides, confidants, and even "father-figures."[21] Undoubtedly, such roles go far beyond the traditional expectations of faculty involved in executive education, business school administrators, or learning and developing professionals.

Managing executive programs founded on the clinical paradigm demands knowledge, skills, and attitudes that are not typically found in a traditional executive educator. Recent thinking on executive development suggests that managers need *to be helped* to recognize their talents and strengths and use them without guilt. They also need *to be helped* to recognize in themselves irrational behaviors that may lead to negative reactions from the people around them.[22] Faculty members and facilitators familiar with clinical approaches can generate remarkable progress in helping program participants bring the learning from the program to their organizations, and personal career and life. Obviously, incorporating such approaches into program design is quite different from, for example, selecting a case study or a set of slides. Ideally, faculty and program directors involved in clinically oriented programs should undertake a process of personal self-exploration and experimentation, and change themselves before they try to help others. A similar recommendation could also be made to the HR and learning and development professionals who want to see noticeable change in the behavior and subjective well-being of the executives in their organizations.

Directing or teaching in an executive course based on the principles of the clinical paradigm requires a deep understanding of the emotional side of human functioning. Staff working in this sort of program will inevitably spend an enormous amount of emotional energy engaging with participants and challenging them, while simultaneously showing empathy and care. Last but not least, the time commitment required from faculty for these programs is much higher than for more traditional programs.

The rewards of working in a clinically oriented program can be very high, particularly when program participants show signs of liberation, enthusiasm, and self-efficacy at the end of the course, but perhaps especially when they contact us months or years after the program. Running such a program may be not for the fainthearted, however. In this chapter, I have identified some of the challenges associated with using clinically based approaches for executive development. Several suggestions have been made as to how to deal with the anxieties of various stakeholders. However, very often the challenges start with the person designing or commissioning the program. Recognizing those challenges may be a good opportunity for all of us who are professionally involved in creating better organizations to start by dealing with our own obstacles to success.

NOTES

1. Day, D. and Lance, C. (2004). "Understanding the Development of Leadership Complexity." In D. Day, S. Zaccaro, and S. Halpin (Eds) *Leader Development for Transforming Organizations*. Mahwah, NJ: Lawrence Erlbaum Associates, Publishers, pp. 41–69; Hall, D. T. (2004). "Self-Awareness, Identity, and Leader Development." In D. Day, S. Zaccaro and S. Halpin (Eds) *Leader Development for Transforming Organizations*. Mahwah, NJ: Lawrence Erlbaum Associates, Publishers, pp. 153–176.
2. Kets de Vries, M. (2006). *The Leader on the Couch*. San Francisco: Jossey-Bass; Kets de Vries, M. (2006). *The Leadership Mystique: Leading Behavior in Human Enterprise* (2nd

edn). London: Financial Times Prentice Hall; Kets de Vries, M., Korotov, K., and Florent-Treacy, E. (Eds) (2007). *Coach and Couch: The Psychology of Making Better Leaders*. Houndmills and New York: Palgrave Macmillan.

3. Kets de Vries, M. and Korotov, K. (2007). "Creating Transformational Executive Education Programs." *Academy of Management Learning & Education*, 6(3), 375–387.

4. See, for example, Mann, J. (1973). *Time Limited Psychotherapy*. Cambridge, MA: Harvard University Press; Rutan, S. and Stone, W. (2001). *Psychodynamic Group Psychotherapy*. New York & London: The Guilford Press.

5. Levinson, H. (2007). "Executive Coaching." In R. Kilburg and R. Diedrich (Eds) *The Wisdom of Coaching: Essential Papers in Consulting Psychology for a World of Change*. Washington, DC: American Psychological Association, pp. 95–102.

6. See, for example, Peiperl, M. A. (2001). "Getting 360° Feedback Right." *Harvard Business Review*, 79(1), 142–147.

7. Kegan, R. (1982). *The Evolving Self: Problem and Process in Human Development*. Cambridge, MA: Harvard University Press.

8. Sosik, J. J., Potosky, D., and Jung, D. I. (2002). "Adaptive Self-Regulation: Meeting Others' Expectations of Leadership and Performance." *Journal of Social Psychology*, 142, 211–232.

9. Klein, K. and Ziegert, J. (2004). "Leader Development and Change Over Time: A Conceptual Integration and Exploration of Research Challenges." In D. Day, S. Zaccaro, and S. Halpin (Eds) *Leader Development for Transforming Organizations*. Mahwah, NJ: Lawrence Erlbaum Associates, pp. 359–382.

10. Kets de Vries, M. (2008). "Leadership Coaching and Organizational Transformation: Effectiveness in a World of Paradoxes." *INSEAD Working Paper* 2008/71/EFE.

11. Korotov, K. (2008). "Preparation for 360-Degree Feedback in Leadership Development Programs and Executive Coaching." In S. Reddy (Ed.) *Leadership Development: Perspectives and Cases*. Hyderabad: The ICFAI University Press, pp. 87–98.

12. Kets de Vries, M., Korotov, K., and Florent-Treacy, E. (Eds) (2007). *Coach and Couch: The Psychology of Making Better Leaders*. Houndmills and New York: Palgrave Macmillan.

13. For example, Kets de Vries, M. (2005). *Global Executive Leadership Inventory: Participant Workbook*. San Francisco: Pfeiffer: An Imprint of Wiley.

14. Schein, E., and Bennis, W. (1965). *Personal and Organizational Change via Group Methods*. New York: Wiley.

15. Kahn, W. (1990). "Psychological Conditions of Personal Engagement and Disengagement at Work." *Academy of Management Journal*, 33(4), 692–724.

16. Korotov, K. (2005). "Identity Laboratories." INSEAD PhD Dissertation. Fontainebleau, France: INSEAD.

17. Goffee, R., and Jones, G. (2006). *Why Should Anyone Be Led by You?* Boston, MA: Harvard Business School Press.

18. Korotov, K. (2008). "Peer Coaching in Executive-Education Programmes." *Training and Management Development Methods*, 22(2), 3.15–13.24.

19. Kets de Vries, M., Korotov, K., and Florent-Treacy, E. (2007). "Introduction: A Psychodynamic Approach to Leadership Development." In M. Kets de Vries, Korotov, K., and Florent-Treacy, E. (Eds) *Coach and Couch: The Psychology of Making Better Leaders*. Houndmills: Palgrave Macmillan, pp. xxxvii–lii.

20. Korotov, K. (2006). *Identity Laboratory: The Process of Going through an Executive Program*. Paper presented at the Academy of Management, Atlanta, GA; Kets de Vries, M. and Korotov, K. (2007). "Creating Transformational Executive Education Programs." *Academy of Management Learning & Education*, 6(3), 375–387.

21. Korotov, K. (2005). "Identity Laboratories." INSEAD PhD Dissertation. Fontainebleau, France: INSEAD.

22. Levinson, H. (2007). "Executive Coaching." In R. Kilburg and R. Diedrich (Eds) *The Wisdom of Coaching: Essential Papers in Consulting Psychology for a World of Change*. Washington, DC: American Psychological Association.

3

ARE YOU FEELING MAD, BAD, SAD, OR GLAD?

MANFRED F. R. KETS DE VRIES

One day an old Chinese sage lost his pearls. Distraught, he sent his eyes to search for his pearls, but his eyes did not find them. Next he sent his ears to search for the pearls, but his ears did not find them either. Then he sent his hands to search for the pearls, but they had no success. And so he sent all of his senses together to search for his pearls, but none found them. Finally he sent his not-search to look for his pearls. And his not-search found them.

We all know about the five senses—sight, smell, hearing, feeling, and taste—and that they are extremely important for our well-being and survival, both individually and in cooperation. Our senses tell us what is happening to our body and what is happening in our immediate surroundings. They tell us whether we are in danger, where we are, whether we are hot or cold. They also tell us if food is good or bad and whether something is enticing or disgusting. They form the basis for all of our actions.

But as this Chinese parable suggests, these senses are not always enough when it comes to interpreting what is going on around us. Much of our mental life—including thoughts, feelings, and motives—takes place at what we might call a subsensory, subterranean level. Neurologists and psychologists have demonstrated abundantly how unconscious processes are activated by emotional stimuli, and neurological studies have supplied copious evidence of the unconscious processes of cognition.[1]

A PUZZLING TALE

One day I was approached by one of the students taking my consulting and coaching seminar to ask if I could help him make sense out of what had been (at least to him) a puzzling incident. This particular student (a partner in one of the leading strategic consulting firms) was called in to discuss a possible consulting project by the CEO of a Fortune 500 organization. My student was eager to meet this CEO as, according to him, if the chemistry was right, he would finally have a real chance of winning some work with the organization the CEO was running. From what he had heard from some of his subordinates, a number of lucrative contracts were there for the asking. But he also realized that it was not going to be a shoo-in, since this CEO was a no-nonsense person and unlikely to be impressed by the latest management fads.

After entering the CEO's office and exchanging the usual niceties, my student and his potential client got down to business. The CEO described what kind of strategic study he was looking for, and what region he was interested in. Just as he finished his general overview, the CEO's assistant entered the office and engaged him in an animated discussion about an issue that had come up earlier that morning. The discussion went on for approximately half an hour. Then the CEO turned his attention back to my student, and asked if he had given some further thought to the question of what his consulting firm could do for them. My student explained that his firm had done extensive market research in the region the CEO was interested in, and that he was sure that they could be extremely helpful. Subsequently, my student was asked to send a proposal, and was told that he would hear from them very soon. He mentioned to me that he had sent the proposal within a week. Now more than a month had gone by without any response. He had tried to call the CEO several times but had not gotten through. He also mentioned that his emails went unanswered. The question he asked me was what I thought had gone wrong.

I asked him if he felt that anything special had happened during the discussion he had with the CEO. What were his feelings in dealing with that person? Was there anything particular that had happened? Was there anything that irritated him? My student was quick in responding to the last question. He mentioned that if there was something he really could not stand, it was being ignored. He noted that he had been quite annoyed when the CEO's assistant had interrupted their discussion. I asked him more about the kind of situations that got him annoyed. On further probing, he mentioned that he came from a large family and had many brothers and sisters. In commenting on his family, he noted that what really got his goat (and still did) was his family's tendency—he was the youngest—to ignore him. It made him furious. I asked if he had shown his anger when he was left hanging by the CEO and his assistant. First he said that, to the best of his knowledge, he had not shown his irritation. I asked him if it was possible that he might have made a flippant comment to the CEO that could have been interpreted as irritating. Giving the matter further thought, he reacted in the affirmative. He suddenly remembered that he had made a rather offhand comment to the CEO when leaving. It had just slipped out but had been instantly forgotten until my questioning.

I explained to him that this inadvertent comment might have cost him the contract. What I did not tell him was that I happened to know the CEO he was referring to. I had once worked with him on a workshop, helping him to develop a high-performance team. At the time, one of the issues he realized he needed to work on to be more effective as a leader was his tendency to quickly categorize people as "winners" or "losers," without giving them the benefit of the doubt. I knew from conversations with him that he had acquired this modus operandi from his father, who had spent all his life striving to do better than his stepbrother. My student (although to the best of my knowledge very competent in strategic marketing) must have been put into the "losers" camp, which explained why the consulting contract never came through.

The "tragedy" of this tale is that both parties behaved like ships passing in the night. What could have been the beginning of a great win-win situation was derailed because the interchange was taken over by unconscious psychological dynamics. My student was unaware of the intensity of his irritation when he felt ignored. The CEO was unaware of how quickly he categorized the abilities of the people he encountered.

In interpersonal encounters, the space between people is filled by what we evoke in one another and, as a result of those evocations, we always seem to be sending mixed messages. To put it another way, when we communicate with each other, we not only explicitly articulate messages but at the same time we communicate in a number of implicit ways, often with a contrary message. For example, the spoken phrase, "I am happy," conveys varying messages, depending on the speaker's body language and emotional tone. The words can be said with all the evidence of great joy, or in a joking fashion, or in a totally cynical manner. These emotional components, received intuitively, supplement the message we receive in the form of direct verbal statements. Thus the tone of a statement always contains an additional, very informative message.

But such messages are generally subtle and thus not always easy to decipher. The five senses alone cannot always pick up implicit signals: attentive observation—as illustrated in the Chinese parable—is required to truly make sense of another person. Frequently, we know that something has happened during the exchange because we are touched somehow deep inside us, but we do not really understand why. We pick up telling cues from body language, sounds, smells, touch, or peripheral vision without being consciously aware of doing so.

Everyday conversation consists of the speaker attempting to provoke feelings in the listener (this presupposes the willingness of the listener to accept these feelings, of course). In more common language, we talk about "putting something across," or giving someone "a piece of our mind." For example, when we are in distress, we may try to convey our distress to the other person in such a way that he or she can literally *feel* it. The normal communication process consists of fairly rapidly oscillating cycles of projection and introjection: as one person communicates with words and demeanor (projection), the other receives and interprets the communication (introjection); then the listener, having understood the speaker's message, reprojects it to the original speaker, perhaps accompanied by an interpretation.

This same cycle of projection and introjection takes place in the psychotherapeutic context as well, and this is what transference and countertransference are all about. A therapist's past is always present in their work. They must pay attention to the symbolic role they play in their clients' fantasy lives because they are not neutral bystanders. The therapist must notice seductive resonances and avoid knee-jerk reactions. They must sort out what belongs to them, and what belongs to others. They will have to engage in an inner dialogue to create an appropriately reflective, interpretive standpoint and, critically, manage boundaries.

In this chapter, I will take the theme of countertransference—that is, the feelings that a therapist has for a client—beyond the couch and apply it to the consultancy or coaching setting. I will explore how coaches and consultants (hereafter "coach") can use themselves as instruments for gathering data—in other words, how they can use their own reactions to help them interpret, in dyadic situations, what the client is trying to tell them and trying to do to them. To clarify that process, I will discuss the concepts of transference and projective identification, concepts grounded in early mother-infant communication and essential to "listening with the third ear." In addition, I will discuss various forms of alignment and misalignment between the sender and receiver of both explicit *and* implicit messages. Finally, I will give a number of suggestions regarding what coaches and consultants should pay attention to when listening to another person.

PROJECTIVE IDENTIFICATION

We can define *projective identification* as the unwanted or unacknowledged feelings of a client that are transmitted to a coach. The "projector" deals with emotional conflict or internal or external stressors by transmitting these unacceptable feelings, impulses, or thoughts to another person. Instead of describing such unwanted thoughts or feelings in a discussion, the projector subtly communicates them to the receiver through actions, facial expression, body attitude, word choice, or sounds.[2] Coaches, experiencing these projected feelings or thoughts in themselves, may understand what the sender is experiencing, even if the sender is not consciously aware of initiating that process. Given the dyadic (and cyclical) nature of projective identification, it eventually becomes difficult to assess who first did what to whom.

Projective identification is more than mere projection. The latter is an intra-psychic dynamic, while the former is in the interpersonal domain; in fact, it is an extremely primitive way of relating to another person. In terms of the feelings experienced by the projector, there is a clear difference between these two phenomena. When projective identification is at work, the sender of the communication feels at one with the other person, which is not the case with simple projection.

As a primitive, preverbal mode of communicating and relating, projective identification finds its prototype in the mother-child interface. Infants cannot *say* how they feel; instead, they have to find ways to get their mothers to experience their emotional state, making for a deep, almost symbiotic connection between mother and child. The infant "speaks" to the mother by evoking emotional reactions in her that, in turn, are received by the infant. The mother may also verbalize what the infant is trying to communicate, thus helping the infant toward verbal concretization of psychological states.

"GOOD ENOUGH" PARENTING AND CONTAINMENT: THE ORIGINS OF SUBLIMINAL COMMUNICATION

The mother-child relationship can be viewed as a co-constructive process whereby infant and mother impact each other on a continuous basis, regulating and aligning their modes of interaction to obtain a satisfactory equilibrium.[3] From the moment of birth, infants communicate their feelings and other internal states through sounds, body movements, smell, and facial expressions. Caregivers generally learn how to interpret these expressions and respond to the infant to provide containment—that is, to keep unwanted feelings from spiraling out of control. Therefore the relationship between the container and the contained can be viewed as a dynamic, mutually influencing process.[4]

The importance of synchronized, dyadic interactions for the developing child cannot be overstated. In fact, the child's satisfactory development rests upon what has been called a "good enough" quality in these early caregiver-child interactions. These "regulatory" interactions are extremely important. Unfortunately, the initial phase of the developmental process is characterized by chaos, confusion, strain, bodily tension, sleep deprivation, eating difficulties, and other problems. It generally takes some time before proper empathic resonance occurs between caregivers and their infants.

Dealing with distress signals

A key factor in good-enough care, and thus in proper alignment, is the way caregivers deal with the child's distress signals. Some mothers have a natural tendency to respond appropriately, others do not. Of the latter category, all but the most heartless mothers attempt to give some form of containment. Many, though, find themselves misaligned with their infant's cues.

Mothers who have a rigid attitude toward childrearing may experience the anxiety of the child but refuse (or not really know how) to respond appropriately. Although such a mother may go through a number of perfunctory movements intended to give generic comfort, she does not truly deal with the infant's distress. This failure of containment creates a state of bewilderment and disbelief in the infant. The infant wants the mother to feel anxiety just as he or she is feeling it. But due to the lack of appropriate response, the infant senses that what he or she tried to convey to the mother has lost its form or meaning.

Other misaligned mothers overreact to the anxiety of their infant. Often inexperienced at parenting, they may panic at their infant's discomfort, thereby aggravating the problem. In such instances, the infant experiences the mother as an unsafe container, unable to tolerate anxiety and distress.

In the third type of containment, there is a high degree of resonance between mother and child. An understanding mother is able to experience the feeling of fear, fatigue, or hunger that the infant is trying to communicate, and yet retain a balanced outlook. She has a knack for feeling what the child experiences and still retains her mental equilibrium. This alignment, unlike containment that is either too rigid or too fragile, makes for an ongoing process of mutual influence and adaptation.

The ability of mothers to be attuned to the needs of their children continues as the young ones grow up. For example, when children are playing in the house, attentive mothers constantly listen to the sounds the children make. Mothers who are well aligned with the needs of their children have a finely tuned ability to distinguish the usual abundant noise from any sign of distress. When their "third ear" (that organ not merely of sense but also of empathy, intuition, and understanding) hears a different sound—something out of the ordinary that may indicate danger—they immediately swing into action and go to the rescue.

We can speculate that mothers who are well attuned to their children are more sensitive to subliminal, non-explicit communication. This talent for picking up subliminal information, for deciphering projective identification as it occurs, stands them in good stead, not only with their children but in any interpersonal situation. In general, experienced mothers have an advantage when making sense of the varied communications that take place in the bi-personal field. Their capacity to really listen—to listen to more than words—may give them a real advantage when they take on the role of therapist, coach, or consultant. Fortunately, nowadays an increasing number of men are breaking stereotypes in the parental role, taking on many of the responsibilities that were once women's exclusive domain. As these men become better communicators with their infants, they can transfer those skills to the workplace.

Listening with the third ear

The interchange between infants and their empathetic caregivers demonstrates the large number of responses—the various forms of empathic resonance—that can occur in an effective coach-client interchange. The ability to make sense of projective identification processes, an ability that we all develop to a greater or lesser extent in infancy as we learn to "listen with the third ear," serves as the prototype for all our future two-way communications and will determine our intuitive capacity. This listening, which bypasses the ordinary senses, has already been part of our repertoire for a long time when we reach adulthood. Because of faulty mother-child communication, however, some people are not well attuned. Others, who resonated well with their primary caregivers in infancy, have been out of practice for so long that they have all but lost the skill.

SUBLIMINAL COMMUNICATION

Remnants of the caregiver-infant dialogue will stay with us throughout life, so aspects of this interactive script are revived in *any* future relationship. Scripts established in childhood color the way we disseminate or gather information, and the way we convey explicit and implicit texts. While explicit texts are out in the open, we struggle to grasp and decipher implicit texts.

As we relate to other people, we are constantly processing large amounts of information. Generally that processing registers in our conscious mind only as hunches. Sometimes, especially when we are totally unaware that this information processing is taking place, we register it in another way: through acting out. Instead of trying consciously to reflect on and process the information deluging us, we act impulsively and offer our emotional response, which is often unconscious and often conflicted. But because the information flooding us has not been properly worked through, the actions that we take are sometimes destructive to self or others, and may prevent us from dealing with the feelings that are aroused in a more constructive way.

While mothers learn to pick up subtle signals by *doing*, psychotherapists, psychiatrists, psychoanalysts, coaches, and other people in the helping professions receive training to listen with the third ear.[5] They learn to use their own unconscious minds to detect and decipher the unconscious wishes and fantasies of their clients. Using their subliminal perceptions about their clients is an important instrument in their repertoire, a way of understanding their clients more deeply. But this activity is not limited to the therapist–client interchange. All of us use our intuition to understand people better. All of us form opinions about others with what seems on the surface to be scanty information. All of us are overeager to verbalize our instant impressions. Coaches and consultants are no different.

TRANSFERENCE

In any form of interpersonal exchange, one person *transfers* his or her own inner experiences to the other.[6] In that sense, frustrations of the past recur in the present. This concept, *transference*, is one of Freud's most important contributions to the field of psychology.[7] According to Freud, transference involves a repetition of infantile prototypes that are lived out with a deep feeling of reality. Although in the past these specific behavior patterns may have been quite appropriate for reasons of psychological or physical survival, in the present they may be inappropriate. Thus, to quote Freud, transferential reactions create a "false connection": the behavior that comes to the fore is inappropriate to the present situation. Though we rarely recognize it, *all* our interchanges revive a vast range of psychological experiences from our past—experiences that are now directed to a person in the present, who becomes the recipient of the interchange. This confusion of time and place implies that all forms of interaction are inevitably both reality- and transference-based.

For example, an executive in a coaching relationship may begin to perceive the coach as if the coach were his father, transferring his feelings for the real father to the coach. Because transference is a largely unconscious process, the executive is not likely to be aware of this—and neither is the coach, at least initially.

It is the unconscious nature of transference that makes it both so elusive and so potent. A well-trained coach will gradually make sense out of what the executive is trying to "communicate." Astute coaches use transference data as a vital source of information. It may help them see that the script a client is following needs to change, because that client is now in a very different situation than that when he or she was a child. Their assignment is to help clients avoid the siren song of simply repeating the past. This time, here in the present, the script needs a new twist, taking the person's current situation into consideration.

The first description of the transference process can be found in the book *Studies on Hysteria*, written by Sigmund Freud in collaboration with Josef Breuer.[8] Anna O. (real name Bertha Pappenheim) was a patient of Breuer's who suffered from a variety of mental and physical symptoms; for example, one of her arms was paralyzed as a result of complex seizures. Today she would probably be diagnosed as having a borderline personality disorder. Through treatment, Breuer and Anna O. discovered that when Anna talked about what had happened when the symptoms started, she often recovered a repressed fact and then managed to do somewhat better. Anna O. called this her "chimney sweeping" or "talking cure." Breuer called it "catharsis." Eventually, while the treatment was still ongoing, Breuer distanced himself from Anna O., because she aroused feelings of sexual excitement in him—feelings that he found unacceptable. He cut the treatment off completely when she announced that she was pregnant by him. Breuer's fast exit due to her false pregnancy, and his panicky decision to go on a second honeymoon with his wife, may be seen as the birth of what now is called countertransference.

The Breuer incident is not the first example of a patient falling in love with his or her doctor, and it certainly will not be the last. But, while others would have left this strange incident unexamined, Freud tried to make sense out of it. In the book *Studies on Hysteria*, he and Breuer (a reluctant collaborator) explored the phenomenon whereby a patient moves beyond strictly professional feelings toward the therapist and allows personal feelings to intrude into the therapy. As Freud described it, these patients had tended to "transfer onto the figure of the physician" distressing ideas that arose due to the content of the treatment. These patients, according to Freud, had made a "false connection" to the analyst. Freud first used the actual term "transference" in relation to a patient of his named Dora, when he belatedly recognized that her feelings for him had led to her abrupt termination from treatment, resulting in a therapeutic failure.[9]

When Freud first discovered the phenomenon by which the patient inappropriately transfers something from his early experiences onto the analyst, he considered it a distraction. A number of years later, however, he acknowledged that such false connections could be used effectively to help the patient unravel his or her neurosis; they could be used to help the patient better understand the script that motivated them. Today, we are interested in the phenomenon of transference because of its diagnostic value as well as its therapeutic use. Transference, through a process of compulsive repetition, reveals in the here-and-now the unresolved and most crucial conflict patterns that remain active in the patient's current life.[10] If the therapist can bring the patient to make his or her own transference reactions conscious, express and acknowledge those reactions, and experience their links with current and past relationships, then transference is a powerful tool for understanding and healing, helping the patient write a new script for their life.

COUNTERTRANSFERENCE

Psychotherapists pay a great deal of attention to transference in clinical training. They go to great lengths to point out to their clients that certain behavior patterns, appropriate at an earlier stage of life, are no longer effective in the present. But this process works both ways. Just as patients unconsciously react to therapists, therapists unconsciously respond to their clients' transference with *countertransference* reactions.

Imagine, for example, a coach who is trying to give advice to one of her executive clients. No matter what she says, the client's response is to repeat how useless he feels in his present situation, how stuck he feels, and how it is unclear to him what he should do. In spite of heroic efforts on the part of the coach to help the executive see things in perspective—see that things are not so bad—he sings the same refrain, apparently ignoring her words. To boot, the executive shows increasing contempt for the coach's advice. The coach, meanwhile, feels increasingly useless, since none of her interventions seem to work. More than that, she starts to feel irritated and angry. As the sessions continue, she has to make a great effort to keep herself from erupting in anger.

The projection by the executive and the introjection of her feelings into the coach are very clear. Depending on the degree to which the coach is a prisoner of this interchange, it may take some time for her to realize what is happening. While the exchange is taking place, she may be too perturbed by the interaction to function properly. Indeed, if she is at her wit's end, she may even "act out" and express her irritation. But it is also possible that she will *not* act out her feelings in a knee-jerk manner. She may take a more reflective pose, engaging in vicarious introspection, trying to understand what the client is "doing" to her, and also asking why she herself feels impelled to be so active. Listening now with the third ear, she may ask herself a number of other questions, such as: Why does she feel such a great need to reassure her client? Why is she feeling useless, irritated, and increasingly angry? As she tries to metabolize these feelings, she may realize that people like her client remind her of an older sister who made it a habit of telling her how useless she was when she was young. Thinking back, the coach may recall how these incidents made her feel not only helpless but also angry. Usually, these situations ended up in a big fight, after which she would run to her mother for reassurance.

The coach, having gone through this reflective process, enters another, more subterranean level in the exchange. Recognizing how the client had made her feel useless, and why she had become so irritated, she sees that she has to do something different to really be helpful to the client. With this awareness, she will no longer get caught up in the kind of *folie à deux* that might eventually have ended in an angry outburst on her part. It is clear that if she had stuck to her own script, the relationship with her client would probably have been doomed.

What we can learn from this example is that one of the compound tasks of coaches is to decipher what the client is trying to enact and how the coach is tempted to *react*, and then help them both not to act out their usual scripts but to create a new, healthier outcome. Coaches should not acquiesce under pressure and buy into the client's script, in spite of the fact that certain lines in a client's script may reverberate with their own. What is needed in these situations is a reenactment, but a reenactment with a twist. The outcome must be different.

Like transference, countertransference includes all of the conscious and unconscious responses aroused by the activities of the client during the interpersonal exchange.[11] And, like transference, it needs to be dealt with. Countertransference *responsiveness* is the coach's ability to hear and deal with the client's infantile past, taking his or her own past into consideration. As the previous example illustrates, countertransference reactions, if not recognized for what they are and responded to, can create serious problems in the interpersonal interface.

Initially, countertransference was viewed as a subject to avoid. The unconscious conflict aroused in the psychoanalyst was something to learn from when it occurred, but to be gotten rid of as soon as possible. Freud viewed countertransference as an impediment to the psychoanalytic process. He felt that it distracted the psychoanalyst from doing his or her therapeutic work effectively.[12]

Since Freud, views of countertransference have generally fallen into two camps; one advocates a rather narrow definition of the term (the impediment position), the other a broader definition. Over time (as with the concept of transference), the broader view has become the more dominant one.[13] Presently, countertransference is no longer seen as a bothersome impediment to clinical work; rather, it is seen as an additional source of data about the client, and as an opportunity to obtain greater insight into the emotions and reactions that occur when two people interact with each other.

While countertransference is undeniably a source of data, it is not necessarily a source of relevant evidence. What the data are and what they can contribute has to be sorted out in the interchange. Complicating the sorting-out process is the fact that the coach needs to operate on two alternating levels: he or she has to be an objective observer of another person's ideas and emotions while also being a subjective receiver. Coaches who are skilled and astute handle the two levels deftly, using their subjective emotional life actively and directly in the dyadic interface.

THE ACTION TRAP: "I ACT, THEREFORE I AM"

It is clear from this discussion that the emotional interface is always a two-way street. The client is always sending subliminal messages (transference), and the coach is always reacting (countertransference). Thus there is always a struggle to make meaning and sense out of what is taking place in an encounter, and both parties are constantly tempted to *act out* perceived meanings rather than verbalize or mentalize them.

In the course of this struggle, every coach will inevitably fall into the action trap at some point. This is especially likely to happen when strong fantasy material emerges during an encounter, prompting a mutual resistance to feeling and working with emotional data. When coaches do not recognize promptly what is going on, do not make sense out of the subliminal messages they are receiving quickly enough, they may succumb to "flight into action"—that is, they may react instantly to information given by the client, without being aware of this acting out. After all, no matter how impeccably trained coaches are, they are still human beings and still have emotions—and probably a number of issues of their own that have yet to be resolved. If coaches unconsciously accept a role ascribed to them by a client, they may respond by placing their own unacceptable feelings onto the client without realizing that they are doing so.

To illustrate, one particular client reminded a coach of her daughter, who had caused many problems at home. This daughter's adolescence had been particularly difficult, and the various family members had gotten caught up in a vicious cycle of escalating destructive communication. Given this association, the coach found it a challenge to keep her cool, maintain sufficient distance, and not to get trapped in parallel behavior.

In another example, a client was perceived as a spoiled, self-centered, manipulative SOB by an executive coach. While that may have been a valid assessment, a much more important issue is why this person evoked such a strong reaction in the coach. Did the client strongly resemble some detested individual from the coach's past—perhaps the father who had separated from his mother, leaving her and their children without any financial support, and was never seen again?

What is important in such situations is that coaches recognize these feelings in themselves and do something about them—or rather, refrain from doing something about them. They need to keep themselves from falling into the action trap. When they recognize such feelings in themselves, they need to be extremely careful of what they say, keeping themselves in the present rather than descending back into the past. For example, the coach in the previous example, looking at her client through a filter of distaste and disapproval, needs to be doubly sure that she is not missing something because of her biases.

Danger signs

Knowing that countertransference reactions can misdirect them and derail their attempts to read another person, coaches need to watch vigilantly for warning signs. The most common sign that countertransference reactions are taking over is when there is a stalemate in the coaching relationship, a feeling that the intervention is not going anywhere. Another giveaway that the client is doing something of which the coach is only subliminally aware is when that coach cannot get a specific incident with the client out of his or her head; fragments of some previous interchange linger on. Coaches often talk about unwittingly bringing clinical situations home, and some even find a particular client's material invading their dreams.

Additional warning signs that countertransference problems are in play include using pejorative language to or about the client; being subliminally aware of becoming annoyed (as in the example above); being overprotective, manipulative, flattered, envious, anxious, fearful, disappointed, or even sexually interested; experiencing a sense of abandonment or hopelessness and depression about the client; fearing engulfment—that is, having a sense that the client is violating boundaries; and, as noted earlier, feeling impelled to do something active. Any of these warning signs should alert coaches that they might be under the influence of a countertransference reaction.

Part of the training for psychotherapists and psychoanalysts (or any other helping professional) is learning to detect signs of subliminal countertransference reactions and to bring these to conscious awareness, in order to refrain from acting upon them unthinkingly. If clients transfer images of parents or other people close to them onto their therapists, coaches, or consultants, and regress to childlike or otherwise inappropriate behavioral patterns, the recipients of these forms of communication need to be able to respond without falling into a countertransference reaction. Such reactions, when they do happen, can seriously distort the communication process.

If a client makes unreasonable demands or declares romantic love, well-trained coaches let these words pass through them. By providing containment, maintaining an attitude of calmness, equanimity, and caring concern, even when they feel themselves reacting out of countertransference, coaches are able to serve as unobtrusive mirrors, permitting their clients to acquire glimpses of themselves without having the coach's own needs get in the way.

Unfortunately, many people never bother to try to understand why they feel the way they do, or to objectively understand the source of their feelings. Indeed, they remember nothing of their internal conflicts but only *express* them—and that too indirectly, through action. They prefer action to facing conflicts head-on.

Choosing reflection over action

If coaches want to avoid falling into the action trap, they need to take a reflective attitude toward the messages projected by clients. A constant challenge for coaches is to identify and decipher the painful and intolerable emotions of their clients—emotions that are likely contributing to problem behavior in those clients—while simultaneously sorting out their own countertransference reactions and providing a "holding environment." Coaches need to guard themselves against precipitate and premature action—saying something unconsidered—simply to reduce their own anxiety, and instead learn to engage in a consistent and constructive exploration of affect and behavior (of self as well as client), no matter how intense those feeling may be, or how disturbing they are to self-esteem.

In the hands of reflective, clinically trained coaches, countertransference reactions are useful tools, helping to reveal the unconscious wishes and fantasies that clients are projecting onto their helpers. In this sense, countertransference reactions fuel their work. That is not the only benefit, however. Well-studied countertransference reactions certainly improve coaches' understanding of their clients, but they also guide coaches in their own journey of self-discovery.

While there is no way to totally overcome the problem of countertransference (since all of us form opinions of others), coaches can learn to use it productively rather than allow it to affect the therapeutic relationship unconsciously. Coaches who are able to recognize what they are feeling and can decipher how those feelings relate to what the client is doing to them, keep their own unconscious processes "inside the equation," thereby preserving the bi-personal frame.

As reflective practitioners, coaches learn to listen to their clients at two levels. While not ignoring the content of what the client is saying, they ask themselves questions such as: How do I feel listening to the client? What is the client doing to me? Am I truly engaged? Do I feel comfortable? Am I bored? Do I feel uneasy? Do I feel in control? Do I feel confused? Am I getting irritated, angry? Do I feel seduced? What do I find disturbing in my relationship with this client? In addition to these in-the-moment assessments, coaches also need to assess how their feelings change over the course of their dealings with the client, evaluating their own emotions and behavior in the light of what is happening with their client's behavior and with the therapeutic relationship as it progresses.

Acquiring a reflective stance is not easy, however. Reflection—the ability to allow ideas to float in our mind without the need for immediate understanding or action—demands a high level of self-awareness on the part of the coach, an understanding of their own thoughts and feelings, as well as a sound grasp of the psychological basis of their work. Above all, they must maintain a questioning attitude toward their own feelings and motives.

ALIGNMENT

As we saw in the mother-child discussion, alignment is the ability to be in sync with another person's feelings and thoughts. That ability to feel and experience what is going on within another person is a prerequisite of reflective coaching; ironically, it is also a by-product of such coaching. The challenge for coaches is to use their own unconscious as a receptive organ—that third ear I spoke of earlier—directed toward the transmitting unconscious of the client. As was noted, the coach needs to listen attentively not only to the explicit text but also to the implicit one. To decipher the underlying text of a conversation, they need to observe the client's overall body language, posture, demeanor, and other factors.

In addition, they need to keep in mind the fact that their own affects, thoughts, associations, and actions are reflections of elicited or awakened conflicts within themselves. Processing those conflicts and reactions is a difficult task, because the accumulation of data from both transference and countertransference is massive. Moreover, data from one area need to be used to make conjectures about the other. In listening simultaneously to both the client and themselves, coaches are in fact attending to communication in three modalities—cognition, affect, and action—as both parties in the therapeutic relationship stir associations and conflict in the other. The good news is that the conflicts and inappropriate feelings that are stirred in coaches—if properly assessed—supplement the information garnered by their eyes and ears. Their challenge is to systematically explore their visceral response to the other person and assess the appropriateness of their gut feelings as they explore their unconscious.

One way of looking at the interaction between the coach and client is to portray the interface in the form of a two-by-two matrix. On one dimension we can place the degree of transference awareness the client has of his or her inner life. On the other dimension we can do the same thing for the coach (see Figure 3.1). We end up with four quadrants.

The four quadrants

In quadrant 1, we are faced with the worst-case scenario of the transference-countertransference interchange. In this instance, both parties are in for a wild ride—one that will most likely end abruptly. Due to their level of unawareness, both parties stick to their own agenda, never bothering to listen to the other

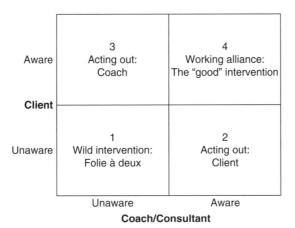

FIGURE 3.1 **The transference–countertransference interface**

party's needs. There is a total mismatch in talent and expectations. Coaches who fall into this quadrant function outside self-awareness: they "act in" and "act out." They advise their client what action to take without considering their client's legitimate needs. Because they are driven by their own needs, the specificity of their intervention is extremely low; quadrant 1 coaches operate according to a general coaching formula they have worked out rather than acting on the specifics of the situation. As a result, they tend to be extremely rigid in their coaching approach.

On the client's side, matters are not much better. Clients who fall into quadrant 1 have little or no awareness of why they act in a specific manner. They may not know what their problem really is, and their coach is not very helpful in discovering what they should focus on. Like coaches in this quadrant, they also "act in" and "act out." With this mutually reinforcing dysfunctional behavior, both parties are out of control, participating in a dangerous *folie à deux*.[14] Usually, this kind of "therapeutic" relationship begins with a temporary honeymoon, in which the interactions resemble an exercise in social form rather than having any substance. It never turns into a true coaching or consulting relationship whereby real, meaningful work is accomplished. Rather, it generally sours quickly, resulting in a dramatic termination of the relationship.

In quadrant 2, there is a degree of awareness on the part of the coach regarding the psychological processes at work, while the client has little or no understanding of the implications of his or her behavior and actions. Given the client's lack of insight—and the lack of progress in acquiring insight—coaches in quadrant 2 know that they are in an impossible situation. They realize that they are stuck but do not know what to do about it. They may try various interventions to achieve some kind of "movement," but to no avail. Realizing that they are not being truly helpful as a coach, some knowingly slip into an unprofessional attitude, not really dealing with the transferential processes of their clients but continuing nonetheless. Instead of choosing to terminate the relationship, they carry on. Generally the reason for doing so is that, despite the lack of progress, despite their frustrations, these coaches get pleasure out of the interface with the client. Material rewards or other perks may also be involved.

Furthermore, the lack of progress notwithstanding, these coaches often remain very popular with the stalemated client. A major reason for their continuing popularity is the client's very positive transferential relationship toward them. Additionally, these coaches often yield easily to the desires and wishes of their client. Unhelpful as this may be, it makes their own life much easier. Because confronting their client with difficult issues is met with negation, many coaches in this quadrant play the role of the Greek chorus, agreeing with whatever ideas their client comes up with. They may even become so close to their client that they become like a friend of the family. Although this kind of relationship can go on for quite some time, it rarely benefits the client at anything other than a superficial level.

Clients in quadrant 3 have acquired considerable insight into their own behavior. They have become astute at making connections between past and present scripts. In this quadrant, it is the coaches who lack self-awareness. They do not seem to realize that they have fallen into the action trap of counter-transference; they fail to recognize that they are acting out. Given their need for action, for a quick word spoken to give themselves comfort, quadrant 3 coaches are poor listeners and quick to give reassurance and advice. They like to make things happen, but whether their reassurance or advice is really helpful is another matter altogether. Initially, however, quadrant 3 coaches often make quite favorable impressions on their clients. Charismatic and almost seductive in their behavior, they enjoy dramatizing certain situations. Given this action orientation and ready advice, their clients may be easily swayed by their pseudo-expertise. Unfortunately, these coaches, stuck in their own scripts, may give their client advice that is totally inappropriate for the specific situation. They often sound like broken records, giving the same advice over and over again. As with quadrant 1 coaches, their recommendations may have nothing to do with their clients' problems. For this reason, their influence can be destructive. Fortunately, this kind of relationship rarely lasts long. The client, who in this quadrant is aware, comes to the realization that he or she has been a victim of positive trans-ference and starts feeling used. When a client arrives at this insight, it does not take very long before the relationship is terminated.

Quadrant 4 represents the ideal state—the "good" intervention—where coaches and their clients are aligned. They are genuinely interested in each other and are able to build a very cooperative relationship. Both parties are aware of the existence of blind spots but also are eager to learn about those blind spots and to do something about them. They know how to listen with their third ear to gain insight into their transference and countertransference reactions. They are on a mutually reinforcing learning curve, one that leads to an authentic relationship. Although there may be some hiccups on the way, generally the intervention is a very successful one.

"Strike When the Iron Is Cold"

Skilled, aware quadrant 4 coaches do not confront their clients with their pro-jections in an abrasive manner, nor do they scold them for thinking or acting inappropriately. Instead, they realize the power of resistance judo, not tackling conflicted issues head-on but reframing them. They also know the importance of timing: they "strike when the iron is cold"—that is, when their clients are pre-pared to hear what they have to say. Coaches who pay attention to transference and countertransference reactions know how to create the right circumstances for their clients to gain awareness and insight into the specifics of situations. They help their clients to recognize their projected fantasies. Furthermore, they keep in mind (while working with their clients) that their own countertrans-ference reactions will not go away, and that they cannot simply ignore their experience of the other.

Humans are both feeling and thinking beings. If we ignore our feelings, we psychologically blind ourselves to important information about the world; and if we ignore our ability to use logic, we do the same thing. If we do not use both faculties together—feeling and thinking—we are not able to integrate our inner and outer worlds.

Going for gold

Understanding and analyzing our own developmental history—exploring our inner world—helps us, as coaches or consultants, to moderate our affects and responses. We need to accept that our emotional reactions will not just go away, but we also need to recognize and process those reactions rather than simply acting on them. If we come to know ourselves better and understand our own weaknesses, vulnerabilities, limitations, and secrets, then our emotional responses to people and to our surroundings can be valuable tools in helping us interpret the world.

In short, an understanding of transference and countertransference is essential to being an effective coach. As coaches, we should always remember that there are (1) things we can know about the client, (2) things we may be able to know if we listen with the third ear, (3) things we will never know, and (4) things that we do not want to know for one reason or another. Being aware of these agendas in the bi-personal field helps coaches explore their clients' wishes and fears, especially those that are not completely conscious and thus contribute to conflict and anxiety. Possessing this kind of awareness, coaches are more likely to view their clients' emotional demands in perspective, thereby avoiding an "acting out" agenda. While mere action can enslave us, reflection goes a long way toward helping us better understand the complex, subterranean interpersonal domain.

NOTES

1. LeDoux, J. E. (1996). *The Emotional Brain: The Mysterious Underpinnings of Emotional Life*. New York: Touchstone; Rizzolatti, G. and Fogassi, L.. (2001). "Neurophysiological Mechanisms Underlying the Understanding and Imitation of Action." *Nature Reviews Neuroscience*, 2(9), 661–670; Stern, D. N. (2004). *The Present Moment in Psychotherapy and Everyday Life*. New York: Norton.
2. Klein, M. (1975). "Notes on Some Schizoid Mechanisms." In M. Masud and R. Khan (Eds) *Envy and Gratitude and Other Works 1946–1963*. London: The Hogarth Press; Ogden, T. H. (1982). *Projective Identification and Psychotherapeutic Technique*. New York: Jason Aronson.
3. Schore, A. N. (1994). *Affect Regulation and the Origin of the Self: The Neurobiology of Emotional Development*. London: Psychology Press; IJzendoorn, V. (1995). "Adult Attachment Representations, Parental Responsiveness, and Infant Attachment: A Meta-analysis on the Predictive Validity of the Adult Attachment Interview." *Psychological Bulletin*, 117, 387–483; Trevarthen, C. (1999/2000). "Musicality and the Intrinsic Motive Pulse: Evidence from Human Psychobiology and Infant Communication." *Musicae Scientiae: Special Issue, Rhythm, Musical Narrative, and the Origin of Human Communication*, 155–211.

4. Bion, W. R. (1970). *Attention and Interpretation*. London: Tavistock.
5. Reik, T. (1948). *Listening with the Third Ear*. New York: Grove Press.
6. Sullivan, H. S. (1953). *The Interpersonal Theory of Psychiatry*. New York: Norton.
7. Breuer, J. and Freud, S. (1895). *Studies on Hysteria: The Standard Edition of the Complete Psychological Works of Sigmund Freud*. J. Strachey (Ed.). London: Hogarth Press and the Institute of Psychoanalysis. Vol. 2; Greenson, R. R. (1967). *The Technique and Practice of Psychoanalysis*. New York: International University Press; Racker, H. (1968). *Transference and Countertransference*. New York: International Universities Press; Luborsky, L. and Crits-Cristoph, P. (1998). *Understanding Transference: The Core Conflictual Relationship Theme Method*. Washington: American Psychological Organization.
8. Breuer, J. and Freud S. (1895). *Studies on Hysteria. The Standard Edition of the Complete Psychological Works of Sigmund Freud*. J. Strachey. (Ed.). London: Hogarth Press and the Institute of Psychoanalysis. Vol. 2.
9. Freud, S. (1905). Fragment of an Analysis of a Case of Hysteria. The Standard Edition of the Complete Psychological Works of Sigmund Freud. J. Strachey. (Ed.). London, Hogarth Press and the Institute of Psychoanalysis. Vol. 7.
10. Luborsky, L., Crits-Cristoph, P., Mintz, J. and Auerbach, A. (1988). *Who Will Benefit from Psychotherapy?* New York: Basic Books; Luborsky, L. and Crits-Cristoph, P. (1998). *Understanding Transference: The Core Conflictual Relationship Theme Method*. Washington: American Psychological Organization.
11. Epstein, L. and Feiner, A. H. (Eds) (1979). *Countertransference*. New York: Jason Aronson; Searles, R. (1979). *Countertransference and Related Subjects: Selected papers*. New York: International Universities Press; Hedges, L. (1987). *Interpreting the Countertransference*. Northvale, NJ: Jason Aronson; Marshall, R. J. and Marshall, S. V. (1988). *The Transference-Countertransference Matrix*. New York: Columbia University Press; Wolstein, B., (Ed.) (1988). *Essential Papers on Countertransference*. New York: New York University Press; Gabbard, G. O., (Ed.) (1999). *Countertransference Issues in Psychiatric Treatment*. Washington, DC: American Psychiatric Press; Hinshelwood, R. D. (1999). "Countertransference." *International Journal of Psychoanalysis*, 80, 797–818; Goldstein, W. N. and Goldberg S. T. (2004). *Using the Transference in Therapy*. New York: Jason Aronson; Maroda, K. J. (2004). *The Power of Countertransference*. Hillsdale, NJ: Analytic Press.
12. Freud, S. (1915). *Observations on Transference Love*. London: Hogarth Press and the Institute of Psychoanalysis.
13. Balint, A. and Balint, M. (1939). "On Transference and Countertransference." *International Journal of Psychoanalysis*, 20, 223–230; Heimann, P. (1950). "On Countertransference." *International Journal of Psychoanalysis*, 31, 81–84; Winnicott, D. W. (1975). *Through Paediatrics to Psycho-Analysis*. New York: Basic Books; Langs, R., and Searles, H. F. (1980). *Intrapsychic and Interpersonal Dimensions of Treatment: A Clinical Dialogue*. New York: Jason Aronson; Casement, P. (1985). *On Learning from the Patient*. London: Tavistock; Bollas, C. (1987). *Shadow of the Object: Psychoanalysis of the Unthought Known*. London: Free Associations Books; Ferenczi, S. (1988). *The Clinical Diary of Sandor Ferenczi*. Cambridge, MA: Harvard University Press.
14. Kets de Vries, M. F. R. (1979). "Managers Can Drive Their Subordinates Mad." *Harvard Business Review*, Jul–Aug, 57(4): 125–127; Kets de Vries, M. F. R. (2006). *The Leader on the Couch*. London: Wiley.

PART TWO: CREATING REFLECTIVE PRACTITIONERS

4

CASE STUDIES OF SELF-AWARENESS AND CHANGE

ELIZABETH FLORENT-TREACY

Identity is the elusive answer to the most fundamental philosophical question that human beings ever ask themselves: "Who am I?" But the more one seeks to grasp identity and pin it down, the more one realizes that it is a chimera. There are myths, ancient and new, which reflect the terror and disarray that confront those who are suddenly faced with doubts about who they really are. It is little wonder that most of us would prefer to navigate from lighthouse to lighthouse in a known world, comforted by the repetitive but familiar nature of our own actions, guided by patterns laid down from birth, bounded by relationships that have grown dull through disillusionment, stuck in jobs that we do by rote, and preferring to be rocked to sleep by security rather than kept awake by doubts or fantasies that could wash away our cherished stability.

And yet, identity is a dynamic, evolutionary process, not an acquired characteristic. Hence many of us feel existential tension and restlessness at certain periods in our lives, without quite understanding why. To make matters more complex, we have not one but many evolving identities, which frame multiple sub-questions: "Who am I at home?" "Who am I at work?" "Who am I when I am alone?" These "master status" identities[1] are interrelated and ultimately inseparable, in that our past and future experiences in one role will affect who we perceive ourselves to be in others;[2] they guide our interactions with others and provide us with an inner sense of direction.

In a sense, our identities form the backbone of our psyche, in the same way that our spinal column allows us to function in the physical world. Most of us never think of our spine until something begins to hurt, and with similar disregard, we do not question who we are until we are visited by a vague and uneasy sense that something is out of line. Pushed by a feeling of inauthenticity, finally we act—at the point when the pain, or fear of imminent pain, becomes greater than our fear of change. A transition begins.

The resulting liminal experience of being between worlds—between selves—has been described as being about a loss of coordinates.[3] But ironically, the very fact of being without a compass—without familiar boundaries and known navigational tools—is what allows transition to occur, as people begin to imagine, and then test, alternative ways of being. These critical periods of identity questioning often coincide with lifecycle stages, occurring commonly in midlife—a passage that Dante described in his *Inferno*, and that Levinson, several centuries later, labeled the Mid-Life Transition.[4]

In general, executive programs are designed for mid- to high-level professionals, typically in their early thirties to late fifties, who are contemplating career change or advancement. Thus, it is not surprising that people join executive education programs not only for the content but also for another, often undeclared motive, which is to create the time and space to take stock of their life and explore their personal agenda.[5] Indeed, taking a class in an educational institution can be seen as an example of *transitional space*[6] as described by Konstantin Korotov in Chapter 2. Mirvis relates a similar observation, suggesting that executive programs may be, under some circumstances, "consciousness raising" experiences which cultivate participants' self awareness, deepen their understanding of others, and help them to relate to society.[7]

To better understand the journey that these mid-life explorers undergo in this type of program, I focused on the experiences of participants in a 15-month, seven-module executive leadership development program at INSEAD. (I was also a participant in this program, but I did not work on this research question until after the program ended.) This program, "Consulting and Coaching for Change" (CCC), is designed to help senior executives improve their coaching and leadership skills. I wondered: Is there any proof that executives in multi-module executive leadership development programs become more reflective practitioners and better leaders?

INSIDE THE IDENTITY LABORATORY

Korotov developed a theory of transitional learning environments, which he calls identity laboratories.[8] He observed that, in some leadership development programs, an identity laboratory (ID lab) is created in which participants begin to experiment with new roles and behaviors. This transitional space is enhanced as participants learn to watch for the irrational, intra-psychic, and interpersonal undercurrents that may influence the way people behave in dyads and in groups. Korotov suggested that the ID lab is a transitional, safe space that is both physical and mental, the boundaries of which consist of a temporal demarcation, a spatial demarcation (a consistent use of the same physical space), and a psychological demarcation (guidelines are set to establish trust). Once inside the ID lab, he found, people are accompanied by, and experiment with, guiding figures (the faculty) and tools they find there (reflection papers, peer coaching, 360-degree feedback, and so on).

And yet key questions remained. The concept of transitional space environments is still ill defined and poorly understood, rooted in individuals' personal experience, complex and conceptually difficult to relate, and delicate, sensitive, and sometimes intangible.[9]

THE RESEARCH SETTING

The pedagogical focus of the CCC program remains on the world of work—in this holistic, systemic approach, both the micro (the individual) and the macro (the organization) are considered to be equally important. Theories of organizational behavior are integrated and explored.

The key pedagogical themes—the warp threads of the tapestry—are deceptively simple. The first theme predicts that true, lasting change can only come through experiences that affect people on both cognitive *and* emotional levels. Lectures and theory building are necessary to set the stage, but deep learning comes through "aha!" moments and tipping points that can sometimes be uncomfortable. The second theme is that successful leadership can only come through authenticity, that is, an alignment between one's own personal leadership style and preferences, and one's role in the organization. Supported by their peers in a group coaching format, participants in CCC learn to become more reflective practitioners and effective change agents.

Group and peer coaching, like group psychotherapy, helps to establish a foundation of trust, commitment to change, and accountability. As individuals work together and observe each other over time within the boundaries of the program, the group becomes the pillar that supports the coaching work; the relationships among learning partners become, and remain, very meaningful. Requiring participants to work on action plans for leadership development in small groups of trusted peers sets up a context of shame, guilt, and hope—three powerful motivating forces. Participants initially feel shame as they admit to certain behavior, which in turn prompts them to declare an intention to change. The sense of guilt they anticipate if they disappoint their peer group is a strong motivator to continue on the path of change. Finally, knowing that their peer group is supportive and empathetic instills participants with a sense of hope that they will be able to meet their goals.

To be sure, some groups work better than others. The process sometimes breaks down, which can lead to even further insights and learning as the group examines the dynamics of the particular situation. Globally, however, all of the emotional experiences that come out of the group setting—in particular as people share and discuss their own feedback on 360-degree survey instruments and their action plans for future development—help to facilitate change.[10]

THE CCC PROGRAM DESIGN

The CCC program consists of seven modules. In the first and second modules, the clinical paradigm is introduced, and basic skills, like effective listening, are tested. In addition, in module 1, participants form small groups, and each person is asked to tell the others in the group about an event, personal or professional, that changed his or her life in a significant way. This early experience of self-disclosure serves to set the ID lab boundary of trust and encourages self-reflection. The professors (the guiding figures in the ID lab) are not present for this exercise, and so the participants are forced to seek safety and comfort in their small group. (Not all small groups have a purely positive experience, however; there are sometimes personality clashes, which the small group must learn to deal with.) Although the participants subsequently change groups several times during the program, most of them are able to quickly recreate a feeling of security when they join a new group. (There is some intentional overlap, such that an individual will always find him/herself with at least one member from a previous group.) Thus, from the earliest days of the program, participants become accustomed to what is in effect a group therapy design.

Drawing increasingly on the support and insights of their peers in small group sessions as the program unfolds, CCC participants re-visit incidents and situations in all areas of their life: from seemingly insignificant interactions with work colleagues to dysfunctional patterns of behavior in their own families, for example. They explore—in case papers, small group meetings, and conference calls—what lies beneath the surface, and use what they discover there to help them reevaluate the authenticity of current life experiences. After each module they go back to the "real world," and often begin to experiment with new behavior or identities. In a feedback loop, they return to the next module, where very often the topic of case papers and conversations will focus on their discoveries and their "experiments."

By the third module, in which the focus is on family and family business, people's emotions have become engaged in the learning process. This is where the hard work begins, as people have a natural tendency to resist the ever-tightening focus on their own motivational drivers and behaviors. Defensive reactions include challenging the professors' competency or commitment to the program, or refusing to write case papers or fully engage in the small group discussions. The fourth and fifth modules are less lecture-oriented and more experimental. In module 4, results of participants' leadership 360-degree feedback surveys are discussed in a group coaching day. In module 5, a two-day simulation on group dynamics forces participants to experience the sometimes uncomfortable experience of regression in groups and other group processes. The professors begin to withdraw to the sidelines in a metaphorical sense, as people turn to their small group peers for support and deeper insights—in fact, it is more likely to be a peer than a professor who provides the catalyst for deep identity work in these modules. Here many participants talk about disorientation, confusion, doubt, failure (their own or program design), or messiness—for a period between modules that lasts several months. In the fifth module, participants experience work through a multi-party simulation that highlights their own behavior in teams. The sixth and seventh modules are designed to be periods when people consolidate their insights and create narratives to help them describe their identity work and their identity discoveries. As this description of the different modules indicates, the CCC program design incorporates a short-term dynamic psychotherapy orientation[11]—not only as a concept to be studied but also as a pedagogical framework.

PARTICIPANTS' STORIES

Twenty-eight of the 35 CCC Wave 7 (2007–08) participants agreed to allow me to use their cases for this study. There were 14 men and 14 women of diverse nationalities (East and West European, North American, South American, and South African) and ages ranging from 36 to 60 (mean about 40). Participants had written a case paper after each of the first six modules; there was no paper required after module 7, which made a total of 161 cases.

WHY USE WRITTEN TEXTS?

Although good interview-based qualitative research on identity transition in executive development programs has been conducted in the recent past, a study of written texts produced during the limited time period of such a program provides a new and different lens.

The case studies capture the experiences of the participants as they unfold. The participants are not responding to a set of interview questions, they are not trying to recollect and reconstruct events after the fact, and have not produced evaluations of the CCC program upon demand. The case study *assignment* was never to write about the group coaching experience, or a personal developmental journey, or even about identity work. In fact the only guideline, after each module, was simply: "Write a case study showing how you have applied the concepts or topics learned in this module to your professional or personal context." Thus the texts are freed from the subject's unconscious wish to give an interviewer, or professor, a socially desirable response.

Participants had a great deal of freedom to interpret the assignment in any way they wished, with only a few rules: the paper should be about seven pages long, and it should be given to the small group peers before their conference call, which was typically scheduled for several weeks after each teaching module and around four weeks before the next one. The papers could (and did) take almost any form the writer felt comfortable with at the time.

Although they were not written to be reflection papers, the case texts were rich and revealing narratives on four levels. On the first level, quite a few of the cases written after modules 1 and 2 followed the assignment fairly closely, recounting incidents at work, and reflecting on them. On the second level, many individual cases were life stories, and some were like fairy tales, with ogres and princesses and dangerous or life-changing events. This level appeared in most cases (but not always) after module 3, the module on families and family business. At the third level, a few of the cases were ID labs in and of themselves: the writer seemed to be playing and experimenting with a new writing style and/or describing a possible new identity. On some cases at this level, I felt as though I was participating in a joyful or fearful exploration of a very private *jardin secret* (secret garden). Finally, I discovered a fourth level that was a surprise to me: reading an individual's case series 1–6 in order, straight through, very often revealed a coherent and complete narrative arc, from prologue, through dilemmas and tension, through new insights and understanding, and finally reaching a state of dénouement and completion. I found this to be true for virtually all 28 of the case series, although none of them, of course, had been written with an overall narrative arc as a fundamental objective.

Many participants reflected on the central importance of the stories they had to tell, an experience that sometimes was accompanied by anxiety:

> F8-3:* "Writing case stories for CCC is about writing something meaningful to me at this moment in my life. Something both business and personal related and something where I can connect both my ongoing experiences and personal challenges into the theory related to the modules."

Knowing that their small group peers would read their narratives and give feedback created a sense of urgency, responsibility, and accountability to move forward and face the confusion. Shame, guilt, and hope: they had to do the work, but then they had an empathetic group to help them make sense of it. This pushed people to experiment and refine their identity exploration. As one participant wrote about a new project he was developing: "I could use the work to write cases for CCC." Some used the cases as a means to collect their thoughts, looking for insights or deeper reflection. Others were forthright in admitting that as they started writing a particular case, they were not sure where the case would end up—an indicator that it was not just a report of ID work in the real world but that *the case itself* was a sort of ID lab. There was evidence of playing *in*, or playing *with*, the case studies in cases that followed all six modules:

> F25-2: "It's a big relief to write everything down and look at it from 'outside' and by doing so try to get answers on some open questions."

> F14-3: "What became very clear to me in writing this down [are] pattern[s] I had not been aware of."

> F12-4 "This paper has also help me to step back. It has been cathartic."

> M20-5: "Through this paper I was coming to terms with my own past, trying to understand it. Perhaps the only thing I can say is that this reflection was a way to regain myself.".

But how do we find greater meaning in these brief narratives of moments of experience? One way is to look for patterns.[12] Because the case studies took a narrative form, meaning appeared through the links the participants made.

---

*Participants' quotes are identified by gender and a number I assigned, followed by the number of the case from which the quote was taken, thus F8-3 is female participant number 8, case 3.

THE REITERATIVE RESEARCH PROCESS: IDENTIFYING ORGANIZING THEMES AND RED THREADS

To begin the process of peeling the onion—working my way down into the different strata of awareness to uncover ever deeper layers of meaning—I looked for evidence of specific emotions and underlying thematic unity. Reading the narrative arcs of the six case studies, I felt not as if I was being given an interpretation or recreation of events but as if I were living through the events with the participant, in a tranquil and private world that contained only the two of us. These were tragi-comic tales told using words not common in a business school classroom: confusion, catharsis, surprise, anger, pain, fear, disillusionment, discoveries, ashamed, worthless, autonomy, hope, freedom, delight, a lifting of heavy burdens, acceptance, serenity, honesty, and transparency.

I listened with my third ear, and not only to my partner in this intimate journey but also to my *own* emotions. Over and over, as I read through the six cases in a series, I had real and sometimes even disturbing sensations of sadness, frustration, tension, or being stuck. Occasionally, I found myself skimming through the first few case studies in a series, feeling somewhat detached or even bored. In the next, or middle, cases, I would sense a tension building up, as if the writer had more to say but was not ready or willing to express it. Then in the last cases, perhaps case 5 or maybe not even until case 6, there would be a dramatic change as the writer turned away from a structured, rigid writing style toward a free-flowing exploration of deeply personal issues. Although quite often there was no clear-cut, narrative conclusion, I had feelings of relief, and I realized I had been waiting for and even desiring that dénouement.

In other instances, after reading case 5 or 6, in which the tone changed or the participant wrote about feeling relieved, unstuck, or happy, or maybe even still confused but optimistic about the future, I would find myself in a state that felt almost euphoric, as if I had lived through the long year that led the writer to this state of grace and resolution *inside his or her head*. The authenticity of the sensations (sadness, fear, boredom, frustration, relief, optimism, and so on) that I picked up from reading the six written texts as a fully developed story are, I believe, a piece of evidence that suggests that the case reports allowed me to enter at least to some degree into the experiential world of the participants. In some cases, I watched as identity experimentation took place on stage. Other times, it was like watching kabuki theatre, or simply hearing "voices off."

What struck me as I read the case series was that, taken as one narrative, they had a real and coherent logic. I had not predicted that a collection of six random essays about individual insights and events would turn out to be one story—not rewritten or reframed as an explanatory narrative in retrospect but a true, complete narrative in and of itself. The unifying narrative theme of these stories seemed to be to search for, or to *rediscover*, one's true self. Many cases circled deeper and deeper around one meta-theme, as people looked for identities that they had somehow lost or had never fully understood.

It seemed that individuals had been writing chapters in a narrative of their future selves, informed somehow by a deeper, subconscious source that connected it all together before the individual was able to articulate it as one story. In other words, the cases were not simply an exercise in sense-making but rather, observed at a meta-level, an exercise in *unmaking* elements of the writers' identities that they now believed to be *non-sense*—the no-longer authentic patterns imposed upon them by the figures in their inner theater.

For the most part, cases 1 and 2 were the introductions or prologues, taking the form of typical business cases with varying attempts to link theories to practice. Case 3, which followed the module on family systems and family business, seemed to take people deeper, where doubts and fears lay. Defenses in some cases began to break down, whereas in others they were reinforced. As F2-3 wrote: "This case was very difficult for me to write and that's why it probably took so long. It still doesn't feel to me as a case, but rather a collection of reflections. The topics mentioned are touching the core of my personality and thus are extremely difficult to work with." The "low point" typically began here as people wrote about feeling that they were prisoners of their past. Cases 4 and 5 were quite diverse, but almost all demonstrated or reported some evidence of identity experimentation. Case 6 was often what I thought of as the "epilogue or dénouement" for most, as they consciously ended their story and talked about their (specific or open-ended) plans for the future.

There were outliers among the writers. Some seemed to have an inherently greater self-awareness, or were more able to control their defensive reactions, or had a stronger motivation to enter the ID lab earlier on (losing a job or a strong desire to change career), and this was apparent even in cases 1 and 2—they never wrote typical business cases. A few cases showed evidence of other kinds of tipping point earlier than most for various reasons. A few people did not write one or more cases at all, which is of course silent but eloquent information in itself. At the other extreme, a few case sets remained at cognitive, "reported" level until case 6, but it was possible to feel tension building from case to subsequent case as I read between the lines. Here, people who had written thoughtful but very focused and structured reports ("on task" in terms of the original assignment) "suddenly" had a complete change of writing style and topic in case 6—the hand on the doorknob effect—sometimes, as they admitted, after hard pushing from their small group peers. This usually took the form of a peer saying: "Who are you really?"

In some cases it was possible to tell almost from the beginning what the person was searching for: emotional freedom and expression, freedom from rigor, freedom from certain responsibilities, an exploration of rank and power—these themes would be repeated over and over again in different forms, as the writer looked both forward and backward in subsequent cases. Sometimes people wrote very movingly about exploring or recovering a part of themselves that had been lost or hurt when they were younger. F8-2 wrote: "His words felt like sharp knives and the look in his eyes made me feel a pain similar to the pain I remembered feeling when my mother verbally punished me for not living up to her expectations during childhood. I felt attacked, ashamed, and worthless. Not being good enough, not doing what was expected from me." And like F8, some would later write about ways to find resolution: "The intention of my life, in this present moment, has to do with living my identity. And by doing so, the intention is to assist others in living theirs. It is about inspiring and helping others, both individuals and organizations in understanding and in living their authentic identity" (F8-4).

To summarize, the six case studies in each series gave me six snapshots of the way people were perceiving and experiencing their time in the ID lab. The meaning that emerged case by case became understanding in retrospect, when the cases were reframed as one set of evolving ideas. Thus the case series, read at a meta-level, helped to answer the question of how the participants "got there"— even though "there" was of course a very individual point of reference.

At the same time, I was sensitive to the fact that, just because I did not see dramatic evidence of ID experimentation, this did *not* prove that it had not occurred. Yalom cautions: "Keep in mind that it is the subjective aspect of self-disclosure that is truly important. . . . Often there is an enormous discrepancy between subjective and objective self-disclosure—a discrepancy that, incidentally, confounds research that measures self-disclosure on some standardized scale. . . . What appears to be minor self-disclosure may be the very first time [a person has] shared this material with anyone. The context of each individual's disclosure is essential in understanding its significance."[13]

An important question is whether or not there is any link between the content of each module and the cases that followed; in other words, does evidence show that the pedagogical framework of CCC affects the outcome? To better decipher what happened after each module, I looked for the emergence of themes and I noted when these themes emerged. I found increasing examples of surprise, confusion, and defensiveness after modules 1–3. The cases that followed modules 4 and 5 reported and/or demonstrated ID experimentation, with many mentions of the importance of the peer group. Case 6 typified the termination or stepping out experience. In addition, I noticed two turning points in terms of narrative orientation: the first most typically in case 3 from "external, present" to "internal, past"; and the second typically in case 6, from "internal, past" to "external, future."

THE LAB REPORT

This exploratory study of a collection of narrative texts supports the proposition that something is indeed happening inside the ID lab. Comparing the emergence of themes to a framework of group psychotherapy gives us a further indication that the CCC modules and intervention phases have successfully integrated an epigenic group psychotherapy process and they have a similar direct influence on participants. The texts show that participants are using both cognitive and affective processes to help them make sense of the material and experiences they encounter in the ID lab and to change their behavior as a consequence. It also appears from reading the case package that there is a secondary epigenic *narrative* process that takes place during the program: (1) prologue; (2) introduction—focus on external, present; (3) identity dilemmas—focus on internal, past; (4) identity exploration and experimentation—internal focus on reframing past and future; and (5) consolidation and dénouement—focus on external, future.

Although the case papers indicated that individuals move through these phases at different rates, the narratives show that for most people identity experimentation begins after the fourth module. However, it appears that the groundwork for the deep change that occurs in modules 4 and 5 is laid in modules 1 and 2 and intensifies in module 3. For some participants, experimentation does not begin until module 6. This suggests that longer, multi-module executive development programs are well suited to identity transition.

Peer support and feedback are mentioned to be a key factor in identity experimentation. For most participants, the obligation to write a case study to be read by a small, trusted group of peer coaches seems to prompt, reinforce, and enhance experimentation in the ID lab. Participants themselves describe cause and effect relationships between their own tipping points and (1) module contents, (2) insights that emerge while writing cases, and (3) peer feedback. This implies that laying the groundwork to train participants to be effective peer coaches in the first modules of the program is worth the time and effort.

The texts also show evidence of internalization. If internalization is said to occur when people accept the influence of a change situation, environment, or other individuals because the content of this change and the ideas and actions behind it are seen as intrinsically rewarding, congruent with one's value system, and useful to meeting one's needs,[14] then, based on an evaluation of the themes in their papers, we can conclude that internalization of behavioral change is indeed occurring for many participants inside the CCC ID lab.

CONCLUSION: WHAT ARE THE SURPRISES?

For many participants, talking over their case with peers was a real call to reflection and action—writing plus discussion proves to be a very effective way to engage the powerful forces of peer groups. The cases also served as "objects" that connected group members and helped to maintain those connections. For example, the group conference calls were often followed by informal telephone calls among specific group members who wanted to elaborate on a point or ask further questions about the case study. In addition, group members would also send their case studies for comments to other participants who were no longer, or never had been, in the current peer coaching group.

The module 3 case studies were a surprise. Here, there was clear evidence of ambivalence in the sample. The cases written after module 3 were *either* professional and family business oriented, *or* took a more internal, past-oriented focus on the writer's own family; some people wanted to explore their own history at that point, and others did not (on paper, at any rate). Of the 28 cases written after module 3, 11 focused on family business (seven men, four women), 11 directly on the writer's own family (eight women, three men), and six had no family orientation at all (three women, three men). In addition, the two writers who had not written cases after modules 1 and 2 both wrote a case after module 3. On average, the cases written after module 3 were the longest of all the cases (in terms of word count). A focus on family history did eventually come up in virtually all of the case series, but sometimes not until case 6. Writing about family seemed to precipitate critical moments—although the definition of "family" sometimes took a different shape than I expected; one person, for example, never wrote a case about his family, but did write about national culture, and this seemed to have the same affect for him in terms of a tipping point as writing about family did for many others. These were all further clues from my interpretive perspective that something significant happens in this module that prepares people for their entry into the heart of darkness—or pushes them into it.

This underscores another important point: these narratives reinforce the proposition that change occurs at different rates for different people. As one Malaysian senior executive put it, some people are like strawberry plants, ready for harvesting within six months; others are like mango trees, which make you wait patiently for many years before you are rewarded with any fruit.

The tremendous importance of the reiterative process of writing in the here-and-now about identity experiments, and then discussing the case with trusted peers after each module, is an element of leadership development programs that has possibly been underestimated. Participants were not *polishing* identity narratives, they were *capturing* emerging narratives. These stories were often very surprising even to the writer. Most significantly, there seems to be some relationship between *not developing* through the epigenic phases of writing cases in parallel to the development of the group psychotherapy progression from module to module and *stuckness* in terms of epigenic progression through the ID lab. I was struck by the discovery that most of the case series, in retrospect, had a logical, narrative arc, in which similar themes kept arising—in these case series, the writer was often able to articulate a new identity-based perspective by case 6. The act of writing the cases seemed to force people to think about themselves more deeply, and over a much longer period of time than they ordinarily would do in our sound-bite, elevator-pitch world.

Surprise, surprise—it turns out that the writing process in and of itself plays a critical role behind the scenes in the identity lab. Writing—something, anything—for most people seemed to be a key pathway for emotion to emerge and be reframed or transformed into something actionable through exactly the process Loewenburg described:[15] a longitudinal repetition of themes in mode or content indicated a *latent unconscious scenario* that, for many CCC participants, was indeed heard and interpreted. In other words, it seemed that they *already knew*, at a subconscious level, who they wanted to be and where they wanted to go. But this reality emerged slowly, and piece by piece, through a long and some-times painful process of internal detective work, shaped by feedback from guiding figures. The new identities were not a *result* of the narratives, they already existed. As M23 wrote: "Odysseus is you. And me. We all make his voyage, we travel from life to life, experience to experience. We taste the sweet fruit of Lotus, ease into the oblivion of the Sirens, struggle between Scylla and Charybdis, with nostalgia. But at last we return to our real home."

NOTES

1. Hughes, E. C. (1958). *Men and their Work*. Glencoe, IL: Free Press.
2. Kets de Vries, M. F. R. (2006a). *The Leader on the Couch*. London: Wiley.
3. Carson, T. (1997). *Liminal Reality and Transformational Power*. Lanhamm, NY, and Oxford: University Press of America.
4. Levinson, D. J. (1977). *The Seasons of a Man's Life*. New York: Ballantine Books.
5. Kets de Vries, M. F. R. and Korotov, K. (2007). "Creating Transformational Executive Education Programs." *Academy of Management Learning and Education*, 6:3, 375–387.
6. Carson, T. (1997). *Liminal Reality and Transformational Power*. Lanhamm, NY, and Oxford: University Press of America.
7. Mirvis, P. (2008). "Executive Development through Consciousness-Raising Experiences." *Academy of Management Learning and Education*, 7:2.
8. Korotov, K. (2005). "Identity Laboratories." INSEAD PhD Dissertation. Fontainebleau, France: INSEAD.
9. Ritchie, J. and Lewis, J. (Eds) (2003). *Qualitative Research Practice: A Guide for Social Science Students and Researchers*. London: Sage.
10. Kets de Vries, M. F. R. (2005). "Leadership Group Coaching in Action: The Zen of Creating High Performance Teams." *Academy of Management Executive*, 19:1.
11. Yalom, I. and Leszcz, M. (2005). *The Theory and Practice of Group Psychotherapy*. New York: Basic Books.
12. Polkinghorne, D. (1983). *Methodology for the Human Sciences*. Albany, NY: State University of New York Press.
13. Yalom, I. and Leszcz, M. (2005). *The Theory and Practice of Group Psychotherapy*. New York: Basic Books.
14. Korotov, K. (2005). "Identity Laboratories." INSEAD PhD Dissertation. Fontainebleau, France: INSEAD.
15. Loewenberg, P. (2000). "Psychoanalysis as a Hermeneutic Science." In P. Brooks and A. Woloch (Eds) *Whose Freud? The Place of Psychoanalysis is Contemporary Culture*. New Haven and London: Yale University Press.

5

SOMETHING FROM NOTHING: THE USE OF TRANSITIONAL SPACE AND HOW GROUP COACHING CHANGES PEOPLE

GRAHAM WARD

It is easy to assume that leaders at the top of their game will adapt when circumstances change in order to retain power and influence. There are many examples of powerful men and women who, under pressure from their followers, made changes to the way they either thought or acted. Nelson Mandela renounced terrorism, Jack Welch overcame his shyness and stuttering to become an iconic organizational leader, and the Dalai Lama renounced his homeland for the good of his people but maintained his integrity. These are all shining examples of leaders who were able to change.

However, the list of leaders who did not make the required changes and have suffered the consequences is far longer. From Richard Fuld at Lehman Brothers to Lord Black at Hollinger, there are plenty of examples of leaders who struggled to get beyond themselves and were hoist by their own petard, a salutary lesson to us lesser mortals of how difficult change is to effect, even if we know it will serve us well. If George W. Bush would not take a simple course in presentation skills and Robert Mugabe is incapable of ceding just one iota of power after nearly 30 years at the helm of Zimbabwe's government, what on earth can make people change when it is so obvious to the rest of us that they are blocked?

Trying to answer this question as an organizational consultant with senior executives is challenging. Of particular interest is how to effect change and improve performance when working not just with individuals but with groups of talented people. After all, no individual exists alone; even a hermit is not a hermit without a group to run away from. So groups are important in organizational life. How can one effectively coach groups of people into winning ways and a positive mindset? This chapter sets out to answer that question.

INSEAD offers various executive management programs to classes of professionals. The executives who attend are handpicked by the faculty according to seniority and suitability. In many of the programs, they are split randomly into task groups to collaborate on projects and assignments. The results, as one might expect, vary. Some groups perform very well together, others fail miserably. From the faculty perspective, it is hard to predict in advance what the outcomes will be.

Some groups, populated with wholly functional individuals, become wholly dys-functional when given collaborative tasks to perform. Squabbling, tantrums, and walkouts are not uncommon, and more subtle resistance techniques like feigned illnesses or "phantom" meetings back at participants' workplaces have been observed. Other groups, populated with seemingly average individuals, perform perfectly well, even outperforming their peers. In these cases, the sum of the whole is greater than that of the parts within the group.

During management programs, coaches from the INSEAD Global Leadership Center (IGLC) intervene in these groups to facilitate a segment on leadership development which uses a group coaching process. As discussed in earlier chapters, the process requires participants to gather 360-degree multi-source feedback, deliver the material in a group coaching context, sometimes participate in a one-on-one meeting with the coach, and very often reconnect with their group via either a conference call or a physical meeting between one and three months later. The point of the exercise is to elicit, discuss, and work on aspects of the executives' leadership behaviors that need to be addressed, for instance by exploring historical weaknesses, or, as has become a recent trend, honing strengths. By improving self-awareness around these issues, research suggests that leaders experience a positive effect on performance.[1]

Why do we use a group coaching process? Why not work one-to-one, the traditional format? Coaching in groups offers participants a number of different perspectives, not just that of the coach. Groups have a more vibrant dynamic than dyads. If facilitated well, they provide lively interactive learning. Individu-als feel comforted when they realize that the challenges they face are shared by other group members, which often happens in the group format. Of paramount importance is that groups hold each other to account for the intended behav-ioral changes.

Executives arrive with a battery of material, some positive, some critical, and during the process they are apprised of characteristics that need improvement or change. Our observation at the end of the process is that, very often, a high percentage of participants do make important changes. Why do so many of the executives on the leadership development program (LDP) make radical changes to their professional and personal lives?

There is an axiom that states: "It's never too late to become what you might have been," yet many of the executives on these programs have spent much of their career watching the clock tick and resisting changes that, strangely, by the end of the LDP process, they are itching to implement. Over the years, we have observed executives making radical shifts in their thinking and activities. These range from one FTSE 100 executive who had not taken a holiday in 13 years but immediately after the LDP booked three weeks' vacation to more subtle changes around leadership techniques, such as delegating authority or adopting more engaging styles with staff and colleagues.

This chapter also sets out to examine the conditions in which change arises so that professional coaches in executive settings might reproduce the circumstances and so optimize outcomes. In particular, I focus on the creation of *transitional space*, which, if used effectively, can generate the will to change, even among people in groups that have not hitherto functioned well and are populated with difficult individuals. Dubouloy comments: "Finding a transitional space is an opportunity to develop further and gain more maturity, but it can also be an opportunity for radical change and new progress."[2]

VARIABILITY

The group coaching scenario is fluid: there is the physical environment and the process, the ability of the coach, the group "as a whole" and its ability to function, and the individual coachees within that group and the level of their desire to interact with the other three elements. Since change is hard to effect and even harder to sustain, it would be easy to assume that these four variables could restrict the impact of group coaching to mediocre at best. Yet a recent exploratory study exposed positive self and observer assessments up to a year after the process.[3] The indications were *particularly* positive in self-awareness, coaching behavior, rewarding, feedback, and team building. To understand how this occurs, we need to deconstruct the process and analyze what actually happens.

In order to make sense of the group coaching process, I have broken down what follows into the critical key concepts that are addressed. When these are put together they create the conditions in which change materializes:

1. Play: using the central notion of "transitional space" as a place where executives can experience their "other" selves.
2. Storytelling: where executives can make sense not only of their career but also of their life, through the medium of revelation and discussion of their own journeys.
3. Feedback: how working through feedback effectively, allowing for the various psychological processes that might sabotage it, can serve to enlighten coachees and help to integrate new ways of being. In this case, feedback is presented not only verbally but also through a variety of psychometrically based 360-degree instruments developed at IGLC specifically for senior executives (described in Chapter 1). These deliver both quantitative and qualitative results.
4. Action planning: taking the executive from the reflective to the practical.
5. Closure: ensuring that the executive can make a healthy transition and return to organizational life unsupported.

TRANSITIONAL SPACE

The notion of transitional space is central to the paradigm for those who want to achieve change in groups. Winnicott introduced the idea of transitional objects and phenomena to the field of psychoanalysis.[4] Transitional objects are, in the purest sense, the playthings of infants who identify with them primarily as things that are "not me." They are symbolic, explained as neither part of the infant's body, nor yet part of external reality. They are playthings but with symbolic importance. They mark the first important delineation between the infant and mother, of reality and of previously assumed reality. They are the first things over which the infant human can truly have power and exercise creativity. But in doing so, the infant needs to relinquish something of the past. As we shall see, this is not without its emotional consequences.

Winnicott stated: "It is in the space between inner and outer world, which is also the space between people—the transitional space—that intimate relationships and creativity occur."[5] The space in which executives find themselves during group coaching days could plausibly be described as "transitional space." What do the supposedly playful aspects of transitional objects and space have to do with this type of coaching environment? As Winnicott said: "Psychotherapy takes place in the overlap of two areas of playing, that of the patient and that of the therapist. Psychotherapy has to do with two people playing together. The corollary of this is that where playing is not possible, then the work done by the therapist is directed towards bringing the patient from a state of not being able to play into a state of being able to play."[6]

Yet leadership development is a serious business, not something that we equate with play. Executives attend management programs expecting to acquire a battery of theoretical tools to apply in the workplace. So what "play" are we talking about? How can that play be extended into the learning environment to facilitate growth? Brown and Starkey make a strong link between professional development and transitional space:

> Play serves to challenge existing belief systems and to restructure cognitions. It facilitates experiments with identity: What kind of a person am I, can I be, and do I want to be? . . . This can best be explained psychodynamically. Play creates what Winnicott calls a transitional object . . . psychologically this play takes place in an intermediate area—a "transitional space" between the inner psyche and external reality—which is a crucial area in the perpetual human task of keeping inner and external reality separate yet interrelated.[7]

Executives generally receive feedback through official channels in their organizations, if they are lucky enough to work in sophisticated organizations with executive development departments. Normally they receive this feedback from a superior during their annual performance review. With luck, they are given a few behaviors to work on over the coming year, to which they might agree. But follow-up is rare, and when the next review takes place, the same issues are often raised again. Change is either occurring at a glacial pace or not at all. Moreover, receiving and integrating any negative feedback (the predicate on which such a meeting is often based) is no laughing matter, as Konstantin Korotov shows in Chapter 2. How one handles such a meeting puts one's professional persona, potential for advancement, and future career opportunities at stake. It is an emotionally loaded gun.

Many executive dyads, or annual feedback reviews, fall into a repetitive game of mental tennis, defined by the history of the superior/employee relationship. Rather than being simplified, the situation is complicated by the transferences within the relationship between individuals and their superiors. For example, too little respect and the executive will not be truly listening; too much and the executive is a metaphorical puppet on a string. Objectivity is a commodity in short supply.

My many years as an executive at a leading investment bank all too clearly illustrated that the internal 360-degree feedback process is more likely to leave employees grumbling about bias and gaming the system than really dealing with the important issues of professional development. Delivering feedback in a group setting with peers makes it possible to reduce extreme polarities of opinion, known as the "halo and horns" effect.

CREATING TRANSITIONAL SPACE: DYNAMIC ADMINISTRATION IN THE LDP PROCESS

In my experience, group coaching is best attempted with groups of no less than four and no more than ten. Too many and the participants can get bored; too few and they may miss the richness of diverse experience.

How the facilitator introduces the LDP day is the key to constructing conditions in which the group can thrive. Group analysis takes place within a carefully constituted setting which is the physical representation of the "group as a whole." As Ettin said, "Knowing, communicating with, and affecting the group as a whole is a task akin to dancing with an alternatively benign and malevolent ghost,"[8] hence the environment needs to be established and managed effectively. The transitional space should be a place where ideally clients might have the opportunity to meet neglected ego needs and allow their true self to emerge. To that end, physical and verbal preparations are necessary.

All detritus is removed from the room. If the room is a classroom, graphics and models left from previous classes are erased or taken down. Computers are switched off and papers and any printed materials put away. Ideally, the room should be small enough to create conditions of intimacy. A circular table is optimal, giving the participants the greatest opportunity to maintain eye contact with each other. It also forms a symbolic center for the group.[9]

The facilitator may then make the following remarks:

- The session is entirely confidential. No information will leave the room or be shared with anyone other than those currently in the room. It is vital that this is observed, if the session is to be successful.
- The facilitator's copies of feedback and any notes he or she makes will be returned to the participants at the end of the day.
- The purpose of the day is for the participants to listen to the agenda set by each participant and offer feedback, coaching, reflection, and advice as appropriate. Care must be taken to do no harm. Everyone will be called on to speak.

- The facilitator will do the same and, moreover, will contain the environment.
- Each participant will be dealt with in turn for approximately 75 minutes. During that period, they will be expected to set the agenda for themselves with respect to the feedback they have recently received. They might want to consider what their key challenges are, and how they want the group to help them address the issues they face.
- Participants are asked to switch off mobile communications devices for the duration of the session, to avoid interruption.
- Finally, the facilitator may ask what the participants want to achieve during the day.

The physical environment must feel contained and containable, comfortable but not informal, open yet intimate, and free from distractions. It must also be a place where the participants feel psychologically safe, in order to facilitate experimentation, openness, confrontation, production of meaning, and understanding of the self and the world.[10] It is a place where the boundaries are absolutely clear and there are no interruptions. To replicate it exactly every time, however, is challenging. Kets de Vries and Korotov describe how it would materialize in an ideal situation,[11] but reality can be different, and the practitioner may wish to reflect on and redesign aspects of the dynamic administration to suit the context. Nevertheless, the underlying principles should hold fast.

EXECUTIVES AT PLAY IN TRANSITIONAL SPACE

Sitting with a package of feedback material weighs heavily on group members. They are often in a state of high anxiety as a result of what their colleagues, safely ensconced back at the office, have said anonymously about them. This anxiety can be exacerbated by the group setting. Often, the participant's individually expressed preference is to work through the material in private with the coach. To allay the anxieties of exposing their feedback in public, we break the ice by asking them to do something playful that removes them from the anxiety, at least temporarily.

We start by asking them to draw a self-portrait on a large piece of paper. This becomes in effect a transitional object. Armed with a *carte-blanche* and a bag of colored marker pens, it is always interesting to see how those who had groaned at the thought of making a drawing only a few moments before enthusiastically bolt for the door clutching their transitional "teddy bears." In truth, while they may hate the idea of drawing something that will be shown to the group, the saving grace is they know that it is something that they are *able* to do. This mitigates thinking about the sessions to follow, where they are less certain and might have to swallow some bitter medicine in front of the group.

Plato remarked that you can learn more about a man in an hour of play than in a year of conversation. Play is creative, liberating, and, for executives with their hectic schedules, unusual. In the context of our executive workshops, the self-portrait is a first step in breaking up formulaic thinking. We ask them to represent dimensions of their life in images only. Future, past, work, and leisure are simple examples, more challenging are the metaphysical dimensions representing their head, heart, and gut. The executives typically spread themselves out around the campus, utilizing floor space and taking over cubicles usually reserved for eight people. It can be like watching toddlers playing with Lego. I often find that the 20 minutes I give them to do their self-portraits are insufficient, so engrossed do they become in this creative undertaking. A useful side effect is it often begins the process of breaking down defenses, as it puts the individual into a reflective mode, bringing unconscious and hidden aspects of the self into the public arena.

Csikszentmihalyi wrote that the following criteria should be present to make free play enjoyable: "Ability to concentrate on a limited stimulus field, in which individual skills can be used to meet clear demands, thereby forgetting personal problems, and his or her separate identity, at the same time obtaining control over his or her environment which may result in a transcendence of ego boundaries."[12] Our observations have been that many of these criteria are often present, making the self-portrait exercise successful and rewarding. It is unsurprising, given the nature of transitional objects, that sometimes participants are reluctant to let go of their portraits and hang them on the walls when they return to the room.

LIFTING THE LID: FIRST STAGES OF TRANSITIONAL SPACE

In the next stage of the workshop, we invite participants to reveal their life stories through the medium of the portrait. Breaking down our life stories, and trying to make sense of them, can provoke a heap of anxiety. After all, most of us operate well within our safety zone, and most of us keep our inner theater a closely guarded secret.

In Winnicott's work on identity, he posits that transitional space in infancy allows the child to become separate from the mother, and become an autonomous and creative individual in the world.[13] In other words, the process drives the child toward self-efficacy. For that to happen, the child needs to experience the ambivalence between what is and what might be, but is being defended against. It requires a trigger. In infants this process pivots on the "good enough mother." The "good enough mother" allows the infant to experience the frustration of becoming self-sufficient in order to facilitate maturation. She does not overprotect. In the executive setting, as we shall see, the coach plays the same role.[14]

Before the storytelling begins, the other participants in the room are invited to comment on, free-associate with, and analyze the portrait of the person to be discussed. The artist listens quietly without comment. Often the unconscious processes that were at work while the portrait was being drawn are elicited by the group. Surprising analysis gives rise to deeper reflection. A portrait drawn in a monochrome for instance, when compared to others in color, might cause the participant to reflect on the inner richness of his or her own life. Or a participant might have placed themselves large, central, and in great detail, with their family represented as sticklike, bit-part players. Often a streak of narcissism is unveiled here, but is made easier to acknowledge by the humorous yet pointed intervention of the other group members.

This first step is helpful in getting the participant to see his or her world through the lens of other people's thoughts and feelings. The superego position is challenged. Strangely, it also fosters trust. If the participants, monitored by the facilitator, are careful in their interpretations, the participant under scrutiny may start to feel others empathizing with his or her story. This is important if the participant is going to take any risks in the next phase, the telling of the story itself.

THE INNER THEATER REVEALED

In the next phase, as the work deepens, we invite the participant to talk the group through the portrait. Great attention is paid to the words chosen, or as Harold Bridger put it, "the music behind the words," the order and emphasis that is placed on events, and the emotions that surface as we begin to understand the participant's inner world.[15] When the participant comes to the dimension of the past, we ask them to go as far back as they can remember and reveal as much as they are comfortable to tell about their personal history. For many people this can be a moving experience. The highs and lows of their lives are often revealed in their entirety for the first time. Participants are often surprised at how far they are prepared to go in talking about very private matters, from family breakdowns and divorce, deaths in the family to more serious career issues that have given rise to both pleasure and pain. Tears are not uncommon. When participants eventually return to their seat, they generally realize that they have entered an unusual psychological space. Executive participants experience the dual benefit of being in a place where they can now confront important issues but with minimal career risk. As one remarked, "The process of talking out loud offered the opportunity for reflection; you get to hear your own voice in a fuller dimension. In addition to hearing the coach's voice, I could hear myself better."[16] Coaches at the IGLC have heard, "I have never told anyone that story," many times.

The other participants engage with the story, ask questions, empathize, tell stories of their own that relate to what they have heard, and all this contributes to an emotional safety net, not only for the person in the hot seat but for all those in the room. As Kets de Vries and Korotov said: "The empathy and support shown by other participants, the appreciation that other people truly care, encourages participants to embrace experimentation and eventually take control of their executive behavior."[17] Typically as each story is revealed, more risks are taken. The transitional space begins to fill.

78

STORYTELLING

Organizational theory has been late in taking an interest in the stories that people tell in and about organizations,[18] but organizational theorists have now become aware that much learning in organizations takes place through story-telling. Whether in or out of organizations, people often recount experiences in story-like forms and listen to the stories of others. By placing themselves at the center of their stories, they begin to make sense of their experiences, whether happy, trying, or painful. Stories can open windows into the cultural and emotional lives of individuals, allowing people to express deep and sometimes hidden or conflicting emotions.

Ibarra talks about the importance of storytelling, how telling your own story over and over, noticing the changes that occur as you tell and retell the story, gradually reveals an insight into the drivers and themes that have led you to where you are.[19] An African proverb explains, "It is the story that outlives the sound of the war drums and exploits of brave fighters, that saves our progeny from blundering like blind beggars into the spikes of the cactus fence." By asking our executives to tell stories, we are trying to help prevent them blundering into their own metaphorical minefields, hence we put great emphasis on storytelling in the leadership development process. It is an accelerator of transitional space.

For many people, their first memories are of lying in bed being read to by their mother or father before going to sleep. These were moments of great comfort, as they slipped into peaceful and childlike unconsciousness. When we tell stories as adults, we unconsciously reengage with that feeling of comfort. It feels safe and engages the often underused emotional "right" brain. Listeners to these stories start to play the role of detectives. In many stories, there are paradoxes, ambiguities, and inconsistencies. The audience not only plays the role of "children at bedtime" but at the same time cross-examines the storyteller about motivations and hidden meanings in the script. If the situation is handled well, the teller will feel the empathetic engagement of the listeners rather than a drive toward pedantic inquiry.

Lest we forget, there is an important side benefit for the listeners too. Listening to stories, whether deeply personal or more generally about experiences in organizational life, gives listeners an opportunity to connect the story to their own experience. As each plot line unfolds, listeners may well begin a process of working through their own issues, either by identifying similarities but dreaming of different endings, or by recognizing these similarities for the first time and lifting the veil on what had hitherto been a blind spot. The stories typically have resonance of some sort. If nothing else, they create an "emotional glue" that binds the members of the group closer together, an important criterion for the risky business ahead.

By the time the portraits have been examined and the stories told, a process that can take each participant up to half an hour, participants are primed to begin the most important phase of the journey. The audience is engaged and typically they are more equipped to face their deepest challenges.

CHALLENGING CONVERSATIONS IN TRANSITIONAL SPACE

Once the transitional space has been created, participants attempt the real work of change. Like the infant child with its transitional object, ambivalence is rife. The 360-degree feedback instruments include both positive and negative commentary about the individual's performance. Most participants naturally focus on the negatives and generally pay particular attention to the critique of their superior. The critique can range from the mundane, "Must learn to truly delegate and not micromanage every outcome," to the downright personal, "Has a tendency toward arrogance and rudeness." In either case, reading the words of one's peers, direct reports, and boss can be a painful and exasperating experience, especially when there is no immediate right to reply.

Like the experimental infant, participants' psychological reactions will be divided. On the one hand, they will want to retreat into their comfort zone and defend their territory, while on the other, their more rational side will be attracted toward making the changes necessary to grow professionally. These are delicate moments. Learning through experience is indeed bitter, but that bitterness can be tempered by emulation and reflection.

In any group situation, whether on the basketball court or group coaching, it is important that the whole team plays—marginalizing any group member is damaging. The facilitator's skill is to bring in every actor and use their experiences to good effect in the space. If they do not do this, the other group members will sit idly by and observe while the facilitator goes through the coaching routine with the person in the "chair." Everyone should fill the space equally. The coach will therefore ask for pertinent reflections, free associations, and experiences from the other participants. The other participants also act as detectives by looking for clues to the sources or triggers of the behaviors, act as friends by offering helpful tips and suggestions, and act as coaches by asking relevant questions and challenging the evidence. If the dynamic is sufficiently healthy, the facilitator almost fades from view and the group takes on a life of its own. Participants will feel challenge, support, and hope that their situation can be successfully resolved.

The task of the group that finds itself in a transitional space is to totally participate in the process, to listen helpfully, and to do no harm. The explicit task of individual participants is to examine their feedback and then, having reflected on it and heard the comments of the group, to decide if they want to react to it and change their behavior. Pressure may be exerted by the group, but in the end the decision to change lies with the individual.

Executives in these learning spaces can exhibit extraordinary behaviors. They can grow angry, cry, argue vociferously, even walk out (and, we hope, back in again). The psychological space needs containment, tolerance, and acceptance that this kind of deviation will lead to development and learning. As Ambrose said, "Each individual needs to be able to feel free enough to express whatever thoughts and feelings occur, however uncharacteristic they may appear. This can lead to strong emotional reactions from the other group members and requires competent facilitation."[20]

Each individual session with each participant needs to be closed properly. To begin the closing process, the facilitator may sum up the content of the session, make his or her last reflections, and invite each member to offer one final piece of advice as a friend as a way of completing the task. Finally, having heard everything, individual participants are asked what they are going to do before they begin the vital work of creating a plan of action.

INTO ACTION: SHATTERING THE SPACE

Executives attending leadership development programs do not want to find themselves in a state of suspended animation, any more than the adult man would want to find himself clinging helplessly to his transitional teddy bear. There comes a time to move on, to break the space, and to allow the executive to reenter and prepare for the real world.

The process of easing participants out of transitional space needs careful handling. The purpose of creating the space was to generate change, but rushing to closure risks ruining the investment. Too fast, and they may find themselves bereft of the tools they need to make the required changes. Too slow, and there is a danger that the momentum for change will be lost in a mire of navel gazing.

The skill of closure in these circumstances is to create a metaphorical snap of the hypnotist's fingers, followed by a lengthier process of reacclimatization. Interviews with people who undergo significant personal change suggest that a good indicator of commitment to change is a public declaration of intent.[21] This can be done in the following way. After the portrait, the questions, free associations, reflections and 360-degree feedback, there comes a need for action. The coach needs to get to the question: "What are you going to do with all this?"

Jarring though it may be, the question has the effect of taking participants out of their reverie. Accompanying this question is a weight of expectation, compounded by the presence of an audience of four or five others. Executives are competitive and in general rise to the occasion and respond with some specifics. Of course there are those who remain vague about their intentions. In this case, the group can be reengaged in a pragmatic effort to pin down elusive participants and get them to commit to some specific goals.

It is important to cross-reference the goals of each participant with the group discussion. Sometimes the effect of the transitional space can cause people to come up with very different action plans than the issues they discussed during their group coaching session. The group must tackle these issues with sensitivity. It is not uncommon for individuals, while reflecting on the challenges facing other executives in his group, to project those issues onto themselves, rightly or wrongly. For example, an executive may have spent most of his time in the group session talking about his need to display more long-term vision as a leader.

When it comes to wrapping up, however, he may concentrate his goals around the need for more work-life balance, exercise, spending time with his family, and indulging personal interests. Possibly, these thoughts will have been provoked by *another* group member facing challenges that the first participant recognized as challenges of his own. The first executive, recognizing these challenges in his own life, prioritizes them.

We give the participants time to draft a written plan of action to cement in their minds, and with the group, what they will actually do differently when they return to work. Armed with this, we appoint a learning partner from within the group to support, coach, and engage with them at regular intervals for a further three months. Finally, we ask all participants to articulate what they plan to do to everyone present. Securing this verbal articulation is a necessary extra step to ensuring follow-through.

THE PITFALLS OF TRANSITIONAL SPACE

Working with groups in this kind of setting poses risks for any coach or therapist. Transitional space is not a scientific phenomenon, it is an abstraction. The facilitator can do his or her best to create conditions wherein the group will thrive, but there are no guarantees. Whitaker and Lieberman noted that we cannot create a feeling of safety by edict.[22] So while some of the conditions listed earlier are useful, they cannot be imposed. If a participant feels anxiety, it is important to give voice to that. If the concerns of participants can be raised openly, this will in the end give rise to feelings of acceptance, which in turn should allow the executive to open emotionally (as described in Chapter 2).

One executive I worked with pointedly refused to draw a self-portrait. She said that she did not see the relevance of drawing on an executive education course and was more interested in leadership theory. Her manner of delivery was extremely forceful and disruptive, leading me to suspect she was very angry. I told her that it was a useful exercise but that I supported her will not to do the portrait if she did not want to. I felt, however, that in order not to disrupt the group further, the other participants would do their portraits elsewhere while we sat and talked. It transpired that she had been stirred up by the feedback from her boss, which she had read the night before, and had barely slept. Realizing that she had transferred her anger onto the process allowed her to open up to what was happening and reengage. She drew the portrait and had a fruitful session relating her issues with authority.

Judging the right amount of pressure to apply to create change in each individual could be seen as somewhat akin to driving a racing car round a tight bend in wet conditions. Too heavy on the gas and the car will spin from the track. Too little, and the car will hug the bend and not take the correct racing line. To manage individuals in a group, each with a differently tuned "engine," is a nuanced process. To change means to give up a part of oneself that was previously valued or, as one executive remarked to me, "giving away my valuable DNA." It raises ambivalent feelings. The participant probably has the following question in mind: "Is changing behavior in the service of that which truly facilitates organizational improvement, or does it in fact relinquish an important facet of organizational sustainability?" Transitional space, because of its nature, can give full vent to the emotions that swirl around these issues.

A group coaching process also undoubtedly gives rise to intrinsic leadership issues. The coach or facilitator is the de facto leader of the group. Bion suggested that any group is likely to be imbued with an encompassing "basic assumption."[23] Bion specifically identified three basic assumptions: dependency, fight-flight, and pairing. When a group adopts any one of these basic assumptions, it interferes with the task the group is attempting to accomplish. In the basic assumption dependency, the essential aim of the group is to attain security through and have its members protected by one individual. The group members behave passively. In contrast, the leader is viewed as omnipotent and omniscient. The basic assumption of fight-flight brings individuals together around the feeling that the salvation of the group and its individual members depends on the fact that their leader will enable them to identify, and then successfully fight or flee, a specific enemy either within or outside the group. The basic assumption of pairing enables the group to come together as such through some of the members' sharing of an implicit, mysterious hope, sparked by the assumption that a couple will give birth to a messiah, a new guide, a new idea, or a new theory or ideology.

In a group coaching scenario, the most likely of the three basic assumptions that Bion postulated is that of dependency. Here the group tends to look to the coach for answers or solutions to their challenges. If this gets out of hand, harm may be done when individual participants eventually cut loose and find that, without the coach or the group to support them, they are adrift. In group coaching, therefore, it is essential that the facilitator sticks stringently to the coaching protocols of active listening and intelligent questioning, leaving solution orientation to the group. Any solutions provided by the coach should be strictly by permission.

BACK TO REALITY: MANAGING REENTRY

Smoothing the path to reentry is a critical last step in the process. Participants may begin to feel separation anxiety or even helplessness at the thought of leaving the group. One often witnesses heavy idealization, the notion that this group above all groups was the best/most successful/most insightful/most creative, etc. There can be a frenetic swapping of business cards and other paraphernalia that represents an unwillingness to relinquish the safety of the environment. Sometimes group members bring presents. Touching though all this is, on a purely mundane level, it is symptomatic of the power of the process.

83

Offering the executives some tools for reentry is helpful in bridging the gap between the "now" and "what is to be." My suggestions to participants are quite pragmatic:

- Thank your observers (providers of 360-degree feedback) for their comments when you return.
- Ask them to expand on any aspects that were not clear to you.
- Create an environment where your direct reports have an understanding of what you have experienced.
- Tell people what you plan to do differently, both at home and at work.
- Keep your action plan visible and refer to it regularly.
- Keep in touch with your learning partner for regular coaching conversations to support, challenge, and encourage.
- Tell your boss what you learned and what you plan to do better.

It is crucial to leave the executives feeling supported emotionally and psychologically. The temptation to revert to old dyed-in-the-wool behaviors is great without the knowledge that there is something to underpin their new experimental operating system.

A study by Marshall Goldsmith, a leading coach, published in 1996 demonstrated that 50 percent of managers who received feedback with no follow-up were deemed 18 months later to be unchanged or less effective, while of those who did receive follow-up, 89 percent were seen as being more effective after the same period.[24] Thus at the very least, we reconvene the group for a two-hour conference call within a few months to discuss progress and help further with any obstacles. Many groups come back to campus and spend a full day together, not only working on some of the old issues but also taking on new challenges. One can see how the behavioral change begun in the group setting becomes self-supporting. Many groups continue to meet literally or virtually for years after the initial event.

CONCLUSION

Creating a psychological transitional space for executives as a form of temporary respite from the rigors of working life can have a salutary and cathartic effect. By opening up emotionally, playing, and being creative, executives generate new ideas for themselves. Many of us have experienced the feeling of taking a plane ride and coming up with an idea for a new business, a book title, a life change, or simply having a self-indulgent yet motivational reverie. Creating structured transitional space can do just this for executives.

With a set primary task, coaches and facilitators can help groups of executives to optimize the probability that they will change for the better. This is beneficial not only to the executives themselves but also to the people who work for and with them, and thus to the organization as a whole. If, as a result, they become happier and self-actualize, the effect in their organizations can be incremental.

Henri Matisse said one should "Derive happiness in oneself from a good day's work, from illuminating the fog that surrounds us." Experiencing a healthy transitional space can feel like the sun warming the mist on a summer morning, clearing the view, and revealing the path to workplace contentment.

NOTES

1. Kilburg, R. R. (1997). "Coaching and Executive Character." *Consulting Psychology Journal*, 49(4), 281–299.
2. Dubouloy, M. (2004). "The Transitional Space and Self Recovery: A Psychoanalytical Approach to High Potential-Managers Training." *Human Relations*, 57(4), 467–496.
3. Kets de Vries, M. F. R., Hellwig, T., Guillen, L., Florent-Treacy, E., and Korotov, K. (2008). "Long Term Effectiveness of a Transitional Leadership Development Program: An Exploratory Study." *INSEAD Working Paper* 2008/24/EFE.
4. Winnicott, D. (1953). "Transitional Objects and Transitional Phenomena." *International Journal of Psychoanalysis*, 34, 89–97.
5. Winnicott, D. (1965). *The Maturational Processes and the Facilitating Environment: Studies in the Theory of the Emotional Development.* London: Hogarth Press & The Institute of Psycho-Analysis.
6. Winnicott, D. (1971). *Playing and Reality* (1st edn). Harmondsworth: Penguin.
7. Brown, A. D. and Starkey, K. (2008). "Organizational Identity and Learning: A Psychodynamic Perspective." In W. W. Burke, D. G. Lake, and J. Waymire Paine (Eds) *Organization Change: A Comprehensive Reader.* San Francisco: Jossey-Bass, pp. 497–498.
8. Ettin, M. (1992). *Foundations and Application of Group Psychotherapy* (1st edn). Boston: Allyn and Bacon.
9. Behr, H., and Hearst, L. (2006). *Group-Analytic Psychotherapy: A Meeting of Minds* (2nd edn). London, England: Whurr Publishers Ltd.
10. Kets de Vries, M. F. R. and Korotov, K. (2007). "Creating Transformational Executive Programs." *Academy of Management Learning and Education*, 6(3), 375–387.
11. Kets de Vries, M. F. R. and Korotov, K. (2007). "Creating Transformational Executive Programs." *Academy of Management Learning and Education*, 6(3), 375–387.
12. Csíkszentmihályi, M. (1990). *Flow: The Psychology of Optimal Experience.* New York: Harper and Row.
13. Winnicott, D. (1953). "Transitional Objects and Transitional Phenomena." *International Journal of Psychoanalysis*, 34, 89–97.
14. Dubouloy, M. (2004). "The Transitional Space and Self Recovery: A Psychoanalytical Approach to High Potential-Managers Training." *Human Relations*, 57(4), 467–496.
15. Amado, G., Ambrose, A., and Edwards, A. (2001) *Transitional Approach to Change.* London: Karnac.
16. Stevens, J. H. J. (2005). "Executive Coaching from the Executive's Perspective." *Consulting Psychology Journal: Practice and Research*, 57(4), 274–285.
17. Kets de Vries, M. F. R. and Korotov, K. (2007). "Creating Transformational Executive Programs." *Academy of Management Learning and Education*, 6(3), 375–387.
18. Denning, S. (2006). "Effective Storytelling: Strategic Business Narrative Techniques." *Strategy & Leadership*, 34(1), 42–48.
19. Ibarra, H. (2003). *Working Identity: Unconventional Strategies for Reinventing your Career* (1st edn). Boston: Harvard Business School Press.
20. Amado, G., Ambrose, A., and Edwards, A. (2001). *Transitional Approach to Change.* London: Karnac.
21. Kets de Vries, M. F. R. and Balazs, K. (1998). "Beyond the Quick Fix: The Psychodynamics of Organizational Transformation and Change." *European Management Journal*, 16(5), 611–622.
22. Whitaker, D. D. and Lieberman, M. A. (1964). *Psychotherapeutic Change through the Group Process* (1st edn). New Brunswick (USA): Aldine Transaction.
23. Bion, W. R. (1961). *Experiences in Groups* (1st edn). New York: Routledge.
24. Goldsmith, M., Lyons, L., and Freas, A. (Eds) (2000). *Coaching for Leadership* (1st edn). San Francisco: Jossey-Bass.

6

A COACH TELLS A STORY OF CHANGE

VINCENT H. DOMINÉ

As a program director and leadership coach at the INSEAD Global Leadership Center (IGLC), I have worked with hundreds of executives in a group coaching format to help them become more effective leaders within their organizations. Of these executives, most benefit in some way from the coaching process, but, as with any endeavor, some use the opportunity to develop and grow more than others.

In this chapter, I illustrate the powerful impact that leadership group coaching can have by sharing the story of Stéphanie (name changed), who participated in a program at INSEAD called "The Leadership Transition" (LT). As we will see, the program, and particularly the group coaching, triggered a major reassessment of some of Stéphanie's basic assumptions in life. By fully embracing the coaching process, Stéphanie initiated a major personal transformation that would positively impact both her professional and private life. At the end, I will take a look at the conditions that made this change possible.

STÉPHANIE'S JOURNEY OF SELF-DISCOVERY

My first encounter with Stéphanie occurred while reading her biography on my way to the European campus of INSEAD, in Fontainebleau, France. As a participant in an LT program that had started a few days before, Stéphanie was to join my group the next morning for the first day dedicated to leadership coaching. LT is an open-enrollment program developed by INSEAD Professor Herminia Ibarra, and was designed to help participants enhance their leadership effectiveness and prepare themselves for transitioning into a new, often more strategic role. It consists of two modules of five and two days respectively, held on campus three months apart, and with various interactions in between.

The biography I was reading had been written by Stéphanie a few weeks earlier, in response to an online questionnaire. The first purpose of the biography is to brief the leadership coach by providing personal and professional background information. The second is to put participants in a reflective mode by asking them very personal questions about different aspects of their lives, including their successes and failures, fears, and fantasies. The questions a participant chooses to answer and the way in which such answers are narrated say a lot about their character.

The first thing that I looked at in Stéphanie's biography was her picture. Her big smile projected a positive and dynamic image. A French national, she lived and worked in Paris. She did not indicate her age, but from reading the chronology in the education section of her biography, I calculated she was in her early forties. She came across as having a strong personality guided by deeply rooted values, and as someone who had achieved a lot in life, particularly considering what she described as her modest family background. When asked about her most interesting feature, Stéphanie simply replied, "my determination." This seemed to explain the professional success she had achieved working for a leading commodity trading company. Her current role was managing a team of professionals that looked after international institutional clients. Stéphanie herself was responsible for defining the market strategy and developing key client relationships. On the personal side, I learned that she had a teenage daughter, but that she was divorced from her husband.

From what I read in her biography, Stéphanie seemed to be someone who was taking the opportunity for self-reflection seriously. It is not unusual for participants in similar programs to skip the difficult questions in their online biographies, to provide answers that are short on information, or even to display defensive behavior in their replies. In contrast, Stéphanie answered all the questions in considerable detail and seemed eager to make the most of the coaching process. In the closing words at the end of her biography, she wrote, "I am sure you and I will discover more about me in a few weeks' time." I interpreted this as further evidence of her willingness to reach a new level of self-awareness.

After going through her biography, I turned to the results of her 360-degree feedback report (the GELI, described in Chapter 1). In Stéphanie's report, her colleagues at all levels recognized that her leadership skills were strong in most areas, particularly her delivery and tenacity. Her direct reports gave her very high marks for her ability to empower and energize them, as well as for her coaching and team-building skills. However, the rating given by her superior suggested that she needed to develop her emotional intelligence, and everyone, including Stéphanie herself, felt that resilience to stress was an issue. Her observers also provided an unusually high number of anonymous comments about her behavior, both praising her strengths and also identifying areas in which she could improve.

When I arrived on campus that late September day, I met the other leadership coaches for a briefing dinner. As I sat down, the program director in charge of the IGLC leadership coaching intervention joined us. She had just come back from delivering a short introductory session to the 29 participants in Stéphanie's class about the upcoming day of coaching. At this stage, many of the participants were not aware of what lay ahead in the leadership coaching process. The purpose of the session was not only to explain how participants should understand the 360-degree feedback instrument but also to get them thinking about change. Since being evaluated by others can be a nerve-racking process, the introductory session tried to prepare the participants for the experience of reading their reports, reduce their anxiety, and help them to interpret their results in a positive and constructive way. Toward this end, the IGLC program director stressed the value of feedback and the self-awareness that it promotes. At the end of this session, Stéphanie and her classmates each received a large, brown envelope with their 360-degree reports. All were probably eager to get back to their rooms, where they could open their envelopes and read the "verdict." The participants then had the evening and night to process the report. As the French say, "*la nuit porte conseil*": to be able to sleep on the feedback for a night is a way of preparing the participant for the day of coaching.

Once Stéphanie was back in her room and finally able to look at her 360-degree report, her first reaction was—as she later confessed—negative and defensive. Although her observers had given her a strong rating overall and had praised her in a number of areas, her frame of mind was such that she did not like what she saw in the report. During an interview three months after the LT program was finished, she said, "I almost completely passed over the positive points and focused on the points that were negative." Stéphanie's reaction was not unique. In fact, most executives concentrate on the less flattering observations in their reports and downplay the good things that people say about them. Rather than trying to think through her observers' critical comments constructively at this point, Stéphanie was taken aback by them and inclined to deny that they were true. These comments hurt; they were "brutal," as she put it. But they also forced her to respond. Stéphanie compared her reaction to the cat that is thrown and lands on its feet. She soon accepted that the comments, though painful, would help her to know herself better and improve herself. Her mood went from one of hurt and shock to one of defiance. She slept soundly that night and felt ready to go to work the next day.

THE POWER OF VICARIOUS LEARNING

I first saw Stéphanie in person in the amphitheater the next morning, when I joined the other leadership coaches and participants for another short introduction from the IGLC program director. I quickly spotted the five participants that had been assigned to me for the day. By this point, Stéphanie was in the third day of her leadership program and was completely immersed in her training. On the first day of the program, she was still checking her emails compulsively, but by now she was no longer even opening her laptop back at the hotel, and was using her BlackBerry as little as possible. She was, as she put it, experiencing "the magic of total immersion," and had created the headspace needed to devote herself fully to the upcoming coaching process.

During the introduction, Stéphanie found out which leadership coach she would be spending the day with, and which participants would be part of her coaching group. Stéphanie was initially disappointed to learn that the coaching would be done in a group, rather than one-on-one. She was concerned that in a group setting, she would be unable to discuss her issues openly and would thus fail to make any real progress. Once again, Stéphanie's reaction was not unusual for participants in her situation. I once coached a senior executive in a company program who was thoroughly dismayed at the prospect of group coaching, and who thought his company had chosen this format to save money. This, of course, is far from the truth. Stéphanie eventually realized the full effectiveness of the group coaching model. "There is a reason for it," she said. "It is not for nothing that you do this, but you discover this later." Though unhappy initially with the group coaching context, Stéphanie said afterward that she had been pleased to hear that she had been assigned a male coach. This preference was not one that she tried to justify with reasons, but was "very personal" and "completely intuitive."

When the introductory session was over, the participants broke up into their assigned groups. Stéphanie's peers came from around the world and were working in a variety of professional sectors. Of the group of five, Stéphanie was the only woman. Once I finished greeting everyone and we had all sat down, I asked them if they could share with me their impressions of the program so far and their expectations for the day. This allows me to get a feel for both the individuals in the group and the group as a whole. In Stéphanie's case, she told the group that she was very pleased with the high quality of the faculty and the overall structure and content of the program. With regard to her expectations, she said that she had been shocked by some of the feedback she had received, but that she wanted to make the most of the day by clarifying what the feedback meant and by finding ways for her to improve. Once again, her message indicated that she had a strong desire to develop.

Stéphanie also shared the reason why she enrolled in the program with the group. In her annual appraisal one of the company directors told her that she might benefit from trying to develop her leadership skills further. She was not sure that she agreed with the director's opinion, but she saw his advice, nonetheless, as an opportunity for change and growth that she promptly seized. Stéphanie decided to look for some form of education to strengthen her leadership abilities and identified the LT program at INSEAD. Although it was not customary for the firm to send people at her level to INSEAD programs, she managed to persuade the company director to support her request internally. Observing her and hearing her speak, I perceived a strong, charismatic personality with a mix of high energy, professionalism, and a good sense of humor that she knew how to use to charm her audience. At the same time, I perceived a slight nervousness in Stéphanie's body language.

The first order of the day was the self-portrait. The five participants were all given colored pens and flipchart-sized paper to draw a self-portrait incorporating images that expressed seven dimensions in their lives: head, heart, stomach/gut, work, leisure, past and future. Unusual as this exercise may appear to the participants, it gets them warmed up for the task ahead by helping them to think about their situation in a way that is supple, intuitive and spontaneous.

Once the participants had completed their drawings, we all reassembled. Throughout the rest of the day, the participants would each take less than an hour to explain their drawings, share their reactions to the 360-degree feedback and discuss their situation with the rest of the group (as described in greater detail in Chapter 5). That day, Stéphanie was the first of the five participants to engage in the group coaching process, and she was about to discover the transformational power of the group coaching model.

Stéphanie's coaching session began, and we focused on her drawing (see Figure 6.1). When the participants draw their self-portrait, it is more than just a preliminary exercise to prepare them for the coaching session. On one level, the participant uses the self-portrait to present a desired self-image, but, at a deeper level, the portrait can also suggest other truths, which can even be contrary to what they want to reveal. For example, someone who is self-centered may draw a picture of himself that takes up most of the page, or may not include anyone else in the drawing.

FIGURE 6.1 **Stéphanie's first self-portrait**

Stéphanie found that her portrait disclosed information about her that she did not intend to disclose. In her words, the self-portrait exercise "is, at its heart, fundamentally innocent, but proves to be absolutely fearsome." Dominated by an imposing, dense forest and a broad, intensely wavy river, Stéphanie's picture was colorful and positive, but also very full and busy. When Stéphanie drew her self-portrait, she wanted to illustrate a number of things that were dear to her—nature, trees, flowers, water, the shining sun, family, and friends—and, having made nature her overriding theme, she intended to infuse her composition with a spirit of peace and serenity. But, as Stéphanie would later acknowledge, this intention was belied by the sheer busyness and agitation that the portrait expressed. In discussion with the group, she came to realize that, far from being an expression of true serenity, her self-portrait indicated a lack of tranquility in her life, or perhaps even an unconscious desire to get away from her current situation.

In discussing her self-portrait, Stéphanie got her first taste of how the group coaching method can help one to achieve better self-knowledge. However, the real transformation, or the major shift in Stéphanie's understanding of herself, took place during the main part of the coaching session, which was dedicated to a discussion of her 360-degree report. By this point, Stéphanie had had a little over 12 hours to process her report and to come to terms with the comments that it contained. I have already indicated that she was able to overcome the initial shock that the comments had caused the night before, but the next day she was still upset and disappointed with what she had read. The comments that she found most difficult to accept were those relating to her control over her emotions. Several of her observers had indicated in their comments that Stéphanie could be too harsh or overly emotional in her dealings with colleagues or clients. Although Stéphanie was generally protective of her team and people close to her, she could also be confrontational when defending her interests. An observer said that she was "territorial," and that she fought furiously in response to anything she perceived as an intrusion.

When discussing the report and the comments it contained, Stéphanie's hurt and frustration came through clearly to the other participants. As part of this discussion, she talked about her superior, with whom she had a difficult relationship. She thought that she was more capable than him and that she knew the business better than he did. Stéphanie explained to us that the position as head of her department had recently been filled after a long search. Stéphanie had not considered herself a candidate for the position, nor was she even interested in having it. However, she was extremely disappointed by the lack of transparency in the hiring process and did not think that the candidate chosen was the right person for the job, since he had very little experience in the required field.

At this point, Stéphanie had not yet accepted that the comments in her 360-degree report were an accurate reflection of her and her behavior at work. She felt they were comments that she, in some sense, did not deserve. When Stéphanie spoke about her superior, she did so in a way that was negative and aggressive, and the other participants picked up on this. They were getting a taste of some of the hot-blooded and combative ways of acting that were described in the report. Rather than being one-sidedly supportive of Stéphanie, they appeared to be shocked by her behavior: by her body language, her tone of voice, and her choice of words. Stéphanie gradually became aware that her interpretation of her report was not in sync with that of the others. With their feedback and their looks of incomprehension, other members of her group were suggesting that there might be some truth to the comments in the report. One participant—I'll call him Alex—even told Stéphanie in a nonthreatening way that he would probably not want to be her superior. An expatriate working as a general manager at an international insurance company in Egypt, Alex personified the type of leader that commands respect with a calm and reflective personality. To some extent, Alex radiated the kind of serenity Stéphanie was aspiring to and had wanted to show in her drawing.

This feedback hit home. Stéphanie's first reaction was what she describes as "almost animal." As in the past, her immediate inclination was to lash out. She said to herself: "Who do these people think they are, saying these kinds of things about me when they don't even know me?" But Stéphanie managed to keep these comments to herself, and her calmer, more objective side soon prevailed. She recognized that the other participants had no reason to like or dislike her and no motivation to resent her or to attack her out of jealousy. The fact that they did not know her outside of the leadership program meant that their comments were likely to be sincere and impartial. This is one of the big advantages of the group coaching model when it is used within an open-enrollment program: participants are able to receive valuable feedback from a number of other successful executives who have no personal interest in either praising or criticizing them. For Stéphanie, the reaction of the others in the group coaching session helped her to overcome her resistance to the comments in her 360-degree report. If the participants were suggesting that she could sometimes be overly emotional and aggressive, then perhaps the comments of her observers from the office were true after all.

To help Stéphanie understand her emotional reactions better, I drew upon the personality theory of Carl Jung, the famous Swiss psychoanalyst. The point of doing so was not to give the participants a dry lesson in psychology. Stéphanie was in the throes of coming to a valuable moment of self-realization, and, to use Socrates' metaphor, my job was, like a midwife, to give her all the help and tools she needed to do this important work herself. Jung distinguishes people who have a preference for making judgments in a detached manner from those who have a tendency to make decisions from "within" a situation. People in the latter group often identify themselves very closely with their work and are often very passionate and value-driven in what they do. Because of that they are more likely to overreact emotionally when their work is being criticized and tend to take such criticism personally. When I said all of this, Stéphanie recognized herself in this behavior. This helped her not only to understand herself better but it also made the revelation less threatening. By seeing her emotional behavior within such a framework, Stéphanie realized that this behavior was very normal, shared as it is by a good portion of the general population.

This set the stage for an even more important discovery that Stéphanie made about herself. During her coaching session, I talked about the analogy of the autopilot, which I often introduce during my coaching sessions. Like today's big commercial airplanes, as individuals we can function on autopilot, performing tasks automatically or without reflecting much on what we are doing. Autopilot mode is incredibly useful, because it allows us to act and react without having to expend too much energy, but the disadvantage of functioning on autopilot is that we give up a certain level of control over our own reactions. When on autopilot, we are not consciously paying attention to what we are doing, and so we act in a way that lacks awareness. We tend to revert most strongly to our autopilot mode in times of stress.

We all have issues that we are sensitive about, and if we are on autopilot and someone comes along and provokes us in one of those areas—if that person "pushes our buttons"—then we will react in the way that we always react in such a situation. Our reaction may not be beneficial or constructive, but it is just what we do, and can leave us open to being manipulated by others. If someone knows how to push our buttons, and if they know how we will react, they can control us in the same way that a puppet master controls a marionette. I like to talk about the Zidane syndrome. In the dying minutes of the 2006 World Cup soccer final, Italy's Marco Materazzi provoked France's Zinedine Zidane into doing something that would hurt his team. Under stress, and frantically trying for the goal that would have lifted his country to victory, Zidane was on autopilot and Materazzi was able to manipulate him with a few words. Zidane headbutted Materazzi in an infamous incident and was sent off. France lost. Stéphanie and the rest of the group laughed at the story, which helped them to assimilate the message. At some point in the session, Stéphanie came to the important realization that, when she reacted emotionally to situations at work, she too was functioning on autopilot, and as a result was not fully in control of herself. She understood that she had been acting in ways that were not always in her best interest. But she also knew that something could be done about it if she switched off her autopilot more often and become more aware of her immediate feelings and reactions.

Another topic relevant to Stéphanie that we covered during the day was the journey involved in moving from a management to a leadership role. To illustrate the difference between the two roles, I gave the following example. If telling someone how to build a boat is a management task, leadership, in contrast, is about inspiring people to discover a new continent. If the leader is successful, people will find a way to build the boat for themselves. Organizations need both effective managers and leaders. Often though, as people move up the ladder, what made them successful as managers does not necessarily make them good leaders. The difference between managers and leaders, Zaleznik wrote, lies in the conceptions they hold, deep in their psyches, of chaos and order. Managers embrace process, seek stability and control, and instinctively try to resolve problems quickly—sometimes before they fully understand a problem's significance. Leaders, on the other hand, tolerate chaos and lack of structure and are willing to delay closure in order to understand the issues more fully.[1] Stéphanie had succeeded in her career by delivering outstanding results within her area of responsibility. She understood that she would now need to "elevate" herself, to develop a strategic vision and to communicate it to both internal and external stakeholders.

At the end of the day, after all five participants had completed their coaching session, they all filled out a Personal Action Commitment (PAC) form. On this form they listed the concrete steps that each of them would take to become better leaders, both within their respective organizations and in their lives outside of work. In her interview with me after the program, Stéphanie had high praise for this step in the coaching process. "For someone who really has a desire to improve himself or to challenge himself, the PAC is worth its weight in gold, because it is now the person's own commitment." Having made important discoveries about herself earlier in the day, Stéphanie now had to decide how best to act. She committed to trying to improve herself in three ways. First, she would try to be more aware of her emotions and to manage them better. Second, she said that she would try to move away from a pure management approach toward demonstrating broader leadership capabilities. Finally, and related to the previous point, Stéphanie said that she would make an effort to expose herself more and improve her communication, not only with the executive committee but also with the members of her peer group, whom she had tended to ignore up to this point.

When everyone had finished preparing a first draft of their PAC, I asked each participant to share the key elements of it with the group. This kind of public declaration adds an element of peer pressure that can strongly motivate participants to make changes, since they know that later they will have to report back to the group on their progress. All had decided to focus on the key development areas identified during the course of the day. In addition, each participant was assigned to one of their colleagues as a "learning partner," to provide additional support and encouragement during the change process.

Before we concluded the day's group coaching session, I thanked the participants for engaging so courageously in the process, wished them success in implementing their action plan, and told them that I looked forward to hearing more about it during the upcoming conference call and in the next coaching session.

TOWARD A MORE AUTHENTIC IDENTITY

By the time Stéphanie's day of coaching had ended, a major transformation in her self-awareness was already under way, but it was far from complete. When participants return to their regular life, they often begin to doubt what they have learned about themselves during the coaching session. Having taken two steps forward, they often take one step back and must come to terms with the truth about themselves once again. Stéphanie said that it took her two months to fully digest what she had learned about herself. The whole experience had shaken the foundations of her being, and the perception of herself that she had taken for granted before the program was now cast into doubt. Like a puzzle that has been broken up, Stéphanie's own picture of herself had been dismantled and needed to be reassembled, piece by piece.

At first, as she continued to mull over the comments that others had made about her in her 360-degree report and in the group coaching session, she still found them difficult to accept. Unfortunately, many people do not manage to get over this hurdle in the coaching process, and so, because of their feelings of hurt, they never fully benefit from the feedback. But with time, Stéphanie was able to step back from the comments, reflect carefully upon them, and recognize the truth that they contained. She was aware that her strong, combative nature had allowed her to be successful so far, but that she now needed to make changes to her behavior if she wanted to progress even further in her career. She also realized that her lack of control over her emotions had probably already set her behind in her career development by a couple of years. For someone as driven and determined as Stéphanie, this was very painful.

As unpleasant as Stéphanie's sense of disappointment was, it was also a strong impetus for change. "I can't be left in a state of transition. I can't be left with a feeling of failure," she said. Having acknowledged that she had some problems to address, she resolved to pick herself up, dust herself off, and try wholeheartedly to improve herself in the areas that required attention. Stéphanie is now emphatic that she has brought about an important transformation in her life, one that is still in progress but that is well established. She likens this transformation to one that a snake undergoes when it sheds its skin. Like the snake, Stéphanie is casting off a skin that has served her well but has outlived its usefulness, and she is assuming a new skin in its place.

To bring about this transformation, Stéphanie adopted what she calls a "quick wins" approach. Rather than getting bogged down in changes that were overly ambitious, Stéphanie tried to react quickly, and to make progress by taking small steps that would bring short-term gain. Foremost on Stéphanie's agenda was dealing with her lack of control over her emotions. She now tries to limit her emotional reactions by being acutely aware of her feelings, not just in the professional setting but also in the rest of her daily life. When she is interacting with others, she generally tries to listen more than she used to and to wait longer before she speaks. If she finds that she has a difference of opinion with someone, she then—to use the flying analogy from her coaching session—stops functioning on autopilot and reverts to manual control. When in a conflict situation, rather than giving in to her inclination to overreact, Stéphanie instead turns inward and questions herself. She asks herself questions like: Why do I feel the way I do? Why does the other person feel the way he or she does? Am I overreacting? Should I give the other person a chance? Regardless of how Stéphanie answers these questions for herself, her battle over her emotions is already largely won. By making these inquiries, she has already taken a step back from the situation and is not simply reacting on impulse. Stéphanie has discovered that, by performing this simple procedure, the people that she deals with feel more at ease with her and are more willing to trust her. She has also seen gains in her personal life, having found that her relationship with her daughter is better now that she reacts to her less quickly and listens to her more.

To help reinforce this way of thinking, Stéphanie recorded the various encounters that she had with people in a notebook, analyzing each encounter in detail. She wrote, for example, how she reacted to the situation, why she reacted in that way, what consequences her reaction had, and how she would try to react when faced with a similar situation in the future. Eventually, once her ability to monitor and analyze her feelings had become well established, Stéphanie was able to put her pen and paper aside. She contends that being aware of her emotions does not mean that she is trying to give herself a new identity. Nor does it mean that she no longer says what she wants to say. Stéphanie is simply trying to control her feelings instead of letting her feelings control her. Paradoxically, saying what she wants has become more of a free choice for her, because when she gives her opinion, she has already had a chance to think about what she is saying and is not just performing a knee-jerk reaction.

The following story illustrates how Stéphanie's new way of handling her reactions has brought about positive results in her professional life. At one point, Stéphanie had given her opinion to a director regarding an important business decision that needed to be made. The director eventually came to Stéphanie and informed her of what he was planning to do. His intention was contrary to what Stéphanie had recommended. In the past, Stéphanie would probably have reacted angrily to the decision, and this is what the director probably expected her to do this time as well. But instead of reacting emotionally, Stéphanie simply told the director that she accepted his decision, that it was his to make, and that she was grateful he had informed her of it. Somewhat bewildered by this unexpected reaction, the director gave his decision more thought and later asked Stéphanie for further input. She was happy to provide it to him, and in the end her advice played a key role in influencing his final choice.

Gaining control over her emotional reactions is not the only element in Stéphanie's personal transformation. She has also made important gains and changes in other areas. One result of Stéphanie's coaching session and the LT program was her growing realization that if she wanted to continue progressing in her career, she needed to broaden her leadership repertoire. This would require her to do things differently than she had in the past and to be willing to step outside of her comfort zone. Before the LT program, Stéphanie had a very strong fear of public speaking. She would be unable to sleep the night before a presentation, and when the time came for her to present, she would be very nervous, lose her voice, and even have difficulty breathing. A session on presentation skills during the LT program, which included role-play, helped Stéphanie learn to deal with her fear of public speaking by rationalizing it. She realized that she was putting unnecessary pressure on herself by setting impossibly high standards. She had implicitly assumed that to be successful she needed to convince everyone of her point of view, but upon reflection she understood that no one, not even a CEO or a senior politician, is ever able to get everyone behind him. This realization helped to calm her fears about speaking in public, and recently she successfully gave an important presentation that drew many compliments from colleagues at her firm. She is still somewhat nervous when speaking in front of a large audience, but not nearly as much as she was before.

Around the time of that same presentation, Stéphanie began to express her femininity more visibly in the way she dressed. When she was growing up, her parents had a very traditional relationship, and her mother was both very feminine and very submissive to her husband. Until recently, Stéphanie had associated being feminine with the way her mother dressed and acted. From a young age, she knew that she did not want to be like that. As a result, the stereotypical "heels and pearls," at least in a professional setting, was something that Stéphanie simply did not do. During her day of coaching, Stéphanie realized that she would gain in authenticity and in stature as a leader if she allowed more of her femininity to be expressed. This part of Stéphanie's transformation is very personal and illustrates well the kind of fundamental change in a person's life and identity that the coaching process can bring about.

Some eight weeks after the first coaching session, we all held a conference call. There is a danger that participants quickly become completely immersed in their work after they have finished the program and find it difficult to keep focused on the objectives that they established during the coaching session. The purpose of the conference call is therefore to check in with them, to help them address any issues they might be facing, and to keep them motivated. During the conference call, it was apparent that Stéphanie had already come a long way since the first coaching session, and she was able to report her progress to me and the group. The last two months had not been easy, but one could sense a great deal of satisfaction on her part for having kept her promise, probably one of the values that Stéphanie cherishes. Her learning partner, the other group members, and I, all complimented her on her impressive development and encouraged her to maintain the momentum. I looked forward to hearing more from Stéphanie in person during the second module, to be held just after Christmas.

For Stéphanie and her classmates, there was one more formal requirement they had to fulfill before the next module. They had to provide the school with a personal written update on their development. In her paper, Stéphanie was both candid and objective, sharing the highlights of her progress. She concluded the paper with the following: "It may sound stupid, but I feel like I am a different person than the one that attended the training program three months ago." While she felt she was still at an early stage in her transformation, she expressed confidence in her capacity to reinvent her business identity and, to some extent, her personal identity, and she now felt much better equipped to handle her leadership transition.

We met again for the second and last round of coaching during the second module of the LT program. For each participant, the day of coaching involved a half-day of group coaching with a second drawing and, in the afternoon, individual coaching sessions with me, a session with each person's learning partner and some time for individual reflection. The day was to be concluded with a wrap-up discussion in the group setting. Following a short reconnection, I asked each member of the group to produce another drawing that would depict the changes each had implemented since the first module. Stéphanie sat there for quite a while, staring at the paper, not quite sure what to sketch. Only in the last five minutes did she decide what to draw, and she quickly produced two graphs (see Figure 6.2).

When I saw the results, I thought that they illustrated the transformation Stéphanie had gone through extremely well. The first graph depicted the journey she had undergone as a gradual, upward slope along XY axes. One axis of the graph measured time, while the other measured her level of contentment. At various points along the slope, Stéphanie had drawn faces showing a continuous

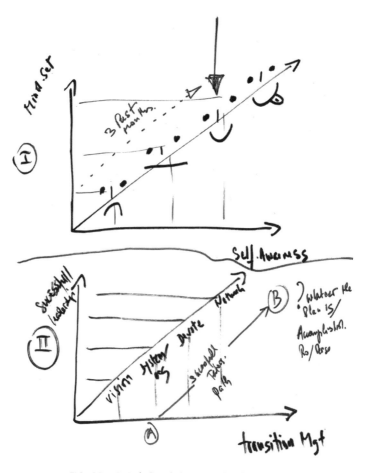

FIGURE 6.2 **Stéphanie's second self-portrait**

progression in her state of mind and self-awareness. At the base of the slope, she drew a face depicting pain and unhappiness, but as the slope rose, each face gradually became happier, with the last of the faces portraying a state of elation at the end of the three-month period. The second graph illustrated the success factors needed to successfully transition from a pure management function into a broader leadership role.

Stéphanie said that the second round of coaching was like "the final step in the self-renewal process." It was an opportunity for her to take stock of what she had accomplished, see where she could continue to improve, and look toward the future. She felt calm, at ease with herself, and clear in her thoughts. "I really had the impression that I had been progressing a good ten years," she said. During the coaching, I challenged her by saying that I thought that the development illustrated by her drawing was almost too good to be true. I wanted to probe how sustainable the metamorphosis was. She told me later that my question had surprised her and that she took it as a challenge. She was taken aback that I would question her ability to stick with the changes that she had decided to implement. Previously I had observed Stéphanie's sense of determination, and the resolve with which she responded to my question dissipated any doubt I could have had. Stéphanie had decided that she would not return to where she had been before the LT program. She is not somebody who looks back, except to measure her progression. She had once again come a long way in her life thanks to her determination and discipline. I was not the only one who was impressed. The members of the group were all pleased to have witnessed her transformation, and the group coaching was, in her case at least, mostly a celebration of her success. We used the one-on-one coaching to connect the dots, so to speak.

When we met in Paris three months after she had completed LT, Stéphanie admitted that she had found it challenging going back to work once her transformation had begun. Having found herself in the same role that she occupied previously, she no longer felt that she was in the right place. This is not unusual for executives who return from a transformational program. They often discover that they have changed as a result of their experience in the program, but their work environment does not change with them. However, Stéphanie has tried to make the most of her situation by taking every opportunity that presents itself to develop her leadership qualities. Probably as a result of her evolution, shortly after she returned from the second LT module, she was offered the opportunity to lead a major strategic project for her firm. In this additional role, Stéphanie is making a conscientious effort to use some of her personal learning to bring about change within her organization. For instance, she uses a coaching style to develop others around her and in her interactions with various stakeholders.

Although her situation in the office prior to attending the program was a great source of anguish for her, she now realizes that it had also been a blessing in disguise. To paraphrase Kierkegaard, we live our lives forward, but we understand them backward. Stéphanie's difficulties unleashed a series of events that led her to a better understanding of herself and a more developed leadership style.

When the next big career opportunity presents itself, she will be better prepared to make the most of it.

CONCLUSION

As remarkable as Stéphanie's transformation may appear to be, particularly considering the short period of time that elapsed between the two modules, many executives in similar educational programs initiate important personal changes. All the members of Stéphanie's group, for instance, identified areas they wanted to develop, and all progressed in some way. However, if a leadership development program is to create fertile ground for personal transformation, a number of elements need to be present.

First, participants selected for the program need to be prepared to engage in a change effort. Stéphanie thought that she was the only one who had to fight to be sponsored for the LT program. In fact, to be admitted, all participants must demonstrate a genuine willingness to involve themselves actively during the program. This is a crucial element of success, since participants learn from each other's experiences. Personal transformation is enhanced by vicarious learning from the stories and feedback of others—an extremely powerful experience, not least because it helps people to realize that they are not alone in struggling with a specific problem. Within Stéphanie's group, each member tried to use the coaching techniques I had introduced at the beginning of the session to achieve the right mix of respectful confrontation and encouragement needed to assess their situations realistically and explore alternative behaviors. Many times during the day, a situation described by one member of the group resonated with others, either because they had experienced similar circumstances or because they were reminded of the behavior of people they knew or of situations they had observed at work or in private. With every coaching round, the group members gained better insight, both into others and themselves. They also started appreciating differences and understanding their own biases better at the affective and cognitive level.

Second, as has been mentioned in previous chapters, the design of the program should allow for the creation of a safe experimentation environment, some sort of transitional space where exploration is allowed and encouraged. Through a rich mix of lectures on topics as varied as leadership styles, fair process, presentation, and networking skills, and combined with group leadership coaching, participants are encouraged to experience a kind of self-renewal.

Third, the dedicated faculty members and leadership coaches need to act as empathetic change agents who provide encouragement and help contain anxieties within the transitional process. As IGLC leadership coaches, we are clinically informed and trained to monitor both conscious and unconscious behaviors and group dynamics. At the same time, we use the business language of the client, enrich our observations with our own experience, use illustrations and metaphors that convey messages in a nonthreatening way, and guide the client in developing change strategies. When combined, all three elements—individual motivation, safe environment, and empathetic change agents—should provide a good setting for transformation.

While the context is essential for personal development to take place, the most important factor by far is the willingness and capacity of the participants to achieve their change targets. Once participants have identified areas for development, they need to create a sense of urgency and build up their confidence so that they can implement the changes. As we know, change is hard to bring about. There are many unconscious drivers and competing hidden commitments that keep people from making the changes they sincerely want to make. Kegan and Laskow Lahey[2] state that a person's environment can often be another source of resistance to change. Miller and Rollnick refer to three critical components of motivation for change that are related to each other in complex ways: readiness, willingness, and ability.[3] In the case of Stéphanie, the program and the coaching helped her to recognize the importance of change in her life, but her level of confidence in her ability to implement change was already very high. This was where Stéphanie's determination came into play. Self-efficacy serves to describe the fact that "people with a high assurance in their capabilities approach difficult tasks as challenges to be mastered rather than threats to be avoided. They set themselves challenging goals and maintain strong commitment to them. They quickly recover their sense of efficacy after failures or setbacks. They approach threatening situations with assurance that they can exercise control over them."[4] Stéphanie's story is that of someone who very early on had developed a strong sense of self-efficacy through utter determination. The eldest in the family, she quickly learned to take responsibility not only for herself but also for her siblings. It is this strong sense of self-efficacy that allowed her to overcome the obstacles that might otherwise have blocked the path leading to change.

So, is Stéphanie's transformation too good to be true? As leadership coaches, we are naturally interested in the sustainability of the changes. In the case of Stéphanie, the stress and the busyness in her life have not disappeared yet. Her efforts to implement change and move out of her comfort zone have increased her level of stress, rather than reducing it. Nonetheless, as part of her journey toward more authenticity and control over her emotions, I believe that she has already internalized a new form of behavior and is evolving toward a more balanced and fulfilling life. Most importantly, I was very pleased to hear that Stéphanie had found a coach within her firm to accompany her on her ongoing journey of growth.

NOTES

1. Zaleznik, A. (1998). "Managers and Leaders: Are they Different?" *Harvard Business Review on Leadership*. Boston: Harvard Business School Publishing.
2. Kegan, R. and Laskow Lahey, L. (2009). *Immunity to Change*. Boston: Harvard Business Press.
3. Miller, W. R. and Rollnick, S. (2002). *Motivational Interviewing, Preparing People for Change* (2nd edn). New York, London: The Guilford Press.
4. Bandura, A. (1997). *Self-Efficacy: The Exercise of Control*. New York: Freeman.

7

360-DEGREE GROUP COACHING FROM THE INSIDE OUT

MURRAY PALEVSKY

Group coaching is an intricate part of many of the open and company-specific executive programs given at INSEAD. As a participant of the "Consulting and Coaching for Change" program, I went through the group coaching process in the program's fourth module. Later, I was a coach in a number of open and company specific programs. This chapter is a distillation of my observations in my role as a coachee, however.

I remember that, before being an active participant in this process, I had asked myself: How is group coaching going to work? Is it going to be a good use of my time? What will be the lasting effects of group coaching on me or my business activities? This chapter gives my account of a 360-degree group coaching experience as a participant in an open executive program, a diverse group of people from different companies, different countries, and a range of cultural backgrounds. It is meant to take the reader through the three phases that make up the process: preparatory (data collection), the group coaching session itself, and the aftermath (the take away).

THE PREPARATORY PHASE

The starting point for the group coaching exercise is the completion of a number of 360-degree survey instruments that focus on leadership behavior and leadership-related personality traits. These questionnaires are completed by the participants and a group of observers whom they select. The process of finding observers and filling in the questionnaires tends to create a certain amount of anxiety about what kind of leader you really are. It starts a thinking process that goes something like: Who am I and how do I perceive myself as a leader? And then: Who do my employees/direct reports/colleagues/superiors/clients think I am and how do they perceive me? And finally: Why am I doing this?

The initial procedures provoke anxiety, as pointed out by Konstantin Korotov in Chapter 2 of this volume, because there is no way of knowing in advance if the observers selected will even complete the surveys on your behalf, and if they do complete them, what will they say about you? I recall that when filling out the questionnaire myself, I would frequently second-guess what I had written down. Would it be better to answer quickly, going with your gut feeling, or think about it for a while? Then I wondered, given how busy executives are, did the observers I chose take completion of the surveys seriously? Although the surveys are not exams, there is something in their nature that made me feel as if they were. They seemed like a form of standardized testing from which a qualitative or quantitative ranking would be drawn. I worried how I would score.

Coming from an entrepreneurial background, and as the founder of my own company, I had very little direct experience of using 360-degree feedback instruments. In the weeks prior to the group coaching day, I spent a lot of time talking to colleagues, direct reports, clients, and other observers. I worried about choosing who would fill out the feedback instruments and what they would say. I knew that trying to influence the data by selecting observers whom I thought would go easy on me would not serve my interest, but I admit that the thought was there. In the end, I tried to select people who knew me and would give honest feedback. "Honest," in my mind, did not necessarily mean flattering. Overcoming this fear of what people would say about me was the first step toward understanding that honest feedback is not a hostile act but a gift for which you should be grateful and, indeed, thank people for.

In general, participants who are preparing for a group coaching session are encouraged to select as many observers as possible. Then the prodding begins, as you have to try and ensure that they complete the survey in a timely fashion. Some simply do not do it, which increases your anxiety about incomplete data collection.

In the corporate world, the use of 360-degree survey questionnaires is much more common than in the entrepreneurial world, and requests to be someone's observer are often reciprocated—you do mine and I'll do yours. In an entrepreneurial enterprise, it is more of an exotic request. Direct reports tend to look at you as if silently asking: Why are you asking me to do this? Getting 360-degree feedback also reminded me of running for elected office, where popularity plays a part in why people vote for you. I fantasized about people's biases toward me, and how that would show up in the report. What will my people say about me? What are the questions going to reveal? How well do they really know me? Do I really show myself to others? When I imagined what this report would be like, I thought about a dissection of some sort. Would I be thought of as a vulnerable human leader with flaws like everyone else? Would my employees label me as an overdemanding tyrant, or some type of touchy-feely fruitcake? I was particularly concerned about what my clients thought of me, since they are the ones who refer leads to future business.

I felt that filling out the feedback questionnaires was going to lead me to uncover hidden truths, revealed either through my own unwitting admissions or the revelations of my observers. I was worried that things I didn't know—or didn't want to know—would be dredged up out of the depths. The "dirt," as one might say. To calm myself down, I tried using some contrarian thinking. I asked myself why I thought that something bad was going to come out. Strangely, I had no answer to this, and yet I still felt a sense of foreboding.

The coaching module finally arrived. In the late afternoon on the eve of the coaching day, the group gathered for a brief introduction to the 360-degree instruments (the GELI, PA, and LAQ questionnaires explained in Chapter 1) and the objective of the coaching session on the following day. It was hard to pay attention, knowing that the feedback results were about to be handed out. One by one, the professor called out our names and gave us a thick envelope of papers to read and digest overnight. I remember a quixotic feeling as I tucked my envelope under my arm and went back to my room to examine the feedback. I sat down in my room and opened the envelope. I framed my curiosity and con-fusion as I read the feedback as two somewhat diametrically opposed rhetorical questions:

1. How well did I do?
2. What is this report supposed to tell me?

After about 15 minutes of failing to make any sense out of the report, I met my group for dinner. This dinner on the eve of the session becomes the first step in a process of team cohesion that occurs in the group coaching context. Since no one really knows what is going to happen the next day and there is no script, it is hard to know how it will unfold. Sitting at the dinner table with your col-leagues, everyone admitting to feeling clueless, all together in the dark, does have a bonding effect. I remember feeling simultaneously quite alone and yet together at this dinner, wondering again what I was doing there and what the others in my group were thinking about. I had no sense at all that I was at the cusp of a transformation that would continue to play out for months after the group coaching session was over.

THE GROUP COACHING SESSION

The next morning, the coach outlined the program for the day. We would begin by drawing a self-portrait. The coach explained that this activity would only take 15 minutes or so, because no one was expected to be a Picasso. We were simply instructed to quickly draw pictures, symbols, or images that somehow showed what was happening in seven areas of our life: head, heart, stomach, past, future, work, and leisure.

Each member of the group in turn would then discuss his or her self-portrait, review the feedback instruments, and tell their own story. It quickly became apparent that this was a much more informal affair than I had expected. As the first person told his story, beginning with his self-portrait, I was listening to him, but at the same time I was thinking about how the group would react when my turn came. I was still nervous about being accepted by these people. They would soon find out who I really was and what I was about. Since I didn't present first, I had to live with my anxiety until it was my turn. However, slowly I was drawn into the stories being told, and my own emotions did not prevent me from being able to concentrate on the other group members' presentations. Quite the contrary, I found myself very immersed and interested in connecting with each presenter. I concentrated acutely, listening to their narratives. I felt the bond with them grow as I realized that they had all felt a lot of anxiety leading up to the coaching day. Now we were beginning to share that stress with each other.

It is at this point in a group coaching session that the participants' anxiety starts to dissipate, just as it is named and brought forth. Having shared the common experience of anxiety leading up to the event, group members then empathize with and trust one another, regardless of the fact that they work for different organizations or have differing personalities or leadership styles.

As the day unfolds, each person has their turn presenting their self-portrait and explaining why they drew what was in it. Then the other group members have a chance to comment on the portrait, bringing in their own insights and understanding of what they see. In our group, the portrait discussion for the first presenter, Alexandre, served as a kind of icebreaker and created the first threads of the web that became the basis for the connection, support, and bonding in the group.

ALEXANDRE'S PRESENTATION TO THE GROUP

The first person in our group to speak was invited to do so by the coach. In other words, he did not volunteer. Although this person was not in any way an extrovert, he agreed to go first to get the ball rolling. Later on, he admitted that he just wanted to get it out of the way.

Alexandre had very strong positive feedback from every one of his assessors. However, this told the group very little about Alexandre as an executive. All the instruments told us was that he was a highly competent individual. What Alexandre, and almost every other member of the group, wanted was to learn how to achieve more, not necessarily in the area of his particular competency but rather by exploring how he could do a better job of managing and leading others. He recognized that different skills might be required to do this, other than those that launched his career. Alexandre seemed to feel stuck, explaining that he was at a crossroads in his career and somewhat lost about what the next steps should be and how to make that transition.

Discussing Alexandre's self-portrait gave the group members quite a bit of information about how he viewed himself. In the images related to his past, Alexandre had included what looked like planets revolving around a sun. Some of the orbits of the planets were so big that they went off the flip-chart page. A group discussion ensued about the inconsistencies this showed. Although a team player, as suggested by his use of constellation imagery, Alexandre seemed to enjoy working in the background and having others in the limelight. Yet, to my mind, the drawing indicated a desire to move away from being eclipsed and be acknowledged for his own important contributions. There was also a conflict in the workplace of, on the one hand, not suffering fools gladly, and on the other, recognizing the wisdom of being patient and understanding.[1] Although Alexandre was recognized as an excellent team player, he seemed ready at any moment to suddenly "go elsewhere" if things were not to his liking. The group discussed the way they felt about this impression of "Don't mess with me, or I will leave," and the antithetical team player statement: "I will go down with the ship." So in spite of the professed team player attitude, which was backed up with ample evidence, there was also an element of: "If things go sideways for longer than I feel is reasonable, I get exasperated and I'm out of here." The seeming contradiction made group members feel a bit uneasy with Alexandre. Was he more like a planet with a defined orbit, or a spectacular comet that blazed quickly in and out? Clues to this behavior came out when Alexandre volunteered a little more about his family background.

He was the oldest of three children. His parents divorced when he was a teenager. At 15, he found a boarding school he liked, applied for a scholarship, and convinced his parents to send him there—because he was fed up with living at home. As I heard this, the leitmotif of frustration and exasperation we had seen in the self-portrait appeared again like a red thread. Central to his story was the issue of finding or losing one's place in the family hierarchy. This person had a conflict about whether he wanted to be seen or be invisible. It seemed as if he wasn't sure if he was happier being noticed, or being eclipsed. In the constellation of Alexandre's current working environment, there was quite a bit of the latter, although it was clear based on what he said that he wanted to have a more visible role. Looking further at how he got exasperated quickly, he talked about an experience where he was falsely accused by an employer. This occurred early on in his career and led him to move to a distant country. Whether described as being blindsided or as sending himself into outer space, the man clearly felt he was *obliged* to start anew (the exasperation theme yet again) and that in his new locale he would be "safer," interacting with his family, friends, and former colleagues from a distance, as though being both observed and observing through a telescope. In hearing this story, the group was touched by the pain and loneliness of this man, as well as his truly intrepid and adventurous nature. Because of his story, I felt closer to him, respected him, and identified with his inner conflicts. I was not alone. The others in the group were similarly moved and the urge to support Alexandre was palpable.

To me, this was the moment where the separate individuals in the group changed their focus from their own anxieties and fears and started to work together to help Alexandre reach some kind of understanding and resolution. It was the point where identification and galvanic support of a fellow team member began, and this was repeated for each person in the group throughout the day. After hearing Alexandre's story, we felt closer to him. In discussing his career development, we were able to understand the challenges he was facing more clearly and help him with suggestions of how to achieve the goals in his action plan. In effect, we said to him, take all the positive comments to heart and accept that people are asking you to take on a more visible role. In what we now knew was his typical way of reacting, he did not show a great deal of emotion, but promised to think about all this very carefully.

Not all the group's narratives went as smoothly as this. In one case, a group member was visibly uncomfortable with the level of self-disclosure that he felt was expected, and he had to stop the group's interaction. Here the coach intervened and offered the participant a chance to reflect a bit on his own and rejoin the group a bit later in the day. This added to group cohesion, in the sense that it illustrated that different levels of participation in the group coaching activity were acceptable. Through this flexible approach, the coach effectively ruled out a performance or participation dogma that would have caused tension in the group. The participants were supportive and gave the group member in question the space needed to decompress. As it happened, the fact that this person had been given "permission" to stop the process and even leave the room, seemed to help him re-center on what he felt comfortable expressing. The group calmly accepted his unwillingness to continue, but this acceptance eventually allowed him to do just that. His session ended on a positive note, with the group encouraging him to realign his priorities and be sure not to overstretch himself.

JENNIFER'S PRESENTATION TO THE GROUP

Another group member was Jennifer, who had distinguished herself by her speedy rise to the highest levels of a global corporation. At the age of 34, she had made it to the top executive team of country managers. Her meteoric rise in the corporate world was a function of her leadership capabilities. Jennifer strongly believed in personal development, work-life balance, and personal reflection. She had a genuine appreciation of soft skills. Although relatively young, Jennifer was already thinking about how to make her company better by helping others with *their* personal development. She frequently mentored less senior executives, especially women in her company. The challenge for her was how to collaborate and at the same time manage differences of opinion with her superiors, who were regional general managers. Her focus in the coaching session, which she expressed as a question to the others in the group, was how to resolve the conflicts and differences of opinion that inevitably arose in dealing with these general managers.

Jennifer talked at length about tension and conflict in communicating with her bosses. She wanted to explore the links between this issue and certain aspects of her childhood experience with our group. In discussing her formative years, she described her parents as intelligent. Her father and mother were both academics and she described herself as coming from a loving family. From a very young age, her parents instilled in her a sense of self-confidence. Why there was a need for her to be strong or perhaps stronger than her parents, had to do, among other things, with a story Jennifer told us about her mother and her infancy. Her mother had told her that she and Jennifer had been separated for health reasons when Jennifer was a newborn. For Jennifer, the message woven into that story was: In order to survive, you need to be not only self-sufficient but strong for both of us. She talked about her struggle to internalize this message. It was almost unthinkable for a child to accept that she needed to be stronger than her mother. How could she be? But in numerous examples relating to challenges she overcame, both as a child and at work, it was clear that Jennifer *had* lived up to the message and that she was stronger emotionally than her mother.

She said that her family was a strange mix of happiness and sadness, which she attributed in part to her father's alcoholism. The atmosphere at home could be quite happy and then all of a sudden it would go black. The unpredictability of this was unsettling and she took upon herself, at a very young age, the responsibility of keeping things together in the family.

The group could empathize with the enormity of this responsibility for a child. We discussed at length how this theme seemed to reappear in her professional life, in the way she felt so responsible for keeping things together in her company. At work, it appeared that this had a parallel in Jennifer's ambivalent relationships with older, more powerful colleagues, including her boss. Who was supposed to be in charge? Her role as a kind of third parent or parent in absentia in her birth family also made it easy for us to understand her corporate role as a kind of ambassador representing her nationality and its distinct culture in a global organization that was not sufficiently appreciative of cultural diversity.

Jennifer became known in her company as an expert in managing change of all kinds. Given her background and her early integration of the need to be strong to survive, it became quite clear to us why Jennifer was great at managing change and helping her company grow through several different restructurings. She was a professional survivor.

Being let down or disappointed by her superiors affected Jennifer's job satisfaction levels. She said that she felt that this had to do with being packed off to boarding school at a young age by her parents. She talked about her boarding school experience, issues of abandonment, conformity, rebelliousness, and bullying. Strangely, she had a deeply nuanced understanding of these difficult issues. She struck the group as being amazingly strong and resilient for someone so young. This was obviously also a core strength in her working life. Jennifer discussed feeling torn about fractiousness within the corporate family and an "us-them" paradigm relating to expatriate executives and indigenous middle management, which was a source of anxiety for her. She also associated that with her boarding school years, where factions and authority figures were quite important and pitted against one another, especially surrounding issues of power.

Jennifer admitted that she was very attracted to power but fair process was something she also felt strongly about. It was essential for her that power be used wisely. She gave impressive examples of the way she had mentored colleagues in her firm and commensurate anxieties and deep disappointment about being betrayed by these same people. Jennifer could not understand why her reward for mentoring these people should be disloyalty.

What stood out as the most unusual trait in Jennifer's personality was her ability as a leader, advancing herself while at the same time empowering others in her firm to advance as well. Whatever life had dealt her, and it was by no means a bowl of cherries, as our group reframed it, she had undergone a form of leadership training from birth. From the neonatal separation in hospital to her mother telling her she had to be strong for both of them, from being a leader at boarding school to a counselor in summer camp, everything that Jennifer did revolved around leadership, helping others and the judicious management of power. She was also a practitioner of *appreciative action*.[2] (The concept of appreciative action is guided by an executive's intention to produce constructive outcomes for himself as well as others in his organization. Appreciative action encompasses the expression of one's own creativity and promotes it in others in the organization.)

The experience of recounting her childhood on the 360-degree group coaching day had a particularly cathartic effect on Jennifer. It was an exercise in *sensemaking* that we were all able to participate in. By talking about her past with the group, she was able to *make sense of her present*. This would not have happened had it not been for the fact that Jennifer perceived the group coaching process as a transitional space and a safe environment within which she could integrate her past to better understand the present. Through this narrative, her corporate persona was better understood by her and by us. We were able to comprehend her resilience and her motivation for helping others. We were able to convince her that, while her core strengths were obvious and would take her far, she also had the right to expect help from key mentors in her company. We encouraged her to identify people who could guide her in specific ways toward her ambitious career goals. (As it happened, she would keep in close touch with our group in the months after our session, frequently checking back with us informally over the next year as she weighed important career decisions.)

MY PRESENTATION TO THE GROUP

When the time came to discuss my self-portrait and feedback, I had already experienced several presentations by other members of the group. I was nonetheless nervous about the ordeal. I explained my self-portrait and then the coach started the discussion of my 360-degree feedback reports. I had thought they seemed "OK," but when we began to look at them in the group, issues about coping with stress and being too harsh on myself and on others came out. It seemed that, while my observers gave me positive ratings, there were many occasions where I did not see myself the same way. In fact there was general congruence among the observers but this diverged from the way I viewed myself, which was not nearly as high. Yet, I did not feel that I was being modest or untruthful in my answers. I felt that the observers did not see me for who I really was. In some sense, I felt like a fake or a fraud.[3] Somehow, to my mind, they were the ones who "got it wrong." They were the ones who were not "sufficiently critical" in their assessment.

My viewing the data as being wrong gave my group a chance to respond and express their opinions. All of them agreed with the assessments made by my observers. Being challenged in this way by the group forced me to slowly recognize that I had some blind spots. Although I had a strong urge to be argumentative, I listened quietly to what the group was telling me. I had already seen them in action with others who had presented before me, and I now trusted them more than I had at the beginning of the day; these people had no hidden agendas or axes to grind as far as I was concerned. They were gently trying to show me that they were seeing a pattern of behavior that I kept repeating. I was reminded of another situation when a group coaching participant was presented with difficult feedback that he didn't want to accept. The coach put a question to the group that went something like: "There are five people in this room who know you and with whom you have shared an intensive and informative day. Would you be interested in hearing their initial impressions about this issue?"[4] The honest answer to that question is: Perhaps not, but go ahead.

In telling my story, I was able to see that a lot of my perfectionist thinking came from an overly demanding father for whom my performance was never good enough, so trying to please him was an impossible task. Suddenly I made a connection: this reminded me of several occasions where overly demanding clients sent me into a frustrating cycle of trying to satisfy their demands and never feeling that I was able to do so. The group members asked me why I felt that I needed to please these people. I was overwhelmed by the simplicity of the question and totally at a loss as to how to respond. On the one hand, my perfectionist temperament had helped me to succeed in my industry and meant I was well respected in my field. On the other hand, I would often get bogged down in the details, trying to satisfy unrealistic and demanding clients. I also had a problem with confronting difficult clients and saying enough is enough. This *folie à deux* seemed to satisfy both parties. The difficult client found someone with whom he was able to fulfill his need to be unreasonably demanding, and I was able to repeat the legacy of endlessly and fruitlessly trying to please my father through my work—a perfect match. As I started to see the connection between my family history and my current problems at work, I was able to share my frustration and the tiresome pointlessness I felt when I was engaging in this kind of interaction. Talking about what I could do to change this behavior, the group suggested I should be less of a perfectionist and accept myself for who I was. I agreed and these objectives constituted my developmental action plan, since I realized that a lot of the stress I had relating to my work was directly related to never believing that my work was good enough. This was going to require much more thinking, but despite this new challenge, at the end of the day I felt that I was going to be able to make some changes.

THE AFTERMATH

Although every group member hopes that the group coaching experience will be a positive one, changing your behavior, particularly behavior that is hidden from you in your blind spot, is difficult work and it is common for the subconscious to try and undermine the process by creating doubts in your mind. In my case, putting my action plan into practice wasn't as easy as I thought. Here is an example of what happened.

A bump in the road

As mentioned in Chapter 4, as part of the CCC program, participants are required to write reflection papers, which are a way of sharing one's thoughts, reactions, and program-related experiences with the program directors. Shortly after the 360-degree group coaching module, I wrote the following reflections about the session:

> It is now almost two weeks since my reentry from the 360-degree group coaching intervention. I am at a loss to explain why it has taken me so long to sit down and write out my action plan. I felt I was in a fog about what exactly I wanted to improve and I experienced a certain degree of forgetfulness regarding some of the observations made about me during the 360-degree group coaching intervention. I felt blocked and unable to understand why I couldn't or wouldn't get started on the action plan. Fortunately, I had written down everything the group and coach had said, but nonetheless it somehow seemed meaningless when I read it over. No reasons for my apparent laziness regarding this task seemed clear to me. What happened to me in the 360-degree that now caused me to feel so derailed? I started to look for reasons why I didn't want to do this assignment but none came to mind. Although I can be a procrastinator, I am generally not lazy.
>
> As I think back on the group coaching days, I recall feeling good about the experience. The time spent with my group was not without a fair amount of anxiety, but the 360-degree coaching was a great release, and we left feeling quite connected and energized.
>
> I feel there is a kind of inner conflict going on that I cannot identify. It makes me question whether I truly benefited from the 360-degree day. I am trying to figure out what is going on, but no insights come to mind. It took me a very long time just to be able to verbalize this confusion.

So what was wrong? I went over the process and the aftermath chronologically in my mind. First, when we did our 360-degree, the group became very close and connected. There was a good feeling of having shared things that normally would not come out in day-to-day work activities. There was a high level of respect in the group and it was a powerful lesson to see how investing in each other and trusting one another motivated us as a team.

But in going back to work, I found myself feeling uncertain about what had actually transpired. Was I really close to my group members? Did they feel close to me? Did we need to somehow shore up our commitment? Was this action laboratory experiment transitory, or part of a lasting change process? I felt myself slipping and maybe even getting a bit defensive now that the group was apart. Although I had a strong desire to continue working with the group on our newly forged action plans, I knew that, because of distance and lack of commonality in our daily work, this was going to be a challenge. This made me feel frustrated because I felt I could not recreate what we had done in the group coaching exercise now that I was back home. Being the boss, there was no one in my company I felt I could confide in. I was starting to have doubts about the relevancy of my commitment to my action plan.

Fortunately, a conference call had been scheduled with one of my group members as a part of the coaching day follow-up. In the conversation, I reconfirmed the feeling that I could open up, and talked about my doubts over what we had accomplished in the group. The really good news about this phone conversation was how I trusted my colleague with my doubts and how he succeeded in reengaging me with what we had done together on the group coaching day and, most importantly, with following through on the commitments to change I had made in the group. The support I received from this phone call strengthened my resolve to go ahead with what I had agreed to do. We scheduled another follow-up call in six weeks to see where I was with my action plan.

In the days after the phone call, my mind seemed to be working through my dilemma in a different way. I no longer felt I could blame the problem on the 360-degree group process, since the conversation with my colleague had reaffirmed the truth of what the group had pointed out. So I asked myself a different question: Why did I feel blocked, empty, and lacking the energy to make the changes I had committed to?

It was at this point that I began to understand in an emotional way, at gut level, the parallels between my childhood relationship with my father and my current endless attempts to please clients, especially those clients that I knew would never be satisfied. I had talked about my late father on the group coaching day and how, despite all my failed efforts to improve our relationship, I never wanted to accept that it could not be fixed. Sticking with the change commitment I had decided to make in my company would mean that I had to draw a line in the sand as to what I was, and was not, prepared to do to achieve client satisfaction. I had somehow convinced myself that it wasn't worth trying to change. I just couldn't bring myself to believe that this change commitment thing was going to work. Yet, I couldn't bear for it to be a failure.

I could see that I was stuck in a double bind. To try and *not succeed* would reinforce old ways of thinking. If I were to try and *succeed*, I would have to let go of the oddly comforting idea that change is not possible. Yes, you read that right; sometimes people feel it's safer not to try. Even though I did not want to abandon what I had achieved in the group coaching session, my second thoughts about putting change into action were probably related to my relationship with my father. Because this was a blind spot in my thinking, at an emotional level I resisted making changes that I truly believed in at the cognitive level. *My unconscious had completely stopped me from putting the action plan in place.*

The phone call to my group coaching colleague was not intended to deal with my unconscious blockage because I didn't understand it for what it was. I just wanted to discuss why I couldn't put my action plan into motion. What the follow-up call did reaffirm for me was that it would be worth the effort to keep trying to understand myself better. Later on, I was able to connect the dots and see that what I had uncovered in my past was preventing me from starting on my action plan.

To tell the truth, I still have doubts about many things. But my resistance to attempting to make small behavioral changes seems to have diminished as a result of understanding my inner workings better. The strange thing about trying to change is that, after the change has occurred, in hindsight it all seems so clear. But it is anything but clear when you are trying to make it happen, and the smaller the steps are, the easier it is to realize the goals.

From talking with other participants in group coaching sessions, I gather that my experience seems to be fairly common. In spite of your best efforts or intentions, barriers can occur that prevent you from accomplishing a goal that you had honestly identified as being a good thing to work on. Other than checking in with a supportive colleague or friend, what can be done? One useful tool to help overcome difficulties in making sense out of the take away from the 360-degree group coaching experience and effecting the action plan can be found in the work of Bob Kegan concerning *competing commitments*.[5] What Kegan points out is that sometimes, in spite of good intentions, the changes that an executive wishes to make do not happen. The reason for this, Kegan suggests, may be a competing commitment that is unconscious and stands in the way of making the changes. What this means is that resistance to change does not reflect opposition, nor is it merely a result of inertia. Instead, even though they might have made a sincere commitment to change, many people are unwittingly applying productive energy toward a hidden, competing commitment. What looks like resistance is actually a kind of personal immunity to change. In order to overcome the competing commitment, the executive might have to admit to painful and even embarrassing feelings that they would not ordinarily disclose to others or even to themselves. However, it is exactly this unmasking or disclosure that disarms the competing commitment and renders it harmless.

SOME INSIGHTS ABOUT THE GROUP COACHING EXPERIENCE

Months after the program ended, all my group members felt that the 360-degree group coaching module had been the most thought provoking of the entire CCC program. I had no difficulty in remembering what I had discovered or the things I had learned due to comments from the others in the group. I knew that when it came to following up on any aspect of our action plan, I would not hesitate for a minute in working with them. An effective method of working together had been forged out of the group coaching experience and this had evolved into supporting one another in each of our particular change agendas.

As I mentioned earlier, after reentering my daily work activities, I had doubts over how I would institute the changes I had agreed to in the group. By relying on my group members, I succeeded in following through. But as an entrepreneur, one of my ambitions was to create a coaching culture in my own organization. As I thought more about this issue, I realized that it might be possible to create a coaching culture in an entrepreneurial organization by sharing my experience in group coaching with others in my company. The way I did this was to make people in my company aware that I had just done a 360-degree group coaching intervention and was actually telling them about it. It was easy enough. After all, your people know that you have been away from the daily activities of the company. In the same way as someone might ask out of curiosity, how was your holiday? they might ask, how was that thing you did at INSEAD? What was it again? Oh yes, group coaching. What became of all those questionnaires you asked us to fill out for you? As the boss, you now have the perfect opportunity to create a coaching culture within your company by sharing what you experienced and telling your people how much you learned about yourself and the way you run your business, and that it in fact impacted not only you but also the way you interact with them. Your responders will feel validated that you are listening to them. The fact that I admitted certain weaknesses to my people and recognized that I was overly demanding or a perfectionist began a dialogue that should lead to better communication at all levels of the company. It guarantees openness because, if the boss is able to be truthful and use self-disclosure about his own strengths and weaknesses, it has the effect of making you more human, better understood, and ultimately stronger.

THE ELEMENTS OF EFFECTIVE GROUP COACHING

After the group coaching module, several members of the group praised the efforts of our coach. As time passed, I remember asking myself: What did the coach actually do? I had some difficulty answering that question, or even remembering much of what he said.

The coach's work continues long after the coaching day. As I mentioned in my own case, happily exiting the room at the end of a group coaching exercise with a mission or an action plan in hand does not guarantee immediate deeper understanding, a successful transformation, or a behavioral change. The process of digesting what happened on the day occurs slowly and can take place over weeks and months. Coachees need to spend time on their own reflecting on what they have learned, and hopefully also share their thoughts with other team members. This period is a time of sense-making for the coachee. Although in most cases the coach is not a part of this, it is the coach who sets the sense-making thought process in motion.

The time that it takes for this sense-making to happen can vary greatly from one person to another. Patience is required, and inevitably one asks the question: What did group coaching do *for me*? It takes some time to figure this out and each of us will have a different timeline. Undoubtedly, this chapter creates certain expectations of what group coaching is about. It would be impossible to write anything without doing so. In living the 360-degree experience, preconceived notions, whether they are realized or not, are far less important than just experiencing the benefits of the group coaching process *as they occur over time.*

Along these lines, I'd like to underline one final point: reflecting on newly and perhaps weakly recognized truths about yourself, whether positive or negative, can cause disruption in routine and in work-related thinking. The tension and anxiety that are evoked in the data collection phase *before* the group session can, and often do, return *after* the group coaching is over, in the sense-making phase. If you are not prepared for this and do not understand that this anxiety is an integral part of working through the issues that have been highlighted, you can begin to feel alone or isolated, and doubts can gallop back. In fact, you can even start to feel worse than before, wishing you had left Pandora's box untouched. Therefore, the most important part of the group coaching exercise is making sure that the action plan you have crafted is fairly simple and easy to follow up. Planning for follow-up contact with the rest of the group is *essential* because the renewed contact can enable a fellow member to stay on track, and see him/herself as a better person for facing the difficult truths and taking action. For this to work, the commitment of the individual to the group, and vice versa, is key—which is a reminder that the coach's role of creating a safe and trusting dynamic in the group is a critical success factor in the group coaching process over the long term.

The group coaching day for CCC participants is a way for us to think about importing our own organizational coaching[6] and instituting a CCC coaching culture. The appreciative action discussed tangentially in Jennifer's case review is part of both the learning and teaching aspects of group coaching at INSEAD. Participants focus simultaneously on improving themselves and in helping their peers. Since CCC participants all go through the same group coaching process, it imprints them with both the specific and the general skill set that makes their particular brand of organizational coaching identifiable. As we were coached, so we coach others in the same way.

CONCLUSION

So what is group coaching really about? It is about supporting one another and challenging one another to promote a transformation in behavior. It is about the powerful tool of telling one's own story within a group. It is about uncovering and revealing things about yourself that you may not normally talk about in the work environment and *not* about leaving you feeling like a beached whale, or naked. It is about sharing things through self-disclosure and then reacting to them and acting on them. It is a process that involves engagement and discussion among a group, facilitated by a coach. Done in a group, coaching can become the basis for an experience that can be transformational for both, for the individual and the group as a whole. The group hears through fellow participants' narratives: how they became who they are, and in sharing that story, it is inevitable that mutual respect will grow and listening will become much easier.

In contemplating the entire 360-degree group coaching experience, it is useful to be mindful of three things:

1. Show your appreciation to those who took the time and made an effort to fill in the various survey instruments on your behalf.
2. Share your gratitude with your group for having supported you and helped you to look at parts of your personality that you do not frequently think about, and for helping you develop an action plan that will make you a better leader.
3. If you evaluate your own strengths and weaknesses with humility and acceptance, ultimately you will be a more effective leader and a better team member.

As for those lasting effects I mentioned at the beginning of this chapter: for executives and those they work with, the 360-degree coaching process is a journey of discovery that continues long after the session ends, for as long as the individual revisits the goals that were set in the action plan on that day. It can take time to absorb what is learned, and implementing your action plan does not happen just because you want it to. The 360-degree day is only a first step. It is a template for working together on each person's individual problems. It includes an exploration of the diversity of the people in the group and leads to a deeper understanding that we all face very similar problems. It provides a richness that would not be possible in a monocultural or homogeneous group.

Taken all together, the portrait, the instruments, the personal narrative, and the group discussions combine and create synergies that give participants a greater understanding of themselves as individuals. When group coaching is done in this way, the whole is greater than the sum of the parts. Going one step further, group coaching creates a galvanizing sense of group cohesion based on mutual understanding through the feeling of being personally understood. The potentiality of such a group and the possibilities of what can be accomplished in leading change are far greater than anything an individual could do on his or her own. Participants come into the group coaching experience as an accomplished executive and soloist, but leave as a first-time chamber player, having learned what it is to make music together as a fully connected group.

NOTES

1. II Corinthians, 11:19
2. Frost, P. J. and Egri, C. P. (1990). "Appreciative Executive Action." In Suresh Srivastva and David L. Cooperrider (Eds) *Appreciative Management and Leadership: The Power of Positive Thought and Action in Organizations*. San Francisco, CA: Jossey-Bass, pp. 289–323.
3. Kets de Vries, M. F. R. (2003). *Leaders, Fools and Impostors: Essays on the Psychology of Leadership*. London: John Wiley & Sons Inc.
4. Nicholas, J. and Twaddell, K. (2008). *Group Executive Coaching in Asia*. Singapore: The AIR Institute.
5. Kegan, R. and Laskow Lahey, L. (2001). "The Real Reason People Won't Change." *Harvard Business Review*, 89, 85–92.
6. Kets de Vries, M. F. R. (2008). "Leadership Coaching and Organizational Transformation: Effectiveness in a World of Paradoxes." *INSEAD Working Paper* 2008/71/EFE.

8

IS THERE ANYBODY IN THERE?

FRANCESC GRANJA

THE FIRST SYMPTOMS

"Well, son, you'll be going to university soon," he said, in a tone pitched somewhere between solemn and proud. "Have you thought about what you want to study?"
"Mmmm . . . I don't know . . ."
"You don't know?" he asked, astonished.
"I don't know . . . I like . . . psychology," I whispered very quietly, as if I didn't want him to hear.
"Psychology?" he said, surprised, and raising the volume a bit.
"Ye . . . yes . . ."
"But that won't earn you a living," he insisted. "And anyway, with unemployment like it is nobody will take you on."
Huh.

This conversation took place early in 1979, when the world was in the middle of the oil crisis. Years later, I still didn't understand why I told my father that psychology was my first choice for university study. It was an instinct, a hunch that came out of the blue, because I'd never considered the possibility before. Some days earlier, I'd read the name of the psychology faculty in a list of universities, and, unlike with most subjects, this one caught my attention. My reaction must have been quite positive, because I can't think of any other reason for such a sudden change—I'd always given the same response when my teachers or pre-university classmates had asked me that million-dollar question: "Engineer," I'd say unthinkingly, "I want to be an engineer." In spite of the certainty of my reply, if I sat down and thought honestly about whether I liked engineering, it was obvious that this subject was nowhere on my list of favorite occupations. I suppose I said it out of inertia, because engineering was what both my father and my older brother had done.

Not to be outdone at this decision-making time, my mother wanted to join in, and suggested that I should study journalism. According to her, my writing showed I had the makings of a journalist. The idea quite appealed to me, but I didn't know how to tell my father, because if psychologists couldn't make a living, just imagine what would happen to a journalist. With psychology and

118

journalism ruled out because of poor job prospects, and agricultural engineering out because the specialist faculty was too far from my home town, I ended up enrolling in a private business school whose qualifications would give me the best chance of finding a good job. Neither one thing nor the other, then: business administration. In the end, one of the most important decisions I've ever taken was decided on purely economic grounds.

Starting at a school like that was quite an experience for me, and it wasn't all positive. My family was lower middle class, and economically wasn't set up to take on such high fees. This meant that I had to apply for loans and do summer jobs as a private tutor, waiter, security guard, and driver. In just a few weeks, my life was turned upside down. I went from living like a king to having to give up my holidays and studying for a career that I didn't find very motivating, and that demanded high, although infrequent, levels of effort. I also played semi-professional handball, but didn't find this stressful. Quite the opposite, it freed me from the tensions caused by academic demands, particularly at exam time, when I had to crush into just a few days all the work I'd avoided doing during the year. Of all the subjects I took as part of my degree, only one, in my fourth year, really awakened my interest. It was called Group Dynamics, and what fascinated me about this program was the way the lecturer managed to explain how teams worked by using all the students' experiences in our interaction as a group. Judging from what I felt for this subject, I shouldn't have hesitated for a moment in redirecting my professional orientation. But just as I had done when choosing my university studies, I ignored this warning sign, and instead concentrated on following the script that someone had apparently written for me.

Four weeks after finishing my degree I did my compulsory military service and immediately after that started my professional career in the world of marketing. I spent the first two years in an industrial company, and in 1988 joined a US multinational, where my rise through the ranks was spectacular. I began as junior product manager, working 14–16 hours a day. In the fourth year, just two months before I was due to get married, I was promoted to head of sales and marketing of the business unit in a small European country. Based in the capital and with a minimum structure, I put in marathon hours trying to get our brand to the top in the only country in the world, apart from one Asian country, where we didn't hold a dominant position. This was the time when I felt the most pressure and stress. My boss hassled me, asking for reports and explanations for our problems, and in a matter of weeks I felt so overwhelmed that I even assumed responsibility for ten years of neglect and disinvestment. My agenda was crammed with travel, meetings, lunches, reports, video conferences, and so on, but our market share still didn't rise. My family and social life were almost nonexistent, while my bank account was rising in line with my anxiety. Unable to enjoy the attractions of the country to which I'd been posted, I lived in the fast lane, at the mercy of events until one rainy day in May 1994, when I found myself trying to avoid a lorry that had broken down on the motorway running between the country's two main cities. My car overturned at 180 km/h and I broke my neck.

From the fast lane I came to a dead stop—and how. I was left quadriplegic, unable to stimulate even one single muscle from my chest to my toes. My neck was immobilized with a titanium plate and I stayed in hospital for almost a year, learning to use the tenth of my body that was still intact. I learned the arts of scratching my nose, cleaning my teeth, and pushing a wheelchair without moving a finger. When the doctors saw they could do no more they sent me back to the habitat I'd come from. A habitat that overnight had become a barren and hostile place. In this new scenario, the first victim was my marriage. Already mortally wounded and unable to adapt to this metamorphosis, it disappeared in a puff of smoke.

I'd left my native city as a winner with a promising future ahead of me, and I went back as a broken, useless toy. In 1996 I moved into a new house, subdued, disorientated, and abandoned. I was only 32 and here I was, with no mobility, no work, and no partner. The only certainty in my life was that the sun still rose every morning. Since I wasn't capable of making decisions I let myself be carried along by circumstances, a modus operandi that had done me so much harm in the past. I put myself in the hands of a naturopath-cum-psychologist, who helped me to deal with the multiple processes of grieving that were knocking on my door. In the depths of despair, I started to cry all the tears I had never cried over the last 15 years, but then I settled for getting through the days as a mere spectator, obsessed by what my ex-wife might be getting up to, and with my only concern being how long it would be before I next soiled my clothing. Consumed by lethargy and loneliness, I started doing other things I'd never done before, like staring at myself in the mirror and asking myself questions that up till then had never crossed my mind. Who was I? What did I want to do with my life? What was I going to do with my time from then on? Given my emotional and physical state, these were questions that I couldn't find a reply to just yet, but they somehow represented the starting point for what would happen to my life six years later.

RAILROAD OF HOPE

It was 2002. I'd had a long struggle to accept the frustration of being unable to control my bodily functions, having to depend on assistance if I wanted to go out or go to bed, and having to ask for help when I was out on my own. And lots of other things, too. But during this period, I also started to work as a consultant for small companies. The initiative came from my older brother, who called me when I was still deep in my pit of despair, asking for my help to rescue his business. "I don't know who's rescuing who here," I thought. After this initial project, I collaborated in a friend's restaurant, then in a head-hunting consultancy and finally in a graphic design agency, in which I became a minority shareholder. And as well as contributing ideas to the two majority shareholders on how to manage the company, I became involved in offering strategic and marketing visions to customers who asked me. These were pretty routine jobs, but there was one big difference compared to what I'd done before the accident: my anxiety had completely disappeared. The urgency, the worry, the pressure—all had gone.

After Christmas dinner that year, all of us from the agency went out to celebrate a year that had brought us excellent results. After the meal we decided to keep the party going by having a few gins and tonic in a bar near the restaurant. By the second round it had started to snow, and the bar filled up with people sheltering from the cold. What with the alcohol, the snow, the closeness of the Christmas holidays, and the atmosphere of the place, I started to feel a pleasant tingling in my stomach that I hadn't felt for many years. I went on drinking and celebrating with my colleagues. During a pause in our lively chat I noticed an older woman offering her services as a fortune-teller at a table toward the back of the bar. Emboldened by what I'd had to drink, I approached her and asked her to read my tarot cards. With a contagious air of brightness and serenity she predicted a year full of transformation and change ahead.

She wasn't wrong. The first of the novelties began that very night, when I decided to go back home on my own. I'd always asked a friend to take me home, but on that day of alcohol and magic, I felt an inner strength that made me forget my problems and set off, driving my chair in a condition that could probably have earned me a fine from the local police. The second change happened in February when, after an honest look at my situation and recognizing how little interest I had in my relationship, I split up with my partner of two years. In my work, the change came in June. After a steep and unexpected fall in income, the graphic design agency's majority shareholders decided to call it a day and start out on their own. However, the biggest change of all happened at the end of July, when I saw an interview published on the back page of a major newspaper. It was to transform my life for ever.

Around that time, a congress on coaching was being held in a town near my home, and the newspaper published an interview with one of the coaches who had organized the event. That very day, a good friend whom I'd got to know at the head-hunting consultancy called me and told me to buy the paper and look at the last page. Before hanging up she said: "You know, you'd make a great coach." This was the first time I'd ever heard the term coaching, and I was so intrigued after reading the interview with the coach and by my friend's premonition that I started to look up information on the Internet. There, feeling like an explorer discovering the remains of an unknown civilization, I found a precious treasure enveloped in words like *motivation, helping people to reach their objectives, listening, trust, not giving advice*—terms and expressions that struck a chord, as if they were part of me. I read all about the functions of a coach and it really was me to a T. And the more I read, the stronger was the tingling in my stomach that I'd first felt in that bar in the Gothic quarter of the city, under the gaze of a 60-year-old fortune teller.

It was as though someone had invented coaching just for me. The more I learned about the discipline, the more I realized that throughout my life, in one way or another, I had been acting as a coach to the people around me: family, friends, teams, work colleagues, and customers. I began to recall times when I'd had a call from a friend who'd just lost his job, or a colleague had confided his problems with the boss, or a relative phoned to let off steam about problems with his marriage. Even a fellow-traveler, a complete stranger, once spent our journey describing the ins and outs of his nerve-racking and difficult relationship with his son. I remembered the conversation with my father on my choice of university course. I thought about my lecturer in Group Dynamics. And I also called to mind the customers whom I'd worked with as a consultant, and with whom I'd created a kind of empathy that went way beyond the project for which I'd been hired. Although these were clearly not orthodox coaching processes, when I turned all these episodes over in my mind, I realized for the first time that I'd developed an innate ability to create confidence in others and open up a space in a conversation where "things" happened. Things that the person I was talking to confirmed with phrases like: "I've never told that to anyone else before," "I like talking to you," "I feel like you're really listening," "You convey a sense of calm," "You help me focus on what's important," "You don't know how much you've helped me," and so on. If coaching is a conversation that accompanies the other person on his or her way toward an objective, it was clear that at least as regards the first part of this process—the conversation—I'd already made the grade. Now I had to develop the second part: learning to motivate people to move in their chosen direction.

On that first week of August 2002, days before the start of the holidays, the weather was roasting hot. My feelings veered from one extreme to the other. On the one hand, I sensed the end of a business to which I'd devoted so much energy and where I'd established solid bonds of friendship. On the other, I was consumed by the enthusiasm I was feeling for the new world I was suddenly immersed in. On Friday, I went out for a drink with my agency colleagues to welcome in the summer, and to start the painful process of dismantling everything. While we were chatting rather inconsequentially, one of the partners asked me: "So when we close the agency, what are you going to do?" The question was so natural that I was at a loss for words. Once again I was facing the same questions that had dragged me down during the early years of my injury, what did I want to do with my time from now on? But fortunately for me, this time they cropped up in a completely different scenario. I hesitated for about a tenth of a second more than usual before replying, but my reply came straight from the heart: "I'm going to be a coach."

I was going to be a coach, there was no doubt in my mind. I believe I've never been more sure of anything in my life. Thinking about it now, this was the first time in 40 years that I'd dared to take a unilateral decision about my professional future, and with such certainty. It had nothing in common with my choice of university or my decision to be a consultant. I'd studied management because it gave me a better chance of finding a job. I'd worked as a consultant because one day my older brother called me to help him solve the problems that were plaguing his business. If a piano tuner or a chicken-sexer had called me, today I'd probably be writing about one of these subjects instead. So that afternoon when I got home I felt like the happiest man in the world. Not only because I'd found what was to become the passion of my life but because I'd been able to commit to it. With my decision to become a coach, I felt I was taking charge of my career, a phenomenon that Fredy Kofman explains very graphically when he describes how people choose between being the victims or the protagonists of their lives.[1] In fact, the feeling I had at the time was that I was becoming the protagonist in my own life. And not only because it was my decision, my passion, but also because for the first time in my life, I could ask myself what my future would be and reply saying exactly where I wanted to go.

After taking my decision, the next stage was to locate the best coaching training my city had to offer. I had no idea where to start, so I decided to look on the Internet for the phone number of the coaching expert who had written the newspaper article. He was a coach but came from the advertising world, so his experience in handling the transition would be very helpful for me. Talking to him confirmed my expectations. He recommended two training programs, the first a taught course that he had developed with a colleague and the second a virtual course.

In September 2002 we shut down the graphic design agency for good, and in October I started my first taught coaching course. I have many fond memories of that program. Like a videogames fan left open-mouthed at the innovations in the latest version of his favorite game, I was fascinated by the distinctions and concepts I was learning. Rapport, limiting beliefs, feedback, active listening, positive mental attitude—some of the other participants had already completely assimilated these notions, but for me they sounded like science fiction.

As well as the theory, the course included group practice sessions where we obtained first-hand experience of the concepts explained in class. And it was during these mini-sessions that I started to experience the power of coaching to facilitate personal change. I also discovered a facet of myself as a student that was completely unknown: it seemed I'd turned into a "swot." I'd become a hard-working student who arrived on time, asked questions, handed in impeccable homework, did all the recommended reading, volunteered for every class exercise, and sat in the front row. In fact, everything I'd never done before, either at school or later at the business school.

Certainly the thing I most enjoyed about this course was meeting Sir John Whitmore, listening to him discussing *Coaching for Performance*.[2] For Sir John, human beings are constantly evolving in an attempt to reach the highest level of Maslow's hierarchy of needs: self-actualization. In his opinion, coaching is one of the best ways to reach this level of satisfaction. It allows you to become aware of your blocks and areas for personal improvement, while also developing the personal sense of responsibility you need to design actions that will lead to well-being. Awareness and responsibility, two words that once again found their echo within me. For wasn't it an immediate awareness when I discovered from the back page of a newspaper that I was a potential coach? And didn't I assume responsibility when I picked up the phone to ask for advice from an expert about the best courses for training as a coach?

I was really excited when I finished the coaching course, and was eager to learn more. I had entered a new dimension, like a painter who discovers a revolutionary technique that will let him express his artistic message more fluently and who stays up for three days on end, producing new works. All through my professional career I'd specialized in calculating price structures, studying market research, analyzing sales figures, and creating business plans. Suddenly I found myself in a world where instead of calculating, I had to ask; instead of planning, I had to listen; instead of evaluating, I had to feel—basically, a world where instead of doing, I just had to be. This was exactly what I learned on that course: how to be. In three weekends, I discovered more about myself than I'd learned in almost 20 years of schooling. And among my discoveries, one was particularly revealing: personal values. It was a simple exercise, and just one of many we were asked to do on the program. We had to choose three values from a list of 50. I chose *being useful to others*, *honesty*, and *love*. I must say it was hard to decide, but once I'd put them down on paper, I was conscious of a deep feeling of relaxation and a soothing sense of relief, as if I'd planted three enormous columns inside myself on which I could set the rest of my life.

This must have been what Elena felt. Elena was the first person who agreed to do coaching practice with me. Elena was the commercial manager of a former client of the agency, and she didn't hesitate to offer to be a volunteer when she heard that one requirement for my coach certification was to have completed 50 practice sessions. She'd been unemployed for two months and had no intention of going back on the employment market until she had a clearer idea of what her next step should be. Elena had had a very varied career. She'd studied tourism and then worked in a foundation, a museum, and finally, a fashion company, as commercial manager. When she turned 30 she realized that nothing she had done up to that point really satisfied her. We did the first session sitting on a terrace overlooking the sea. The feeble sunlight meant we had to keep our coats on. The discovery of my own first three treasures, my three personal values, was still very fresh in my mind, and because I didn't know how to deal with this first session, I asked Elena to start there, by writing down her three most important values. She chose *solidarity*, *love*, and *education*. I asked her to explain why she'd chosen these three and not others. And of the three values, I noticed that she had hesitated most on the third. We spent two more sessions trying to discover her passion, delving into her favorite hobbies, which included ceramics, fashion design, decoration, collaborating with an NGO, and so on, but that got us nowhere. The answer came during the fourth session, when an enthusiastic Elena showed me an article in German that she explained talked about the benefits of the Montessori method of educating children. "I've got it, Francesc," she said with a big smile "I've got it: I want to be a primary teacher!" In only four sessions, by simply becoming aware of what her personal values were, Elena had discovered her passion. Less than a month later she'd enrolled at university to study primary teaching, where she got top marks. I also know that at the moment she's on a course in Italy, learning the Montessori method that so inspired her. Personally, I can never thank her enough for her trust in opening up to me in a coaching conversation. Thanks to her openness, we achieved a result that increased my confidence as a coach enormously and was a great starting point for the career I was about to embark on.

DESTINATION: NEVERLAND

From that first conversation with Elena to the present, almost four years and nearly 500 sessions have gone by; some better than others, but all entered into with passion. During this time I've attended a couple of training programs that have helped me extend my knowledge and mold my way of engaging in and understanding coaching. The first was at a business school, where I collaborated in the leadership development program created by Richard Boyatzis, and taught on MBA and executive education courses. Here I discovered (among many other things) how important it was to have a motivating vision as an agent of change, and the different ways that people can learn.[3] It was also on this course that I realized that we do not all learn in the same way, and that the complete lack of interest I'd shown in classes at school and university was not due to my incompetence as a student but because my learning style was more focused on experience than on conceptualization. It was certainly a relief, and above all a lesson that gave me a new tool for use in future sessions with my clients.

I did the other program in 2004. This was a course on ontological coaching, which completely changed the course of my new life. The methodology of Rafael Echeverría,[4] who ran the program, helped me to discover the power of language as a vehicle for achieving well-being and, more importantly, opened the door to a new universe that had remained hidden for 40 years: my emotions. I learned to forgive myself for destroying my body at 180 km/h and leaving it immobilized. I came into contact with the wisdom of Maturana and his theory of love.[5] I learned to show emotion without shame. I became aware of my corporal nature and discovered how I could use it to create emotional changes. I learned to say *I love you*. I learned to embrace. In short, I learned to be a better person and so a better coach.

After this marvelous program, my perception of coaching changed completely, and instead of being a profession, it became a way of life. Thanks to ontological coaching, I overhauled my vision of what it meant to be a coach. I brought new practices into my sessions: grounding for judgments, posture, emotional management, declaration, silence, etc. I became an apprentice and went on many different seminars and workshops to engage in further self-exploration. Many coachees recognize that they want (and need) to change, but they don't know how to face a change process, or even more disheartening, they don't know what exactly they are supposed to change. Traumatic experiences may trigger a feeling that the time has come for change, but triggers for development can take many forms and they may also look much more prosaic. Executives may be alert to subtle hints in their professional and personal lives urging them for change to make sure that they do not go unnoticed and become a source of pain and anxiety. Coaching is about being aware of the need for change and about creating tipping points for self-development. No more excuses. No more delays. Tipping points are accompanied by a sense of urgency that brings discomfort, but also by hope and optimism. Recognizing the call to managing this tension of fear and hope effectively makes coaching processes unique and extremely powerful.

Building trustful relations is crucial to push people toward self-development processes. When the coach guides the examination of executives' values, assumptions, and behaviors, it can be like using a new lens to rediscover familiar stories. But I increasingly recognized that the coach should also be equipped with the appropriate psychotherapeutic tools to illuminate hidden or suppressed areas of people's identities.

I became familiar with psychotherapy, learning how psychodynamic concepts may be used to help coachees to make links between past and present and thus becoming aware of previously useful patterns that need to be changed.[6] I also learned about how the different psychodynamic schools of thought may be even more effective if they are used in a complementary way. I received some exposure to Gestalt—seeing its use in making coachees more aware of their phenomenological present condition.[7] I dabbled in Rogerian, person-centered therapy,[8] as well as rational-emotive, cognitive therapy.[9]

Carl Rogers had a pioneering role in psychotherapy and in his client-centered therapy he sets the basis for understanding healthy coaching relationships. From a coaching perspective, psychotherapeutic concepts such as "empathy," "congruence," and "unconditional positive regard" may set the stage for understanding the ingredients that establish fruitful coach-coachee interactions.

I was also exposed to Perls' Gestalt therapy, which emphasizes personal responsibility for the management of challenging events. Gestalt therapy schools have mushroomed during the past few years and they have welcomed a huge number of new adepts coming from a wide variety of disciplines, mainly because of Perls' appealing bid for integrating body and psyche to obtain psychotherapeutical results. Gestalt focuses on the present moment and, during its interventions, everything the coachee does and says is pointed out by the coach to gain new insights in real time and to explore how the coachee feels about them. I also found Albert Ellis's rational-emotive cognitive therapy useful. Cognitive therapy relies on how the coachee makes causal connections, finds alternative paths of action, and reflects on their possible outcomes.

My main takeaway from my exposure to all these therapies was that it is useful to adapt your style as a coach and the techniques that you use to ensure they fit with a coachee's particular needs at a particular moment. I increasingly realized that having a broad repertoire of techniques is the most valuable asset

126

for effective coaching interventions. These techniques may include motivational interviewing, paradoxical interventions, positive reframing, behavioral interventions, and appreciative inquiry, to name only a few.

I became fully aware that by combining some of these I could obtain a much more complete vision of the individuals I coach. Being aware of these various techniques also triggered a self-reflection process on my preferences as a coach and the situations and circumstances in which I could be most effective. Additionally, it drove me to discover my blind spots as a coach. Thus I engaged in a developmental process to enhance my coaching skills and to understand whether and to what extent I could develop coaching styles and techniques that differed from my natural preferences while remaining authentic with my clients.

My search for the appropriate coaching tools to help executives throughout their careers led me to the group dynamics technique. Throughout my career, I understood that vital aspects of executives' success, such as communication, influence, or teamwork, may be addressed in a comprehensive way if both coach and coachee take advantage of groups and the relationships between group members.

I intend to continue on this inner journey for a long time. I believe that you do not start to live your life to the full until you discover your vocation. On the basis of my experience, and shared exchanges with other coaches and therapists, I believe that good coaching happens when a strong bond forms between the coach and the coachee; and as I see it, this bond will occur more often when the coach has done more personal work. Coaching is a multidisciplinary art. The greater the repertory of tools the coach offers, the more effective the final results.[10] Every person is unique because our behavior is determined by the laws of cerebral development, and every life experience leaves a unique and unrepeatable mark on the subconscious that is used to build our future.[11] So coaches should be prepared to face the great variety of "life experiences" they will meet. I've seen people who in one single session of visualization managed to break down beliefs that had been entrenched in them for years. Some of my coachees have confessed that just my presence as a coach helps them improve their state of mind. Others make a radical change in how they perceive their problem with one simple question. Unlike some colleagues, I don't think there are any impossible cases in coaching, just professionals who have many skills to learn. To deal with this plurality of situations, I suggest that coaches should be in constant evolution, always adding new angles to their professional practice.

This is the point my personal story has reached so far. As a coach, I have often witnessed in other people the moment that I myself experienced—that almost magic moment when someone discovers that life could be different, fuller, and more meaningful. In an instant, fear disappears and a universe full of opportunities takes its place. A bored IT specialist becomes an avant-garde gallery owner, a chatty businesswoman becomes a teacher, a discontented doctor becomes a creative chef—and an aggressive executive becomes a personal coach.

It's very difficult to give a recipe or method for how to do this. Buddhists recommend the Noble Eightfold Path. Steve Jobs, in his 2005 Stanford Commencement

Address, spoke of joining the dots. Others say that you should listen to your stomach. But whatever the answer, each one of us is free to explore when and how we can attain that vocation we were born for. I don't have any other rules or guidelines for finding the meaning of life. All I can really say, from the certainty that my experience has given me, is that it is possible. You can change your own life. You can find the path to happiness.

NOTES

1. Kofman, F. (2001). *Metamanagement, Tomo 1*. Naucalpan: Ediciones Granica.
2. Whitmore, J. (2002). *Coaching for Performance*. Maryland: National Book Network.
3. Kolb, David (1984). *Experiential Learning*. New Jersey, NY: Prentice Hall.
4. Echeverría, R. (1994). *Ontología del Lenguaje*. Santiago de Chile: Dolmen Ediciones.
5. Maturana, H. (1996). *Biología del Emocionar y Alba Emoting*. Santiago de Chile: Dolmen Ediciones.
6. Etchegoyen, H. (2005). *The Fundamentals of Psychoanalytic Technique*. London: Karnac Books.
7. Perls, F. (1969). *Ego, Hunger, and Aggression: The Beginning of Gestalt Therapy*. New York, NY: Random House.
8. Rogers, C. (1995). *On Becoming a Person: A Therapist's View of Psychotherapy*. New York: Mariner Books.
9. Ellis, A. and Dryden, W. (2007). *The Practice of Rational Emotive Behavior Therapy* (2nd edn). New York: Springer Publishing.
10. Blanton, B. (1996). *Radical Honesty*. New York, NY: Dell Publishing.
11. Punset, E. (2008). *Porqué somos como somos*. Madrid: Editorial Aguilar.

9

BECOMING A BETTER COACH: A STORY OF TRANSITION

ANDREAS BERNHARDT AND KONSTANTIN KOROTOV

This chapter is based on a case study by Andreas Bernhardt, a professional psychologist and consultant involved in management development and executive coaching in a business school setting. Andreas realized he would become a better coach by deepening an understanding of his own inner theater, exploring the driving forces behind his behavior, and experimenting with new opportunities to increase his effectiveness with clients and personal satisfaction from work and beyond. The story of Andreas's own development as a coach parallels his experience of serving his clients better and discovering new opportunities for using himself as an instrument to help others. The chapter also touches upon an important issue of professional development and personal growth for people professionally involved in developing better leaders and creating better organizations.

While the practice of executive coaching and the literature concerning it are mushrooming, there is still not enough codified information about how coaches grow and develop, how they move through various stages of effectiveness and professionalism, and how they reinvent themselves. Helping others develop is part of the coach's job. However, coaches are often subject to the same developmental challenges as their clients. Developing means changing—giving something up, trying and accepting something new, claiming and being granted a new identity. In this chapter we offer the reader an opportunity to witness and think about the development of an executive coach whose growth was assisted by a transformational executive education program.

A LEADERSHIP COACHING INTERVENTION WITH RICARDO—A TRIGGER

It was very early in the morning of a sunny day in September. I was making the final preparations for the day, sitting in the program director's office in the beautiful moated site of a business school campus and getting myself into the right mood for that day's group leadership coaching session. And at that early hour, there was little else to hear than the dawn chorus. I had no way of knowing at that time that the day ahead would be one I would remember for a long time

129

and that it would have a significant influence on my development over the next two years.

After 17 years in leadership development in different organizations, roles, and responsibilities, I was heading a leadership development program, designed for senior executives just below board level in a global corporation. As program director I was responsible for the success of the program and for exceeding the expectations of the participants, the head of management development, and, ultimately, the executive board. The participants came from five different continents, making it a truly international group.

It could have been just another successful, if routine, executive education week. But this time it turned out to be significantly different—at least for me. We had a smooth start, and after two days the participating executives seemed quite happy with the program. In the afternoon of the third day, I was facilitating a group leadership coaching session, using the results of a 360-degree feedback tool. Tension and expectations were high on all sides, as the participants were competitive, despite the generally harmonious company culture. On my side, the tension was increased by the members of my coaching group, who were all at the upper end of the hierarchical level I was used to dealing with in coaching assignments. The group was a colorful mixture of high-caliber leaders: a regional CEO from Latin America; a senior vice-president from India; two country operations heads, one from Russia and one from the Netherlands; and a head of a global function within the client organization. After a very constructive first round with the country head from the Netherlands, it was the turn of Ricardo, a Brazilian and the regional CEO from Latin America, to be in the spotlight for about an hour. Ricardo reported directly to a very influential executive board member and he was recognized as one of the opinion leaders in the company. The group discussed his self-portrait (a tool used in leadership group coaching—see Chapter 5) and the first impressions conveyed by his apparently well designed, fast-track management career path; then I started to lead the discussion toward Ricardo's 360-degree feedback report results: "Thank you very much so far, Ricardo. Would you like to look at your report now? I think it contains some valuable information that could support you in planning the next steps in your leadership career."

Immediately, Ricardo's mood changed significantly. The temperature in the room seemed actually to drop. He replied: "The report? You mean the results of this hair-splitting questionnaire that tries to judge my effectiveness as an executive by reshuffling my colleagues' random clicks of a mouse? I don't think there'll be any value in looking at it." He continued to voice a strong critique of the instrument, questioning the whole process of 360-degree feedback and group leadership coaching in general, arguing that this type of intervention might be suitable for young or middle managers, but was superfluous for executives at his level. He would not accept any of my explanations about its suitability for his level and examples of the many senior executives who had benefited from this kind of intervention. All my arguments provoked only counterattacks against the intervention, the overall leadership development program, and the company's leadership development department. Ricardo started to invite other group members to back him up. The strength of his emotions made me feel very uncomfortable, particularly as I considered myself "on stage," with several heavyweight program participants watching and evaluating me in my role as leadership coach and as a representative of my business school.

I knew from instinct and years of management development experience that this situation could escalate and affect the motivation of the rest of the group. My stomach cramped and I felt a strong impulse to run away, to get out of the room, to avoid the looming conflict in any way I could. My mind was racing: *What did I do wrong? What can I do now? How do I get out of this? I can't handle this guy. He's way too powerful—and senior.* And then: *Why am I doing this? Why did I agree to take on a group like this by myself? Why didn't I let a more senior coach do the job?* I felt I couldn't handle coaching executives at this level; that I was the wrong person for the role, and that someone else, someone with more clout and even more years of experience and wisdom, should be discussing feedback results and coaching with this man. I was flooded with self-doubt: *Why do I pretend I can do this? How long till they find out I'm not skilled or competent enough to handle executives at this level?* In short, I felt like a fake. Manfred Kets de Vries[1] calls this common phenomenon the impostor syndrome, the fear that reasonably skilled and accomplished people feel when they begin to doubt whether they are good enough, and start to undervalue their talent, risking their career and psychological well-being. But at the time, I had no idea I'd become a victim of this syndrome. In an attempt to ease the situation—while unconsciously fleeing the conflict—I offered Ricardo an individual one-on-one coaching session with me after the group intervention, suggesting that we could discuss his arguments then, and skip group discussion of his 360-degree feedback report. He paused for a moment—one of the longest moments in my professional life—and finally said: "I don't think it will change anything, but why not? Let's meet after dinner, then." My relief that he had accepted the deal was cut short when he added, "But you can be sure that I will talk to Luis [the head of management development] about this."

Unsurprisingly, I couldn't eat much dinner and felt more than a little tense when we started the one-on-one session that evening. I tried to create an atmosphere of trust and let Ricardo articulate his criticism of the 360-degree method and process once again. "This instrument is unprofessional. People mix up ratings when they fill in the questionnaire and the system reports ratings incorrectly." "Why do you say that?" I asked. He replied: "Look, it's obvious. Here, for example, on the overview chart—the purple line that's supposed to represent my boss is way too low. I know exactly what my boss thinks about me and this line here is definitely wrong. So how can I trust this system?"

Ricardo was very frustrated by the feedback from his immediate superior, as well as some of the qualitative comments from his boss and colleagues at the end of the report. His boss rated Ricardo significantly lower on dimensions like "visioning," "empowering," and "tenacity"—dimensions that are typically seen as critical for senior executives—than he himself and most of the other observers did. Ricardo thought this evaluation was incorrect, unfair, and that it would be offensive to share it with the other group members. He would be exposed to colleagues he suspected to be interested in the role of head of US operations, which he was aiming for and which was shortly to become vacant. He couldn't accept that his boss would give him a low rating and so rejected both the feedback instrument and the whole intervention.

After releasing his frustration, speculating about possible reasons for the unpleasant results, and exploring different options about how to proceed, Ricardo was taken with the idea of having a direct conversation with his boss. At this point, fortune was on my side: his boss was visiting the program for a fireside chat with participants later that week and Ricardo seized the chance to have a one-on-one session with him.

After their meeting I had a quick follow-up with Ricardo. To my relief, he behaved like a completely different person. He was relaxed, happy, and full of positive energy. Apparently, his boss had wanted to give Ricardo a clear signal that if he wanted to make the next step, he would have to develop his competencies in particular leadership dimensions that his boss considered very crucial for the new role. His boss had rated Ricardo on those dimensions not according to his performance in the current role, but according to the expectations related to his next career step. Ricardo received a clear signal that his boss wanted him to make the next step, that he believed in him, and wanted him to be prepared for hard work to make a successful transition to the new role and new expectations.

Ricardo thanked me for the one-on-one follow-up session after the leadership group coaching intervention and regretted that he had failed to use the potential of a group session for serious reflection on his case. He knew other participants were highly impressed with the outcomes of their group coaching experience. However, Ricardo also kept his initial "threatening" promise and talked to Luis. He urged him to offer this kind of development program to other management levels within the company. In the formal program evaluation, Ricardo wrote honestly: "I frankly did not think the coaching session would be valuable. I was wrong. It was excellent and provided me with valuable insight."

Although this looked like a happy ending, I had sweated a lot throughout the whole week, which to me had been an emotional roller coaster. In the week that followed I woke several times in the night, having dreamed about catastrophic derailments of coaching interactions with high-level executives. My experience with Ricardo and a possibility of similar challenges in the future gave me real headaches. I knew I had to do something about my ability to handle clients and myself better in similar situations.

In a supervision session with a very seasoned leadership coach I worked through the unpleasant experience and came to the conclusion that I had done more or less the right things. Different perspectives, a competitive company culture, and a forcefully defensive participant had given rise to strong emotions and reactions, even if the overall outcome was apparently satisfactory. However, I certainly didn't want to go through that kind of thing on a regular basis. And I was about to face the possibility, as I had just been asked to think about building up professional coaching services in my institution. One of my major objectives was to set up excellent executive coaching services for programs at all executive levels, from aspiring high potentials to seasoned leaders. So it looked as though the future might hold even tougher situations in my executive coaching and program director roles. I felt that experiencing emotional turmoil too often would not be beneficial either to the professionalism of the services, or to my own mental health.

But how should I prepare for this scenario? How could I handle the potentially explosive mixture of senior executives' emotional arousal, strong personalities, and substantial egos more professionally? How was I going to deal with the multilayered dilemmas senior executives face when leading large organizational entities in tough times, when executive coaches are asked to be sparring partners, in the hope they will help executives to find solutions? And, importantly, how could I overcome the feeling that I was not skilled, competent, or senior enough to deal with this clients at this level? How could I look these clients in the eye and be a more suitable and effective partner for senior executives and their organizations?

These were very pressing questions for me. I had the impression that I had reached a kind of a glass ceiling in my career, where I was bound to coach and teach mostly young and mid-level managers and would have to leave the majority of coaching and teaching assignments with higher levels of executives to more senior coaches. I felt stuck. And I felt that there should be a way out of the situation. Part of the coaching value proposition is helping executives get "unstuck," using their own resources. If I was going to be successful coaching others, I needed to find a way to help myself grow personally and professionally to the level that would make me comfortable and successful helping others grow and develop.

EXPLORING PERSONAL DEVELOPMENT OPPORTUNITIES

I was convinced that I needed sound and enhanced development, but could not immediately figure out what the right path would be. I strongly believe in the power of continuous education for the development of professionals. However, on the basis of my education and experience (a master's degree in psychology with specialization in organizational and clinical psychology, training in psychotherapy, and many years of successful professional coaching practice), it was quite obvious to me that another "normal" coaching training would not add much value. It would not address the specific challenges I faced. The option of just pushing myself into new senior executive assignments and learning from experience appeared to me too risky, too expensive (for me and the clients), and probably irresponsible, particularly in view of senior executives' expectations. There is a good reason why trial and error is also called learning the hard way.

Intensified individual or group supervision was another option, but I didn't want to wait for other incidents to happen and then analyze them in hindsight, I wanted to prepare myself proactively. Besides, I had come up with a number of issues that I wanted to address through my further development options. I wanted to focus on individual change at senior executive level and pay more attention to organizational change. I wanted to enhance my international focus in my work with executives. I wanted to increase my portfolio of approaches to helping managers deal with their challenges, and, through that, feel better equipped to manage my own professionalism and personal satisfaction.

Thinking about options available, I realized that I wanted to be involved with a longer-term program, not just a short seminar, that would allow me to learn in class, try something out in "real life," receive para-supervision from faculty and fellow participants, and have an opportunity to experiment with coaching approaches and my own emotions and behavior. I also realized that to be successful with senior executives, I would benefit from having a strongly branded institution and faculty involved in my professional development. I also wanted to be in a program that attracted other experienced professionals looking for further growth and development.

After an intense preselection I ended up with a small sample of long-term programs that seemed to fit most of these criteria. I contacted the institutions that offered the programs and some of their former participants. I received a strong recommendation from a good friend and alumnus of INSEAD's executive program, Consulting and Coaching for Change (CCC), a modular course that runs over 17 months, with additional graduation thesis work (see Chapter 4). I decided this was the program for me. But if I thought I'd already come far making this decision, I was wrong. There was an extra mile to go to make my way into this program. First of all, I really had to apply myself—twice over.

First, I had to convince my managing director that such an expensive program was worth the investment of money and time, and that it would contribute significantly to my own institution. Second, I had to apply for a place in the program, which involved providing written recommendations from at least two recognized authorities and deliver no fewer than 16 short essays for approval at the final selection interview with one of the program directors.

This was a tough application process for an executive education program. Why did I have to write 16 essays before I could even start the program? What was the point? They would be very time consuming and I had my time cut out for me already, finishing some important projects to clear time for the course modules. I had to write about my extramural activities, international experiences, personal achievements and failures, the sort of person I was, the stories people tell about me, my fantasies, and my experiences of personal growth. And while I was writing my last essay on a Sunday afternoon before the submission deadline it began to dawn on me that the first part of my journey had already started, that I was just experiencing the first intervention of this program while I was reflecting on my past experiences in my professional and personal life, about important relationships, and patterns of my personality. I opened the program brochure once again and saw a sentence that I had read at least a couple of times already, but only now really understood: "During the program, you will be . . . encouraged to reflect on your own behavior and on your interaction with others." And here I was, already reflecting on my past behavior and important interactions, even before the program officially started. Later, having had an interview with a program director, attended initial course modules, and explored literature on executive development, I understood how that pre-entrance experience set the tone for further program work and gave applicants the opportunity to decide whether they really wanted to embark on a journey with such a strong emphasis on personal reflection.[2]

Those essays and that interview were the first occasions for a long time that I had consciously paused for a significant period of time and reflected so intensely on my life and career, as well as my dreams for the future. It brought back a lot of memories and feelings that had been buried under the pressing duties of day-to-day life.

ENTERING TRANSITIONAL SPACE

More than happy at having secured one of the very last slots in the CCC program, I was on my way to INSEAD's campus in Fontainebleau, France, and couldn't wait to meet the other 35 participants who, according to their biographies, seemed to be an exciting mix of highly qualified executives, professionals, and entrepreneurs from all over the world. During my flight I sat next to a well-known TV presenter, who facilitated a prestigious weekly show with top-level politicians and CEOs. I took this as an important sign that my journey would be special.

And it did become special, but not exactly in the way I imagined. After the initial phase of getting to know some of the other participants, I attended the first introductory sessions on psychodynamic concepts, deep listening, and different clinical approaches to helping executives succeed. Although I was familiar with a fair proportion of this content, listening to it was refreshing, and it confirmed my belief in the importance of the clinical perspective in helping people change. However, I soon realized that discussing psychodynamic concepts was one thing. Applying them to oneself was a very different one. Until that point, I had been feeling reasonably comfortable, as I had mainly received what I expected: confirmation of familiar theories and approaches and insights into new ones. But quite soon I felt the focus of the module had shifted. I found myself in a small group of participants with very different backgrounds, sharing our life experiences in the process of exploring our individual core conceptual relationship themes (CCRT), while practicing the art of deep listening.[3] As we seemed to do quite well at this form of highly concentrated listening and reading between the lines, and the faculty did everything to ensure a safe environment, we all shared at least some aspects of our past that we had shared with very few people—some not even with our partners. Emotionally, the exploration process turned out to be a very powerful intervention; it was not uncommon for participants to shed tears. Surprisingly to me, we embarked on a path of deep reflection right in the first module. I had anticipated some elements of reflection in the program, but this experience went far beyond my expectations.

But was this really what I wanted? I'd joined the program to learn more about the challenging characters of senior executives, about their shadow sides, and how to coach them and their organizations to bring about change. I'd invested a great deal of effort into becoming enrolled in this program to harvest the wisdom of top professors and CEO coaches; instead I was sharing stories of the past with other participants and sometimes even bursting into tears when the memories became too strong. Throughout my flight home, one inner voice nagged at me, "Are you on the right program? What can you get out of it? Is it really worth the investment?" while another said, "They know what they're doing, they're all world-class experts. If you want to help others to change, it's critical to 'know thyself.'"

My inner struggle went on, even after a telephone conference with the other members of my participant group, facilitated by one of the program directors. The conference was set up as a means to discuss individual cases; the participants documented the implementation of their learning in the "real world" after each module by writing cases (see Chapter 4). Although I thought the approach itself was excellent, writing these cases was a challenge for me. I couldn't relate to the exercise as, at this point, I still hadn't found a proper relation to the program itself. I learned later that I was not the only one to struggle in the first phase, and that the struggle itself was an important part of my transitional journey. Only with hindsight did I realize that while we were discussing the clinical paradigm cognitively in the classroom, I was simultaneously experiencing some of its major themes—unconscious motivation, defense mechanisms, and intrapsychic and interpersonal conflict. For example, my unconscious motivation was my irrational fantasy that I would master the challenge of coaching high-caliber executives more self-confidently simply by acquiring the "right" knowledge, acquiring a new and adapted skill set, and by using the new approaches presented by the program faculty. As far as defense mechanisms were concerned, I was playing with the idea of quitting the program, or at the very least questioning the value of the sometimes painful deep reflections on my past. In effect, I was repressing the threatening implications of some of the insights—that we are all products of our past and cannot alter the fact that the past will have an impact on our future opportunities. Finally, when I had to open up in the group reflection sessions my tension and anxiety rose rapidly. My strong wish to be liked conflicted with the need to be open and honest. I was making an unconscious assumption that other people's liking was conditional on presenting myself as a perfect professional. This conflicted with the fact that reflection demonstrates that no one is perfect all the time, and of course I am no exception.

So paradoxically, all the time I was thinking about distancing myself from the program, emotionally I was already in the thick of it. This experience has proved invaluable to me ever since, and today helps me to deal with the anxieties and defenses of the executives who embark on my executive programs in a much more relaxed and confident way.

The friend who initially recommended the CCC program to me also helped me to overcome my doubts by framing the program as a "transitional journey" that might be bumpy from time to time, but in the end would certainly pay off. His affirmation helped me to relax and be more open to the experiences that followed.

THE FIRST TIPPING POINT

Once reassured, I was curious about the next part of the journey. Module 2 turned out to be a highly interesting if particularly bumpy ride. Its official title was "Interpersonal Interaction" and the special focus was emotional intelligence. My expectations for this module were very high—these were topics I considered key to handling senior executives' big egos—so inevitably I set myself up for frustration, unconsciously expecting much more content than could possibly be covered in the time available. But my frustration was more than compensated for by the real-life inter- and intra-personal interaction we experienced. Apart from the extremely interesting group dynamics of the larger group, we took our reflections in our subgroup to another level while exploring the ways mentalizing and empathy can fuel understanding of core conflictual relationship themes (CCRT). As we dug deeper, strong emotions were evoked, and one particular situation became the first real tipping point in my personal journey. With the support of my colleagues, I was in the process of exploring my personal CCRT (avoiding conflict, based on the strong wish to be liked by others) when one of the program directors, Erik van de Loo, briefly joined the group to observe our interactions. One of my typical behavioral patterns, while in conversation with others, was to smile most of the time, masking my real emotions. Erik seized on one short moment when I was not smiling and told me that he liked what he saw very much: "I had the feeling I was seeing the real person, 'the real Andreas.'"

This very short intervention triggered intense reflection and an ongoing change of mindset in me. From that point I observed myself more consciously and realized that I did indeed smile most of the time when I was in contact with others. I started consciously to experiment with limiting my smiling in subsequent interactions and could literally see how this change of behavior influenced other participants' responses to me. I had more conversations about topics that were of particular importance to my dialogue partners, and people opened up more and shared more of their inner theater with me than before. The feedback I now started to receive was that people perceived me as more serious and genuinely interested in their issues. This was a very pleasant finding. Not only did I feel more natural, I recognized that I had discovered one of the keys to becoming a more respected and trusted sparring partner in coaching interactions with executives. So far, my smiling (as a representation of my CCRT) had interfered with my ambition to handle senior clients confidently. However, I also realized that it would not be enough just to smile less if I wanted to establish relationships of trust and cooperation with my coachees and other important stakeholders in my personal and professional life.

Our patterns of interaction with others are rooted in our past and hark back to how we were handled in childhood by our caretakers. To effect a long-term change, I would have to dig deeper and deal with the root causes of my behavior. Erik's intervention was first and foremost an excellent example on how to "use yourself as a tool," a concept that underlined the philosophy of the CCC program, and which has since become a foundation for my work with senior executives. By paying close attention to his perceptions and to personal reaction to my behavior, Erik had been able to conduct a short but strong intervention. Manfred Kets de Vries[4] argues that "using yourself as a tool" also implies that when working with executives "leadership coaches have to use their own unconscious as a receptive organ for the unconscious signals the other person is transmitting. They have to learn to look out for transferential and counter-transferential reactions—when they and their client respond to one another following archaic responses founded on past relationships."

From that time on, my attitude toward my participation in the CCC program started to transform. I started to see the program as an opportunity to change myself in a significant way, instead of just learning new concepts, skills, and tricks. The program started to become what Korotov[5] calls an "identity laboratory"—"a transitional environment, demarcated temporarily, spatially, and psychologically from the rest of the identities-granting world . . . 'equipped' with identity exploration and experimentation opportunities, guiding figures or facilitators, and tools, such as transitional objects that participants need to learn to use to go through the laboratory productively."

LEARNING TO USE TRANSITIONAL SPACE

Now that I was concentrating on developing myself as a tool, I started to use the modules and the time between them differently. Module 3, with its focus on family businesses, inspired me to analyze and to reflect on my relationships with my clients from family-owned companies. In some areas I had become stuck in the customer relationship, having reached a kind of a plateau after a phase of constant progress. But it was not until I made an additional journey into my own past, an exploration of my own family story and the analysis of family rules and relationship patterns, that I achieved a breakthrough in my understanding of why the relationship with the client organization was unfolding in this specific way. After experimenting with breaking my ties with some dysfunctional family patterns in the safe environment of the CCC community, I determined to apply what I had learned in the "real world." I had an opportunity shortly after the third module, in a meeting with my business partners on the client side of a large Europe-based, globally operating, family-owned company. A senior board member attended the meeting and requested a procedure that would provide the board with what he considered to be valuable information about the perceived potential of their top managers. However, gathering and passing such information to the board would put the psychological safety of the company's management development program, and the mutual trust between managers, program faculty, and the management development department, at risk. The board member stressed the importance of the program's assessment component and seemed to expect me, and management development, to accede to the request without question. I was keenly aware that, given this particular company's culture and my own family rules and patterns, I would previously have avoided opposing this request directly by circumventing any confrontation or conflict and trying to find a compromise. But this time I didn't shy away and addressed the issue immediately, voicing my strong concerns about implementing this process, and presenting the potential negative consequences for the people involved and the organization as a whole, supporting what I said with examples from other companies. I also offered an alternative solution.

Initially, everyone was taken aback by my reaction, which was atypical of the company's culture and the type of consultants it usually hired. But after a short silence the board member bought into the idea, appreciating my comments and concerns, and asked me to elaborate on the alternative solution. He finished by saying, "It's excellent that we have such experienced consultants. That's what we pay them for." Instead of a heated discussion and potential anger from the board member, I earned respect and appreciation. In retrospect, he was probably looking for a real sparring partner with whom he could discuss the pros and cons of this kind of decision, rather than a yes man who would accept his demands without challenging them. Needless to say, I felt good about myself.

After this insightful experience and the impression that I had made some developmental headway, I couldn't wait to explore further my deeply rooted behavioral patterns and potential for greater change, to experiment with new behavior, and investigate opportunities to develop as a leadership coach. So it fitted in nicely that in the fourth module we had the opportunity to use three different feedback tools (developed by Manfred Kets de Vries for the INSEAD Global Leadership Center and described throughout this book) and to have a group leadership coaching session to discuss the results. But when I invited the observers—my boss, colleagues, direct reports, and friends—to give me feedback on 12 different leadership-related dimensions, I started to have mixed feelings. How would they rate me? Had they been honest with me up to now or would the feedback include some unpleasant surprises, which would be obvious to my co-participants and to the coach? Was I in danger of losing face?

Although not entirely pleasant, experiencing these feelings and the entire process with a group of my peers was like being in my clients' shoes, as I use

360-degree feedback with follow-up coaching on a regular basis in my work as coach. It helped me to get a better sense of how my clients feel when I put them through the process, and the kind of thoughts, feelings, anxieties, defenses, and fantasies accompany this kind of intervention.

LEADERSHIP GROUP COACHING: EXAMINING PAST AND CURRENT IDENTITIES AND EXPERIENCING THE SECOND TIPPING POINT

The group leadership coaching session itself was far more intense than the previous modules. I realize now that it had a significant impact on my professional development, on the way I work as an executive coach, and a surprising impact on my personal life. I experienced important impulses to change critical behavioral patterns, to work on my CCRT, and to challenge what Kegan and Lahey call "big assumptions."[6]

Manfred Kets de Vries[7] points out that, despite the effectiveness of one-on-one coaching, leadership coaching in a group setting is more likely to lead to durable changes in leadership behavior. I did not need convincing of this, as I had experienced the positive impact of group settings many times in my work as an executive coach. But my belief in the effectiveness of this method was pushed to another level by my own experience both as a coachee and during the first implementation steps I took after the module.

I received my feedback reports in the evening of the first day of the fourth module, following a sound preparation by the CCC faculty. I appreciated having some time for myself to go through the report, reflect on my first impressions, and start to digest some of the rather surprising messages. I had an uneasy night, as I was wondering what direction we would be heading in the following day. The combined results from the IGLC feedback tools—the Global Executive Leadership Inventory (GELI), Personality Audit (PA), and Leadership Archetypes Questionnaire (LAQ)—offered me a comprehensive and in-depth analysis of how I was perceived by my observers. Briefly, the key messages were: (1) You have excellent people skills. Build on these and expand further your activities as executive coach. That's what you are particularly good at. (2) Try to increase your self-esteem and assertiveness. This will have a positive impact on several other leadership areas and your professional role. (3) Improve your time and energy management. Your self-esteem and assertiveness seem to be related to it and changes here could be key to your making headway in these areas.

This is an oversimplification of the feedback I received, but it identifies the important issues. However, the intervention created an unexpected impulse regarding my private life that had a significant impact on me. The leadership group coaching session was a unique opportunity to explore my own development, from early childhood on, in a safe environment, reflecting on how I was brought up, what kind of family system I experienced, what kind of values I developed over the course of time, and what kind of relationship patterns evolved through personal and professional experience. I discovered something astonishing: over time the organizations I worked for had all become a kind of family substitute for me and so played a dominant role in my life. From the background of my parents' divorce and a strong need to "care" for my mother, left alone at that time, I seemed to have unconsciously adopted a similar pattern in my relations to the organizations I worked for, so that I was frequently busier helping co-workers with their issues than with achieving the objectives for my own area of responsibility or working on my professional development. In the further coaching process I discovered that some of these relationship patterns were quite dysfunctional, in terms of enhancing further development in my professional roles. The critical questions related to how to diminish the dysfunctional impact of the past on my current functioning and, eventually, how to change those deeply ingrained patterns that no longer worked.

The answers my peer-coaches gave sounded quite logical and obvious to them, but really surprising to me: "Create your own family!" At first I was flabbergasted by the suggestion that starting a family might provide a solution to a professional challenge, but after some further inquiry, clarification, and reflection, I became more and more taken by the idea and began to think of ways to make it happen. When it came to defining the priorities for my action plan, I was again pushed out of my comfort zone by my peers: "When are you going to propose?" they asked. They had hit the nail on the head. For many years I had been "happily-unmarried," living with my girlfriend Madeleine. My philosophy—"Why should I get married?"—seemed to have gone unquestioned. With the support of the coaching intervention I became conscious that early relationship experiences might have triggered this unconscious defense against the formal creation of my own family and its application to other fields—with consequent implications for my professional role.

My answer to my inquisitive colleagues was, "Before Christmas." And in the middle of the week before Christmas, during a specially arranged vacation, I organized a trip to the summit of a hill, where we had a breathtaking view over the Alps. I knelt down and asked Madeleine to marry me. The tension I felt at that moment was greater than what I had experienced with Ricardo—even though that incident had turned out to have triggered changes far beyond my professional life, in an extremely positive way. Fortunately I didn't have to wait long for an answer. Our wedding took place six months later and it was the best thing that could have happened to me. My "new family" had a lasting effect on how I defined my relationship with my company from then on. By marrying Madeleine I shifted the caring part of my behavioral patterns toward my new family, freed myself from an unconscious feeling of being tied to an organization in an inflexible role (just as family members sometimes feel stuck in their role and cannot see opportunities to change inflexible relationships), and established a more professional and mutually beneficial relationship with my colleagues and the business school I work for at large.

It goes without saying that the feedback from my CCC colleagues during the coaching session was extremely valuable and created a second tipping point for me. The feedback reports from the 360-degree tools alone would not have been nearly as effective without their attention, feedback, helping questions, hypotheses, probes, and supporting advice. Excellently facilitated and enriched by the leadership coach, they helped me to gather additional insights and to set up a personal change action plan.

After I returned from the fourth module I started to work on the other aspects of my action plan and experimented with some of the ideas generated during the session. After a truly dynamic fifth module, some months later, I took some time off over a long weekend in Barcelona to take a helicopter view and reflect on my experiences with CCC and my development since beginning the course.

Korotov[8] examines the role of a transitional space that gives participants in executive education programs an opportunity to reflect and to change their perspective about themselves. It helps participants to revisit their concept of their professional identity and to embark on a journey to explore potential new identities and possible selves. The CCC program seems to be particularly supportive of people who have become stuck in their development and experience so called impasses. Gianpiero Petriglieri[9] points out:

> Impasses occur each time we encounter a situation that our current adaptions cannot make sense of or handle meaningfully. The result is a difficulty in experiencing or in making sense of experience. I suggest looking at the perception of "being stuck" as the manifestation of such an impasse, one that emerges when our cognitive frameworks, emotional capacity, and behavioral repertoire do not allow us to make sense of, be within, and deal with our present intrapsychic or social reality.

Reflecting on the time before module 4, my experiences in the group coaching session, and my development after the module, I had to admit that I seemed to have been in a serious impasse in my professional role for quite some time. Interestingly, I felt I had probably been stuck for nearly two years, deadlocked in a professional identity where on the one hand I felt comfortable, but on the other hand had insufficient opportunities for further growth.

In my professional role as executive education program director I was responsible for developing and delivering courses for various clients and for executives at all levels, in association with excellent faculty. Although this role satisfied me to a certain extent, I increasingly missed the feeling of having a strong direct impact. With target groups of managers above a certain level of seniority I typically found myself facilitating sessions given by other speakers and executive coaches; I only rarely conducted the sessions myself. Yet my heart is with developing others—I often felt I could have a more direct impact on the development and growth of these clients when I was either executive coach or lecturer. But something held me back from stepping out of the shadows and increasing the number of coaching and teaching assignments I did in senior executive programs. What was preventing me from defining myself as an executive coach for more seasoned executives and communicating this internally and externally?

Until I joined CCC, I believed that the circumstances, my job description, lack of time to design and prepare sessions and interventions, and the toughness or (perceived) arrogance of senior executives and their use of power were to blame. But through intense reflections and interactions during the program I discovered that my own defenses were to a large extent responsible for creating this invisible ceiling from which I bounced back for longer and longer periods of time. The group coaching session in module 4, different interactions with my CCC colleagues and faculty, as well as feedback and reflection from a good friend helped me to get a much clearer perspective of my impasse. One of the real reasons seemed to be a disproportionate fear of negative appraisal by others and a hidden fear of not being liked by others. Using Kegan and Lehay's framework,[10] this can be described as follows:

1. *Fear of negative appraisal.* My stated commitment ("I will coach and teach in more assignments with senior managers") constantly had to compete with my hidden competing commitment ("I must always get perfect evaluations"). I identified the main big assumption as "I am not 'good enough' for this level of senior executives. They will not respect me and therefore I will not get perfect evaluations."
2. *Fear of not being liked by others.* My stated commitment ("I will be more assertive") constantly had to compete with my hidden competing commitment ("I must not harm the feelings of my coachees but create harmonious interactions with these executives"). I identified the main big assumption as "When I am assertive in coaching or teaching sessions I hurt the feelings of these executives. This will ruin our working relationship, they will dislike me and turn against me."

Identifying these "big assumptions" was just one step toward sustainable change. In the next step I challenged these assumptions and made some reality tests in different settings. When I relaxed and did not force myself to exceed the (perceived) expectations of my coachees immediately—and even started to carefully challenge some of their initial expectations—I discovered that these executives not only still respected me but that their level of respect often increased after a while. This happened especially when coachees felt that some of their initial expectations were partly dysfunctional for them and that some of the interventions they disliked in the beginning turned out to be very beneficial for them. Through further conscious experimenting with coaching assignments at executive level, I started to develop a thicker but more sensitive skin. This helped me to not panic when an executive showed strong emotions, but to interpret these as a normal reaction to a special situation, by trying to step into his or her shoes and being very respectful, empathetic, and sensitive in the whole interaction.

Through controlled reality testing of the second assumption ("I hurt the feelings of executives when I am assertive") I gained much more confidence and realized that executives' feelings are not necessarily harmed when I challenge them during a coaching session. I started to challenge some of my coachees more than I would have done previously, but also announced and framed these interventions accordingly. Bit by bit, I increased the level of assertiveness and could see that high-level managers in particular want a true sparring partner in coaching interactions and therefore appreciate a certain level of challenge from my side, when it is framed in the right way. Executives perceived me as being much more on equal level with them, when I didn't show any sign of fear or overly gentle behavior but behaved in a positively challenging and natural way with them. In these exploratory experiments I gained much more respect than formerly, when I tried simply to be friendly to them. It made for a lot of fun and it was very satisfying to get more and more positive feedback from clients.

The outcomes of my development through the CCC program at that point were:

- I was perceived as being more relaxed, more serious, more self-confident, and more authentic.
- Clients gave more positive feedback to my teaching and coaching; senior executives in particular clearly valued the mix of support and challenge.
- I received more requests from fellow program directors and faculty to coach in their senior executive programs.
- I felt very good and had a new feeling of purpose in my professional life.

Because of these developments I can candidly say that the transitional space that the course offered had an increasingly transformational effect on me, just as suggested in the literature on transformational executive education.[11]

Inspired by the outcomes of my first exploratory experiments with changed behavior I felt very much encouraged to test further my potential as coach and program faculty for high-level managers. As a first step, I concentrated on exploring how to shape my role in leadership group coaching and team coaching assignments with this target group. A discussion with Manfred Kets de Vries about the future of leadership coaching triggered my curiosity to look further, to experiment with my potential as a researcher, and to elaborate on my research plans in the field of coaching. I took what Korotov[12] calls identity experimentation further by applying new approaches and changed behavior in senior executive education programs, embarked on coaching research attempts, and took a more active role in shaping the leadership coaching practice at the European School of Management and Technology (ESMT) in Berlin. I experimented with combining team coaching interventions and group leadership coaching, flanked by further interventions in the course of a multimodular executive program as a first step to increasing the effectiveness of my coaching interventions.

STEPPING OUT: INTERNALIZING TRANSITIONAL SPACE

After seven modules of CCC it was time to step out of the program, to cross the border between experimentation and the implementation of new behaviors and mindsets in a sustainable way, and to act upon my newly shaped professional (and personal) identity.

Some experiments were helpful in this respect, as positive feedback from several executives confirmed that I was being granted the new identity. I began to feel that I was now suited to my new role and to dealing with this challenging target group. But it turned out that I had at least one more hurdle to clear. I learned that some colleagues and clients, who had known me for a long time, were finding it difficult to perceive me in my new role. Although I felt I had gone through a substantial change process, some still saw me in my previous role. They could not imagine me successfully coaching experienced executives or teaching a group of seasoned managers from global corporations. I found this frustrating at first, but was reminded of a discussion we had had with Professor Herminia Ibarra at INSEAD, who was in charge of one session in the CCC program. We explored the idea that people to whom we are close can sometimes unintentionally hinder our development—in much the same way as parents find it difficult to recognize that their children have already become adults themselves. It needed another initializing event to change this perception on the side of my colleagues, and luckily fortune was on my side. A colleague invited me to join a team of very successful senior professors and seasoned executive coaches as senior lecturer and executive coach in a program delivered to a group of senior managers from a global corporation. The managers, some of whom had quite challenging personalities, were in transition to higher executive positions. After a full week of demanding teaching and coaching interventions we received excellent feedback from the client and I was thrilled, if surprised, to learn that my coaching and teaching sessions were evaluated in the formal assessments in line with some of the most senior faculty members. After this program, words of my performance spread quickly through my business school—the effectiveness of this informal news distribution cannot be underestimated. I received requests to join the faculty teams of other executive programs shortly after.

But I also experienced a temporary backslide into old thinking patterns. The faculty and target group of one of the upcoming programs included the CEO of a major global player, and I initially thought it would be beyond my scope. When the program director asked me if I would like to join the program faculty, I actually hesitated. Fortunately, the stepping-out interventions of the final CCC module had prepared me to handle this backslide. I could frame these doubts as part of my longer transitional journey, using one of my peers from the program as sparring partner. When I reached this point, I felt I had not just survived, or even merely succeeded—I felt I had graduated.

I'm sure there will be future situations where I will be aware of potential backslides and have to prove the change to myself and others, pushing myself out of my comfort zone. My co-author, Konstantin Korotov, offered me such a "test" as we took a taxi to Hong Kong airport, after a workshop for a challenging group of future partners of an international professional services firm. Discussing this chapter, which we had originally intended to write as though about a third person, Konstantin asked whether I would be prepared to make it clear that I was telling my own story. My instant response was that that would make me feel too exposed and vulnerable. I had an immediate inner impulse to reject the idea. Konstantin went on: "Think for a moment about the different options. What would you find more interesting and useful as a reader, the story of a fictional third person or the real story of the author?" The only possible answer was the latter. In that case, Konstantin pressed me, what was I afraid of? Why was I reluctant to be that transparent?

Our short exchange triggered a quick reflection and decision process and is also a nice example of the principle that the development of an executive coach never ends and of the benefit of constant peer-coaching and supervision. In one of my coaching supervision sessions, while I was recounting my transition story, the supervising coach remarked: "I think you have become a different person." I thought about it for a while and then replied, "I don't know. Perhaps I just learned to be more myself."

FROM ANDREAS'S STORY TO THE ISSUE OF COACHES' DEVELOPMENT AND GROWTH

Andreas's story is a reminder to all of us who work in coaching, leadership development, consulting, teaching, and the like, that we are also subject to concerns, anxieties, fantasies, hopes, and developmental needs. It is also a reminder that from time to time we should experience what our clients, coachees, or program participants go through when engaged in developmental interventions. This chapter is also an invitation to all interested readers and the professional community at large to engage in a discussion of our own growth and development and its role for the success of our clients.

Andreas's experience also illustrates what Korotov[13] describes as the process of going through an identity laboratory, a transformational learning experience. Personal transformation assisted by executive development programs often starts with a powerful preentry experience that both engages the participant in anticipatory self-exploration and cements the intent to engage in the challenging work of personal change. However, participants, like Andreas, are sometimes genuinely surprised at the implications of having to go deeper in learning about self. This type of surprise is frequent in all kind of programs involving self-assessment and self-development. The move from discussing others toward discussing oneself, although rewarding eventually, may be a difficult step to take, even for experienced coaches and consultants. Eventually participants in interventions similar to those described in this chapter realize that before they can help others to change, they should experience change themselves. Importantly, participants need to learn to use the resources available to them, like Andreas learned to use the small group interactions, leadership development instruments, and coaching process for achieving success not only in his professional but also in his personal life.

The opportunity to explore one's identity and experiment with new possibilities is critical for the success of change. In the context of a multimodular executive education program, Andreas had a chance to stage experiments between modules and discuss them with faculty and fellow participants in class. His experience supports our call for the multimodular design of transformational executive programs.[14]

The process of stepping out of the laboratory is also very important for achieving sustained change in identity and behavior. As we learn from Andreas's case, it is critically important not just to claim a new sense of self but also to be granted this new identity.[15] Andreas's case demonstrates the importance of guiding figures (e.g., faculty members, coaches, or bosses) in supporting changing individuals' desire to try something new and giving them a chance to succeed.[16] As the last paragraphs in the case suggest, "graduation" from a program does not mean that the process of change has been completed. The internalization of the identity laboratory means that we have to keep looking for opportunities to explore and experiment.

In this chapter we wanted to draw attention to the issue of helping professionals whose mission is to create better organizations *become better themselves*. We showcased one way of engaging in becoming a better coach, participating in a program that created an identity laboratory for its participants. In conclusion, however, we would like to emphasize once again that the issue of becoming better coaches and practitioners helping to create better organizations is still a very fruitful arena for both practical experimentation and academic analysis.

NOTES

1. Kets de Vries, M. (2005a). "The Dangers of Feeling Like a Fake." *Harvard Business Review*, 83(9), 108–116.
2. Korotov, K. (2005). "Identity Laboratories." INSEAD PhD Dissertation. Fontainebleau, France: INSEAD.
3. Luborsky, L. and Crits-Christoph, P. (1998). *Understanding Transference: The Core Conflictual Relationship Theme Method*. Washington, DC: American Psychological Association.
4. Kets de Vries, M. F. R. (2008). "Leadership Coaching and Organizational Transformation: Effectiveness in a World of Paradoxes." *INSEAD Working Paper* 2008/71/EFE, p. 26.
5. Korotov, K. (2005). "Identity Laboratories." INSEAD PhD Dissertation. Fontainebleau, France: INSEAD, p. 268.
6. Kegan, R. and Lahey, L. L. (2001). "The Real Reason People Won't Change." *Harvard Business Review*, 79(10): 85–92.
7. Kets de Vries, M. F. R. (2005b). "Leadership Group Coaching in Action: The Zen of Creating High Performance Teams." *Academy of Management Executive*, 19(1): 61–77.
8. Korotov, K. (2005). "Identity Laboratories." INSEAD PhD Dissertation. Fontainebleau, France: INSEAD.
9. Petriglieri, G. (2007). "Stuck in a Moment: A Developmental Perspective on Impasses." *Transactional Analysis Journal*, 37(3): 185–194.
10. Kegan, R. and Lahey, L. L. (2001). "The Real Reason People Won't Change." *Harvard Business Review*, 79(10): 85–92.
11. Kets de Vries, M. and Korotov, K. (2007). "Creating Transformational Executive Education Programs." *Academy of Management Learning & Education*, 6(3), 375–387; Petriglieri, G. and Wood, J. D. (2005). "Behind the Mask: The MBA Personal Development Elective." IMD Working Paper 2005–10.

12. Korotov, K. (2005). "Identity Laboratories." INSEAD PhD Dissertation. Fontainebleau, France: INSEAD.
13. Korotov, K. (2005). "Identity Laboratories." INSEAD PhD Dissertation. Fontainebleau, France: INSEAD; Korotov, K. (2007). "Executive Education from the Participant's Point of View." In M. Kets de Vries, K. Korotov, and E. Florent-Treacy (Eds) *Coach and Couch: The Psychology of Making Better Leaders*. Houndmills: Palgrave Macmillan, pp. 127–141.
14. Kets de Vries, M. and Korotov, K. (2007). "Creating Transformational Executive Education Programs." *Academy of Management Learning & Education*, 6(3), 375–387.
15. Bartel, C. and Dutton, J. (2001). "Ambiguous Organizational Memberships: Constructing Organizational Identities in Interactions with Others." In M. Hogg and D. Terry (Eds) *Social Identity Process in Organizational Contexts*. Philadelphia, PA: Psychology Press, pp. 115–130.
16. Korotov, K. (2005). "Identity Laboratories." INSEAD PhD Dissertation. Fontainebleau, France: INSEAD.

PART THREE: CREATING BETTER PLACES TO WORK

10

IMAGINING BETTER PLACES TO WORK: INDIVIDUAL-ORGANIZATIONAL INTERFACES AND COACHING PRACTICES

LAURA GUILLÉN

In 1936, Karel Câpek ironically illustrated in his satirical science fiction novel *War With the Newts* the difficulties and occasional incoherencies of communities without a shared vision and a sense of trust and collaboration. He described how a new kind of animal has been discovered by a pearl diver. The strange beasts walked on two legs and, in addition, they were able to talk. In their attempts to describe what they were, the scientific community hypothesized about their nature. Their conclusions were:

> Of course, there were some people, who because of their scientific knowledge, were sure that the pictures showed that they were not prehistoric lizards, but salamanders. Even more expert people then claimed that this type of salamander was not scientifically recognized and therefore did not exist. Long debates were held in the newspapers. Long discussions about priorities and other purely scientific questions. But finally, the Natural History Department of each country created its own salamander, cruelly criticizing the salamanders of other countries. This is why a scientific explanation for the problem of the salamander was never found.[1]

As funny as we may think this story sounds, it can also resonate strongly with us. We can probably find, without digging very deep in our personal and professional experiences, projects that were turned into tournaments to win, and work colleagues turned into rivals to defeat. In fact, organizations are riddled with examples of group envy and conspiracies where the *others* (other departments, other members of our own department, or our closest work neighbor) are translated into quixotic enemies to beat. Wouldn't it be simpler to recognize other people's work? Wouldn't it be more rewarding to be able to work in teams and create trusting bonds with our colleagues, to share a sense of community with them? Wouldn't working in such places be more satisfactory? Even if we answer these questions with a categorical yes, we may still think that pretending to create such a type of healthy organization is a little naïve, to say the least. Life is hard. Work is tough.

When considering alternative ways of making the workplace more attractive, we have already advocated the creation of "authentizotic" organizations,[2] which have a vision, structure, and culture that provide a compelling connective quality for their employees. They are places where people feel at their best and are invigorated by their work. In authentizotic organizations, people are provided with learning opportunities, encouraging their self-development and self-expression. While improving the level of caring, new trusting relationships with people throughout the organization can be created. Again, is this idea so disconnected from daily job realities? Is this an unrealistic wish? Maybe, but new managerial discourses have already started to emphasize how increasingly important it is for executives to do something meaningful at work.

We need to go far beyond managerial stereotypes and allow ourselves to be creative and playful, imagining new organizational architectures that invest in values, meaning, and collaboration. Perhaps we may not reach our highest aspirations, but certainly we can look up and see them as a source of motivation, believe in them, and try to follow where they lead us. So, let's imagine for a second that creating authentizotic organizations is actually possible. The objective of this chapter is not to offer a recipe for that but to comment on what the creation process of authentizotic organizations may look like. I will illustrate this process with two cases of organizations attempting to create better places to work. This will allow me to review how coaching practices affect the creation and sustainability of this type of healthy organizational cultures.

INGREDIENTS FOR CREATING BETTER PLACES TO WORK

Organizational cultures are highly susceptible to the influence of leaders. In fact, one characteristic of authentizotic organizations is that "leadership walks the talk."[3] The role of senior executives is to provide a supportive leadership that fosters a shared vision and mindset, and to encourage people to be more sensitive to human relations and managerial development. Leaders may in addition ensure that the appropriate organizational changes are put in place and institutionalized in the daily social practices to actually experience a healthy organizational culture. Two variables affect the creation of a healthy organizational culture: the type of leadership within the organization and the socialization practices in place.

Type of leadership within the organization

Leaders characterizing authentizotic organizations tend to care more about their people than about power, status, or prestige. They are prepared to delegate, listen, and trust others. But in fact, this type of leader is rare. Why would something so simple to describe on paper be so difficult to translate into leaders' actions? To a great extent it has to do with a hidden agenda guided by unconscious, and sometimes not socially acceptable, motives and desires. It also has to do with leaders' natural inclination to work with selected people with whom they happen to feel more secure and comfortable. Often, loyalty supersedes competence. These people usually share objectives and ways of doing things with the leader, and the bonds they are able to create are difficult for less similar colleagues to match. As a result, the leader creates a cohort of "mini-mes" that serves to reinforce the leader's basic assumptions about human nature and work functioning. The problem is that such alliances may end in paranoid reactions, separating, in a de facto way, "good" from "bad," and who deserves attention from who doesn't. It is also not uncommon to find that executives who have not been able to identify improvement areas for themselves are all too capable of pointing out areas their colleagues should work on. Finally, leaders' narcissistic tendencies often result in battles for power and recognition, whatever the cost. Even if new flatter and flexible organizational structures are replacing old-fashioned pyramidal ones, the "there can be only one" leitmotif—as in the movie *Highlander*, where the characters are condemned to fight each other until only one is left—is still a basic assumption of many executives.

This view of leadership inhibits the development of skills such as active listening, empathy, or effective communication, the very skills that drive best places to work. But the good news is that these skills are increasingly appreciated not only by academics and HR professionals but also by executives themselves. Being more open and honest, allocating time for regular meetings with direct reports, working on communication skills, and moving to a more reflective approach are usually cited as improvement objectives in executives' wish lists. The recent turbulent economic times have reinforced more than ever the importance of being able to trust our leaders and of conducting business in an ethical and socially responsible manner. Thus the type of leadership needed for creating and sustaining healthy organizations is a very appealing one. This has led to a growing interest in authentic leadership,[4] which is closely related to the idea of leaders proactively fostering positive, healthy environments. And in turn, this has led executive development programs to be reframed so that they can offer curricula attuned with authentic leadership.

Socialization practices in place

Andrés Hurtado, the main character of *El Árbol de la Ciencia*,[5] (*The Tree of Knowledge*) by Pío Baroja, embodies the feelings of hopelessness and alienation that recur in all types of modern artistic expression. Hurtado is paralyzed behind a shield of excuses. "I'm just a man. What do you expect me to do?" This discouraging feeling echoes life in modern societies in many different ways, from social responsibility to taking environmentally friendly initiatives. Poor Andrés Hurtado feels overwhelmed by everything he has to deal with. Worse, the more he experiences life, the more futile everything seems. He cannot even begin to imagine how to act in his environment, let alone how to change it. But as difficult as it might seem, leaders are required to do precisely that. Despite their self-doubt, they must influence others; they must reinvent their context in a continuous way instead of advocating an indifferent, contemplative attitude.

Thus leaders influence, consciously or unconsciously, the practices that support a particular organizational culture. They are responsible to a great extent for the creation of an organizational ideal and the corresponding values that people at all organizational levels internalize. Building shared values and a common-sense-making process, having role models consistent with organizational values, sharing a folklore that is repeated and that reinforces the core values and norms of the organization, and making attempts to "unfreeze" people to make them more understanding and open to learning are senior executives' responsibilities in order to impact organizational culture.[6]

Thus a crucial leadership task is to provide people with a healthy vision that fosters a shared mindset focused on appropriate organizational values. It is the responsibility of top management to practice and reward behaviors that are attuned to the desired culture. The organization's communication, both internal and external, should be consistent with these values. Additionally, new members who join the organization should be aware of these values throughout the selection process so that they conceive the right expectations of the organization. In short, values (apart from some core values) are not a static list to be hung on some dusty notice board or stored in an inaccessible drawer of an HR professional's desk; they should be experienced, constantly revisited, and communicated to members of the organization. Seniors managers reinforce values by defining clear performance goals and job descriptions that include behaviors aligned with strategic values. They can also put in place appropriate reinforcing organizational structures and policies. For example, if the organization is trying to be perceived as more open and less bureaucratic, designing a flat structure as a substitute for a more hierarchical one may help to reinforce the message.

Another way of communicating a particular organizational culture is to make it demonstrable to observers. Role models are powerful motivators because they generate greater emotional involvement.[7] They guide us as we set our personal standards, and are a major motive for self-development. Even if there are substantial differences in the way people respond to role models, their influence has long been noted, both in popular and academic literature. Junior managers look for heroes to emulate. Their role models are usually at intermediate or top levels of the organization. If executives in these positions remain aware of the effect they have on younger people and manifest a genuine interest in supporting their development, they are in a splendid position to disseminate their values. Middle-rank executives look for role models who complement their skills or leadership styles. Executives at this level realize that moving up often involves displaying a more sophisticated repertoire of social skills, and they seek to benchmark their styles against those of their colleagues. Having opportunities to meet and work with people at the same level has a refreshing effect on them. Finally, senior executives look for negative role models mainly outside the organization, who display specific attributes or values they would like to avoid. Doing so, they boost their ego while confirming their own way of doing things.

But if vision alignment and role modeling are to do more than scratch the surface of any transformational effort, all members of the organization need to be involved in the process. Top management should provide a roadmap that helps other executives to internalize a participative culture, but it is the employees' reaction to it that constitutes the key success factor in crafting a particular organizational culture. Being perceived as authentic is crucial to this. A sense of collective commitment (an unwritten and informal way to set behaviors), decision processes, and a code of action to distinguish what is right or wrong are the only ways to align rhetoric with corporate actions.

Finally, providing learning opportunities for employees may demolish defensive attitudes that often perpetuate a toxic status quo and outmoded winning formulas. The need for development should be recognized and valued by people in the organization and they should be brave enough to jump into the unknown and challenge their own standards. A safe environment that encourages playfulness and creativity should be in place to "unfreeze" people and to make them feel an urge for development.[8] Setting appropriate spaces and moments for coaching experiences provides safety and anxiety containment. I will now illustrate how coaching practices may help in the establishment of better working relationships.

At this point, it seems pretty clear that the skeleton that vertebrates the creation of healthy organizational cultures is the emotional contagion provided by authentic leadership and trusting work relationships. Thus it is not surprising that leaders are increasingly asking for ways to improve skills that lie far beyond technical or strategic knowledge. They need to work on their emotional and social intelligences, to learn how to interact with others more effectively, and to become aware of their own emotional states. They need to face the psychological side of the organizational life and that is precisely where coaching-oriented programs are of invaluable help.

COACHING PRACTICES: INSTILLING HOPE AND TRUST IN THE ORGANIZATION

Nowadays, individuals jump from organization to organization throughout their life and career. The very first organization to which we all belong is the family system. To understand our personal development, we should look at all the social hosts where we spend most of our time. In this sense, organizations may be seen as successive wombs—or "holding environments"—in which we recreate patterns of past behaviors and create new ones for the future. The clinical/systemic paradigm addressed in earlier chapters in this book is particularly relevant for undertaking this task. Organizations can be converted into learning spaces where people are encouraged to learn without fear of punishment—and this type of conversion should be at the very top of an organization's priorities.

Executives tend to view coaching programs as an opportunity to focus on themselves. They feel that the time has finally arrived for them to reflect upon, and talk about, their life and experiences—*me, me, me, and a bit more of me, please.* Therein lies a dilemma, however: too intense a focus on "me and mine" can give rise to extremely unrealistic expectations about coaching methods and outcomes. Executives who only see coaching as parenthetical self-reflection, squeezed into their busy agendas with a goal of personal gain, may lose track of the bigger picture. They underestimate the defining and limiting characteristics of their organizations and how mutual individual-organizational interdependencies and influences impact the development of self- and organizational constructs. Executives often become so excited about having someone who really listens to their stories that they forget that the coaching session is about change and not merely about reconfirmation of themselves based on past achievements. But without contextualization, expectations of the coaching sessions often become unrealistic, and quick paybacks from coaching investments are impossible. But coaching used appropriately—that is, holistically and systemically—also promotes development at a broader organizational level, thus helping to create the kinds of healthy culture referred to by the contributors to this book.

A coaching attitude creates the sort of supportive atmosphere within an organization that is needed to help others change, by allowing them to try out new behaviors without fear of marginalization or punishment. A culture grounded in a "coaching mindset" will not only serve individual development purposes but also set the foundation for creating a better place to work. Awareness of individual-organizational interfaces, and how leadership challenges and coaching practices may change the organization's attitude toward creating a coaching culture, will facilitate the establishment of new patterns of relationships among organizational members and help eliminate patterns that are no longer effective.

As a leadership development method, coaching can be internal or external, or a combination of both. When coaching occurs outside the organization, it may extend beyond immediate realities and job requirements to broader professional, career, and personal issues. After being coached outside the organization, most participants report that they are more aware of themselves, often experiencing a sense of self-renewal that helps them to reset goals and priorities and triggers new attitudes toward their direct reports, colleagues, and other stakeholders. They become more in tune with a "coaching attitude" that includes, for example, practicing active listening, empathy, or open communication. They may see new paths and centers of interest that help them enlarge their professional networks. Participants bring back learning takeaways from the educational settings of programs to their organizations. Coaching can also take place inside the organization, through in-company programs or individual coaching assignments for organizational key players who are facing a job transition or a specific challenge at some point of their careers. Regardless of location, coaching processes can use a one-on-one[9] or group methodology.[10]

It is also important to note that coaching practices can be formal or informal. Informal processes often arise from, and are facilitated by, trusting relationships between individuals in the organization. These relationships develop when people are aware of their colleagues' and superiors' support and accessibility. They receive the implicit message "I'm there when you need me" through such simple conventions as leaving an office door open. Informal processes may also occur outside the organization, for example in forums (electronic or otherwise) where experience and knowledge are exchanged, networks provide social support, and new insights and perspectives are lent to everyday routines and functions. Within the organization, more formal coaching practices can take the form of mentoring or peer and senior coaching. Mentoring describes the process by which more experienced members of the organization share insights and cues with less experienced members.[11] Peer coaching is the establishment of a cooperative relationship between two or more executives of similar experience.[12] Senior coaching is similar, but indicates a cooperative relationship between executives with different amounts of experience.

The selection of the appropriate coaching practices for a specific organization must be aligned with the targets to which the development efforts are aimed. While internal methods are invaluable for novices, external coaching that promotes critical inquiry may be more useful for senior executives. Middle-rank executives may benefit from methods that emphasize real-life learning and involve the creation of a learning community that helps participants question their goals and priorities.[13]

At an early career stage, executives are more likely to adopt the role of coachee without resistance and take advantage of mentoring processes and informal coaching practices that help them tackle their weaknesses and polish job-related skills.[14] This also facilitates their acceptance of feedback from more experienced leaders in the organization. In the mid-career phase, coaching practices among managers with different functions and from different levels increase the motivational power to attain a successful career in the organization, increase understanding of relevant behaviors linked to organizational values, and guide self-development.

As executives become more experienced and confident, they gain special benefit from peer and external coaching and networking processes. Coaching practices may help to address the ambiguity of their future career and help them reinterpret their personal goals.[15] Peer interaction and group experiences may be extremely helpful in making sense of the overlapping boundaries of nonexplicit organizational routines. In general, seniors are more interested in investing time in nurturing talent within the organization. At their level, they become increasingly concerned with organizational challenges such as talent retention and succession and legacy building. And as a bonus, in these coaching sessions senior executives often find they can explore innovative ideas with their junior colleagues in parallel with seniors' sharing of organizational vision and knowledge.

But how to convert these aims into practice? In the next section I illustrate how two middle-sized companies—the Navarra and Zaragoza Chambers of

Commerce in Spain—orchestrated some socialization and coaching practices to create a coaching culture within their organizations.

THE CASE OF THE NAVARRA AND ZARAGOZA CHAMBERS OF COMMERCE

The Navarra Chamber of Commerce (NCC) and the Zaragoza Chamber of Commerce (ZCC) are medium-sized public institutions with around 100 employees each (executives and others). They are public corporations whose mission is the representation, defense, and promotion of the general interests of the trade, industrial, and service organizations located in the region in which they operate. Some years ago the NCC and ZCC realized that their public status—they were completely dependent on public funding—was no longer aligned with the evolving needs of their clients. They needed to transform their institutions into independent organizations offering professionalized services and new, profitable initiatives. The two senior management teams recognized the need to get rid of bureaucratic and static mindsets and replace them with more dynamic, creative, and result-oriented ones. As the change initiative began, the values associated with individual performance, achievement orientation, and efficacy were transmitted to the workforce successfully, but the effect of making explicit this cultural switch created pressure, stress, and anxiety among certain people.

Employees in both organizations tended to have a high level of organizational commitment. Paradoxically, high employee satisfaction of employees constituted a barrier to acknowledging the need for change and for questioning the current status quo. In addition, both companies were facing internal leadership issues. They realized they needed to define and find the right leadership skills to strengthen the new organizational culture they were advocating.

In parallel, and aligned with their new cultural values, they recognized the importance of giving all employees the opportunity to develop managerial tasks and to assume project responsibilities. They believed that the cornerstone for undertaking successful cultural change lay in people's attitudes toward it.

Thus NCC and ZCC decided to run external training programs to enhance self-development of people at all levels of the organization, with a special emphasis on emotional and social competencies, and to encourage a vivacious communication process among employees at all levels to reinforce their organizational values. Both training programs were carried out by the same external consultancy and were exact replicas, with the same structure and objective, but took into account contextual specificities regarding culture, strategy, or structure. The primary objectives of the senior executive teams of both companies were to reinforce the change message and to create a culture that promoted continuous personal and organizational development, with special emphasis on the personal and interpersonal aspects.

The model used for designing the program adopted a broad perspective that urged managers to reflect on three interrelated aspects: (1) the organizational context and the characteristics and particularities of the organizational culture, values, and desired behaviors; (2) the job positions and responsibilities they entailed in terms of skills, values, interpersonal styles, and time allocation; and (3) who were they as individuals and what their personal ambitions and life priorities were.

Before implementation of the program, senior managers discussed their vision, corporate values, and the corresponding leadership behaviors associated with them at different organizational levels. The revised statements were included in the training program material to spread them throughout the entire organization.

The training program was voluntary for members at all levels of the organization and combined theoretical, personal, and on-the-job learning approaches. The program used individual and group methodologies to help the internalization of individual development initiatives and consisted of four main stages: (1) setting the stage and 360-degree assessment; (2) a training program that offered participants a general overview of the conceptual, operational, and developmental issues associated with emotional and social competencies and a chance to reflect on their own style, values, vision, and developmental priorities; (3) individualized feedback and coaching sessions to identify learning objectives and/or improvement areas for a one-year period; and (4) follow-up.

Stage 1: Setting the stage and 360-degree assessment

The senior executive team discussed in groups the key organizational issues in terms of development. A debate was held to identify what characterized an efficient leader in order to articulate a model of development that was tuned to the organizational culture and would be transmitted to the rest of the organization in the next step of the training.

In parallel, all organizational members attended an information session and were asked to complete 360-degree assessment instruments via intranet. The instruments used rated emotional and social competencies like teamwork and collaboration, influence, self-confidence, flexibility, or initiative. Additionally, all participants were assessed on the same dimensions by other observers who knew them well (superiors, colleagues, subordinates, others). All were assessed by their immediate superior and had the opportunity to choose further observers from their professional environment for additional assessments.

To capture the richness of how individuals were perceived by others, all the participants in the study held a session in which the two versions of the 360-degree instrument (self-assessment and informants' assessment) were discussed openly and frankly by the individual participants and the informants who worked with them on a daily basis in a session led by the participant and his or her immediate superior. Participation in this stage was voluntary and individual participants could decide to change their default profile discussion partner for a valid reason (e.g., they had worked together for only a very short period of time). In addition, they could include other people from the organization in the discussion.

The objectives of this step were to engage in more open communication with direct reports, provide qualitative feedback for supporting the employee's development, and to identify skills, behaviors, and attitudes that could be more effective. As these organizations had not had formal performance evaluation policies in the past, this step generated great expectations among those who saw it as an opportunity to find out what their bosses actually thought about them. A few, in particular employees who had worked in the organizations for many years and had internalized their expectations and understanding of their own role in bureaucratic institutions, might have been reluctant to engage in the process but did not express their discomfort openly.

Stage 2: Training sessions

The transparent, reassuring, and motivating statements about the program's objectives on the part of the senior executive team helped to create a trustful and safe environment in which personal and professional issues were discussed openly. The training sessions were open to all employees who voluntary agreed to take part in the project, regardless of their experience in the company or their organizational level. Thus, in a given session, the CEO might find herself sitting close to a newcomer who had just joined the organization, or people from the marketing department could share a table with people from HR, thus enriching everyone's overall perspective about the organizational system. The methodology used in the sessions combined theory on leadership development, career development, and competencies with experiential learning exercises that gave room for self-reflection at both individual and group levels.

The objectives of this stage were to motivate participants and highlight the importance of managing development on a daily basis, to clarify how to evaluate and interpret the 360-degree profile, to unify language about leadership behaviors throughout the organization, and to reflect on personal development opportunities within the organizational setting.

The training sessions helped to establish the basis for a self-directed development process, by focusing more deeply on interpersonal style and identifying strengths and areas for improvement. Numerous exercises were used to promote self-awareness. Reflecting on legacy and vision, completing a values questionnaire, assessing their learning styles, and simulations to reflect on their role in work groups, are all examples of exercises used during the training sessions. All the exercises were discussed in peer groups to obtain feedback and draw on the images that participants were transmitting to their colleagues through their daily interactions. These sessions also served to contain anxiety about the development process; discuss organizational values, strengths, and shortcomings regarding development policies and desired managerial behaviors; and to explain how the results of the project were not meant to be used for performance or reward purposes. The sessions ended with an exercise in identifying development objectives and sketching a learning agenda for the following months.

At this point, members of the organizations felt obliged to take part in this massive training initiative. But during the process the cultural clash with members embodying the *old* organizational culture became obvious, and therefore easier to manage. To some people it seemed that an organization that had for a long time been successful at producing apples, so to speak, was now being asked to become a paradigm of orange production. Bridge building was needed to trace connections between the old and new cultures, making explicit not only the need for change but also how to get there. To communicate the transition, the executive management presented it as a natural evolution rather than a revolution. The construction of this bridge was facilitated through reinforcement of the communication processes in the program and the opportunity to participate in them. Intense debates and careful attention were devoted to accompanying, rather than forcing, a change in people's mindsets. To reinforce this, after the training sessions, participants were divided into discussion forums (with four to five members in each) to share reflections on topics intimately connected to the organizational culture such as strategy, structure, human resources policies, and opportunities for self-development. The new values were stated explicitly, and their internalization was encouraged by the subsequent stages in the process. A report that guaranteed the confidentiality of the participants was written by the external training consultants to summarize impressions and reflections that appeared during the training and cultural sessions and to debrief results of the 360-degree assessments at the collective level on strategic competencies, such as achievement orientation, influence, or initiative.

Before the one-on-one feedback and coaching sessions with external coaches, participants in both organizations decided voluntarily if they wanted to move on to the next step of the project. Those who chose to move on to the next step were asked to reflect on the materials used in the training sessions and in their 360-degree feedback and devise an action plan with objectives for personal and professional development. From the positive response to the sessions it was clear that the organizations' leaders had been successful in creating a safe and flexible context in which employees were able to engage in self-development. Feelings of optimism and enthusiasm—or at least a high degree of expectation—expanded rapidly, thanks to informal conversations and practices that facilitated an emotional contagion among organizational members. A huge majority of the organizational members decided to move on in the training program and enroll for the coaching sessions. Even people who had had doubts at the beginning of the process were increasingly intrigued about what more it could offer them.

161

Stage 3: Feedback and coaching session

The feedback and coaching session was focused on development goals and actions to improve personal and social skills and/or leadership styles. All participants had an individual 90-minute session with an external coach to discuss their feedback and the different tools introduced earlier in the program. In general, participants showed satisfaction with their own levels of empathy, teamwork, and collaboration. Among the top priorities for development were improving conflict management, being more assertive, increasing self-confidence, and developing a client orientation. This may be indicative of members' realization that they needed to reinforce these competencies to be able to transition toward a more professional and results-oriented culture. Individual participants were made responsible for their own progress: from writing down the resulting learning objectives and actions committed to achieving them and sharing them with their bosses if they considered them pertinent. All understood that control of the process was in their hands, which helped to establish a climate of trust and commitment.

Although employees' attitudes toward the process were positive rather than negative, a quantitative study revealed an unexpected challenge. The competencies included as developmental objectives in members' action plans were aggregated to identify their alignment with organizational strategy. Interestingly, only a few people showed interest in improving their leadership and influence skills. Enhancing an achievement orientation and taking new initiatives were also accorded a low level of importance. A high need for affiliation and conflict avoidance prevented members, as a whole, from trying to find ways to stand out and reinforced friendship and team spirit above other things. People appeared to be satisfied to perform exactly as they were asked, no more, and no differently. But in the drive to create a dynamic and change-oriented culture, these tendencies were unnecessary ballast.

In response, the executive management team engaged in a deep reflection process about what leadership in these organizations meant and how to develop it on a continuous basis. Their dilemma was how they could change perceptions to prioritize achievement and initiative orientations without losing the sense of affiliation and community that their employees obviously appreciated and needed. The identification of individual learning objectives at this stage constituted the trigger for a continuous developmental process within the organization. The senior management teams realized that they needed to equip the organization with the means to keep the developmental project alive.

Stage 4: Follow-up and keeping the project alive

Continuous improvement requires continuous attention and support. A number of actions were taken at this stage to assure the continuation of the project, including the provision of Internet resources to support emotional and social competencies; regular organization-wide workshops on strategic competencies (one workshop every two months); establishing electronic platforms for employee discussion forums; and, last but not least, more coaching sessions for those interested. At an organizational level, management decided to run a satisfaction survey to deepen their understanding of the sources of employees' satisfaction and dissatisfaction. Additionally, they decided to run a 360-degree assessment with subsequent discussions with the immediate bosses and identification of individual learning objectives on a regular basis (once a year).

At this point the NCC and ZCC projects diverged. Even though both CEOs shared the ultimate objective of promoting individual development, while creating a coaching culture in a continuous way, they decided to follow two opposite strategies. NCC decided to train coaches internally while ZCC hired external coaches to provide support to high potentials in the organization.

The senior management team at NCC selected an external coaching program to train their internal coaches. Participants for this new program were selected among all NCC employees who had shown interest in the previous development project and were considered to have appropriate skills—including motivation to develop others in the organization and coaching competencies (empathy, active listening, self-awareness, nondirective attitude, assertiveness, and sensitivity). Senior executives and HR professionals identified the pool of candidates from all organizational levels. Two external coaches were asked to meet the candidates to reassess their motivation and coaching abilities and proposed the final candidates for the training program. Thirteen participants were selected, including the CEO and two other board members (three senior, nine middle, and one junior executive altogether).

The training program for internal coaches combined theories of coaching and practical tools and exercises and was presented in four modules spread over six months. The 13 participants were involved in all the activities and attended all the sessions. In the case of the CEO, the time and energy she devoted to the project gave a clear signal of commitment to the coaching project to the whole organization. Once the program ended, the teachers and facilitators deemed 11 of the 13 participants were ready to run internal coaching sessions.

The senior management team ran two information sessions for the rest of the organization in which they officially presented the internal coaching project. To establish a stable coaching relationship, those who wanted to participate in the project as coachees (around 85 percent) were invited to select their preferred coach from the 11 candidates. The coaches received the list of people who had selected them and they scheduled an initial session only if they felt they could build a trusting and open relationship with the coachee. Once the coaching process started, it was quickly established as an organizational routine and has successfully become part of the organizational culture. Interestingly, the CEO seemed to be quite sure that no one was going to select her as a coach, but surprisingly she received numerous requests from people who wanted to be coached by her.

Conversely, the CEO of ZCC decided to hire external coaches to take charge of the development of high potentials in the organization. He chose a pool of participants at all levels of the organization who could decide voluntarily whether or not they wanted to continue with the process. If they were in, they were expected to follow a coaching process that was guaranteed to be confidential, but to come up with some developmental objectives aligned with the organizational priorities. The participants were ultimately to be responsible for writing the development plan that would be circulated at senior executive level to agree the efforts that the organization would make toward supporting the development plan (which included external training, job rotation, and new job responsibilities). Twelve participants were coached and supervised directly by the CEO, who had personal interviews with all of them to discuss the developmental opportunities for the next few years. The participants who had completed the first coaching sessions (to Stage 3), but were not selected among the high potentials, were not forgotten. Their development plans were available online (for them and their immediate bosses) through a tailored software solution and were discussed and updated after regular meetings with their supervisors.

The coaching sessions the selected participants undertook were confidential, and at the same time allowed communication channels to be opened between them and their immediate superiors. In this way, there were three main responsibles along the development process, providing a continuous perspective: the coach (either internal or external), the coachee, and the immediate superior. Through the sessions held in Stage 1, the coachees and their immediate superiors had the opportunity to discuss development linked to job positions and further career development. At this point, the immediate superiors were able to communicate their impressions about the coachees' developmental needs. With this information, the 360-degree profile and the exercises carried out during the training session, participants were equipped to engage in a coaching process that was directed to the areas that were most significant for them. They were able to work on the objectives that they chose, even if these did not converge with their superiors' impressions. The coach and the immediate superiors had a relationship of trust and an attitude of noninterference to allow personal development goals and job performance goals diverge. These would be included in subsequent annual revisions of the action plans (see Figure 10.1).

Even if they opted for different follow-up strategies, among the success factors that provided the basis for continuous development in both organizations was the implementation of a software platform that supported communication and easy access to all development resources. Other key aspects were the commitment of the senior management team and the opportunities for interactions between managers in all levels and departments. When the projects were launched, perceived tension between development and performance was a major threat to the process. Many people were reluctant to believe that their organization was genuinely interested in their development, especially if this could open new horizons beyond organizational boundaries. They were worried about being manipulated and guided toward including the "appropriate" objectives in their learning plans. "If the organization is paying for this, it's because they see

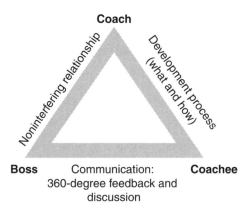

FIGURE 10.1 **Roles in the development process**

pay-back from it," some believed. Because of this, the organizations' leaders took time to confront this barrier and convince people that the organizations really did care about them. Confidentiality and trust were absolutely crucial for this purpose. The overall result, beyond progress in individual development, was the creation of coaching cultures in both organizations that were not only effective at supporting change but also self-renewing.

FURTHER REFLECTIONS

The cases of NCC and ZCC illustrate how the senior management team instituted organizational routines that introduced coaching attitudes at all levels of the organization. They highlighted the importance of their leaders' commitment to the new values and the efforts to make them part of the organizations' cultural package. The actions taken by NCC and ZCC also reflect their attempt to provide their employees with better places to work—an effort to create authentizotic organizations. Senior management made this happen through a systemic approach: sharing values and giving opportunities to discuss them, showing commitment and authenticity by supporting and participating in all stages of the organizational development program, clarifying the separation between performance evaluation and development, creating software platforms where information could be shared, and providing individuals with the resources to work successfully on their self-designed action plans.

Training internal coaches or hiring external coaching to support development are not the only ways of creating a coaching culture, and organizations may explore numerous options and alternative routes. They can decide to build informal coaching relationships between more and less experienced executives, to use peer groups to meet regularly and discuss their own worries, or to use external coaches (to name a few options). But the commitment of senior managers' support for employees' development and the creation of practices to make this commitment explicit are absolutely essential for getting the rest of the organization behind the initiative of enhancing a coaching attitude.

CONCLUSION

Our purpose in talking about authentizotic organizations and the use of coaching practices has been to infuse the management field with some hope and vision. Imagining better places to work, and how coaching practices in all their forms constitute a powerful organizational tool to accomplish this task, has guided us in this creative process. In this chapter, I have taken coaching as a tool for both individual and organizational development. As the cases demonstrate, while providing guidance, confidence, and social support to executives throughout their professional career, coaching can also become the skeletal structure on which a healthy organizational culture flourishes and develops.

My fellow contributors to this book and I want to promote our firm belief that it is possible to wake up in the morning and look forward to going to work. We want to challenge the human tendency to be pessimistic and defeatist when it comes to thinking about changing organizations for the better. Why is this? Leo Tolstoy wrote that "happy families are all alike, every unhappy family is unhappy in its own way."[16] People often find tales of unhappy families more interesting; human beings are seduced by drama and misfortune. Management literature has been devoted, in great measure, to wide-eyed observations of sickeningly heroic leaders that create anxiety and dysfunction in their surroundings. The great mythologist Joseph Campbell also noted the human tendency to see the world full of suffering and tragedy. It seems that many of us are unconvinced that it is possible to live a fun life with a happy ending. Happy tales are usually scorned as an oversimplification of human experiences. The main character of Mike Leigh's film *Happy-Go-Lucky* was created explicitly to caricaturize overoptimism and perversely enervate the audience, provoking us to admit that we can stand extraordinary happy people for a very short period of time before they get on our nerves. Consequently, it is much more difficult for many of us to imagine people living life in peace than tripping each other up. It is much easier to empathize with people who are facing problems than with people who do not have any, and with stories that deal with pain and misery rather than comedies.

The psychology and management literatures have also been influenced by this trend and have given all forms of pathology high priority in their research agendas. However, some scholars have recently counterattacked this tendency and have focused attention on positive psychology,[17] addressing issues such as happiness, meaning, and creativity at work. Following this trail, one of the objectives of this book—and this chapter in particular—was to focus on the bright side of management. For a change.

NOTES

1. Câpek, K. (1990). *War With the Newts*. Highland Park, NJ: Catbird Press (first published 1936).
2. Kets de Vries, M. F. R. (2006). *The Leader on the Couch: A Clinical Approach to Changing People and Organisations*. San Francisco: Jossey-Bass.
3. Ibid, p. 254.
4. Cooper, C., Scandura, T. A., and Schriesheim, C. A. (2005). "Looking Forward But Learning From our Past: Potential Challenges to Developing Authentic Leaders." *Leadership Quarterly*, 16, 475–613.
5. Baroja, P. (1968). *El Árbol de la Ciencia*. Madrid: Alianza Editorial.
6. Schein, E. H. (1992). *Organizational Culture and Leadership*. San Francisco: Jossey-Bass.
7. Gibson, D. E. (2003). "Developing the Professional Self-Concept: Role Model Construals in Early, Middle and Late Career Stages." *Organization Science*, 14(5): pp. 591–610.
8. Kets de Vries, M. F. R. and Korotov, K. (2007). "Creating Transformational Executive Education Programs." *Academy of Management Learning and Education*, 6(3): 375–387.
9. Hackman, J. R. and Wageman, R. (2007). "Asking the Right Question about Leadership." *American Psychologist*, 62(1), 43–47.
10. Kets de Vries, M. F. R. (2006). *The Leader on the Couch: A Clinical Approach to Changing People and Organizations*. San Francisco: Jossey-Bass.
11. Blass, F. R. and Ferris, G. R. (2007). "Leader Reputation: The Roles of Mentoring, Political Skill, Contextual Learning, and Adaptation." *Human Resource Management*, 45, 5–19; Higgins, M. C. and Kram, K. E. (2001). "Reconceptualizing Mentoring at Work: A Developmental Network Perspective." *Academy of Management Review*, 26, 264–288.
12. Korotov, K. (2008). "Peer Coaching in Executive Education Programmes." *Training & Management Development Methods*, 22(2): 3.15–3.24; Parker, P., Hall, D. T., and Kramer, K. E. (2008). "Peer Coaching: A Relational Process for Accelerating Career Learning." *Academy of Management Learning and Education*, 7(4), 487–503.
13. Guillén, L. and Ibarra, H. (2009). "Seasons of a Leader's Development: Beyond a One-Size Fits All Approach to Designing Interventions." *Best Paper Proceedings of the Academy of Management*, Chicago: Academy of Management.
14. Harrison, R. T., Leitch, C. M., Chia, R. (2007). "Developing Paradigmatic Awareness in University Business Schools: The Challenge for Executive Education." *Academy of Management Learning and Education*, 6(3), 332–343.
15. Hermans, H. J. M. and Oles, P. K. (1999). "Midlife Crisis in Men: Affective Organization of Personal Meanings." *Human Relations*, 52(11), 1403–1426.
16. Tolstoy, L. (1984). *Anna Karenina*. New York: Bantam Dell. (First published 1877).
17. Seligman, M. E. P. (2002). *Authentic Happiness: Using the New Positive Psychology to Realize your Potential for Lasting Fulfilment*. New York: The Free Press.

11

COACHING TEAMS FOR SUSTAINED, DESIRED CHANGE

RICHARD E. BOYATZIS

INTRODUCTION

Team development, like any sustained, desired change, is a multilevel phenomenon[1] and, therefore, coaching teams necessitates a deep understanding of the various parameters at work. This chapter focuses on the emotional aspects that drive the team toward a change process; it zeros in on the complexity of systems and discusses the "multileveledness" in which teams are socially embedded. Clearly team development can be viewed as an intentional change process.

To explore the forces that influence teams, intentional change theory (ICT)[2] is introduced as a way to help conceptualize how a coach decides how, when, and why to best intervene. Three major coaching interventions for team development are explained: (1) the importance of shared vision in developing and reminding the team of its purpose; (2) the importance of team identity to create emotional glue; and (3) the need for multiple levels of resonant leadership (and resonant coaches) for team development and performance to be sustained. Resonant relationships, in this context, mean those that are in tune with each other on many levels and are often characterized by shared vision/hope, compassion, and mindfulness.[3] These three factors establish and maintain team emotional and social intelligence (EI and SI, or E/SI), which support team development and sustained team performance.

EMOTIONAL ATTRACTORS

Our experiences invoke emotional and physiological states. These states determine the way we react, our thoughts, feelings, and behavior. Two of these possible states are fundamental to our functioning and performance: arousal of the positive emotional attractor and the negative emotional attractor. Thus it would be difficult, if not impossible, to understand team development without appreciating the influence of these two forces: the positive emotional attractor, or PEA, (which is composed of our hopes, dreams, possibilities, strengths and is indicated when the parasympathetic nervous system is aroused and related endocrines are in our blood) and the negative emotional attractor, or NEA, (which is composed of our fears, problems, defensiveness, shortfalls, pessimism and is indicated when the sympathetic nervous system is aroused and its related endocrines are secreted into the blood).

PEA pulls teams toward their shared vision or purpose, encouraging them to focus on future possibilities and experience hope as a group.[4] In this case, group members are capable of shared cognitive performance surpassing what occurs when they are in the NEA. They also feel proud, good about the group and excited about the future. Because they are able to be more perceptually and cognitively open, they are aware of their shared identity and dreams. This reduces stress, facilitates learning, increases the sustainability of the team,[5] and helps team members to adapt, innovate, and be resilient in difficult situations.

The good side of experiencing negative emotions is that they may force teams to reflect and explore alternative ways of acting. Without alternation between positive and negative emotions among the team members, no change occurs.[6] Thus in team development, the interplay of PEA and NEA may determine the potential and direction of the change process—both PEA and NEA can become destabilizing factors, either pulling the team toward a better sense of their shared vision, and a greater ability to learn, or in the other direction, toward defensive protection.

In the study of team change processes, the primary focus has been on the reduction of negative emotions rather than on how the experience of positive emotions is an essential component for improvement. The PEA opens the team and people within it to learning and adaptation. Thus positive emotions may modulate and deepen team development processes. In this chapter, I focus on how to coach, that is to facilitate or inspire PEA within team members. In the following section, I offer a coaching guide that can do this. It identifies team development as an intentional change process. Groups can be described as complex systems that move through phases of equilibrium and disequilibrium, tipping points between PEA and NEA states.

TEAM DEVELOPMENT AS INTENTIONAL CHANGE: A COACHING GUIDE

Some approaches to understanding group development, like the progressive models by Bennis and Sheppard,[7] the recursive models by Bion,[8] and morphing models,[9] have focused on the problems facing teams as they evolve. I take another angle, however, and propose that the team development process is predominantly teleological (focused on a specific end) and nonlinear. For example, if the relationship between team practice and team performance were linear, each team interaction session would be followed by a noticeable and predictable improvement in performance. But in reality, any team member knows that you may see no improvement over three sessions and then, in the fourth, everything comes together perfectly.

To be viable, a group needs to adopt new behaviors that help them to maintain the internal levels of trust and awareness that facilitate the change process. More specifically, the application of emotional and social intelligence to establish positive emotions and to pull the PEA among the team members is key to establishing a mindset that focuses on opportunities instead of fears, and curiosity instead of shame. Coaching practices that use these skills create the emotional glue among team members needed to sustain the team development process.

In group coaching, coach and clients work together to move closer to a desired future, by building on strengths and values and minimizing gaps or weaknesses. Furthermore, coaching is a helping profession, distinct from other helping roles, such as therapy, counseling, mentoring, teaching, management, consulting and so on, even though the boundaries can be fuzzy. Group coaching is unique in that the coach works with the clients, with less authority distance or power difference than in other forms of helping.

Also, in group coaching the coach may be an expert, but their role as a facilitator is primary. Coaches do, however, come to the coaching relationship with particular training that allow them to ask powerful questions and to listen intently to their clients. The coach and the team work together to arrive at a learning agenda—helping the team to build on its strengths and reduce the gap between where it is and where it wants to go. Many studies have shown that building on your strengths is more productive and success-enhancing than overcoming weaknesses and trying to learn something that is a struggle to you, or trying to be someone that you are not. Working with a coach provides individualized support in these areas, specific to the situation the clients find themselves in.

In the coaching conversations, groups usually come up with new ideas for action, things that they would like to try. This is the experimentation stage and clients try to practice these experiments in the "real world," doing something different in meetings, acting differently in the face of a stimulus, and so on. When the new action results in success, that is, it produces something that the client wants, the client will practice to mastery.

This entire change process unfolds supported by resonant relationships, which include the coach, and may also include partners, family, friends, work colleagues, and any significant other in the client's life, as the client chooses. The coach and the group work closely together to create the best possible scenario to help the team move closer to its desired future.

The process of sustained, desired change can be conceptualized as being part of the ICT, a term I use to illustrate a nonlinear, self-organizing model for team development. Clients typically come to coaching because they are dissatisfied with something that is going on currently—clients often have a vision of how they would prefer the situation to unfold and how they would rather be and act in that situation. Working with the coach, clients can define their desired situation more clearly. But even if clients have a pretty good handle on where they are or if they have a sense of their strengths and gaps, working with a coach can help them gain better insights into their values and strengths, which are the building blocks for coaching for a better team.

"Desired change" is something that a person or group would like to happen. It is not accidental or inevitable. It has features of sustainability, self-perpetuation, repeated reinvention, or replication. Sustainable, in this definition, means that the components do not atrophy or become exhausted during the change process. A desirable, sustainable change requires intentionality to happen or to be sustained.

Desired sustainable changes in a team's norms, shared beliefs, purpose, roles, and identity are, on the whole, discontinuous. That is, they often appear as dramatic changes that are experienced as a surprise or discovery. If team members learn to become more mindful of the group's dynamics, thanks to coaching interventions, changes may be anticipated and so appear more as a set of smooth transitions. For example, an observant team member may notice a particularly close, personal relationship developing among three team members and not be surprised when these three people begin to act toward team issues as a coalition (with the same perspective on issues). But to a less observant team member, the appearance of a coalition within the team may seem puzzling and sudden. As a complex system, team development has moments of surprise even for the most observant members or coaches.

To describe group coaching interventions, I will first use the concept of self-organizing and self-directed change to describe change as a dynamic process that is fueled by PEA and NEA, bringing balance and imbalance to the group change dynamics. More concretely, ICT proposes a sequence of discoveries that produce sustainable change by these specific attractors. Second, I will comment on the importance of the influence of the different social systems that influence the team. ICT predicts how the interrelationship across levels (individual, dyad, team, organization, etc.) enables people to become attuned to each other and maintain this attunement throughout the developmental process. Third, nonlinear and discontinuous dynamic systems include tipping points, which can illustrate how evolutionary patterns emerge throughout a team developmental process. Tipping points, as described in earlier chapters in this book, are moments where teams find that it's time for change.

THE FIVE INSIGHTS OF INTENTIONAL CHANGE THEORY

Team development involves a sequence of discoveries that function as an iterative cycle in producing sustainable change. In ICT, these discoveries are: (1) a shared vision (a shared image of the ideal team); (2) the norms and practices of the team that constitute its real team, and comparison to the ideal, resulting in an assessment of team strengths and weaknesses—in a sense, a team balance sheet; (3) a learning agenda and plan; (4) experimentation and practice with new behavior, thoughts, feelings, or perceptions; and (5) trusting or resonant relationships that enable members of a team to experience and process each discovery. An effective coaching intervention will involve the team in a reflection process that encourages enlightenment of these five discoveries (see Figure 11.1).

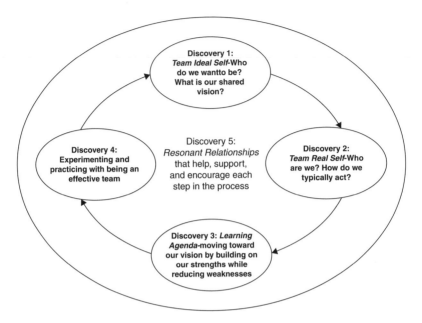

FIGURE 11.1 **Team Intentional Change Theory**

The first discovery and potential starting point for the process of team development is the discovery of what the group wants to be (the team's ideal self-image). The team's ideal, or shared vision appears to have three major components: (1) an image of a desired future; (2) hope that it is attainable; and (3) aspects of the team's core identity, which include enduring strengths on which they build for their desired future.[10] This team dream engages the power of positive imaging or visioning, which is well documented in sports psychology, meditation, biofeedback, and other psycho-physiological research.[11] Although purpose was at the heart of Bennis and Shepard's[12] theory of group development, in most work teams discussion of shared purpose is skipped. A positive vision may include the team seeing itself as high performing or successful, incorporating an important drive to outstanding performance.[13] The first discovery supports PEA.

The second discovery, the self-awareness of the team's norms and values and how others see them (the team's real self-image), is often elusive. At the team level, this has been labeled "group think." The greatest challenge to an accurate self-image is an open flow of evaluative information within the team, as well as between the team and the external environment. For example, one group norm that predicts lower learning in teams is the practice of not openly confronting internal conflicts, such as unequal contributions to the group's work.[14] Group EI helps to create team identity and relationships among team members.[15] The second discovery can be achieved by using multiple sources for feedback, such as climate surveys. Insights may also come from behavioral feedback (for example, video- or audio-taped interactions).

172

For teams to truly consider changing a part of themselves, they must have a sense of what they value and want to keep. Those areas in which their real and ideal self-images as a team are consistent or congruent can be considered strengths. Areas where these team self-images are inconsistent can be considered weaknesses. Acknowledging discrepancies between the team's real and ideal self-images can be a powerful motivator for change. Again, the team's real self-image is its view of how it acts, its norms and practices, and how its members relate to each other and with others outside the team. The team's ideal self-image is its shared dreams and aspirations for what the team might be and can become.

After identifying and comparing the team's real and ideal self-images, the third discovery that a coaching intervention may facilitate is the development of a team learning agenda, which focuses on development, exploration, and novelty. A learning orientation arouses a positive belief in our capability and the hope of improvement. It brings a team back into the realm of PEA. But coaching interventions at group level need to overcome at least two challenges at this point. First, there is often confusion about the team's ideal self and what can be termed the "ought self" (that is, the expectations of performance imposed by others often in supervisory positions with regard to the team). The "ought self" typically arouses NEA and diminishes performance, innovation, and adaptability. Second, all too often, teams explore growth or development by focusing on deficiencies, especially when survey scores are made public. Many team training programs, periodic reviews, and even coaching interventions often make the same mistake. What was intended to help a team develop, may in fact result in the team becoming stuck in an NEA state, feeling beleaguered, and neither helped nor encouraged. Thus invoking "ought self" expectations invokes anxiety and doubts about whether or not we can change.

The process of desired, sustainable change requires behavioral freedom and permission to try something new and see what happens. This permission comes from interaction with others, as the fourth and fifth ICT discoveries demonstrate. The fourth discovery is to promote active experimentation in safe environments and then practice desired changes. During this part of the process, intentional change looks like a continuous improvement process because it is actually cycling through ICT with increasing speed. For example, Dreyfus[16] studied managers of scientists and engineers who were considered superior performers. She pursued how they developed some of their distinguishing competencies, one of which was team building. She found that many of these middle-aged managers had first experimented with team-building skills in high school and college, in sports, clubs, and living groups. Later, when they became bench scientists and engineers working on problems in relative isolation, they still used and practiced this ability in activities outside work. They practiced team building and group management in social and community organizations, such as 4-H clubs, and professional associations in planning conferences and such—and then were able to bring these newly developed skills back into the workplace.

The fifth ICT discovery is about resonant relationships. Resonant relationships are characterized by a high level of emotional and social competencies. They are

173

an essential part of our environment. The most crucial relationships are often a part of social identity groups that give organizational participants a sense of identity, guide them about what is appropriate and good behavior, and provide feedback on behavior. The type of resonant relationships among group members I refer to here drives the team to change. One tipping point that is particularly relevant for group coaching interventions is the emergence of a new leader in a team.

For example, a study of the impact of the Professional Fellows Program at Case Western Reserve University's Weatherhead School of Management (a year-long executive development program for doctors, lawyers, professors, engineers, and other professionals) found that participants gained self-confidence during the program, illustrating the importance of accompanying development with personal relationships.[17] Although at the beginning of the program the participants were described by others as already having very high levels of self-confidence, the graduates of the program explained that the continued increase in self-confidence during and after the program was related to an increase in their confidence in their ability to change. Ironically, their existing social identity groups (family, groups at work, professional groups, community groups) had a vested interest in the participants' staying the same, which hindered individual participants' desire to change. The Professional Fellows Program allowed them to develop a new social identity group that encouraged change. This illustrates that belonging to (feeling a social identity with) a supportive team or group reduces stress and mitigates the effects of NEA.[18]

MULTIPLE LEVELS OF RESONANT LEADERS/COACHES

Sustained, desired change occurs at all levels of human and social organization. These levels are: individual; dyad or couple (including boss, subordinate relationships); team, group, or family; organization; community; country/culture; and global. A chain of resonant relationships that link desired change from the individual level to the community level is necessary to enable change. Positive emotions are contagious and can create a momentum for change that spreads quickly to other members in the team and to other social entities to which the team is related. If they are missing, team performance suffers and its ability to improve performance or sustain current performance is dramatically reduced. Resonant leadership does this between individuals, dyads, teams, organizations, and communities.

Leaders especially have a huge influence on emotional contagion that occurs from level to level. Thus the first degree of interaction between levels (individuals, teams, and organizations) is leadership. Much has been written about leaders trapped in endless cycles of stress and dissatisfaction, but leaders can also take advantage of empathetic and trusting relationships to encourage team openness, curiosity, and awareness at different levels. To illustrate this with a sports metaphor, ICT would claim that no sports team can succeed in sustainable performance improvement without a resonant leader within the team (see Figure 11.2).

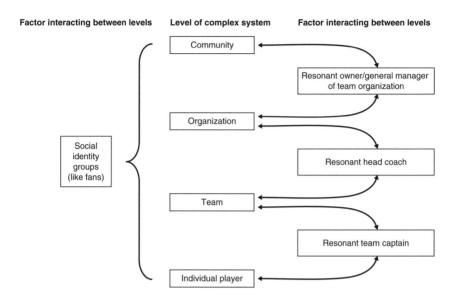

FIGURE 11.2 **Multilevel model of team development and the other role of leadership**

The team captain provides the emotional glue that keeps people working together. The captain is the link that fosters the contagion between individual and team levels and excites them about change. Meanwhile, the coach is the person who links the team and organization levels, with the organization often represented by the team management and ownership. The team owner or general manager has to move between the organization and the community, managing public relations, fans, and the political community.

EMOTIONAL AND SOCIAL INTELLIGENCE: A COACHING CHALLENGE

To establish resonant relationships, leaders and those around them need to employ emotional and social intelligence competencies to motivate their teams.[19] These behaviors enable leaders to get in tune with the group and maintain this attunement along development processes. Leadership works best when everyone is participating through collaborative and trusting relationships rather than through authority. This allows a communication flow that creates a more cooperative and productive environment.

Group coaching interventions can be a platform for practicing interpersonal and leadership competencies from which the entire team might benefit. People cannot be effective coaches without building resonant relationships with the teams and people they are coaching. They need to create safe and empathetic rela-tionships to allow emotions to be accessed and expressed. Here again, a balance of selected competencies from emotional, social, and cognitive intelligence clusters appears to be needed. EI and SI competencies are sets of behavior with an organizing, underlying intent that enable people to "manage their own emotions . . . and understand and manage the emotions of others and their relationship."[20] One EI competency that is crucial in coaching teams is emotional self-control, that is, controlling one's impulses or needs for the good of the group. Another is adaptability, being flexible in your approach to goals or others. An important SI competency for team coaches is empathy, understanding others. Others are influence, getting others to do what you want them to do, and inspirational leadership, creating a shared vision and team pride. The use of these competencies by coaches enables them to help a team develop its vision, identity, and multiple levels of team leaders.

COACHING FOR TEAM DEVELOPMENT

Hackman and Wageman defined team coaching as "direct interaction with a team intended to help members make coordinated and task-appropriate use of their collective resources in accomplishing the team's work."[21] Group coaching can be a path to renewal by incorporating mindfulness, hope, and compassion. One of the many things a coach can do to help a team develop is to draw attention to the emotional aspects that pull the team toward a change process and to the dynamics between multiple levels in which the team is socially embedded. These considerations point to three major coaching interventions that might be expected to be most effective.

Coaching a team toward a shared vision

Iterating or reiterating a shared vision can be a benefit at numerous stages in the team's evolution and development, not just at the beginning. The challenge is to provide a constant reminder of the purpose or context that drives the team's functioning. To help a team (and its members) develop, the coach should invoke PEA to maximize the team's openness, cognitive ability, and readiness to consider alternatives and new ideas. Helping a team develop a shared vision and purpose is a potent way to do this. There are many techniques to begin the exploration of a shared vision. For example, the coach could ask team members to explore:

- their shared values or philosophy;
- the stage of development or maturity of the team itself;
- the purpose (reason for existing, not merely team goals);
- the desired legacy or contribution to their organization and its mission; and/or
- dreams of what the team could become and do.

But a shared vision is just the beginning. The team must also explore and specify its goals and measures to ensure it meets performance expectations from those in authority. Exploring the shared vision and reminding everyone of it should be a continuous pursuit and a key element of every meeting.

Appreciative inquiry[22] is another technique that can help build shared vision. Using this technique, a coach asks the team members to remember:

- a time when they felt proud to be a part of the team; and
- a time when the team was at its best.

The coach can then ask team members to form trios and share their stories of these moments. Once that task is complete, the entire team shares observations from these trio discussions. The themes emerging from these discussions become key elements in the shared vision. This process is a powerful arousal of PEA and energizes a team to move ahead into discussions of strategy, goals, and tasks.

Coaching a team identity

Moving toward a shared team identity can also be a trigger for development. Identity refers to the various meanings attached to a person by "self" and "others." The team members' sense of "who" and "what" they are can be called their shared identity and embodies the dreams, sense of distinctiveness, purpose, beliefs, values, and experiences through which a team defines itself. In this way, identity is close to shared vision and may emerge from the same exercises. But teams can also explore their identity through metaphors and symbols that make aspects of their self-concept overt.

Many of the techniques I discussed in the section on establishing a shared vision will also help a team develop a shared identity. By recounting proud moments, and discussing values and purpose, members of a team create an awareness of the shared elements of identity that excite them. Leaders sensitive to this use success stories as evidence of group effectiveness to counterbalance difficult tasks, overcome obstacles, set a new standard of performance, innovate, or create something new. Such leaders may even create symbols, such as baseball caps, jackets, medals, or posters, to strengthen the symbolic value of the event or accomplishment.

Once an identity is established and shared, the team can become a social identity group for its members. A social identity group helps its current and aspiring members to find a sense of belonging and shared beliefs. They share a sense of what they are, and what defines them. Social identity groups are vehicles for moving information, emotion, and relationships across levels of the complex system within which the team exists. To illustrate, the emergence of groups of faithful fans of sports teams, bands, television shows, or movies can be described as the emotional bonding of strangers. They are brought together because of a commitment and belief in a sports team, like Manchester United, or their love of a group, like the Grateful Dead, or a fantasy in the form of a TV show, like the Trekkies, fans of *Star Trek*, who created a force that brought the television show back into prime time in the US, and then launched four sequel series, 11 movies, an animated cartoon series, and myriad other media vehicles.[23] Social identity groups often display their distinctiveness proudly in the clothes they wear, photos in their homes and offices, and talk about it often in social settings—ask any football fan how their team is doing.

Thus team development is facilitated by the emergence of a social identity group or the incorporation of elements that enrich the identity of the existing team. For example, there was a poignant moment in the emergence of the 1980 US Olympic gold medal winning hockey team when individual members began to introduce themselves to others not as players from their hometown or college team but as members of Team USA. This was the signal Herb Brooks, the coach, was waiting for: they had begun to see themselves as a team and a group to which they wanted to belong.[24]

Coaching multiple levels of resonant team leaders

Helping a team leader move emotions and relationships across levels requires a deep, emotional intervention with the leader and possibly the team. Leaders' moods affect the team's mood. In the same way, when coaches build resonant relationships they affect the mood of the team—positively or negatively, sometimes in a quasi-therapeutic way.[25]

Teams need leaders, both formal and informal. They need leaders within the team to create purpose and excitement and provide social glue. They need leaders outside the team to help communicate and link across levels, as I discussed earlier in this chapter, a task that Hackman[26] called "bracketing." Team researchers, such as Hackman and Wageman,[27] even contend that many teams need rotating leaders for leadership development purposes, a feeling of equality within the team, and shared responsibility for team norms and performance.

Resonant leaders are able to build trusting, engaged, and energizing relationships with others around them. Just as teams need resonant or effective leaders to perform and develop, and multiple resonant leaders to function across the multilevel system within which they operate, it is also clear that teams need coaches who are resonant and can help move information, emotions, and relationships across levels. The leaders can be the coaches, but it is likely that the team needs both resonant leaders and coaches. If the team has no resonant leadership, it is adrift in many ways. Dissonance can become its modus operandi. Then the team begins to dissolve.

CONCLUSION

Sustainability of desired change in teams is the key to effective change. Without intentionally maintaining desired team development, atrophy, entropy, and dissonance will dissolve the progress and may even return the team to a less desirable condition than the one it was in when it started the change process. Intentional change theory and a variety of concepts from complexity theory help us to understand what is occurring, when, and why it occurs. Concepts like the emergence of leaders, the pull of attractors, and the multiple levels involved light the path to sustainability. Coaching team development can involve many activities, but from this perspective three of the most potent interventions would be to help the team develop a shared vision, shared identity, and the multiple resonant leaders needed at various levels within their system.

NOTES

1. Hackman, R. (2003). "Learning More by Crossing Levels: Evidence from Airplanes, Hospitals, and Orchestras." *Journal of Organizational Behavior*, 24, 905–922.
2. Boyatzis, R. E. (2006a). "Intentional Change Theory from a Complexity Perspective." *Journal of Management Development*, 25(7), 607–623.
3. Boyatzis, R. E. and McKee, A. (2005). *Resonant Leadership: Renewing Yourself and Connecting with Others Through Mindfulness, Hope, and Compassion*. Boston: Harvard Business School Press.
4. Boyatzis, R. E., Smith, M., and Blaize, N. (2006). "Developing Sustainable Leaders through Coaching and Compassion." *Academy of Management Journal on Learning and Education*, 5(1), 8–24.
5. Haslam, S. A. and Reicher, S. (2006). "Stressing the Group: Social Identity and the Unfolding Dynamics of Response to Stress." *Journal of Applied Psychology*, 91(5), 1037–1052.
6. Howard, A. (2006). "Positive and Negative Attractors and Intentional Change." *Journal of Management Development*, 25(7), 657–670.
7. Bennis, W. G. and Shepard, H. A. (1956). "A Theory of Group Development." *Human Relations*, 9, 415–437.
8. Bion, W. R. (1961). *Experiences in Groups*. New York: Basic Books.
9. Bales, R. F. (1970). *Personality and Interpersonal Behavior*. New York: Holt Rinehardt and Winston.
10. Boyatzis, R. E. and Akrivou, K. (2006). "The Ideal Self as a Driver of Change." *Journal of Management Development*, 25(7), 624–642.
11. Goleman, D., Boyatzis, R. E., and McKee, A. (2002). *Primal Leadership: Realizing the Power of Emotional Intelligence*. Boston: Harvard Business School Press.
12. Bennis, W. G. and Shepard, H. A. (1956). "A Theory of Group Development." *Human Relations*, 9, 415–437.
13. Hackman, R. and Wageman, R. (2005). A Theory of Team Coaching." *Academy of Management Review*, 30(2), 269–287.
14. Druskat, V. U. and Kayes, D. C. (2000). "Learning Versus Performance in Short-Term Project Teams." *Small Group Research*, 31(3), 328–353.
15. Wolff, S. B., Pescosolido, A. T., and Druskat, V. U. (2002). "Emotional Intelligence as the Basis of Leadership Emergence in Self-Managing Teams." *Leadership Quarterly*, 13(5), 505–522.
16. Dreyfus, C. (2008). "Identifying Competencies that Predict Effectiveness of R&D Managers." *Journal of Management Development*, 27(1), 76–91.
17. Ballou, R., Bowers, D., Boyatzis, R. E., and Kolb, D. A. (1999). "Fellowship in Lifelong Learning: An Executive Development Program for Advanced Professionals." *Journal of Management Education*, 23(4), 338–354.
18. Haslam, S.A. and Reicher, S. (2006). "Stressing the Group: Social Identity and the Unfolding Dynamics of Response to Stress." *Journal of Applied Psychology*, 91(5), 1037–1052.
19. Goleman, D., Boyatzis, R. E. and McKee, A. (2002). *Primal Leadership: Realizing the Power of Emotional Intelligence*. Boston: Harvard Business School Press; Boyatzis, R. E. and McKee, A. (2005). *Resonant Leadership: Renewing Yourself and Connecting with Others Through Mindfulness, Hope, and Compassion*. Boston: Harvard Business School Press.

20. Boyatzis, R. E. (2009). "A Behavioral Approach to Emotional Intelligence." *Journal of Management Development*, 28, 9, 749–770.
21. Hackman, R. and Wageman, R. (2005). "A Theory of Team Coaching." *Academy of Management Review*, 30(2), 269.
22. Cooperrider, D. and Whitney, D. (2005). *Appreciative Inquiry: A Positive Revolution in Change*. NY: Berrett-Koehler.
23. Neo Art and Logic Production (1999, 2004). *Trekkies* and *Trekkies 2*, DVDs distributed by Paramount Classics.
24. O'Connor, G. (2004). *Miracle: The DVD (with the supplementary interview with Coach Herb Brooks)*, Disney Entertainment.
25. Kets De Vries, M., Korotov, K., and Florent-Treacy, E. (2007). *Coach and Couch: The Psychology of Making Better Leaders*. London: Palgrave Macmillan.
26. Hackman, R. (2003). "Learning More by Crossing Levels: Evidence from Airplanes, Hospitals, and Orchestras." *Journal of Organizational Behavior*, 24, 905–922.
27. Hackman, R. and Wageman, R. (2005). "A Theory of Team Coaching." *Academy of Management Review*, 30(2), 269–287.

12

CONNECTING THE SCIENCE OF MANAGEMENT SYSTEMS WITH THE CLINICAL PARADIGM

CHRISTOPH LOCH

The clinical paradigm of psychology, as described in Chapter 2, seeks an integrated understanding of a person's motivation that incorporates biological "need systems" (such as physiological needs, security, sensual needs, and attachment needs) as well as the effect of the individual's environment—in particular, important interactions with other people, including childhood experiences. The premise is that there is a rationale behind every human act, even those that are apparently irrational, but that this rationale (stemming from thoughts, feelings, and motives) is not entirely conscious.[1] In short, the clinical paradigm focuses on understanding the *individual*.

The management discipline, in contrast, examines *systemic collective action* in organizations. How can the organization induce its members (with all their individual differences) to behave consistently in a way that allows the organization to succeed and profit? Management focuses on processes, incentives, shared knowledge, and culture, all of which are systems that unite people in collective behavior and de-emphasize individual idiosyncrasy.

These two areas of study have not interacted much, but each holds a part of the key to understanding organizational performance. Clinical psychology helps individuals to become effective, but that in itself does not solve an organization's performance problems. (Similarly, hiring only creative people does not guarantee a creative organization; the trick in making an organization creative lies in using collective processes to enable its "normal" members to release their own creativity.) On the other hand, management theory helps in the setting up of organizational routines that coordinate the behavior of *groups*. It has no answers for *individual* dysfunctionality; anecdotes abound about powerful managers who single-handedly lead an organization astray, throw its routines into disarray, or de-motivate its people.

The clinical approach is not widely accepted among management practitioners. It may be fashionable for managers to have a coach, but does this express a genuine understanding of the clinical approach or the mere pursuit of self-importance? In this chapter, I offer arguments for why the clinical approach should indeed be introduced into management science and show where and how the two approaches can be fruitfully combined, as well as the potential benefits. Toward these ends, I first give a brief overview of three fundamental themes in the management discipline, followed by a brief introduction to the clinical paradigm. I then outline where the two approaches can complement each other.

I argue that the clinical paradigm can help improve management processes in at least three ways: leadership group coaching can help top management teams to become more functional; individual coaching can help employees in middle management roles to resist stress and overcome performance limitations; psychology can be introduced into business process design efforts, improving the track record of change management; and the clinical approach can help individuals to identify both hidden personal relational conflicts and half-conscious motives for resisting a change in behavior.

THE MANAGEMENT SYSTEMS VIEW

It is still acceptable for managers to view psychological support and intervention as a luxury: a benefit for sensitive employees when funds are available but a mere distraction to be pushed aside during lean times. If we want to introduce the clinical paradigm into management, we must explain its benefits in management terms; hence this section offers a short introduction to three fundamental management themes.

The management discipline is concerned with the laws that govern the behaviors of organizations—for example, the economic laws of performance, the sociological laws of cooperation in large groups, and the physical laws of the transformation of materials and information into goods and services. Figure 12.1 describes three fundamental themes of management science that have a considerable effect on an organization's performance: the *strategic position* that the organization occupies in its competitive market space; the organization's *execution effectiveness*, or the ability to translate its strategic priorities into consistent and advantageous actions; and the organization's ability to *change* in response to changes in its environment. I shall briefly describe each in turn.

The strategy system

A key performance driver is the organization's strategic position. This allows it to thrive in a hostile environment, to occupy the central zone in Figure 12.1, even though surrounded by the dangers of hostile winds (trends), predators (competitors), fires (customer fickleness), and corpses (acquired companies).

The strategy is a battle plan that gives the organization clear guidelines (high-level directions and priorities) on how to best their competitors and "conquer" the customer's preference. Having a battle plan requires clarity on four questions.[2] *What* is the organization's market offering? *Who* are the customers: what are their characteristics (income, tastes) and whose example do they follow? *Why*

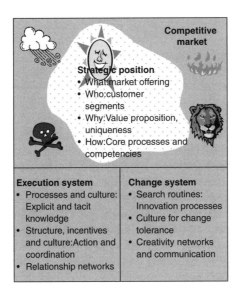

Competitive market

Strategic position
- What: market offering
- Who: customer segments
- Why: Value proposition, uniqueness
- How: Core processes and competencies

Execution system
- Processes and culture: Explicit and tacit knowledge
- Structure, incentives and culture: Action and coordination
- Relationship networks

Change system
- Search routines: Innovation processes
- Culture for change tolerance
- Creativity networks and communication

FIGURE 12.1 **A management systems view of the organization**

should a customer buy from this organization (i.e., what is its value proposition) and not from another? *How* can the value be delivered—in other words, what are the core processes (activities) and competencies (knowledge) that enable the organization to provide its particular value?

It sounds like straightforward common sense that an organization should have a battle plan (whether it is explained in these terms or differently). But it is surprisingly hard to have a good plan *and* to live by it. Company A has a brilliant boss who intuitively holds a great strategic position, but no one else understands it and the boss cannot explain it. In company B, there are several competing versions of a battle plan and different players in the organization fight over whose version will win, which may cripple the organization's ability to act. Company C, a large organization, has a "strategy department" that develops battle plans according to the latest rocket science from the hottest textbooks—but it never manages to connect those plans to the reality of line executives, who then fail to follow them. And some (smaller) organizations may simply happen upon a favorable competitive position without knowing why it occurred and how it works (the market may have turned in their direction, or perhaps an advantage was "inherited" from decisions made by a previous generation of managers).

A strategy serves as a coordinating device that helps the various parts of an organization act consistently. A strategy that unites an organization can have powerful effects even if the strategy itself is not "smarter" than other organizations. The ability of an entire organization to pull together is, in itself, powerful. Strategies are useless without the organization's actions, which are driven by the execution and change systems.[3]

183

The execution system

The execution system includes all sources of knowledge and mechanisms of action available in the organization. Knowledge resides in explicit form in the organization's *routines and processes* and in its decision rules[4]—for instance, in the way strategy is formally deployed, the supply chain is organized, investment proposals are judged, and personnel are developed.

Knowledge also resides in tacit form in the organization's *culture*: the collection of its values and beliefs.[5] For example, in one organization the R&D engineers know that, "of course," one must check with colleagues before freezing a component design into prototype form; in another organization, the engineers know that, "of course," one must get the boss's approval before freezing a component into prototype form. At business school A, professors know that research published in journal X is better, while the professors at business school B know (with equal certainty) that research published in journal Y is better. Different values and beliefs enable organizations to do certain things but can be a hindrance in other areas. Values and beliefs are not "decided" by anyone; rather, they evolve by trial and error through social processes in the organization.

In the end, the organization makes decisions, sets priorities, and allocates resources under the influence of explicit processes and implicit cultural habits. Knowledge is filtered through formal structures, which define responsibilities, resource ownership, and reporting relationships, and also through incentive systems, which encourage desired actions by rewarding them. Typical rewards include money, promotion, and/or public praise (e.g., an employee of the month award).

Culture influences action, often tacitly, by defining "how things are done here" and by shaping not only what motivates people but also the extent to which they feel accountable to one another (e.g., by emphasizing group solidarity, or relationship reciprocity, or simply economic transactions). People are also influenced by their relationship networks. Thus I consider the wishes of friends more than those of strangers (or enemies), and I pay more attention to information, or innovation opportunities, that are brought to me by friends than by others. Management can shape these networks—for example, by job rotation, mutual benchmarking visits, and internal conferences and training.[6] Finally, culture also influences how much the members of an organization identify with it, whether they have a feeling of "us" (versus "them" in that company over there), and whether they will commit to mutual trust and acts of solidarity. Management of the organization influences culture over time by giving consistent messages (backed up by action), enforcing certain standards of behavior, and leading by example.

The change system

No strategy, no matter how brilliant, lasts forever because the environment rarely remains stable for more than half a decade, so the execution system and often the battle plan, too, must change. This is difficult because the organization, as a system, consists of many partially decentralized parts (such as functional departments, product lines, geographic regions, project organizations) that interact. For example, if the production facility wants to introduce a new process technology and material, then product development must redesign the parts and field service must change its maintenance and replacement processes and criteria. Complex interactive systems possess inertia, which is exacerbated by the well-known tendency of employees to prefer the status quo for many reasons: risk aversion, complacency, or lack of trust in management's good intentions.

Therefore, organizations that perform well over long periods of time tend to have mechanisms that enable and promote change. This includes formal processes that search for improvements over current routines and the current position: examples are technology scanning processes, road maps, product development processes (e.g., the "stage gate" process), process development processes, Six Sigma initiatives for continuous improvement, and many more.

Again, explicit routines are accompanied in some way by a culture, one that may be conservative and discourages change, or one that actually welcomes change. A culture may encourage change in several different ways: making role models of those who have changed their surroundings, showing tolerance of risk taking and some forms of failure, bluntly ordering from the top, "Change, or else." An interesting, if extreme, example of the latter is Microsoft, which found itself behind the curve when, in 1994, the World Wide Web suddenly came to prominence. Bill Gates essentially ordered his organization to drop everything else, putting thousands of people and hundreds of millions of dollars behind his order; this allowed Microsoft to offer a competing product (Explorer) within a year.

Such purely top-down change is rare, because the best ideas do not usually come from the top. New ideas and changes often emerge through (internal and external) networks of information exchange combined with organizational "experimentation spaces," which take the form of some extra time, budget, or other types of unassigned resources—as well as some allowance for failure without being judged. Such networks and spaces can be provided by managerially determined structures.[7]

THE MANAGEMENT SYSTEM VIEW: ROLES, NOT INDIVIDUALS

So far, I have briefly described three management systems that help organizations to perform: strategy, execution, and change. Two lessons leap out. The first, discouragingly, is that effective senior managers apparently need to be superheroes. They must be more than analysts who can deduce a battle plan from a hardheaded industry analysis; they must also be "clock makers" who are able to shape an intricate system of interlocking procedures and incentives, processing pieces that must work smoothly together without smashing one another to bits. Moreover, managers must also be orators and role models who can shape action by subtly biasing people's standards, convictions, and moods. And if that were not enough, a top manager must be able to orchestrate a network of artistic idea generators who produce ideas that the orchestrator may not even understand; and these ideas must be shepherded into evaluation and then implementation, so that the clockwork system of the organization can evolve over time.

But do not despair. We can, once again, exclude the tyranny of the individual by devising personnel development plans that encompass education and recruitment, socialization, leadership and cross-cultural training, job rotation, and leadership development. These approaches are designed to produce, in the end, the heroes needed to make the organization behave.

The second lesson is that the management sciences have amassed evidence suggesting that organizations have a better chance of performing well if the systems of strategy, execution, and change processes are well designed—that is, if the components of these systems function reliably and if they fit together and reinforce one another. Someone has to chat up the customer, no matter who has flu or who is currently being mobbed by other people. No matter how different the people in an organization, certain roles must be filled and certain problems solved. The organization goes beyond the individual; indeed, those who insist on being "too individualistic" become enemies of the organization's functioning. This is Weber's view of the perfect bureaucracy.

Adding a psychological view of individual personalities

The management systems view is quite broad and flexible. It has, over time, developed to encompass not only economic drivers but also formal decisions, work flow, and incentive systems as well as informal influences from the culture of the organizations, the networks that spread information, and the systemic and shared emotional needs of people (e.g., fairness, recognition, and belonging). Thus the management systems view explicitly includes people but simultaneously avoids individual personalities. People and their desires, errors, and needs are included as categories but not as individuals. Even when people are viewed in the context of processes or incentive systems, we look at them as sociological "masses"; organizational psychologists consider "typical" needs of people and "typical" decision biases. The individual personality is rarely acknowledged.

There are many reasons for this. First, considering people *qua* individuals would throw sand into the gears of the system, as I discussed earlier. The organization designer with a management systems view does not want individuals to have a strong influence on system behavior or performance. On the contrary, the organization seeks to be robust and so needs "replaceable" individuals (we cannot be held hostage by one person who could leave, encounter a personal crisis, or otherwise become nonperforming). Therefore, such systems are indeed designed to function on the basis of roles rather than individual heroism.

186

Second, besides being inconvenient, individual differences (when averaged) tend to wash out in an organization with many people. The lone individual is seen as too inconsequential to make a difference; what counts are the aggregated behaviors and needs of the population. For example, we talk of risk aversion as applying to an (averaged) category, not to a given individual's attitude.

But this view is, of course, incomplete: it fails to accommodate not only a bit of noise but some large effects as well. Even if the effects of different personalities do wash out in large organizations, many endeavors and change processes still involve critical interactions with individuals who might speak for, or be central to, an informal network and whose personalities matter crucially. Process rules shape decisions in many routine situations, but no process can foresee all exceptions. It is at these exceptional moments when individuals really matter.

Moreover, as one approaches the top of an organization, the personalities of the leaders become more important. (An old idiom expresses this negatively as "a fish rots from the head down.") Senior managers have a large impact on their organizations because they have many degrees of freedom, their decisions are too unstructured to be ruled by procedures, they have themselves set up the organization's processes and incentive systems, and they are the role models after whom many junior employees fashion their own behavior. To ignore the personalities of senior people is to risk misunderstanding important aspects of an organization's dynamics. As a consequence, the management systems view should be combined with a psychological view of the individual (see Figure 12.2).

Although individuals influence management systems in important ways at crucial moments, the counter argument is that personalities do not develop randomly but are rather influenced, in turn, by the management systems. First, selection is at work: only certain types of people make it to the top (we like to believe they are the most capable, ethical, and flexible ones). Second, the organization's culture unifies behavior: once a person has internalized the organization's values and norms, there is less room for individual deviation. Third, conditioning further limits aberrations—for example, the internalized fear of sanctions following certain behavior (such as cheating or taking a reckless risk) will inhibit such behavior.

This is known to be true: there is a feedback loop of influence between management culture (and systems) and the individual behavior of people in the organization. However, personalities are not actually formed during the time employees work in the organization; people bring their individual characters and life experiences to the job. Personalities are not determined by the organizational culture. The more exceptional the situation (when the processes and culture do not have routine action recipes available) and the more powerful the person (as with one who "stands above" the processes and culture), the more important it becomes to understand why an individual behaves in certain ways. A leader who

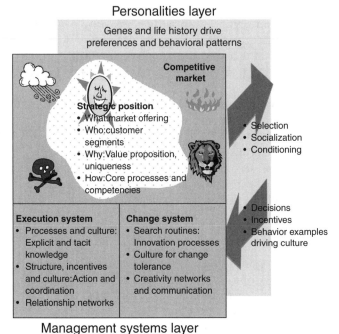

Personalities layer

Genes and life history drive
preferences and behavioral patterns

Competitive market

Strategic position
- What:market offering
- Who:customer segments
- Why:Value proposition, uniqueness
- How:Core processes and competencies

- Selection
- Socialization
- Conditioning

- Decisions
- Incentives
- Behavior examples driving culture

Execution system
- Processes and culture: Explicit and tacit knowledge
- Structure, incentives and culture:Action and coordination
- Relationship networks

Change system
- Search routines: Innovation processes
- Culture for change tolerance
- Creativity networks and communication

Management systems layer

FIGURE 12.2 **A management systems view that accommodates individual personalities**

is (say) narcissistic, controlling, or paranoid will skew decisions and radiate poor behavior examples into the organization.[8]

The systems view of the organization—in which people are seen only in terms of the roles that they play, or perhaps as archetypical categories that have certain "biases" and "psychological needs"—does not offer ways to understand the behavior of individual leaders. Conversely, the pure psychoanalytic view misses the organization's system aspects. The organization is not simply an expression of the personalities of the leadership team; assigning several smart people to a department does not yield a smart department if, say, current group processes set those people up for runaway arguments without any external correctives. The organization's systems and culture do indeed partially socialize people into functioning appropriately irrespective of who happens to hold the job.

These observations imply that each approach, management and clinical, holds an important clue to understanding an organization but that both approaches are required to gain a full understanding. Thus we need a marriage of the two views. When is it accurate to describe the organization as a system populated by "roles" rather than individuals? When should we apply a clinical approach to examine the possibly hidden motives of individual leaders? I turn to these questions in the rest of this chapter.

INTEGRATING THE CLINICAL APPROACH AND THE MANAGEMENT SYSTEMS VIEW

What the clinical approach can offer

My aim is to propose a few ways in which an organization might integrate individual clinical psychology into its systemic procedures and culture. An anecdote illustrates what such integration could mean. A few years ago, one office of a large management consulting firm employed a brilliant senior partner capable of providing relevant, elegant solutions and of building relationships with clients. However, he tended to be rough with his internal teams: he pushed them too hard, he was nasty and dismissive, and he had burned out several consultants. The office manager reacted by reducing the senior partner's bonus, requiring him to undergo "team leadership" training and insisting that his team management behavior needed to be supervised for a certain period. In response to this (individualized) approach, the errant partner's behavior changed markedly. He began to treat even junior consultants with respect; when he pushed the team hard, he now gave an explanation (in terms of client and project needs) and a target for when the high-pressure period would end; he solicited opinions from all team members in team meetings; and he even learned how to induce junior consultants to participate, think more broadly, and develop themselves.

This senior partner was able to transform himself into a more effective leader by changing his behavior. He could do so because the problem was explained to him and he was motivated to correct it (the reduced bonus was a strong indication that the need for change was serious; the signal worked, although it certainly did not make him poor). As for the cause of his destructive behavior, was it lack of knowledge, undeveloped emotional intelligence, or heavy baggage he carried from childhood? We do not know, but in fact he accomplished the change without psychotherapy; change occurred simply as the result of understanding the behavioral problem and mustering (with help) the urgency to make an effort. Some leaders, of course, carry such heavy emotional baggage that coaching or therapy is a prerequisite of accomplishing a change in behavior.

This anecdote holds two important lessons for bringing the clinical paradigm into management systems. First, the process cannot be about making everyone conform to personality standards that are used to define the ideal leader or team member. For example, the senior partner in this anecdote was, and remained, an introvert who did not excite his teams with charisma. He was effective in his own way. Of course, the organization needs certain roles fulfilled and certain requirements met. A leader must be able to articulate a direction, engage with subordinates, apply fair process, give feedback, and follow up. A team needs an ideas generator, an organizer, a planner, one or more experts, a finisher, social "glue," an external networker, and a decider.[9] But none of these roles requires specific personalities: many personalities can fill a given role, each in its different way. The contribution the clinical approach can make is to identify (a) the strengths of an individual, which should be used and reinforced in his or her role; and (b) the weaknesses of an individual, which might be mitigated by self-development, help from others, and/or delegation of responsibilities. The clinical approach helps executives understand and leverage their strengths and minimize their weaknesses.

Second, our anecdote illustrates that the solution to bringing individual psychology into management systems is not to force everyone through therapy (this caricature of psychoanalysis is nothing but a straw man for lazy critics). What is needed is enough of the clinical approach to look beyond the roles and official self-serving statements of managers and to diagnose those who, for some reason, are not effective. Then, the clinical approach helps to find the reasons and take appropriate measures. It may turn out that solution measures fall within standard management systems—for example, a structure change that ensures certain information flows and resource availability. But the solutions may also lie in the psychology of the individuals involved. In these cases, psychoanalytical tools can be applied to recommend measures that improve the management system and behavior within it.

Psychological researchers have developed a range of tools that can be used to assess and understand an individual within the context of an organization. There is not enough space in this chapter to elaborate on all of them, but a few important tools are listed here.

- Individual assessment with formal tools, such as an emotional intelligence inventory or a 360-degree feedback tool with personality and leadership styles frameworks.
- Identification of core conflictual relational themes (CCRTs) in the individual's behavior that is used to study recurrent relationship patterns and identification of hidden competing commitments, for example, goals that a person clings to, perhaps unconsciously, based on memories of long-past events where the failure to fulfill the commitment led to bad consequences.[10]
- Personal background analysis, such as family genograms.
- Role analysis: identifying gaps or weaknesses in how individuals perform in their roles.
- Coaching: a helping relationship between a manager and a coach who uses behavioral techniques, in accordance with a coaching agreement, to help the client manager improve his or her professional performance and personal satisfaction.[11]

In the next section, I illustrate applications of these tools to the three themes of the management paradigm (strategy, execution, and change systems) in complementary ways that can enrich our understanding of an organization.

THREE APPLICATIONS OF THE CLINICAL APPROACH IN MANAGEMENT SYSTEMS

Applications of the clinical paradigm in the strategy system

I have already pointed out that the top management team is where personalities matter most, because it is here that individuals are the least constrained and the most influential. The following anecdote may illustrate this point. Several years ago, I held a workshop with a consultant to help him develop a method for managing the portfolio of a company's strategic R&D initiatives. This consultant sought an automated procedure (algorithm), but I argued that automation is not possible for key strategic decisions, such as selecting innovation initiatives. At best, a tool can facilitate a common understanding and offer a basis for a decisive discussion within the top management team; no tool can relieve the team of its responsibility to make the decision in the light of ambiguity, incomplete information, and conflicts of interest. Yet the consultant insisted: "The CEO office members of my client do not want an intelligent discussion; they don't need the best possible decision. Each of the individuals has worked very hard to get into this position because they like to be right (and tell others what to do), and if there is a real content discussion, then each fears he might be proved wrong. And he has no interest in that happening. Therefore, they want an algorithm that chooses initiatives, because then, the algorithm decides, and no one is right and no one wrong." I declined to collaborate further on this initiative because no incentives, structures, or processes could possibly overcome such flawed decision-making attitudes.

Unfortunately, such (or worse) dysfunctional top management teams are more common than one might expect, and they can have severe effects on the organization. Under these circumstances a group coaching intervention may be the best way to help the organization, one in which tensions among members and/or individual dysfunctionalities are brought into the open and worked out. We should also consider the other extreme: the conscientious CEO who is all too aware of the crushing responsibility and exhausting workload that may leave him estranged from any support network. Such a person may slide into a negative spiral, since CEOs are frequently alone and often have no one they can trust or talk to. Indeed, one such CEO (of a successful small financial institution) recently committed suicide, a desperate act that no one had foreseen.

Group coaching interventions in top management are difficult, prone to explosions, and require extensive coaching experience. However, they are certainly possible (if management decides that they need to make a change) and have been amply documented.[12] An intervention that works well can create a large improvement in the functioning of top management, which is obviously of great value to the organization.

It is interesting to speculate on how feedback to the organization's top management could be made "systematic"; after all, it is in the management system's interest to remain robust against any damage that could result from unconstrained idiosyncrasies. Regular assessment of leadership behavior would enable an organization to articulate the responsibilities of leaders and build a culture of consistent leadership over time. Executives are measured in terms of their business performance, so why not also in terms of their leadership behavior?

Such assessment of senior managers is still the exception, as far as I know. However, I have seen one example of an effective articulation of leadership culture—with measurability and bite because it can be used to hold top managers accountable for their behavior. The company is a European power-tool manufacturer that has made four core values explicit and measurable: integrity, regularly breaking old habits, teamwork, and pursuing both company and personal growth. Every manager has been trained in those values (representing a large investment), and senior managers are accountable for (and measured in terms of) exhibiting them on a daily basis. Leadership according to these values has become the main determinant of career progress in this company.

Applications of the clinical paradigm in the execution system

By their very nature, clinical methods do not contribute to the clockwork of processes and operational routines. Nonetheless the clinical approach—in particular, coaching—can still contribute to the performance of individual employees. Consider an investment bank in France that offers its overworked-to-exhaustion professionals a coaching service. The coach helped several employees regain their sense of control ("I have chosen this lifestyle because of the financial benefits and intellectual challenge, and when it becomes too much, I can decide to make a change"), to identify and safeguard havens of personal privacy ("Saturday morning is for my son"), and to negotiate real or perceived gender conflicts. No processes and structures changed, but employees' coping abilities improved.

Clinical psychology has another important contribution to make to the execution system. Performance evaluations are becoming more widespread; they are no longer based solely on technical outcomes and now also assess team building and leadership behavior. Whenever performance is measured seriously, some managers are identified as underperforming and are either demoted or removed. However, a performance appraisal system judges behaviors and outcomes, not the underlying reasons for an individual's behavior. Thus an evaluation might state that a manager "did not achieve the numbers" and/or "did not motivate and develop his/her team." The implicit assumption is that low performance is due to a lack of ability (insufficient mental or emotional intelligence).

However, the reasons for an individual's low performance may well lie not in a lack of ability but rather in specific psychological blocks that prevent that person from performing. If the blocks were removed, the individual could perform at a high level. This is a win-win scenario because it avoids traumatizing the employee by moving him/her aside and ensures the retention of someone in whom the organization has invested.

Examples of psychological blocks include a CCRT, transference, hidden competing commitments[13] and other subtle, half-conscious fears that prevent an individual from effectively engaging with peers, a boss, or a certain class of problems. Think of the stereotypical genius programmer who cannot relate to others because he is an insecure introvert who is terrified of other people. If such a person can be enabled to share his capabilities with others in the organization, there may be a large payoff in terms of increased organizational performance (and a more satisfied programmer). I have not witnessed any coaching program targeted to low performers, but why not try it?

Applications of the clinical paradigm in the change system

Finally, the clinical approach can also contribute to the ability of organizations to change. Before I go on to describe two methods from the clinical approach that can augment management system approaches, I would like to make a historical note on the management systems approach they can complement.

An established and widely known method for organizational change, in the context of the management systems paradigm, is business process reengineering (BPR). Since the beginning of the 1990s, BPR has been a prominent tool used to help organizations achieve radical improvements in cost, quality, time, and customer satisfaction. Indeed, the engineering tools of BPR—the flow principles, process structure improvements, and IT platforms—have been widely applied and become part of the tool kit of well-managed organizations. Even so, the promised revolution has not occurred, empowerment has proved elusive, and most BPR implementations have failed.[14] The reasons given were "soft factors," so change management methods have been introduced that improve the way the BPR rationale is explained to employees and that use "influencing networks" to achieve higher acceptance.[15] Although part of management's standard tool kit, BPR has yielded mixed results and a fair amount of skepticism.

More recently, clinical psychologists have developed a method for integrating the consideration of individual personal views into process redesign; this method is known as organizational role analysis (ORA).[16] It is a group process in which individuals can explore, with the help of others, their role in the process as it is understood by the organization.

On the one hand, the focus is on the role, not the individual. The role is the defined activity and function that links the individual to the organization (e.g., the organization needs "a cost accountant," not the individual John Doe). On the other hand, ORA helps individuals to look at themselves as observers from outside the box. In addition, ORA is structured around hypotheses, not opinions; at no time does one try to pin the truth down. This serves to contain tensions and conflict and to facilitate a focus on performing the tasks at hand after considering all influential issues. Thus ORA has the potential to bridge the gap between BPR and personality issues and to address better the idiosyncratic reasons why individuals (or groups, with their internal tensions) sometimes resist process changes whose benefits are self-evident. There are already some prototype applications of ORA, and additional ones are underway.

I now turn to the second clinical approach method, hidden competing commitments.[17] This goes well beyond the change management methods I have described so far, as it seeks to uncover hidden psychological sources of resistance. Employees may resist following or supporting a change for entirely rational reasons: it runs counter to their interests, its long-term effects are uncertain, and/or the organization cannot be trusted to look out for them. Change management methods address those sources of reluctance within the management systems paradigm, by offering transparency, fair process, and a realistic vision of where the change leads—a vision that engenders trust.

It is often said that employees do not want to change because of inertia. This means preference for the status quo, but it is also a broad residual category into which any otherwise inexplicable reluctance toward change is placed. Such explanations presume a learning-based model of change: if I could just explain the change's rationale in a sufficiently compelling way, you would accept it. Yet the reason for reluctance may be inner barriers of a different kind, mentioned above as "hidden competing commitments."[18]

A hidden commitment is similar to a CCRT in that it concerns the maintenance or protection of something that is related to a person's past but is triggered by present events. For example, someone may wish to avoid uncertainty or being controlled by authority; if these commitments are unconscious, the employee may act out, undermining what he and his team are consciously trying to achieve. This dynamic can be brought out in the open with exercises from clinical psychology (in an environment of guaranteed safety). Consider the manager who wanted to develop his relationship-building capabilities but kept getting into trouble for behaving aggressively toward fellow managers and superiors. In a coaching workshop, it turned out that he had a hidden commitment to challenge authorities and hold them accountable for doing their duty. Identifying this hidden motive allowed the manager to avoid reacting on autopilot and to reduce his aggressive behavior.

By targeted interventions of this kind, key employees or small groups of employees may be brought out of their inertia and helped to make positive contributions. This is clearly valuable to the organization and, in addition, employees are typically relieved to be rid of the stress caused by their unwitting sabotage of their own desired ends.

FINAL THOUGHTS: INTEGRATION

In this chapter I have discussed the integration of the idiosyncratic individual into the management systems of an organization. However, this still leaves the question of how to square the circle. How can we attend to the individual amid the turning gears of robust organizational processes? Who is responsible, and who can drive the integration?

One might say that this is precisely the role of middle and frontline managers: they are supposed to know their teams well, be sensitive to personalities and events in team members' lives, and accommodate individuals' needs within the work processes of the team or department. This is true, and indeed a minority of exemplary and naturally people-oriented managers does exactly that. But the majority does not. There are huge differences in managers because of the natural variation in people's sensitivity to others, and leadership training does not usually encompass this fraternal role of caring for others' personal problems or helping others to develop their personalities. A massive upgrade in management training—coupled with more stringent selection of people-oriented managers— would be necessary for an organization to take care of the individual in this way. I believe this is unlikely to happen in the foreseeable future.

An alternative answer is that top management is responsible for driving the integration. This is also true, to a certain extent. There is no doubt that any application of the clinical approach at the strategy level, a top management team coaching intervention, must be driven by the top management team itself; such an intervention is too personal and unsettling to be forced upon the most power-ful people in the organization. However, the top management team will not normally be the driver of incorporating the clinical approach into the execution and change systems of the organization. Its members can issue a mission state-ment and put in place some priorities and incentives, and they can even lead by example, but someone else must assume responsibility for actually doing it.

Thus we arrive at the third answer: I think that the most natural owner of the clinical approach in the execution and change systems is the human resources (HR) function. "Strategic HR" is much talked about but seldom used by organizations. Even when HR does have an important role in developing the management ranks, it usually stops short of holding senior managers account-able or assessing them.

Human resources could become involved in process design and BPR by helping to introduce new methods, such as ORA. HR could also introduce and advocate the practice of coaching individually people who are underperforming in their leadership activities. This would be an additional (costly) HR activity, but one for which a viable business case could be made. HR could even take on the respon-sibility of facilitating efforts to coach the top management team; over time, this could evolve into a culture within which a top management team is implicitly expected to improve its own functioning via team coaching.

All this would, indeed, be a valuable and powerful responsibility of the HR function. It would require wise HR managers who are able to exert the pressure of good practice without threatening top managers with the dreaded fate of being steered by HR people. Moreover, injecting HR people into BPR efforts (and allowing them to add methods) requires that they possess operational knowledge and credibility. As a result, HR managers should collaborate closely with line managers when making individual assessments or addressing change fears within BPR. I know a few organizations where competent operating people routinely transfer to HR and back, but all too often a transfer to HR is the one-way street of low performers. If HR is to assume strategically critical activities of the type discussed here, an upgrade of personnel (and an associated change in how HR people are recruited and promoted) will be required.

This change in the role of HR can occur if there is clear awareness and a mandate by top management to bring clinical psychology into the management of the organization's personnel, especially if accompanied by widening the HR mission and by encouraging line managers to become more involved in leadership development. Top management teams who have witnessed the importance of bringing their half-conscious barriers and fears out in the open may be sufficiently wise to initiate such a change.

NOTES

1. Kets de Vries, M. (2004). "Organizations on the Couch: A Clinical Perspective on Organizational Dynamics." *European Management Journal*, 22(2), 183–200.
2. Markides, C. C. (1999). "A Dynamic View of Strategy." *Sloan Management Review* (Spring), 55–63.
3. Loch, C. (2008). "Mobilizing an R&D Organization through Strategy Cascading." *Research Technology Management*, 51(5), 18–26.
4. Nelson, R. R. and Winter, S. G. (1982). *An Evolutionary Theory of Economic Change*. Cambridge, MA: Belknap.
5. Boyd, R. and Richerson, P. J. (1999). *The Origin and Evolution of Cultures*. Oxford: Oxford University Press; Schein, E. H. (1992). *Organizational Culture and Leadership*. San Francisco: Jossey-Bass.
6. Ancona, D. B., Kochan, T. A., Scully, M., Van Maanen, J., and Westney D. E. (1999). *Managing for the Future: Organizational Behavior & Processes*, 2nd edn. Cincinnati, OH: South Western; Krackhardt, D. and Hanson, J. R. (1993). "Informal Networks: The Company behind the Charts." *Harvard Business Review* (July/August), 104–111.
7. Hansen, M. T. and Birkinshaw, J. (2007). "The Innovation Value Chain." *Harvard Business Review* (June), 3–13; Van de Ven, A. H., Polley, D. E., Garud, R., and Vankatamaran, S. (1999). *The Innovation Journey*. Oxford: Oxford University Press.
8. Kets de Vries, M. and Miller, D. (1984). *The Neurotic Organization*. San Francisco: Jossey-Bass.
9. Goffee, R. and Jones, G. (2006). *Why Should Anyone Be Led by You?* Boston: Harvard Business School Press; Roberts, E. B. and Fusfeld, A. R. (1997). "Critical Functions: Needed Roles in the Innovation Process." In R. Katz (Ed.) *The Human Side of Managing Technology Innovation*. Oxford: Oxford University Press, pp. 307–319.
10. Luborsky, L. and Crits-Christoph, P. (1998). *Understanding Transference: The Core Conflictual Relationship Theme Method*. Washington, DC: American Psychological Association; Kegan, R. and Lahey, L. L. (2001). "The Real Reason People Won't Change." *Harvard Business Review* (November), 85–92.
11. Kilburg, R. R. (2000). *Executive Coaching*. Washington, DC: American Psychological Association, p. 65.
12. Kets de Vries, M. (2006). *The Leader on the Couch*. San Francisco: Jossey-Bass.
13. Luborsky, L. and Crits-Christoph, P. (1998). *Understanding Transference: The Core Conflictual Relationship Theme Method*. Washington, DC: American Psychological Association;

Kegan, R. and Lahey, L. L. (2001). "The Real Reason People Won't Change." *Harvard Business Review* (November), 85–92.

14. Hammer, M. and Champy, J. (1993). *Reengineering the Corporation: A Manifesto for Business Revolution.* New York: Harper Business; Hammer, M. (1996). *Beyond Reengineering.* New York: Harper Business.

15. Kotter, J. (1995). "Leading Change: Why Transformation Efforts Fail." *Harvard Business Review* (March/April), 59–67; Ghoshal, S. and Bartlett, C. A. (1996). "Rebuilding Behavioral Context: A Blueprint for Corporate Renewal." *Sloan Management Review,* 37(2), 23–37.

16. Borwick, I. (2006). "Organizational Role Analysis: Managing Strategic Change in Business Settings." In J. Newton, S. Long, and B. Sievers (Eds) *Coaching in Depth: The Organizational Role Analysis Approach.* London: Karnac.

17. Kegan, R. and Lahey, L. L. (2001). "The Real Reason People Won't Change." *Harvard Business Review* (November), 85–92.

18. Kegan, R. and Lahey, L. L. (2001). "The Real Reason People Won't Change." *Harvard Business Review* (November), 85–92.

13

FAILURE IN FAMILY BUSINESS COACHING

RANDEL S. CARLOCK AND ELIZABETH
FLORENT-TREACY

As coaches, we have all failed with clients, or will fail one day, but we tend to keep our failures to ourselves. As one wit said, success is a public affair, failure is a private funeral. It is human nature to react defensively to failure: by shutting it out of our mind as quickly as possible; by consciously or unconsciously seeking to avoid putting ourselves into a similar, failure-prone situation ever again; or even reframing it so that we can say that we were not responsible. As Benjamin Franklin argued, "I did not fail the test! I just found 100 ways to get it wrong."

And yet the way we perceive and deal with our own failure is one of the most accurate predictors of our progression in growth and maturity as coaches. If we can deconstruct failure and, through experience, become accustomed to its inherent, complex ambiguities and paradoxes, then not only might we become better coaches but we can also protect ourselves from a paralyzing fear of failure or its emotional fallout. When we accept that failure is just another potential element of any coaching intervention, to be examined through a protocol of self-reflection and support from supervisors or peers, we can be less afraid.

Admittedly, part of the complexity arises because it is not so easy to define concrete standards of success and failure. Psychotherapists come to grips with this ambiguity by differentiating between *normative* and *excessive* failure. This can lead to greater clarity, as practitioners reflect on whether, in a specific context, they were on the normative or excessive side of the fence. As Shovolt points out, "Practitioners must realize that all our best intentions, all our work, all our competence, will sometimes not be enough. We must learn to accept lack of success—that is, normative failure—as a component of the work. Being able to come to this realization, accept it, and incorporate it into one's professional self-concept is important for long-term, high-quality professional functioning."[1]

How do we learn to accept lack of success? Primarily through experience, which is not acquired simply through longevity, seniority, or the passage of time, but in living through actual situations in such a way that the experience informs our perception and understanding of all subsequent situations.[2] We can learn from failure if we are willing to ask ourselves some tough questions. What was the cause of the failure, and for what factors am I responsible or not responsible? How could I have been more effective? What techniques could have created a different outcome? Did my ego, fears, or desires get in the way? What does this failure teach me?

In framing this discussion about failure, we must emphasize that this kind of analysis cannot take place entirely through internal monologue. To act ethically and responsibly during the coaching intervention, and to learn from both successes and failures, it is very important to work with a supervisor or partner. Supervisors play a containment role, helping the coach experience the world of the "other" (the client) without being overwhelmed. They encourage exploration of uncertainty and ambiguity within the client and the coach, while giving advice in areas where the coach may lack perspective and/or insight. Supervisors become partners in evaluating client motivation and readiness for change, boundaries, and successful or unsuccessful outcomes. Most important, perhaps, is the supervisor's role in facilitating the reflective process that allows a coach to make sense of his or her professional experiences and transform this knowledge into internal signposts.[3]

In this chapter, we bring some insights about psychotherapeutic failure into the world of family business coaching. We focus on family business coaching because this is a context in which emotions and repercussions are magnified by enmeshed business and family systems, and there are evident underlying parallels to family therapy. We demystify failure—what it is, and what it is not—and introduce it as a concept that family business coaches should expect and confront. We tell the story of a failed family business intervention that had disastrous consequences.

We conclude the chapter with ideas and tips on how coaches can recover their equilibrium in the aftermath of failure. The negative emotional effect of failure is often denied or repressed by coaches in an instinctive form of self-protection, but we believe this is not only harmful but also irresponsible. It is essential to protect the psychological health of the coach, as well as the family client. Ultimately, we believe that coaches, like therapists, should not be ashamed of the specters of their failures, or try to repress them, but rather should expose them to the light of day, learn from experience, and share their insights with others.

FAMILY BUSINESS COACHING: WHAT IS FAILURE AND WHAT IS SUCCESS?

Conflicting forces within an organization can restrain or drive a change process. Experienced family business coaches, aware of the potential for failure in any assignment, will often begin by assessing the ability of the business and the family to change, both at individual and group level. Is there one member of the group who plans the meetings, with the support and cooperation of the others? Do family members greet each other in a friendly way when they arrive at the meeting? Are there obvious alliances among family members who sit together, or is anyone subtly excluded? Do people listen to each other? The group's willingness and ability to work together—something that should be fairly obvious in early meetings with the coach—can be a factor in predicting successful implementation of changes in behavior.

People will respond far better to change initiatives if the need to change becomes apparent through a group discussion, rather than being imposed with specific instructions. On the other hand, if key players in the organization are not involved in developing the change agenda, the organizational system will resist change. The task is made more difficult for a family business coach, by the fact that two systems—family and business—must be engaged in parallel interventions, at three levels: the individual, the family, and the organization. This means that, typically, a coach working with a family in a situation that requires significant change—such as leadership or ownership transitions, or the potential sale of the business—needs to take a participative approach that includes multiple key players and systems.

There is often a triggering event or crisis that drives the family to meet a coach and identify the objectives for a change process. The intervention begins the minute the family business coach picks up the telephone to answer that initial call. From this first contact it is critical that the coach engage with the family or business *system* and not with an *individual*. In the next phase, the coach collects data and shares them with the family to assess the current situation. Another key factor at this stage is the coach's ability to build alliances within the group. After these engagement and assessment phases, the real work of developing action plans begins. This often involves creating task forces that use the feedback to explore change-related issues in detail and begin implementation. Later in the process, the family and coach/consultant evaluate progress, and ultimately the coach disengages from the family, who are now able to carry on autonomously.[4]

This is a description of a best-case family intervention. Unfortunately, the hard reality is that, to paraphrase the common wisdom of psychotherapists, there are two kinds of family business coaches: those who have worked with a family business that failed, and those who will work with a family business that fails. Failure, in other words, is an ever-present specter that we should be aware of, plan for, and face squarely when it happens to us—as it surely will—in family business coaching. The most experienced coaches plan and work to implement a best-case change process, but are also psychologically prepared to accept and learn from failure.

One of the most difficult issues to deal with in any coaching or consulting relationship is the failure of a client or family to achieve a satisfactory outcome. In many cases, a root cause of failure is the individual's, family's, or organization's inability to change. In a family business, change is even more complex because the organizational and family systems are enmeshed, and conflict arises from different values, goals, and expectations. Failure to reach a satisfactory outcome may also be caused by a breakdown in the leadership transition process, and this failure can have many consequences, including blocked or damaged careers, unresolved conflicts, hurtful relationships, or even loss of control of the business. Finally, the ebb and flow of human life cycles, as children mature and parents age, have a tremendous but often invisible influence on decisions and actions in a family business.

In some cases, the coach or advisor's inability to see or assess the potential derailment of the engagement and assessment process during the intervention may lead directly to a drastic outcome failure for the client. Two of the most serious challenges a coach can face are the symbolic "death" of a client through the loss of the business or an unresolved conflict that splits the family, following an intervention. Outcome failure for the family business client includes:

- Business deterioration: family owners and management cannot work together to develop effective strategic plans, affecting business assets and value negatively.
- Loss of the business: losing family control through events like forced sale or transfer of ownership.
- Unresolved conflict in the family: where individual family members, or the unity of the family as a group, are damaged even though the family business functions well.
- Individual family member's career failure resulting in self-harm or destructive behavior.

A crucial point to consider, when evaluating the fine line between normative and excessive failure in this context, is what does a failure in a family intervention mean to this particular family? How do they experience the failure? Do they even agree that it is a failure? Or is apparent failure in fact a desired outcome, at a much deeper level? Families often want homeostasis—maintaining things the way they are—while claiming that they want to make a change in the family system. They might not even be aware that the change may be too frightening for them to make. How many younger generation family members complain about not being given full leadership responsibility, but at the same time, at an unconscious level, are relieved that their father retains control and takes the heat off them? The source of motivation for change can be a classic red flag signaling potential trouble. If change is imposed externally on an individual or family—for example, when a bank becomes involved in managing the finances of a family's business—then it is likely that the larger change process will not be successful. Therefore, a careful examination of the underlying motivations for maintaining the status quo, and the potential secondary gains to be achieved by doing so, are critical factors in evaluating outcomes (as we will explore in detail in the case story that follows).

One of the dilemmas faced by coaches is that they want a very positive outcome for their clients, but they must be realistic in the engagement and goal setting steps of the intervention or coaching process. Reflecting upon failure after the fact, we may find that the problem lay not in the intervention but in the initial engagement. Did the client fully understand that a successful outcome might mean dramatic change in the family, in terms of restructuring hierarchy, power, influence, roles, and status? When family members say they're going to "take some more time" to think about a proposed action, they might really be saying, "We're not ready to change yet." What the coach might interpret as failure, because of continued ineffective patterns of behavior on the part of the client, could be a signal that the coach needs to reengage with the client to redefine or clarify the family's understanding and expectations of the outcome. Sometimes the family business coach may need to take a harder line, using a paradoxical intervention, or even disengaging, saying, in effect, "You're wasting my time, and I'm wasting yours."

Experienced family business coaches measure the success of their interventions and activities on three levels: how the outcome has affected the well-being of individual family members; the family's level of effectiveness in accomplishing critical tasks; and finally, whether business performance has deteriorated or improved. Forced sale or bankruptcy, with conflict in the family or management team, clearly indicates failure. Less evident, but equally negative over the long term, is slow death by suboptimal business performance, which may be caused by one or more family members' inertia or actions to undermine the process of change or transition. For example, the Bancroft family, owners of Dow Jones (*Wall Street Journal*) through several generations, never "failed" but they were eventually forced to sell the business after years of hands-off family leadership and declining stock prices left them without much choice.

Although the family business coach cannot be held responsible for changes in market conditions or other events that might contribute to the loss of a business, there are several factors related to the coach that can directly result in failure of outcome. It is somewhat unrealistic to think that, as coaches, we are going to be able to untangle many years of personal conflict and family experiences in a few sessions. So the engagement process should have a very strategic focus on realistic outcomes, to ensure that coach and client are working toward the same goals. If outcome failure occurs, it may well be that the coach did not properly engage with the family, including the powers behind the throne; the coach may not have established a therapeutic alliance with all the key players; or the coach may have lacked proper expertise or supervision.

Although context is important and each family is different, normative failure— that is to say, lack of success for which the coach is not directly responsible—in family business coaching can be attributed to three principal causes.

Lack of engagement. The client (or some members of the family) does not show up for the first meeting, or never comes back for another meeting—no therapeutic alliance is established.

Failure to continue. The clients begin the process, but some disconnection keeps them from finishing it—they see no improvement, and may have doubts about the coach's methods or relevant experience.

Outcome confusion. The family is unable to define realistic strategic goals, and the coach is unable to determine underlying motivation and the influence of secondary gain—leading to disengagement by coach or client.

Excessive failure—in other words, failure that may be partly attributed to the coach—can include the following:

Ineffective stable state. The client or the coach does not see change over time, but rather than reassessing or terminating, one or the other wants to continue indefinitely—in effect, the coach is acting as an enabler, allowing the client to continue in established patterns of behavior.

Relief of symptoms. Coaching removes pain from the system, and so removes motivation to change, but does not address the underlying problems.

Lack of self-reflection or supervision. Coaches fail to recognize their own limitations or countertransference issues.

Misplaced affiliation. Coaches allow themselves to feel like "a member of the family" in fulfillment of their own need for affiliation or control, not respecting boundaries.

Dramatic punctuation. A (theoretically foreseeable) incident occurs that terminates the coaching relationship abruptly—eruption of open conflict in the family, legal actions that cause the family to lose control of the business—indicating that the process was not working.

To be clear, selling the family business at the right time for a good price is *not* a failure for the family, if the decision is reached through fair process.[5] Equally, if the coach recognizes that the relationship is failing for the reasons described above and proceeds to terminate the relationship cleanly and/or make referrals to other advisors, this is not failure in terms of the coach's responsibility to the family. Finally, if the coach must refer the family or individual family members to other professionals for help on specific issues—including therapy, medication, or hospitalization—this should not be considered a failure. To put it succinctly, if coaches act ethically, putting the highest priority on the requirement to "do no harm," then they have not failed.

THE COACH'S EXPERIENCE OF FAILURE

Despite the best efforts of even experienced coaches, the reasons for the failure of a coaching intervention usually become apparent only after the event. It takes a great deal of courageous self-reflection, aided by a supervisor when necessary, for a family business coach to conduct an "autopsy" of what went wrong. Like psychotherapists, coaches can experience outcome failure as a professional injury that affects them at a level of narcissistic vulnerability. This does not facilitate the analytic process. Less experienced coaches are even more likely than experienced coaches to bury their head in the sand, affecting the way they assess and work with other clients. They fear that their colleagues and future potential clients might say, "Why should we take you seriously? Look what happened to the last family you worked with." Even experienced coaches can be blindsided by the suddenness of unforeseen events, despite knowing that the situation was risky—in fact, they may have been drawn to the project in the first place because it looked particularly challenging. After the fact, they second-guess themselves, wondering why they once considered that they had the process under control. They are surprised by the intensity and duration of their own emotional reaction to the failed intervention.

Although there is little written about how family business coaches experience failure, the effect of failure on the therapist is a growing area in psychotherapy literature.[6] The ultimate outcome failure for a psychotherapist is when a patient commits suicide. Therapists are increasingly aware that even if they cannot prevent an excessive failure, they must protect their own mental health in the aftermath of such a deeply disturbing event.

In family business coaching, a catastrophic failure of the highest magnitude would be when a family leader or family member acts (or fails to act) in such a way that it leads to the loss or destruction of the business, or causes serious damage to the well-being of other family members. The emotional fallout of a failed family business intervention can be devastating for a family business coach, given family members' potentially intense explosions of anger or denial. There can be permanent damage to family relationships, financial collapse or bankruptcy, and covert or overt blaming of scapegoats—all directed frequently toward the family business coach.

However, the ability to rise again from the ashes of an excessive failure is a quality of the mature, professional coach. What is it that often prevents us, as coaches, from looking more closely at our own failures? We have found in our practice that failure can have a debilitating and long-lasting negative effect on the coach, with reactions similar to those experienced by psychotherapists, who report feelings of self-blame, inadequacy, and serious loss of confidence in their abilities.[7] Compared with many coaches, psychotherapists, as a group, are better prepared for failure. They are aware of the certainty that they will fail to help one or more clients at some point. In addition, they accept that supervision is a sine qua non, and therapeutic "autopsies" of failed interventions, with the help of supervisors and colleagues, are an important part of the protocol for dealing with the effect of failure on the therapist.

Tillman[8] established a categorization of the experiences of psychotherapists who had experienced excessive failure, as reported by the clinicians themselves. Each described reactions that fell into five main categories.

- Traumatic responses—dissociation, avoidance, somatic symptoms.
- Affective responses—grief, anger.
- Risk management responses—fear of lawsuit.

- Narcissistic responses—grandiosity, shame, humiliation, guilt, blame.
- Sense of crisis—loss of faith in professional identity, psychodynamic methods, personal competence.

The clinicians in the study also reported that their overwhelming perception of failure had affected their own relationships with colleagues and supervisors and their work with other patients. Tillman derived three general themes from the categories in her study that can also help us to describe and deconstruct the experience of family business coaches. They are: traumatic loss and grief, disruption of personal and professional relationships, and professional identity concerns. Ultimately, psychotherapists and coaches who have experienced an intervention failure are faced with a dual loss: of the patient or coaching client and of the professional ideal. This loss is often accompanied by mourning, depression, self-reproach, and criticism of others.

As Tillman pointed out, post-event analysis is complicated when the fracturing of the professional ego ideal activates a number of personal and professional defenses.[9] The patient or family may become an object of fear or a container for anger and blame. The clinician may come to believe that the patient's decision to take a drastic or irrational action was somehow right—just as a family business coach might argue that losing the family business would probably turn out for the best in the end. Some psychotherapists and coaches will work through an "autopsy" of failure and learn from the process, but others will avoid facing it, with the ongoing negative consequences this implies.

A FAMILY BUSINESS COACHING FAILURE?

Family background

The Sanchez family, controlling owners of a multimillion euro retail distribution company located in southern Europe, was referred to Richard Albertson, an experienced family business advisor, by a large international consulting group that had been working unsuccessfully with the family for several months. This consulting group had faced serious issues with the client family and had determined that the problems were probably related to dysfunctional dynamics within the family. The consulting group felt that their organizational and strategy-focused approach was not proving effective. They believed that Albertson, who was also a practicing psychotherapist, and had trained under the supervision of senior member of the group in the past, had the psychological perspective required for a successful intervention.

Previously, after several years of deteriorating performance in the business, the family had sought advice from a respected investment bank that looked at the family's brand and other assets and came back with the recommendation to sell the company or look for a merger and acquisition, which would give outside shareholders majority control. The family had rejected this proposal with little consideration. The family's lawyers had advised them that they needed better governance and a process to deal with the family conflict if they planned to manage the business together successfully. After talking with lawyers, the family contacted Albertson.

Albertson agreed to meet the family. He developed a genogram (a family tree that includes symbols that illustrate relationships between individuals) and learned that the family group included six family members: two daughters and two sons, plus the parents (see Figure 13.1). The family business had been in operation for 75 years. An ownership and leadership transition had been completed five years previously, with the father passing the ownership to the four children: 30 percent each to the two brothers and 20 percent each to the two sisters. The two brothers and older sister were executives in the company; the older brother was the CEO. The younger sister did not work in the company.

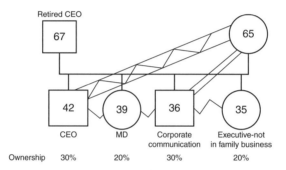

FIGURE 13.1 **Sanchez family genogram**

In this genogram, the jagged lines represent a conflict between the oldest brother and his siblings, the two solid lines between the youngest son and mother means a close relationship and the jagged and two solid lines between the oldest son and mother represents a fused or "love-hate" relationship.

The family informed Albertson that they wanted him to provide them with some processes to improve relationships and try to develop an operating structure around vision, decision-making, and governance. The family was struggling with chronic conflicts among the four shareholding siblings. A major problem for the business was that the minority shareholders were able to block any actions because corporate bylaws required a super majority of 75 percent of the shares to take any significant business decisions. This meant that at least one of the sisters had to vote with the two brothers to ratify management's or board actions. They had been unable to agree on a long-term vision and at one point had even been unwilling to ratify the actions of the board of directors, which in effect meant that the company was not operating legitimately. They had come to the conclusion—as they told Albertson—that a lot of their issues centered on relationships and aligning family values and family behavior in a way that would support the business. Albertson's mandate was to find a way for the family to maintain profitable control of their business.

The intervention

Albertson took an action research model approach, beginning with individual interviews with each of the family members, except the parents, whom he interviewed together. These in-depth interviews allowed all family members to share their observations about the family business, family relationships, and what they saw as the issues and challenges the family faced. Additionally, there were structured questions related to the board, business performance, and other business activities.

In the interviews, Albertson learned that the transition between the father and siblings had been somewhat strained, in the sense that after completing the transfer of ownership, the father had walked away from the business and ceased to participate as a board member or advisor. There had been a series of apparently minor conflicts about strategy and future vision between his two oldest children—the son who became CEO, and his older daughter, who was managing director of one of the subsidiaries. The father's absence had created an opportunity for his wife, who had not previously been involved in the business, to extend her role unofficially, particularly in relation to her two sons. She now offered endless advice on the business, as she had previously done on every other aspect of their personal lives.

The mother's involvement in her children's lives was a major issue for her two sons and at times for the daughters. The oldest son broke his first engagement because his mother did not approve of his fiancée. He soon married another young woman, but ended that marriage within months and returned to live with his parents. The mother was adept at using emotional blackmail, and frequently warned her children that the stress caused by their behavior was affecting her health.

The family members seemed to have very different views about the business, their roles, and their responsibilities. The older brother, the CEO, saw the business as his: his creativity, energy, and ideas were the driving force. Unfortunately, his management skills, while adequate, lacked vision and he constantly seemed to be reacting to the competition rather than working to sustain the firm's traditional market leadership position. The younger son, who was not deeply committed to a business career, did not always agree with his brother but supported him out of respect for his seniority and dedication. The older sister worked in the business and did an excellent job as managing director of the least glamorous but most profitable division of the company. She had limited technical business skills but was excellent with people, especially customers, and managed to contribute some 60 percent of the group's operating profits. The younger sister, who had never worked in the family firm, had a successful career as a marketing director in an international consumer products firm. She remained very interested in the family company in her role as minority shareholder. One of the reasons she had chosen not to work for the family firm was her very strong resentment, bordering on hate, toward her older brother, whom she saw as an incompetent who had been handed control of the business by her father simply because he was the oldest son. She frequently criticized her brother's decisions and was ready to argue with him about everything from the simplest family matters to very complex governance or board issues, which she inevitably tried to block.

Following the interviews, Albertson wrote a report that outlined each individual's thinking without revealing who had said what. After reading the report, the family acknowledged that communication was ineffective and often ended in conflict; they did not work together to make decisions for the business or the family; and that some of the family members acted as if the business was theirs alone, annoying the other shareholders, who tended to overuse their blocking votes as a result. They also admitted that there were deep personal resentments in the family over ownership and control, with the daughters feeling they were treated unfairly in receiving fewer shares than their brothers. Each of the siblings seemed to have an issue. The oldest son felt burdened with the CEO responsibilities and frustrated by having his actions blocked by his sisters; the older sister felt her contribution in running the most profitable subsidiary was not recognized; and the younger sister felt she had been unfairly prevented from joining the family firm despite having excellent skills and leadership potential. There was also general agreement that the younger son was free riding and did not deserve a 30 percent ownership position—but his mild-mannered personality and the intensity of the other issues greatly overshadowed this problem.

Following this family meeting, Albertson decided in consultation with the family to focus on the sibling subsystem and not involve the parents in any further discussions, because they were no longer shareholders and their involvement seemed to create significant tension. They had officially stepped away from the business, and the mother's involvement tended to escalate minor issues into major conflicts. For example, if there was a disagreement between two of the siblings, the mother would inevitably take the side of one of them, and then confront the other, creating a triangle that made it impossible for the siblings to resolve the initial issue themselves.

The family, including the mother, reluctantly agreed that working with the sibling group made sense because in the future they were the ones who would have to make the decisions and develop a vision of how they were going to work together, both as a family and in the business. The intervention continued with a series of sibling meetings to address the issues in the report and to develop a rough outline of family agreements, including a family code of conduct, governance roles, and decision-making processes. Family communication and fair process were underlying themes as an attempt was made to improve trust by learning to be more transparent and consistent in family actions.

Albertson also met with the nonfamily chairman of the board to discuss the siblings' plans for improved governance processes. The board, particularly the external members, had been discouraged by the failure to have their actions ratified by the ownership group, so they strongly supported the family's actions. The plan was to involve the board in the business issues and the family in the ownership issues and attempt to create clarity and alignment around strategy and decision-making. The board had taken a passive, more advisory role in the past, but Albertson felt that if the board demanded more accountability from the CEO, it would lessen the criticism the CEO received from his shareholders (siblings) and create an opening for improved family relationships.

The siblings' work resulted in several concrete agreements and after about six months of meetings between them, a document was developed that outlined procedures for decision-making and consensus on spending, control of business assets, and the role of the board, the management team, and the ownership group. Fair process was a central theme that went beyond the formal structures and process of governance in an attempt to ensure that the three younger siblings had a voice and received accurate information, and that their brother was committed to treating the others in the fairest way possible. The siblings and board believed that formalizing these agreements signaled a new start for the family and the business.

Seeds of failure

After a brief honeymoon period, several issues triggered new conflicts within the sibling group. The CEO, despite his full endorsement of the family agreements, violated many of the understandings that the family had agreed were fundamental to working together. He appointed one of his friends to a senior management position and redirected company resources and assets into his pet projects without discussing them with the board or informing the shareholder group. The board reneged on their agreement to provide serious accountability by claiming that they worked for the CEO, and it was pointless to challenge his actions. It was evident that there was a complete disconnect between espoused intentions and actions.

The breaking point came sooner than the sisters had expected. The CEO felt that a solution to the business dilemma was to use company stock to acquire another retailer in their industry, and was approaching a tentative acquisition agreement—one that, incidentally, would change the ownership structure and dilute the sisters' control. The sisters found out about this through another contact in the industry. When confronted, the CEO initially denied the plan, and then in a burst of anger, told his sisters that it was none of their business. This incident convinced the sisters that their only recourse was to seek legal counsel and attempt to force their brother to comply, at the very least, to strict legal governance regulations—they had given up on the family agreements—and to force him and the board to recognize their rights as minority shareholders.

At this point, Albertson decided to stop working with the family. His rationale was that, with the lawyers involved, the situation had shifted from family business advising to a legal conflict. It made little sense to attempt to do any more work around the family issues at that time because every communication and action required review by legal council, who strongly resisted any attempts at reconciliation. During this period, Albertson had no further formal contact with the Sanchez family group, although the sisters called him from time to time to give updates and share their concerns.

A second intervention attempt

Five months later, the CEO sent Albertson an email reporting that he and his parents wanted to reengage him in an attempt to come to some agreements and resolve the family's conflicts. The legal processes were still continuing in the background, with strongly worded letters and positioning around different legal actions and threats, but no formal court case had been brought.

Albertson replied with an email stating that as a matter of fairness and professionalism he did not feel that he could provide any additional services. However, if the family was willing to agree to some rather strict guidelines, he would consider working with them once again. The exchange of emails did not lead to agreement, and there was no further contact between Albertson and the family.

The process continued on the legal front with family lawyers, family members, the board of directors, and the bank, which had been involved as a substantial commercial lender. A court case was imminent, even though there was some uncertainty whether a court would force the CEO or board to take any action to protect the rights of the minority shareholders.

At that point the bank informed the CEO and board of directors that it was unwilling to continue providing a line of credit, and demanded that the company repay its entire €75 million loan. The bank's reasoning was simple and based on the continuing deterioration in the company's performance. It also cited the shareholder disputes and lack of shareholder approval of board actions as serious threats to the company's survival. The bank's legal position was reasonably strong because it had not been involved in the family dispute in any way and was simply exercising its rights, under the loan covenants, to demand payment or additional assets to protect its loan.

Later, the bank informed management and the board that it was willing to support the transfer of ownership of the business to another group—a client of both the family firm and the bank—in lieu of repayment of the loan. As the discussions continued, it became clear that the family business was unable to repay the loan, so would have been in default and eventually bankrupt. The bank's offer to accept the substitution of a new debtor, which would then take ownership of the business with a small cash payment for the family's stock, was the only viable option on the table for avoiding bankruptcy, which would have damaged the family's reputation and destroyed the company's brand and market position.

Failure on all fronts

A few weeks before the final sale was due to go through, the CEO contacted Albertson and met him privately to discuss options. Against his better judgment, Albertson agreed to talk to him. The CEO explained that one possible option was to inject private equity into the firm as a way of pacifying the bank's claims, maintaining at least a large ownership, if not a majority ownership, position for the family and protecting the viability of the business. Albertson referred the CEO to a private equity investor. But the CEO did not follow up the idea—it was unclear whether he ever discussed this option with any other shareholders—and a few weeks later the bank took possession of the company. The family received a small cash settlement and gave up control of the business, which still exists under its new owner, and is once again profitable.

ALBERTSON'S COACHING AUTOPSY

Several years later, we were told this story by Albertson, who said that he realized that he had not yet been able to reach a sense of closure about this intervention. It was still bothering him. We suggested that a coaching autopsy might be helpful, and he agreed.

From a coach's perspective, what options could have led to a different outcome? It was clear from the outset that there were significant emotional and business problems in this family. The fact that they had sought outside help from an investment banker and then from a trusted lawyer showed that the family members were aware that the situation was serious. The business was losing substantial amounts of money. Key employees had left and some had been replaced by the CEO's closest friends. The whole process was clearly on a downward slide before Albertson was ever engaged. Was there anything Albertson could have done differently?

There are several elements in this case that, in retrospect, clearly contributed to its outcome failure. After the early discussions about family agreements, the sisters said they were convinced that the CEO would not honor his commitments to any of them. This was a gray area: in his dual roles as senior corporate executive and family shareholder, the CEO had to deal with some degree of conflict of interest between the business and the owners. In addition, it could be argued that perhaps the CEO did not want the business to survive: if he experienced it as a burden that his parents had forced on him after his father's abrupt departure, this might have been a subconscious attempt to free himself from it. If so, this was another factor—a hidden secondary gain—that had set Albertson up to fail from the beginning. The CEO's motives and actions had merited greater analysis than Albertson had given them at the time.

Albertson should have brought in a co-advisor or supervisor to work with the CEO individually, since Albertson's client was the family system. In addition, it would have been helpful for Albertson to meet privately with a supervisor to reflect on his own motivations, as well as to test his interpretation of the situation and the many complicated issues in this case. The referral to Albertson was made by one of his own mentors, a senior partner at the consulting group that had worked with the family for several months and got nowhere. Albertson had felt some pressure to meet his mentor's expectations, and even surpass him by succeeding where the consulting group had failed. In addition, Albertson had once been the CEO of a large company himself; here again, a supervisor could have helped Albertson sort out his motivation for taking the assignment.

Albertson admitted that many times after leaving meetings with the Sanchez family, he felt he was inadequate—there was so much toxic emotion—anger, resentment, and hate—between some of the family members. A key event occurred after the initial intervention had broken down, when the CEO contacted Albertson by email to ask about starting over. Albertson's reply could be interpreted in two ways, either as a very factual, straightforward document outlining his requirements for restarting the process, or as a kind of power play: "You didn't live up to your agreements before, but now you realize you need me. I'm in charge, you're going to play by my rules." He not only found it hard to help the family but their emotions also disturbed him. He had probably overrated the importance of the family agreements; although they were concrete demonstrations of action, the family's core dynamics had not changed. They were acting out the willingness to work together and develop agreements, but fundamentally they did not want to be there together. But Albertson did not examine the clues provided by his own emotions and uncertainties closely enough to uncover the fundamental instability of the family system.

A decision had been made to exclude the parents in an attempt to create some stronger subsystem boundaries and to reduce the amount of conflict and anxiety created by the parents in their interactions with their children. No attempt had been made to include the parents in the process, expand the group, and attempt an intervention involving all six family members. Given the mother's hold over her older son, perhaps Albertson had overlooked a potential ally, or underestimated a possible adversary.

Although he was a very experienced family business advisor, Albertson knew this had been a failed coaching intervention, with outcome failure for the family. Although he had assessed the family carefully, and designed an action research change process, his actions had contributed more to removing the pain in the system than to a radical shift in the way the family interacted. He had not established a solid therapeutic alliance with the family, and had excluded two key members of the family system. He had not worked with a supervisor to test his ideas and interpretations, and he had been influenced by his desire to prove himself to his old mentor. He admitted that he had blocked the whole story from his mind, which had prevented him from analyzing the degree of his responsibility for the outcome.

LEARNING FROM FAILURE

As Albertson's story illustrates, to avoid failures, coaches should reflect constantly on their own motivations. Because self is the most important tool of the therapist or coach, self-awareness is a key part of developing an effective therapeutic relationship. At the same time, it is critical to seek different perspectives outside the self through interactions with colleagues and supervisors. In most coaching situations, and particularly in family systems, there will be multiple agendas, manipulation, and hidden motivations of which individuals are unaware, and which the coach could easily miss.

After an intervention like this, how can coaches evaluate their work? The Sanchez case is complex because a strong argument can be made that the family, and the CEO in particular, were well aware of the risks their behavior created. They were competing in a tough industry and using bank debt to support their financial position. Additionally, the family had met an investment banker who had advised them to sell the business for competitive reasons. They had also had legal advice about resolving their governance issues. But despite these warnings the siblings, led or pushed by their brother the CEO, did not take any action to protect the business from the family's conflicts and self-dealing. It could be argued that Albertson's real mistake was to have missed what the family really wanted as an outcome: to be permanently disentangled from one another and from a business that had been a tremendous source of conflict. In this case, although the coaching intervention was a failure, the outcome for the family, seen through a psychodynamic lens, might well have been what they had truly desired all along, although this desire seems to have included the seeds of self-destruction for the business.

Failure is never easy to accept, but it is a missed opportunity if we do not use it as the basis for learning and personal growth. So, what is the protocol for learning from failure? Typically, coaches ask themselves to what extent they were responsible for what happened. If we do everything in our power to help clients look at their situation in new ways, yet they are unable to do so, does this mean that we have failed? If a coach realizes that a client has problems beyond the scope of their mandate, makes a referral and follows up with the client several times, is it their responsibility if the client is unwilling to engage? The people who own family businesses are usually highly trained, educated, wealthy, experienced adults; should coaches blame themselves if their clients do not take the actions identified?

These are tough questions—yet they may not be the right questions when dealing with failure. If coaches find they are asking themselves questions like these, it may be an indication that they are feeling emotional distress or doubts about their professional ability. Questions like these should be discussed with a supervisor *during* the intervention, to help coaches evaluate the effectiveness of the process. When conducting a coaching review, it is more productive to return to the most fundamental guidelines that any responsible coach will have learned during training, and which we outlined at the beginning of this chapter. Did I establish a therapeutic alliance? Were the key actors in the family in agreement about desired outcomes and the measures of success? Did I, the coach, remain neutral and free of transference issues, using a supervisor as a sounding board? Did I help the family/ client identify multiple options and scenarios to improve their performance?

A mistake is not a mistake if we use it to help other clients or families—as the proverb says, a stumble may prevent a fall. But outcome failure can be very difficult for a coach to accept, because in coaching, the self is the primary tool and there is an often a blurring of the boundaries between personal and professional identities. Just as psychotherapists analyze their own capacity to deal with catastrophic outcome failure, family business coaches need to be aware of their own distress in similar situations and the effect this may have on their work. Although fear of failure is common, it is very important to see failure as an opportunity to learn, through examining our own contribution, as coaches, to the failure. A clear understanding of what is failure and what is not, as we discussed earlier in this chapter, can be very helpful. In addition, there are several questions that coaches can use to examine their own reaction to client failure and develop new strategies to improve client interventions in the future.

- What kind of clients distresses me most? Rigid, strongly enmeshed, or chaotic? What does this tell me about my family of origin and my transference and countertransference reactions? What should I be aware of?
- What are my typical patterns for engaging the family? Do I work on a hierarchical model? Do I find myself forming an alliance with certain parts (genders, generations . . .) of the family? In what situations are these patterns more or less effective?
- How willing am I to ask for help? How often do I seek the support of a colleague or supervisor when I am in a difficult or stuck situation with a client? Am I fully aware and accepting of my own needs for a sounding board and outside perspectives?
- What other sources of assistance, such as professional organizations or academic institutions, are available to me when I am struggling to help a family client? Do I know whom to call for support?
- What are my personal stressors, and what can I do to manage the stress that I feel in certain kinds of coaching relationships?
- What are my limits and boundaries as a coach? What additional training or experience would make me a more effective coach?
- How do I deal with failure in the coaching context? Do I quickly move on to the next project, or take the time to do a coaching autopsy?

Thinking about these questions can help coaches reconsider their own reactions to failure, and help them develop better strategies for dealing with difficult client situations in the future. It is important for coaches to remember that they are human, and they need to appreciate fully their own anxiety. One useful tool for building self-awareness is to keep a log of short reports or narratives explaining each case, identifying successes and potential issues that coaches can reflect on when dealing with the current client or new clients in the future. Some coaches create their own personal code of behavior, saying for example:

- I am the right coach for some clients, and wrong for others. I will try not to let my ego get in the way.
- When I feel overwhelmed, I will attempt to figure out why.
- I will seek to clarify who owns the problem I have been asked to solve, and to understand their real motivation.
- I will constantly delve into my own inner theater, to identify what or who in the current intervention reminds me of my past, and what that means in the present.
- I will reflect on every intervention and try to learn from it.

Finally, it is good to keep in mind that confronting failure is more cathartic than running from it. Tillman points out in her study of clinicians who have lost patients to suicide that all of them except one contacted a supervisor for containment and support.[10] Through analysis and reflection on how such a terrible event could have occurred, they reached a greater acceptance of the paradoxes around helpfulness and helplessness, and around feeling both more and less responsible for their patients. After reflection, many said that such a terrible failure had instilled in them a greater sense of fallibility, and ironically, they found some comfort in that.

By seeing the seed of failure in every success, we remain humble. By seeing the seed of success in every failure, we remain hopeful. And as the philosopher Kierkegaard reminds us, "To dare is to lose one's footing momentarily. To not dare is to lose oneself." At the end of the day, when we hang up the phone after a call with a potential client, walk out of a family meeting, or conclude a coaching intervention, the questions should be, each and every time: How has this client affected me? What does the client really want? Have I been effective or ineffective in helping this family today, and how can I be even more effective tomorrow?

NOTES

1. Skovholt, T. (2001). *The Resilient Practitioner*. Needham Heights, MA: Allyn & Bacon.
2. Benner, P. and Wrubel, J. (1982). "Skilled Clinical Knowledge: The Value of Perceptual Awareness, Part 2." *Journal of Nursing Administration*, 12, 28–33.
3. Skovholt, T. (2001). *The Resilient Practitioner*. Needham Heights, MA: Allyn & Bacon.

4. Kets de Vries, M. F. R., Carlock, R. S. with Florent-Treacy, E. (2007). *Family Business on the Couch.* London: Wiley.
5. Kaye, K. (1996). "When Family Business is a Sickness." *Family Business Review*, 9(4) 347–368.
6. Valente, S. (2003). "Aftermath of a Patient's Suicide: A Case Study." *Perspectives in Psychiatric Care*, 39:1, 17–22.
7. Valente, S. (2003). "Aftermath of a Patient's Suicide: A Case Study." *Perspectives in Psychiatric Care*, 39:1, 17–22.
8. Tillman, J. (2006). "When a Patient Commits Suicide: An Empirical Study of Psycho-analytic Clinicians." *International Journal of Psychoanalysis*, 87, 159–177.
9. Tillman, J. (2006). "When a Patient Commits Suicide: An Empirical Study of Psycho-analytic Clinicians." *International Journal of Psychoanalysis*, 87, 159–177.
10. Tillman, J. (2006). "When a Patient Commits Suicide: An Empirical Study of Psycho-analytic Clinicians." *International Journal of Psychoanalysis*, 87, 159–177.

14

COACHING FOR WORK-LIFE BALANCE

KATTY MARMENOUT

Achieving work-life balance has been increasingly recognized as crucial in preventing the damaging effects of stress on one's health and reducing the risk of burnout. Over the last few decades, both men and women, particularly professionals, have seen increasing pressure of work interfering with their personal life. As the demands of work increase, time spent at home is often sacrificed to satisfy job requirements, resulting in feelings of guilt, inadequacy, and overall dissatisfaction. Work-life balance issues are particularly significant after major transitions in an individual's life, such as an important career move, starting a family, the end of a relationship, or when children leave home. These events have a profound impact on our self-concept and may lead us to do some soul searching, trying to find meaning in our life, and may affect our priorities in terms of work and family.

I personally became interested in work-life balance after just such an important transition in my own life: having a baby. While I had managed my demanding career as a consultant, my MBA and PhD studies, and a dual-career household for 15 years, when work-life balance was a nonissue, the arrival of this little person suddenly filled the concept with meaning. This transition, coupled with a move from Europe to the Middle East and a new job, resulted in significant challenges to find a way to make things both workable and enjoyable. As a researcher with IGLC in Abu Dhabi, I managed to integrate my personal struggle and my work, while doing something I believed to be useful for the community. As part of my research I organized work-life balance workshops for Middle Eastern women. As my female target audience frequently voiced their concern for their husbands to acknowledge what they liked to call their "lack of balance," I came to believe that my experience in coaching these women for work-life balance could be equally relevant for men. The purpose of this chapter is to take the reader through a number of concepts and tools related to work-life balance as I have used them in the workshops I have conducted. I start by defining work-life balance, and then go on to discuss why it appears difficult to manage competing demands and multiple roles and why we feel an imbalance. This understanding will set the stage for action in discussing coping strategies, self-leadership, and energy management.

WORK-LIFE BALANCE REDEFINED

Work-life balance has generally been conceptualized as equal involvement and investment of time in work and family. Under this frame of reference, people investing all their waking time in work would be considered imbalanced, having no "life," and to be leading a lifestyle that would inevitably lead to burnout. However, more recent research has moved away from this restrictive view of work-life balance and defines balance more in terms of fit or harmony between our situation and our priorities. As such, it is more a matter of harmony than equality. This approach to work-life balance allows the acceptance of both the "happy workaholic" and the self-realized stay-at-home mom or dad.

This view of balance, however, makes two important assumptions: first, individuals know what they value most and where their focus lies; second, individuals are able to act upon their values. First, we may value both spheres to a great extent, feel torn, and have difficulty establishing our priorities. Second, it might not be financially feasible to focus entirely on our family, nor may it be practically feasible to focus on both work and family simultaneously. Therefore, our awareness of our values, and our ability to act upon them, should not be taken for granted. This is crucial with respect to coaching for work-life balance and should be at the core of the coaching contract.

JUGGLING WITH MULTIPLE ROLES AND IDENTITIES

Both men and women occupy multiple roles in society. While our most important roles in our adult life are those of worker, parent, and spouse, throughout our lives we remain linked to extended family as children and siblings. We may also adopt significant roles related to our communities at large. These not only affect how we distribute our time and efforts but also largely define our identity and self-esteem. Indeed, what we do defines who we are and how we think of ourselves. Thus it becomes clear that finding the right balance between the different roles we desire or are expected to play in life is critical; struggling with work-life balance entails much more than just "time management," as it is commonly perceived. Coaching for work-life balance can help establish self-awareness by assisting in the soul-searching aspect and in unlocking the potential to achieve a better balance, measured in terms of efficiency and satisfaction.

Indeed, to achieve work-life balance it is crucial to undertake some soul-searching to determine our priorities. Pie charts, with each role allotted one slice of the pie, can be an effective aid to provide insights into competing roles and multiple identities. Pie charts can be usefully thought of in two ways: first in terms of time, more in line with the traditional view on work-life balance (for example, how much time is actually spent on each role or with each stakeholder); second in terms of perception (for example, pregnant women may already feel they are a mother while the actual time spent in that role as observed by others is zero). From my experience, individuals with a quantitative background (for example, engineers and bankers) often feel more comfortable with the first approach and may be unable to draw the pie chart based on feelings. Others will intuitively approach the pie chart in a more fluid way, considering the figure more in terms of commitment or emotional investment in a particular role. For both approaches, drawing a second pie depicting a desired or future state is useful. The future state pie may be particularly important for individuals facing a life transition and needing to envision how it will affect their roles and activities. The coach will find this especially beneficial for individuals starting a family or retiring. On the other hand, the desired pie would be the starting point for addressing complaints concerning work-life balance. Gaps between current and desired states can be examined and will stimulate self-reflection on the roles, their value, and their impact. The pie charts can also be a starting point to reflect on our priorities in life and the shifts we would like to see. Group discussions can also be useful at this stage—comparing charts and explaining rationales for the desired state. One interesting question to emerge can be whether there should be a slice allotted to the self. Among the women in my seminars, it was rare to meet any who had a space for self in the current chart; and most did not have one in the desired state chart either. Most women would try to squeeze a small slice for themselves into the desired state pie after discussing this point. Some coachees will need to go through the pie process in a more detailed manner than others or over several iterations.

Looking at such pie charts it becomes clear that we have many domains and roles in our lives. However, most individuals tend to struggle with the integration of the two broad domains of family (which may include friends or hobbies) and work (which may include other public roles or studies), so I will concentrate mainly on this dichotomy. We can also use the work/nonwork distinction, refer to home and nonhome roles, or talk about the spheres of work and life. If we first consider the two dominant spheres in life (work and family), three focus options arise: focus on work, focus on family, or focus on work and family. As individuals face transitions in their life, these priorities may shift from one domain to the other over time. A young graduate may focus mostly on work, and then enter a phase of starting a family, during which this aspect may become more prominent, while parents of college students typically see a reversal of that situation and often become more involved with work or community activities as children leave the home. People go through cycles during which their priorities may change. Similarly, unexpected events or illnesses may dramatically affect priorities in life. Being aware of our priorities should provide us with a frame when we are faced with having to make decisions between competing spheres.

The women I encountered frequently stated that work was essential to them, that they could not imagine staying at home, and that they could not abandon their professional identity. However, they also stated that on occasions they would have preferred to work less or have more flexible work arrangements to enable them to cope with unexpected demands from the family. Thus even establishing clear priorities at a certain point in time does not diminish the need to learn to cope with the competing demands of work and family. Competing demands originating from home and nonhome roles emphasize the need to prioritize the demands we face and to manage and distribute our resources effectively.

Our societies are built on the concept of reciprocity. Indeed, life is all about give and take. Depending on the number of roles we play (our multiple identities) and the number of people we deal with (we could call them our stakeholders) we will be expected to give back more than we take. Many of these demands go unnoticed, as they seem natural and are part of our daily routines. However, there are times when these demands appear unmanageable, out of proportion, or simply in conflict—when everybody seems to need something "right now." Why are these situations difficult to manage? Two root causes are at play here. First, the competing demands originate mostly from stakeholders from different domains, who are therefore unaware or lack understanding of the other demands on us. When two stakeholders belong to the same domain, they can easily see and understand that we have to attend to something else first. Competing demands among siblings or family members can often be resolved easily (unless one party feels, perhaps rightly, that he or she always gets the worse deal). It can be far more problematic at work, where employees in many matrix organizations are exposed to the competing demands of different superiors in the overlapping structure. However, if two colleagues come to you with an urgent request, it should be less difficult to sort out an understanding and prioritize those different demands together. Second, competing demands often relate to a crisis, and are therefore unplanned and unexpected. For example, you have arranged to spend the evening watching the final of a favorite sporting event with friends. You have planned to leave work at a certain time, when your boss calls you with an urgent request to prepare a report to justify a decision taken on a whim two weeks earlier. Unless your boss is also a sports fan (and can therefore understand the other domain), it will be difficult to convince him to wait for the analysis until after the game. If unplanned demands of this kind occur frequently, especially if related to crises in competing domains (for example, an urgent report and a sick child) they will result in a considerable amount of strain and stress for the individual.

COMPETING DEMANDS AND COPING STRATEGIES

To deal with or, better still, to avoid the tensions of competing demands, individuals can be trained and coached with respect to a number of coping strategies. Two types of coping strategy can be distinguished, one reactive, the other proactive. Reactive role behavior is characterized by relying on existing roles and behaviors, while trying to meet all demands simultaneously. Proactive coping strategies, on the other hand, are based on redefining the roles of the actors involved. First, starting with awareness, coachees will benefit from recognizing their reliance on reactive coping strategies and the self-reinforcing patterns resulting from them. Reactive behavior, or what we often refer to in the corporate context as "fire-fighting," merely attends to upcoming demands in sequence. These responses will deal with the current situation but not provide a systemic solution, as the same challenges will come up again and again. These behaviors are counterproductive as they reinforce expectations from others and may lead them to reiterate those demands in the future. Indeed, reactive role behavior is more likely to contribute to the feeling of imbalance than change it, and only increases dissatisfaction and physical exhaustion.

Reactive role behavior can readily be acknowledged when individuals complain of similar recurring instances of competing demands they face. Therefore, identifying and reflecting on situations involving stressful competing demands is critical to creating the awareness of the inadequacy of reactive behavior. The next step is to realize that there are recurrent patterns associated with these behaviors. As discussed earlier, one of the reasons that competing demands are difficult to manage is their unplanned nature. Of course, some events are truly unexpected, but many could be anticipated and therefore planned as well (even as a Plan B). If you invariably respond to last-minute requests by colleagues, they will never learn that they have to plan and place requests well in advance, to allow you to execute them appropriately. Setting clear rules and managing the expectations of others are essential to providing a sustainable solution. Moreover, as our role will tend to evolve and expand over time, we cannot rely solely on reactive role behavior. We need a proactive approach to manage the different demands our different roles imply.

Two proactive coping strategies can be used, structural and personal role redefinition. Structural role redefinition involves redrawing the boundaries of expectations and duties and relies on direct negotiations with other social actors (partner, boss, child) to adjust the mutual expectations linked to the role. This coping strategy may require a significant amount of energy and time but can greatly reduce the conflict that arises from competing demands, as it results in an agreement over an issue once and for all. Not all people feel comfortable with this approach, or are skilled at it, so coaching individuals to become skilful in structural role redefinition will play an important part in the coaching for work-life balance process. It is crucial to convey the power of this strategy. From the coachees' perspective, a recurrent issue that could be easily settled through structural role redefinition may act as a powerful quick gain, allowing them to appreciate the benefit and potential impact of this approach. I recall the example of an Emirati woman in my seminars, who had negotiated a reduced workload but whose boss consistently held team meetings in the late afternoon so that she either had to stay late or skip the meeting. One day she decided this had to change and sent him an email formally requesting that all team meetings should be held before 2 p.m. He replied: "Yes."

Not all instances of structural role redefinition may be as easily settled as this one, and some may require constant renegotiation. Consider the struggle of Malika, a single Pakistani woman, the only remaining child living at home with her retired parents. Her father refused to have dinner alone and would wait for her to come home from work so they could eat together. She felt guilty for making him wait, but also felt it was unreasonable for him to expect her to have dinner with him every night while she had a demanding job and activities outside the home she wanted to pursue. The tension apparent in this situation could not be resolved through structural role redefinition alone. While the father needed to adjust his expectations, Malika also had to adjust her own attitude and role expectations. Feelings of guilt and inadequacy are good indicators of situations that can benefit from personal role redefinition. Although perfectionists may be particularly prone to these feelings, most of us struggle with guilt and "feeling bad" in relation to something we value a great deal. Women in particular can benefit greatly from this coping strategy. Women all over the world are socialized and prepared from early childhood to become a good mother (much like the "good daughter" standard Malika had set herself). The good mother stereotype, and women's own values centered around striving to uphold this ideal, create a great deal of guilt for women pursuing work outside the home. Personal role redefinition can greatly reduce the psychological stress experienced by the individual. A feeling of work-life balance may well lie closer within reach than many of us may believe.

FEELING IMBALANCED

While juggling different roles and competing demands requires time and practice, other tools can be helpful to address feelings of overload and imbalance. As I mentioned earlier, recent definitions of work-life balance state that it is not about equality but about fit and harmony. How, then, can we measure or evaluate work-life balance? The best indicator of fit would be that it should "feel right," so feeling imbalanced may be enough of a sign that something needs to be addressed. I propose two criteria to assess work-life balance: are you effective and are you satisfied? Identifying barriers to effectiveness on the one hand and to satisfaction on the other can be a useful framework to assess our situation. Individuals start by reflecting on whether the current situation allows them to reach their goals and objectives, or even simply achieve what needs to be done. Then the question arises about whether they are happy with this situation and what may hamper their satisfaction. As both aspects are related (you can be unhappy because you feel you cannot achieve your goal), I advise people to make two columns on a sheet of paper, the first labeled "Effectiveness," the second "Satisfaction," as the first may spill over on the second. Indeed, it is valuable to try and understand why effectiveness and satisfaction fail to meet expectations. One often-cited barrier is the continuous distraction of email, BlackBerry, and mobile phones, interrupting the flow of our activity (a barrier to effectiveness) and leading to a sense of overload (a barrier to satisfaction). Those barriers could then be examined from a systemic perspective and integrated into an action plan.

SELF-LEADERSHIP

While many human capital development programs focus on honing participants' leadership skills, a much-neglected area is that of self-leadership. Just as we need to develop a vision, set goals, and motivate followers to be successful, we also need to be skilled in leading ourselves. Complaining of insufficient time to fulfill all our obligations is often a prominent sign of a lack of self-leadership. However, the sense of drowning and lack of time experienced cannot be mended merely by tackling the symptoms through time-management tactics. Self-leadership goes beyond the time-management approach. While it is true that we need to make better use of our time, what is often more important is that we should focus our efforts on our goals. Thus coming to an understanding of our goals is key. First, the coach can initiate exercises in self-reflection with respect to goal setting. Goals should be considered in the short (coming months), medium (one to two years), and long term (over the course of the next ten years). Some individuals may feel more comfortable starting with the short term, while others may have a long-term vision, from which they can work backwards. Either way, this exercise may take several iterations before a SMART (specific, measurable, attainable, realistic, and timely) set of goals is defined. Many coachees will be overfamiliar with the SMART approach from their working sphere, so coaches need to know how to counter "So what?" First, this exercise is different than a corporate goal-setting exercise because it concerns personal career goals and aspirations. Thus wild dreams are allowed, if they can be developed and formulated in a SMART frame. We are increasingly discovering a world with "boundaryless careers," that is to say, careers that evolve beyond the traditional boundaries of organizations. With this in mind, it makes sense to reflect on individual skill sets and career aspirations and set goals that are in line with those. Some coachees will readily embrace this frame of reference as they may have already switched careers a number of times and do not see their future linked to any particular organization. Their current position may be merely a stepping-stone for the next transition. Other individuals may be more reluctant to adopt this new career perspective. Coaches have an important role to play here in sensing where the individual would be most comfortable. It makes no sense to force a public sector employee to think of life outside the organization if that person is happy in the present environment and on the current track. However, when coachees indicate a sense of uncertainty or a need to explore, it may be well worth pushing the limits and trying to make them think outside their present working context, challenging the status quo or the suitability and desirability of the path they are on.

While setting short- and long-term professional goals is where to start, the challenge usually increases significantly when it comes to extending the same exercise into the personal realm, setting goals for the other roles we play in life (spouse, parent, community representative, or simply self). "What does it mean to have goals as a mother?" was a question often raised at the start of the exercise. However, after some reflection, stories and examples emerged. There was then discussion about the need for such goals: without them, time is taken up by other things and we do not feel like doing what we should have done. Indeed, most of us have some implicit personal or family goals, but their implicitness often leads to their being relegated to the bottom of priority lists. As they are only in the back of our mind, they are frequently sacrificed for seemingly more important or urgent matters. For example, one participant's simple short-term family goal was first expressed as, "I try to spend some quality time with each child." Following the exercise this goal was reframed in more SMART terms as, "My objective is to spend at least one hour of quality time with each of my children every week." Granted, "quality time" was still a bit fuzzy, but it was good to start with an explicitly stated goal from which several stakeholders would benefit and which could be tracked on a weekly basis. The statement also acknowledged that "quality time" was to mean something different for each child (ranging from going shopping to a game of table tennis).

While making goals explicit and updating them regularly is key to effective self-leadership, we also need to motivate ourselves to achieve those goals. Some of them will be closely aligned with our personal values and may therefore generate a great amount of intrinsic motivation. In other instances ("Why should I do this?"), we may need to remind ourselves of the bigger picture. Take the example of the Egyptian woman in her late forties who complained of always feeling tired while her teenage children were full of energy. One of her personal goals was to change her lifestyle to improve her health and live a longer life. Broken down into smaller, actionable statements, her SMART goals included "going to the gym three times a week." While her demanding job and hectic family life often made it difficult to generate the necessary motivation, recalling the bigger picture (I am doing this for my children, to be there longer for them) could help. In other instances, self-reward and punishment can give an extra nudge. Effective use of this self-leadership strategy again requires adequate self-awareness. First, it is crucial to know our tendencies. Do you tend to reward yourself (with an ice cream, say, or a new accessory) every so often or are you the kind of person who frets for hours over a lost opportunity or a word unsaid? Most of us have a fairly good sense of where we lie on the spectrum of self-reward and punishment. Moreover, in the group setting, with a show of hands, or through the chuckles or specific examples shared among group members, the coach can quickly gain a sense of who could benefit from some extra punishment and who could focus more on rewards. Once again, self-awareness is the key here. Also, as when motivating subordinates, finding the right rewards for yourself may require some creative thinking. Obviously an ice cream would be counterproductive if you want to reward yourself for a step toward your weight-loss goal. You need to find intrinsic rewards, that is, intrinsic to the activities you pursue toward your goal. If your goal is to spend time with your child, then enjoying that time may be your biggest reward. Listening to music while doing a menial job can add some intrinsic reward to the activity and make it easier for us to complete.

Finally, as emotional intelligence is increasingly considered crucial to successful leadership, self-leadership requires emotional regulation and self-awareness about tendencies and situations that may cause emotional distress. The Positive Affectivity Negative Affectivity Schedule (PANAS) scale can assess whether individuals display more positive or negative affectivity overall. But while such scales may be useful, they may also have the drawback of labeling coachees—not always desirable, as it can lead to helplessness reactions. Therefore, self-awareness about feelings of optimism and pessimism (self-identification) may be another viable alternative to recognizing patterns and drawing conclusions about our tendencies. This approach is also particularly useful for people who score at the mid-point on instruments like the PANAS scale, and who are often left in limbo after such an assessment. Persons high on positive affectivity can benefit from coaching toward better self-leadership, in the sense that awareness of that trait may reduce upward spirals toward unrealistically rosy outcomes. Reality checks may help these individuals to avoid becoming too confident in their perceptions. Conversely, people with negative affectivity can benefit from self-awareness by recognizing instances of overly negative outlooks. Putting things in perspective in the face of adversity, thinking about the long-term impact of an event, counterfactual thinking ("What if I do not hand in this report on time this week?"), and simply reminding oneself to "be positive" can effectively lead to better outcomes.

Other than personal affectivity tendencies, it is also important to become skilled at understanding how your emotions are affected by others. Indeed, when you feel you are not in a good mood it may be worth avoiding encounters with people you know will only make you feel worse. Some individuals are better at this than others. A timid young woman in one of my groups shared her self-leadership story. Aisha was the mother of a six-month-old child. Her husband was in the military and away most of the time, and she lived with her husband's family. Aisha used to receive frequent phone calls at the office from her mother-in-law who took care of her child while she was at work. The mother-in-law would lament that the baby was missing Aisha and refusing to eat. Aisha was deeply affected by these calls, which fueled the feelings of guilt with which she was struggling. Leaving her job was not an option. So one day, under pressure at work, she told her mother-in-law, "I don't want to hear you complain any longer. If you don't want to take care of Ali, that is fine, I can find a nanny but I need to continue my work. Please only call me if it is an emergency." She hung up. The group exploded with admiration. Aisha had solved a major, recurring, and emotionally stressful issue, using a proactive coping strategy. Although she still faced the same negative influences after work, she had taken one important step toward increased satisfaction and effectiveness in her work life. Other steps would be needed on the family side.

ENERGY MANAGEMENT

Aisha's story highlights a common misconception about work-life balance and work-life stressors. Close your eyes and think of the good things in life. The chances are that you thought of a nice candlelit dinner with your partner, a walk in the forest, or a recent vacation—pleasant, restorative experiences related to your free time. Now think of the not-so-good things in life. The chances are you thought of deadlines, piles of files to go through, and lists of emails, exhausting and frustrating matters, and all work-related. Indeed, we commonly think of work as depleting, and activities in the nonwork or family realm as restorative. But is this really true? Aisha's story illustrates the misconception quite clearly. Her work was her haven in which she could invest herself and feel a sense of purpose and enjoyment. Her family was a strain, and interaction with family was depleting in many ways. This is an important point to clarify when coaching for work-life balance. Examples of depleting family activities are numerous and will be shared with humor and relief. Indeed, family life is not always as restorative as we would like it to be. This is important to acknowledge because it allows us to see the other side of the coin, which is often more difficult to convey: work is not all bad either. We can experience instances of flow, deep involvement, and genuine satisfaction while working on an interesting or enjoyable task alone or with a stimulating group of people. To allow people to visualize their life from this perspective, in the workshop two axes are drawn on a piece of paper. The vertical axis reflects the restorative versus depleting dimension; the horizontal axis represents work versus family. Participants are asked to fill each quadrant with appropriate examples. Most people will readily recognize a couple of depleting experiences in the family realm and a couple of restorative activities in their work. However, I have also come across individuals who tried and tried in vain to come up with any restorative or rewarding element in their job. These cases are difficult to address in a work-life balance coaching group and will require further counseling on career goals and aspirations. We may at least have established a more explicit sense of lingering dissatisfaction, which may lead to action, once the problem is pinpointed. Far worse, however, is the case where no restorative experience on the family side can be recalled. I encountered just one such instance with a middle-aged man in an executive seminar where I also used this framework. All his restorative and flow experiences were related to work and self-development. No comparable experiences were found on the family side, and he had no restorative experiences to share with his young second wife and his small children. This realization would call for a complete questioning of the family system and might need counseling well beyond work-life balance coaching in a corporate setting.

Once made aware of what drains their energy levels and what gives them a boost, participants can be introduced to the techniques of energy management. The first and most obvious approach is to delegate or avoid depleting activities. While driving is a depleting activity for many of us, only a limited number of us can call upon chauffeurs. However, car-sharing and taking turns could be a viable option. With a complementary partner or colleague we can find ways to exchange/delegate activities for which we feel less affinity. While we try to avoid or delegate depleting activities, we can also seek out more restorative activities. Of course, this technique has its limitations as many depleting things simply have to be dealt with (for example, a teething baby or a nagging customer). In these instances, sequencing is the name of the game. Sequencing means addressing issues or tasks in order so that you never reach burnout—so a depleting activity should be followed by a restorative one, to avoid slipping further into depletion. This approach can readily be illustrated by charting a typical day. Starting with an average energy level, a cup of coffee may give us a boost, driving to the office may be depleting, but then with luck some interaction with colleagues will bring our energy levels back up. By lunch-time we are usually running low again, so it is important to take a break and refuel with some food and social interaction— and so on. Allowing participants to graph their own typical day (both working and weekend) gives them a feel for the approach and can generate insight into better choices in terms of sequencing.

Ultimately, the major reason to include a discussion on energy management in a work-life balance coaching program is that many individuals complain that after a long day at work they do not have enough energy to enjoy anything outside of work; they just crash in front of the TV. An awareness of how our energy levels are depleted and restored during the day (or even over the week)—proper energy management—can be a great contribution to better work-life balance.

CONCLUDING THOUGHTS

Of course, we could tackle many more issues to facilitate and enhance work-life balance. Depending on the life cycle of the coachees, we may have to address different personal and professional needs. Families and workplaces are systems that influence each other. We may experience negative (but also positive) spillover effects from one to the other. Spillover effects can also occur between couples or colleagues.

With their self-awareness heightened, and armed with a set of tools, coachees often make a good start at improving their work-life balance. However, experiment-ing and exploring, and setting new boundaries, may not come easily. Eventually, some new routines may be set in place and some old patterns abandoned. The coaching sessions themselves are a window of opportunity, providing space for participants to reflect and create action plans for better work-life balance.

15

CULTURAL DIVERSITY IN GLOBAL LEADERSHIP—GROUP EXECUTIVE COACHING IN ASIA

JACKI NICHOLAS AND KATHERINE TWADDELL

The essence of global leadership is the ability to influence people who are not like the leader and come from different cultural backgrounds. To succeed, global leaders need to have a global mindset, tolerate high levels of ambiguity, and show cultural adaptability and flexibility.

GLOBE Project[1]

Group executive coaching (GEC) is a way for individuals to witness and explore contemporary leadership issues in a safe and supervised arena. It has the potential to accelerate awareness, behavioral shifts, and results relating to a leader's development. The group context can act as a microcosm of an organization and the interplay of its numerous human dynamics. The trust and support engendered within the group cohorts can open participants to new possibilities, perspectives, and learning that tend to take much longer in the normal work environment. Group coaching can accelerate the pace at which executives explore and assimilate the issues necessary for them to become effective global leaders.

We begin with a general overview of group executive coaching, drawing on global data and examples from our experiences of GEC in Asia. We address the critical success factors we have found important as well as how to evaluate GEC effectiveness—all within the context of the more common issues playing out in the diverse leadership landscape of Asia today. This chapter offers the reader some initial coordinates from which to begin to chart their own group coaching journey.

GLOBAL OVERVIEW OF GROUP EXECUTIVE COACHING

Although coaching has been around for many decades, it has burgeoned over the last ten years into one of the fastest growing human capital initiatives around the globe. Despite a small lag effect, Asia has been no exception. The bulk of executive coaching is one-on-one, and group coaching, despite its immense potential for impact, remains on the fringe of today's coaching explosion.

In 2008, we surveyed 171 executive coaches from 40 countries* who employed group executive coaching on a regular basis.[2] The majority had coached in countries and cultures other than their own and over 50 percent of respondents had practiced group coaching for five years or more. These coaches predominantly implemented GEC in the following arenas:

- executive leadership (71 percent)
- executive team effectiveness (61 percent)
- developing high potentials (51 percent) and
- change leadership (45 percent).

The survey was undertaken as an online questionnaire run between August and October 2008. Group coaches from around the world were invited to participate. Survey invitations were sent to professional coaching associations such as the Association of Coaching, European Mentoring and Coaching Council (EMCC), International Association of Coaching (IAC), International Coaching Federation (ICF), Worldwide Association of Business Coaches (WABC), and so on, as well as institutions known to be involved in group coaching. Invitations were also extended to numerous regional, national, and local coaching groups. Coaches were encouraged to forward the invitation to other coaches in their professional networks.

The survey consisted of 17 closed and open-ended questions, the latter used for discussion-related topics to encourage the full, unbiased expression of respondents' professional experiences in group executive coaching. An initial finding was that the duration of group executive coaching varies considerably. Programs typically range from one day to two years, the most prevalent being between three and twelve months. The length of coaching sessions varies from one hour to a whole day.

What constitutes a "group" in group executive coaching? While the jury is still out on the ideal group size, the survey showed that there is some variation in the number of coachees per group:

- 2–6 (48 percent)
- 7–12 (48 percent)
- 13–20 (16 percent) and
- over 20 (6 percent)
- (some people surveyed did not have a precise answer).

These statistics seem to indicate that, in GEC, less can be more. It is easy to see how the lines between coaching, facilitating, and consulting could

---

*Australia, Belgium, Brazil, Canada, China, Czech Republic, Denmark, England, France, Germany, Hong Kong, India, Indonesia, Ireland, Israel, Japan, Luxembourg, Malaysia, Mexico, Netherlands, New Zealand, Peru, Philippines, Poland, Portugal, Puerto Rico, Romania, Russian Federation, Scotland, Serbia, Singapore, South Africa, South Korea, Sweden, Switzerland, Taiwan, Thailand, Turkey, United Arab Emirates, and USA.

become blurred as group size increases. This can be further affected by the fact that there are different approaches to GEC. Some involve the coach providing relevant content on an issue and then posing coaching questions to the entire group. It is then up to individual coachees to respond. This may be managed via a spontaneous and voluntary approach, or by a systematic, orderly one-by-one method. Contrarily, the IGLC approach primarily seeks to generate insights, clarify participants' focus on development, and enhance the coaching skills of coachees themselves. It takes a reflective stance, and uses a different methodology. Participants take turns in the "coaching chair" and are coached by their peers, with the IGLC coach acting as both head coach and group facilitator, as described in earlier chapters. IGLC's clinical approach (see the Introduction to this book) gives busy leaders the space and time to look within, back, and across personal and interpersonal divides, to gain awareness, and move forward. This approach favors small group sizes, and we work in groups of four to six coachees per coach for a full day. Coachees will often regroup for follow-up, in situ or virtually, sometimes with and sometimes without the coach, over the next six to twelve months. Thus GEC group size seems to be influenced by GEC methodology, objectives, and the role of the coach.

DIVERSITY VERSUS HOMOGENEITY

Diversity, in its essence, means difference or variety. In a societal and organizational context, diversity typically consists of at least eight people-related dimensions. These include age, gender, race, disability, sexual orientation, religion, ethnicity, and language skills.[3] The acknowledgment and respect of diversity have been important in global and forward-thinking organizations for many years, driven initially from a perspective of equality and inclusivity. The importance of working and leading with diversity, however, has spread and escalated. Whereas a mere five years ago the ability to work effectively with people "other than ourselves" might have been advantageous, in today's highly globalized corporations it is more a necessity or critical success factor.

INSEAD is a global business school and its programs typically include a diverse mix of executives. On its campuses, the majority of IGLC's coaching groups comprise leaders from highly diverse cultures. In a small group, it is not unusual to have participants from three or four continents. Each cohort is selected to optimize diversity of culture, gender, industry, professional function, and other prevalent criteria.

Exploring and becoming more familiar with diversity can be a powerful component of the group process. When you are working with any group of at least four people, there is a good chance you will find similarities and differences in their characteristics, behaviors, and issues. One person's strength can be another's challenge, a source of creative insight, and a trigger for learning potential. The power of diversity is even greater when participants from different cultures, genders, generations, or professional functions find, through the group coaching process, that they share similar traits, issues, or attributes. Thus there can be diversity in homogeneity and similarity in heterogeneity.

In a recent program held in Singapore for a multinational pharmaceutical, five ostensibly very different participants came together from three continents and five professional functions. As each of the four men and one woman told their respective stories throughout the day, sharing the "portrait" of their life, it was gradually revealed that the Japanese, American, and French participants, despite very different cultural traditions and upbringing, had experienced uncannily similar parenting. This had significantly impacted the lives of each of them and been a strong force in shaping their personal and professional identity. This surprising common thread of shared experience united and bonded the three in a tacit but very real way.

THE IMPACT OF DIVERSITY AND HOMOGENEITY IN GEC

The Air Institute GEC survey sought to explore coaches' experience of diversity in terms of generation , cross-cultural, and gender issues, within the group executive coaching context.

Of the three, we have found that cultural diversity trumps generation and gender as the most frequently observed form of diversity at IGLC. The coaching cohorts typically comprise professionals at similar leadership levels and so, by proxy, generation. Although cross-generational challenges often arise as a thematic leadership issue[*] shared by the group, we rarely see significant generational diversity in group composition.

As women continue to form a relative minority at senior executive levels, it is rare to have more than one woman in a group, particularly in company-specific programs. This equates to approximately 20–25 percent of the leadership population on any given program. So, while there is some gender diversity in such groups, it is difficult to accumulate sufficient data from which to draw conclusions about the impact of gender diversity. In a situation where "the other" is just one, it would be premature to pinpoint the cause of any observable behavioral differences. For this reason, we focus on culture as the main form of diversity in the group coaching context.

As one of the first global surveys on group executive coaching, the Air Institute GEC survey was intentionally investigative. The majority of the questions were open-ended to glean as much unbiased data as possible from diverse group coaching sources. Examples of questions included:

- "From your experience, what are the advantages and disadvantages of coaching cross-cultural groups?"

[*]Common thematic leadership issues often emerge in group executive coaching, including interpersonal communication, work-life balance, influence, executive presence, navigating matrix organizations, leading change, cross-generational challenges, virtual teams, resilience, priority management, ethics, and so on.

- "Have you noticed any gender differences in group coaching in your experience, and if so, what?"
- "What have you found are the key issues of working across generations in group executive coaching?"
- "What can get in the way of, or derail, a successful group coaching experience?"

The results of the survey indicated that coaching in diverse groups can be both positive and negative. Responses suggested that, while homogeneous groups are in some ways easier to coach, heterogeneous groups can bring significant benefits to compensate for the additional challenges posed. Just as in work scenarios, in the group executive context diversity must be handled with great skill and respect to derive maximum benefit from it.

We present some of the key advantages and disadvantages of coaching homogeneous and diverse groups in Tables 15.1 and 15.2.

TABLE 15.1 **Coaching homogeneous groups**

Advantages	Disadvantages
• Shared societal norms that require little or no explanation, for example, excessive work hours in Japan, collective social time with male executives in Saudi Arabia, after hours work-related drinking and socializing in Korea.	• Groupthink
	• Potential positioning and jostling to be seen as the leader or the best in the group, in strongly individual oriented groups, for example, alpha males.[4]
• Shared platform from which participants can explore a multitude of relevant topics.	• Less creative (fewer perspectives).
• Less risky to make assumptions.	• Collective complaining—viewing an unwanted situation as inevitable or unfixable.
• People are less guarded and less "politically correct." They are likely to say what they think.	
• Easier communication as participants "speak the same language" and use readily understood verbal and nonverbal communication patterns.	• May be less trusting and more concerned about confidentiality being maintained.

TABLE 15.2 **Coaching diverse groups**

Advantages	Disadvantages
• Unexpected learning from deeper exposure to "the other" can lead to widening of perspectives.	• Language barriers.
	• Communication problems can lead to confusion.
• Potential spark for creativity.	• The pace of discussion can be slower.
• Breaks down perceived barriers.	• Potential limitations of stereotypes.
• Surprise and bonding from noting very real similarities between people initially perceived as very different.	• An individual who feels the odd one out might be isolated and take longer to draw out.

SETTING THE STAGE WITH A DIVERSE COACHING GROUP

Our experience and research have shown that some specific factors enhance the effectiveness of GEC, regardless of a group's homogeneity or diversity. The most fundamental of these are:

- rapport and trust between all coachees, and between coachees and coach;
- the coach's expertise—in coaching, facilitating group dynamics, and remaining present;
- the mindset of coachees and their will for self-disclosure and commitment to contribute to their own and fellow coachees' growth.

The first step in any group coaching is to establish rapport and trust within the group. Building a bridge and bond, both between participants and with the coach, serves a multitude of purposes in the group coaching context. It establishes the cornerstone of the coaching experience by creating a high level of trust. Indeed, an overwhelming number of coaches in the Air Institute GEC survey emphasized the criticality of confidentiality and openness as key success factors. These can be even more important when coaching in a diverse group.

We use creative, yet probing icebreakers as a nonthreatening way of illustrating the self-disclosure necessary for effective group coaching. This creates the opportunity for leaders to take a risk, play with the unfamiliar, and become more at ease with uncertainty and ambiguity. Engaging corporate individuals in a more right-brain perspective (through activities like drawing, symbolic metaphors, or storytelling) encourages coachees to delve into the emotional and creative side of their brain. At IGLC we ask coachees to draw a portrait of themselves, depicting what is currently in their head, heart, and stomach, their work and leisure, and their past and future. We never cease to be amazed by the creative, symbolic, and emotional depth of this seemingly simple exercise. Everything from traditional portraits and caricatures to landscapes, creatures, storyboards, cartoons, and still lives can emerge. However, it is the discourse that follows, when the individual explains the portrait to the group, which is most revealing.

This kind of exercise heralds that it is no normal day at the office. When dealing with executives from highly structured, top-down organizations, who are used primarily to applying their left (logical) brain, such an activity both disrupts their normal way of operating and allows the individuals to bond as a unit. This is a necessary and sometimes challenging shift to make for corporate cultures dominated by rational, left-brain thinking and allows for more integrated and balanced ways of processing and interacting. Other factors work in parallel with bonding and trust in GEC success. One, clearly, is the coach's coaching expertise; the other is the mindset of each individual in the group. A coach must be able effortlessly and fluidly to shift between coach and facilitator roles, continually calibrating the energy and emotion of the group. So too must the individuals be open to embarking on the deep dive into their own "inner theater."

233

"Our inner theater results from a combination of nature and nurture. Although our brains are genetically hard-wired with certain instinctual behavior patterns, this wiring isn't irrevocably fixed. Through the nature-nurture interface, highly complex motivational need systems determine the unique inner theater of the individual—the stage on which the major themes that define the person are played out."[5] For it is within the inner theater that exploration and awareness truly begin.

HOW CULTURAL DIVERSITY PLAYS OUT IN GROUP EXECUTIVE COACHING

Cultural diversity is by no means a new concept in the study of leadership and organizational effectiveness. Various well-known cultural dimensions have been identified over the years, such as those propounded by Hofstede and Hampden-Turner and Trompenaars.[6] More recently, the Global Leadership and Organizational Behavior Effectiveness (GLOBE) Project recognized the importance of understanding its impact on leadership. In a ten-year study, 170 GLOBE researchers gathered and analyzed cultural and leadership data from 17,000 managers in 62 societal cultures. They identified nine cultural dimensions that have managerial and leadership implications, irrespective of specific culture.[*] We expect these are likely to be relevant irrespective of generation or gender.

In the GEC survey, coaches were specifically asked about the advantages and disadvantages of working with cross-cultural groups.

ADVANTAGES OF CULTURAL DIVERSITY

Twenty-nine percent of respondents cited diversity as the main advantage of cross-cultural groups. Figure 15.1 shows the advantages of cross-cultural diversity in group executive coaching.

Comments focused on the themes of awareness and new perspectives:

- "One of the beauties is getting people to realize that the basic needs and wants of humans expand neatly across varied cultures."
- "Celebrating differences."
- "Different perspectives and points of view are always enriching."
- "Learning more about how others think, feel, work, and live."
- "Diverse groups share same problems—enlightenment!"
- "Learning, respecting other cultures."
- "Celebrating sameness."

---

[*] The nine cultural dimensions that the GLOBE project identified are performance orientation, assertiveness, future orientation, humane orientation, institutional collectivism, in-group collectivism, gender egalitarianism, power distance, and uncertainty avoidance.

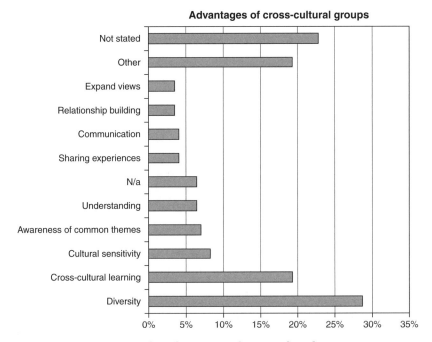

FIGURE 15.1 **The advantages of cross-cultural groups**

DISADVANTAGES OF CULTURAL DIVERSITY

Diversity, however, is not always seen as a positive by all coaches. "Cultural difference" was identified as a disadvantage by 15 percent of survey respondents. This included cultural factors such as:

- "losing face";
- directness versus reticence of different cultures;
- the dominant/submissive behaviors of specific cultures;
- a troubling issue to some may not be perceived as a problem at all in other cultures.

Respondents cited various disadvantages of coaching cross-cultural groups for the coach:

- It is more challenging.
- It is difficult to generalize.
- Can be harder to focus the group.
- It usually takes more time.
- It is more difficult to explain principles.
- Requires a variety of communication strategies to be effective.

More specifically:

- "It can become very demanding and the coach needs to be extremely aware."
- "Need to get their point across in several ways to reach all."
- "Requires constant feedback about whether everyone in the group is in a learning mode and that language is accessible to all."

In our experience, however, these disadvantages can be alleviated through the coaches' application of their intercultural understanding and group coaching skills.

Some 27 percent of GEC survey respondents stated that "less effective communication" was the biggest disadvantage when coaching cross-cultural groups. Language barriers and misunderstandings ("same words, different meaning"), message dilution, and missed cues can all undermine effective communication between cultures. As one survey respondent commented, "Language may mean different things depending on your frame of reference and where you learned the language. You may think you are speaking the same language, but how it is used can create cultural clashes."

We frequently face this language challenge when coaching culturally diverse groups in IGLC Singapore. We have witnessed potentially derailing confusion about comments in participants' feedback. In one group, Tashi, a Japanese sales executive, was praised several times for his aggressiveness in his written 360-degree feedback from friends and colleagues. He came to the coaching session the following day still in shock after a largely sleepless night, and was very upset and ashamed. When he took his place in the coaching chair, he kept insisting, quite emotionally, that he was not aggressive. He was almost pleading with us to agree with him. The culturally diverse group, which included executives from the United States, France, India, and the Philippines responded in different ways. The three western or western-educated executives could not understand why Tashi was so upset. From their perspective, it was clear that aggressiveness was a strength of which he should be proud. They thought he was confused between the sections for behaviors to stop and behaviors to continue. Michel, the French executive, was encouraging: "They want you to carry on being aggressive," while the American asserted, "It's good to be aggressive." Meanwhile Bayani, the Filipino executive, was quiet but shook his head vigorously, and, when prompted, shared his own dilemma. "This isn't right. I know what is happening here. My American boss keeps telling me that I must be more aggressive. But he doesn't understand. I explain to him that it just won't work in the Philippines. If I am aggressive, I will not succeed. No one will listen to me. It is not good in our culture. But he just won't listen. Tashi must only be pretending to be aggressive at work to please his boss—it's not right." As the group shared their different perceptions of the term "aggressive," from both cultural and work function perspectives, the room filled with laughter and relief. Tashi ended his session with a happy face and upright posture, assured that he was seen as a strong and determined sales executive, and Bayani realized he could retain his preferred leadership style in the Philippines, yet needed to supplement it with different styles according to the situation, his purpose, and the people with whom he was communicating. The English-speaking executives realized they needed to be very specific about language and explanation when providing cross-cultural feedback. The whole group left with a new perspective and understanding—all over a single word. Clearly, language can have significant implications for 360-degree feedback in diverse cultures and potentially for diverse genders and generations as well.

CULTURAL DIVERSITY IN 360-DEGREE FEEDBACK

Historically, cross-cultural research focused on highlighting differences between cultures. More recently, there has been a shift to identifying and focusing on similarities. But there is a third way—the integration of these two viewpoints. It is not simply about what is the same and what is different, but rather, the mutuality of human existence. This concept has been explored in the leadership arena through the GLOBE project, which has systematically researched how different cultures value and define leadership, to identify universal facilitators of effective leadership and impediments to it. They include perceived attributes such as integrity, charisma, vision, inspiration and good team building. Conversely, universal impediments to effective leadership include being perceived as autocratic, a loner or noncooperative.[7]

Each of these dimensions represents a powerful vantage point for working with diverse cultures in GEC, as diversity is always at play in multicultural groups—within and between coaching participants, in the narratives they relate, and in the 360-degree feedback that is discussed. In the IGLC group approach, it is interesting to see how these universal attributes play out as participants comment on their own and other participants' feedback.

Comments from some GEC survey respondents indicated that some cultures, for example, Asian, Latin American, and some southern European, are viewed as likely to be uneasy about doing 360-degree feedback. The main cultural difference cited in the GEC survey was that Asians were seen as less forthright in their feedback by 26 percent of coaches who provided comments. Conversely, Westerners were seen as more direct and willing to provide feedback by 9 percent of responding coaches. Some respondents believed this stemmed from cultural norms: in many Asian countries, for example, it is not polite to criticize someone, especially an elder. The GLOBE project cites that in the Chinese culture, which is distinguished by its high performance and institutional orientation, and in-group collectivism,[8] "managers seem to like leaders who are fraternal and friendly with their subordinates and who have an indirect approach to communication, using metaphors and parables to communicate their point."[9]

What is not clear, however, is the extent to which this perceived uneasiness about giving feedback could be related to the amount of previous exposure executives and their stakeholders have had to providing 360-degree feedback. From our experience, cultural reluctance can be neutralized by greater positive exposure to multi-rater feedback methods. Although it is not unlikely that people from collectivist and/or hierarchical cultures might well be more reticent or cautious in their feedback, other factors, such as method novelty, may also contribute to this reaction.

In the GEC survey, and from a feedback perspective, Asians were generally seen as:

- less critical of superiors;
- culturally uneasy about undertaking 360-degree feedback;
- providing fewer comments; and
- giving themselves low self-scores.

Westerners were generally viewed as:

- more assertive, clear, and direct in their feedback;
- more comfortable giving feedback, even to bosses; and
- having higher self-scores.

Specific GEC survey comments include:

- "Feedback from Asian people is more modest, polite, less direct."
- "Asian people's tendency is to protect the status quo."
- "North Americans are more direct, while Asians may be less willing to criticize directly."
- "People from Confucian cultures may be more reticent in giving feedback, especially to their superiors."
- "A Westerner's notion of assertiveness may be very different from an Asian's perspective of it."

In our Asian experience, we have noted two telltale signs of potential uneasiness with giving feedback: first, a lack of open-ended comments and second, higher than usual ratings. While a low level of comments could be related to language challenges, we still observe it where feedback technology allows for comments in the participant's own language. When participants feel less comfortable about giving feedback, the comments they provide tend to be very general, skewed toward the positive, and sometimes take on the nature of overarching praise and gratitude for working with someone, almost like a personal message of thanks.

We have found that one way of tackling the second issue—consistently high ratings—is to note the lower end of these. For example, in a Japanese multinational, many Japanese respondents rated their managers at very high levels, consistently 5, 6, and 7 (out of a possible 7). While these are pleasing results for an executive to receive, at first glance there seemed to be little to work on, as respondents provided very few comments. It could have been a bland coaching dialogue, at least from a data perspective. In this case, we flagged the lower ratings for each respondent—5 for those who gave 5 to 7, and 6 for those giving only 6 or 7. We suggested treating them as potentially lower—as we might normally view a rating of 3 or 4. This treatment opened up the opportunity to uncover development themes that would not otherwise have been noticed among the highly complimentary ratings. In fact, the approach lent additional weight to what had looked like small, outlying ratings received from one or two non-Japanese respondents. It is always important, however, to do a reality check with the executive and group, to see if any themes that emerge from this more detailed treatment resonate with their personal observations, as relevant areas for development.

OBSERVATIONS FROM THE FIELD IN ASIA

At first glance, one might think that GEC in Asia would differ vastly, as the region comprises such diverse and distinctive cultures. To further hone our exploration of GEC issues in Asia, we compared and contrasted the set-up and rapport building phase of five recent assignments in the region:

- four Japanese executives from a high-tech manufacturing company;
- six Thai executives from a large industrial conglomerate;
- four British executives in an international bank in Asia;
- five non-Asian executives from different countries and organizations; and
- six Asian and non-Asian executives from a pharmaceutical.

As we discussed earlier, this phase is crucial in developing the trust necessary for creating the safe arena in which to explore universal leadership attributes. It needs to be clear, understood, and agreed, yet in an almost contradictory way, low-key.

Our observations revealed that, in the Japanese and Thai groups, building intimacy and trust took longer and required greater patience. This could be related to several causes:

- English language challenges;
- the coach's cultural background—might it have been different with a Japanese or Thai coach?
- moving beyond the polite faces or public veneer that are so fundamental to interaction in these two cultures.

Linked to this was the issue of the coach being viewed as a guru or expert, with the authority and "responsibility" to provide coachees with "answers." This is particularly common in Confucian-based societies and in cultures where institutions and leaders exert a somewhat parental influence over their people. In such contexts, it is even more important for coaches to establish professional credibility up front, to explain the critical success factors (which effectively become the rules of engagement), and actively to embody the desired coaching skills they want coachees to adopt.

Conversely, when working with British and non-Asian executive groups, trust and collaboration were noticeably more readily established between participants. As the icebreaking process later revealed, however, this apparent intimacy can sometimes be little more than a social nicety occurring at relatively superficial levels. The self-disclosure process created greater intimacy and interpersonal commitment, which then allowed for safer revelation of core issues, as the group progressed with the coaching.

With some Asian groups, the coach needs to lead the initial "curious questioning" for a longer period of time than with many non-Asian groups. The coach's questioning in the early stages may need to be more focused, persistent and, at times, directive with an Asian group. In some Asian cultures, asking questions is seen as disrespectful to the "leader" or "teacher," as is admission of a person's own foolishness. The self-disclosure offered by some Asian coachees can be more indirect and layered, requiring further questioning to get to the deeper level, much like sequential separation of Russian dolls, until we uncover the core issue.

The coaching tenet of "enlightenment through questions"—a cornerstone of both Buddhist philosophy and the Socratic method—is often far removed from the everyday ways of operating in traditional, hierarchical cultures, corporate or ethnographic, Asian or non-Asian. Some of the more common topics with which our group coachees in Asia grapple include:

- traditional conservative cultures interacting with international corporate philosophies and ways of working; for example, Japan with work-life balance, Saudi Arabia with trust, secrecy, and transparency;
- differences between generations and cultures in dynamic emerging markets with strong tradition-based cultures (like Vietnam, India, China) and established economies.

In any culture, it is a challenge for both parties when an older person reports to a younger. When strong cultural expectations and values about hierarchy are factored in, an even greater challenge arises. This is an increasingly common issue for Asians working in multinational organizations, especially in emerging Asian markets. It can cause people to lose face and even derail teams. On occasion, the struggle can surface during group coaching in Asia when the group contains participants from different generations. An older executive can sometimes find it insulting to be in the same coaching group and treated as a peer of a younger executive—it can feel like a demotion or a slap in the face.

It is equally awkward for the young executive wanting on the one hand to show respect for the older colleague, and on the other, to be an active participant, challenge the status quo, and be visibly connected to the international corporate community. We have found this phenomenon to be most extreme in dynamic and emerging economies such as Vietnam, China, and India, where the traditional cultures are still highly conservative and believe in honoring and obeying elders. In these situations, the coach needs to allow both parties to reflect, express, and discuss. Sometimes this is the first time the issue has been openly acknowledged and shared, let alone done so in public.

A review of these five culturally different coaching groups tells us that coaches must be mindful of remaining sufficiently open to allow each group to proceed in its own way according to its composition and the issues that arise. The IGLC's clinical approach has the flexibility to do this. Our experience in group coaching across diverse cultures supports Richard Nisbett's tenet that "human cognition is not everywhere the same" and that "two utterly different approaches to the world have maintained themselves for thousands of years. These approaches include profoundly different social relations, views about the nature of the world, and characteristic thought processes. Each of these orientations—the Western and the Eastern—is a self-reinforcing, homeostatic system."[10] As Western coaches in Asia, we must remain alert to how this might play out, in our own coaching and within each group we coach.

Increasingly, however, we see exchanges between Asian and Western views in executives' thinking and behavior. When working with millennials and some generation X in Asia's emerging economies, we sometimes see evidence that could support Francis Fukuyama's[11] view that the world's societies are converging with the "westernization" of younger generations. Yet, at other times, we also see an increasing cultural pride in being able to maintain and even expand Asian culture in an increasingly modernized world, which could support Samuel Huntington's[12] theory of cultural divergence. In our group coaching, we encourage cross-fertilization and influence between the various cultures represented.

EVALUATING GEC EFFECTIVENESS

Group coaches always ask themselves, "How do I gauge how effective the coaching experience has been?" With a culturally diverse group the answer may appear more ambiguous and subtle. We have found some indicators, which are a combination of process and results. They include:

- The energy in the room—this can vary from an excited buzz to an empathetic silence, creating profound human sharing.
- Greater individual clarity and personal commitment to values, goals, and priorities.
- Implementation of action or development plans.
- Improved individual and/or group performance.
- Ongoing, spontaneous collaboration between group members over time.
- Coachees disseminating their experience and learning by building a coaching culture—down, up, and across—in their organizations.

Sometimes, however, the answer can be plain and simple, as the following example shows. During a recent group coaching day in Singapore, involving six banking executives from around the world, there was a lot of discussion among a mainly extrovert group. Sanjay, an Indian participant, although clearly engaged, had noticeably little airtime compared to his colleagues. Fairly early on, the coach started to prompt him during discussion: "And what are your thoughts, Sanjay?" Each time, Sanjay would neatly summarize and provide a definitive observation or question to the group in one or two laser-like sentences. The first time, the group fell silent, simultaneously surprised and impressed by the usually quiet Sanjay's insight. The second time they started to laugh and said, "He's good!" The third time Sanjay was asked for his input, he paused and said, "Well, I just have one question . . ." and then delivered a question that cut to the core of the issue and shifted the group significantly in a different direction. The group laughed, "He's *really* good!" The real breakthrough, however, came when the group was just about to launch into its usual energetic discussion. Sebastian, an Australian executive, stopped mid-sentence and pleaded, "Actually . . . Sanjay . . . it would be great if you could save us all a lot of hot air and time . . . and tell us what's your take on this?" The group then worked with Sanjay to help him uncover the motivation and develop the strategies that would enable him to volunteer his views, observations, and questions more readily, without waiting for an explicit invitation. The Australian, who had perhaps previously viewed his Asian counterparts as more compliant, had the opportunity to interpret that apparent behavior in a new and more favorable light. The genuine concern of the Western colleagues also gave Sanjay (and the other Asians in the group) the opportunity to see how his colleagues genuinely valued his contribution and cared about his development.

This story exemplifies how, through the process of group coaching, executives from diverse cultures and with diverse personalities can work through many of the leadership challenges faced in today's ethnographically complex organizations. As the Air Institute GEC survey showed, cultural stereotypes abound and can permeate the expectations and perceptions of executives as well as coaches. The process of creating the time and space to observe and discuss behaviors in a noncritical setting allows an expanded view of individuals and their cultures.

CONCLUSION

If we accept the GLOBE project's findings that, to succeed, global leaders need to influence across a diverse group and demonstrate cultural adaptability, GEC is certainly a dynamic forum in which to practice and embed these traits in a safe and supervised setting. The initial discomfort felt by most diverse GEC groups soon transforms into greater ease with uncertainty and unpredictability, as the notion of ambiguity becomes less threatening. This space of "not knowing," which seasoned executives are often loath to entertain a notion of, let alone enter, is subtly explored. This is most likely to happen when the group coaching process has been orchestrated as a reflective and developmental pursuit, in stark juxtaposition to the critical, high-stake context that prevails in corporations.

The IGLC's powerful approach of combining a symbolic, agenda-free portrait activity with the more concrete analysis of 360-degree feedback data allows for a holistic picture of the individual to emerge. Interestingly, executives are often fascinated that the largely unstructured portrait process, which calls for coaching staples such as curious questioning, deep listening, and suspending all judgment, often leads to just as rich and revealing a dialogue as the more familiar formal structure of reports and data. The exercise can free executives to use more informal and less linear approaches more spontaneously and frequently in their conversations with people. The reflective space and process of understanding these nuances in the group coaching context increases participants' self-awareness when they return to the workplace, sharpening their sensitivity and acuity in observing and addressing the inherent potential that diversity offers.

When executives are thrown together in a room, for an hour or for a day, they are automatically tempted to move into task focus and problem solving. Add cultural diversity and the potential for miscommunication is high. A good group coach needs strong facilitation skills, a thorough understanding of the differences and possible interplay between directive and nondirective coaching and facilitation, and the ability to judge if and when to shift between these different roles—all the while maintaining a safe holding environment in which coachees explore, reflect, and take their own path toward becoming more effective global leaders.

NOTES

1. Javidan, M., Dorfman, P. W., de Luque, M. S., and Hourse, R. J. (2006). "In the Eye of the Beholder: Cross Cultural Lessons in Leadership from Project GLOBE." *Academy of Management Perspectives*, February 2006, pp. 67–90.
2. Nicholas, J. and Twaddell, K. (2009). *Group Executive Coaching: 2008 Global Survey*. Singapore: The Air Institute.
3. Kluttz, L. September (2002). SHRM/Fortune Survey on the Changing Face of Diversity.
4. Ludeman, K. and Erlandson, E. (2004). "Coaching the Alpha Male." *Harvard Business Review*, 82(5), pp. 58–67.
5. Kets de Vries, M. (2006). *The Leader on the Couch*. San Francisco, CA: Jossey-Bass.
6. Hofstede, G. (1980). *Culture's Consequences: International Differences in Work-Related Values*. London: Sage.
7. Javidan, M., Dorfman, P. W., de Luque, M. S., and Hourse, R. J. (2006). "In the Eye of the Beholder: Cross Cultural Lessons in Leadership from Project GLOBE." *Academy of Management Perspectives*, February 2006, pp. 67–90.
8. Javidan, M., Dorfman, P. W., de Luque, M. S. and Hourse, R. J. (2006). "In the Eye of the Beholder: Cross Cultural Lessons in Leadership from Project GLOBE." *Academy of Management Perspectives*, February 2006, pp. 67–90.

9. Javidan, M., Dorfman, P. W., de Luque, M. S., and Hourse, R. J. (2006). "In the Eye of the Beholder: Cross Cultural Lessons in Leadership from Project GLOBE." *Academy of Management Perspectives,* February 2006, pp. 67–90.
10. Nisbett, R. E. (2003). *The Geography of Thought: How Asians and Westerners Think Differently ... and Why.* New York: Simon & Schuster.
11. Fukuyama, F. (1992). *The End of History and the Last Man.* New York: Free Press.
12. Huntington, S. P. (1996). *The Clash of Civilizations and the Remaking of World Order.* New York: Simon & Schuster.

CONCLUSION: TURNING THE COACHING KALEIDOSCOPE

MANFRED F. R. KETS DE VRIES, ELIZABETH FLORENT-TREACY, KONSTANTIN KOROTOV, AND LAURA GUILLÉN

A young Zen student approached his teacher, and asked, "If I work very hard and conscientiously, how long will it take for me to find Zen?" The master thought hard, then replied, "Ten years." The student said, "But what if I work very, very hard and really apply myself to learn fast—how long will it then take?" "Well, in that case," said the master, "it will take 20 years." "But, if I really, really work at it. How long would it take then?" "Thirty years," replied the master. "But, master, I do not understand," said the confused student. "Each time I say I will work harder, you say it will take me longer. Why is that?" "Because," replied the Zen master, "when you have one eye on the goal, you only have one eye on the path."

Like the quest for Zen, the kind of coaching we advocate is neither a quick fix nor an easy undertaking. It takes time to understand the underlying dynamics affecting individual and organizational behavior. We are not interested in Band-Aid remedies. We want people to take a systemic view and look beneath the surface. The ability to do this necessitates using ourselves as an instrument and listening with the "third ear." We see coaching processes as platforms for this type of self-development, helping leaders to manage their careers throughout the professional life cycle.

We have always argued that human behavior is much less rational than is assumed by traditional students of organizations. As we have set out to explain in this book, executives are not rational decision makers. An increasing number of people are asking themselves whether conventional teaching in management has become obsolete. The *Homo economicus*—that incredible optimizer of benefits and costs—is no longer a believable concept. One of the chapters in this book specifically discusses how management science and the clinical approach can be productively combined for addressing the needs of the ever more complex executive work. Recent findings from neuroscience, contemporary psychoanalysis, cognition, emotions, and network contagion, clearly demonstrate that we have to pay more attention to out-of-awareness behavior. There is more to all of us than meets the eye. We are very susceptible to cognitive and affective distortions—as the recent financial meltdown has proved.

Modern managerial thinking proclaims that management development means becoming better, more autonomous, more authentic and more aware as a person. As the traditional models of organizational analysis alone did not provide us with the tools to obtain deep insight into individual and organizational functioning, we have advocated the use of a more clinical model, thus accepting the presence of unconscious processes and defenses, and the impact of early influences on our development. Leadership coaching practices within this clinical paradigm can promote small inner revolutions that augment the understanding of self and others and trace an accurate picture of how to face career challenges, and make the most of professional and personal opportunities. Adopting this perspective reflects the new vision of management and gives prominence to individuals and their inner theater, motivations, values, goals, and beliefs.

The clinical paradigm that we are advocating is based on the assumption that many aspects of the individuals' inner theater remain in the shadows. And coaching is precisely about shedding light onto these unaware spots that are intimately related to our notion of self. Thus coaching is about increasing people's awareness, which requires patience and involves raising uncomfortable and challenging questions. When questions about careers, behavior, needs, fears, or hopes are raised, a coach has to deal with the work-related identities of a coachee, while maintaining a holistic view, looking at the individual as a whole, including the complexities of personal developmental history, family, culture, and societal expectations, as well as team and organizational realities. At high levels of responsibility in organizations, the separation of work and life is more illusory: executives continue working when they are away from their office, and ignoring issues beyond the office walls may lead to missed challenges and opportunities. However, coaching discussions that involve the whole person are much more complicated at higher levels for the coach and the coachee. This is also an issue for the organization, which in many cases is the coach's client.

The process of self-enlightenment that we advocate is especially important in times of economic crisis and turbulence. Organizations no longer have sole responsibility for managing individuals' careers; professionals must take charge of their own development. With this in mind, the objective of this book, a continuation of our previous work,[1] is the better understanding of organizational life, executive coaching, and leadership development. We hope to contribute further to the conceptual understanding and descriptive accounts of what it takes to help people maximize their potential and create better places to work. We have tried to show that leader and leadership development need organizations and individuals to be attuned, and how they can work together to render personal and organizational growth.

BRINGING THE INDIVIDUAL BACK INTO THE ORGANIZATION

To achieve a communion of individual and organizational developmental needs, we go to great lengths to bring people in all their complexity back into the organizations. We want to encourage executives to strive to create authentizotic organizations, places where people feel at their best, and give their best.[2] And hope, optimism, trust, self-efficacy, resilience, and a "can do" attitude are what characterize such organizations.

Apart from coaching executives to pay attention to the psychological processes that affect the individual, we also make a great effort to imbue them with obtaining a systemic outlook; to have them recognize existing interdependencies. In our desire to help create authentizotic organizations, we encourage creative, out-of-the-box thinking. We want to contribute to organizations where people are prepared to try new things, with the implicit understanding that mistakes are acceptable. Learning is impossible without accepting mistakes. Learning is hindered by blame and fear, leading to paralysis and protective inaction; we can only learn from failure if we face it squarely. We want to be part of, or contribute to, organizations where people can fail forward.

We are astutely aware of the fact that executives in authentizotic organizations are in pursuit of excellence, and never satisfied with the status quo. They have an ongoing commitment to learning and development at all levels. In these organizations, there is a climate of openness and information is accessible to all. Furthermore, executives in these organizations retain the ability to play. They like being with each other; they like working together. As we have pointed out in the final part of this book, coaching may help individuals and teams engage in creating organizations where these conditions are met. Moreover, it is precisely the coaching culture that encourages learning and experimentation, helps people deal with mistakes creatively and productively, and turns work into discovery and fun.

Many of the contributors to this book have noted that to create a coaching culture, senior managers need to recognize the advantages such a culture will bring to today's highly complex, diverse, and global organizations. If leadership is distributed, and coaching offered on all organizational levels to leaders with varying profiles, the benefits are much more likely to cross barriers and demolish individual, team, and organizational resistance.

The chapters in this book have explored various aspects related to the place and role of psychodynamic/systemic approaches to leader and leadership development, talent management, and executive coaching. We have learned from experience that taking this perspective provides executives with more insight about themselves, other people in their organization, the organization itself, and the world at large. Such knowledge establishes a foundation to help them embark on transformational journeys, transforming their attitudes and behaviors. Furthermore, the book illustrates how this transformational energy extends beyond individuals to create better work cultures, where people can be, and perform, their very best.

In this book, we have explained our particular affinity for techniques of group intervention, although we do acknowledge the value of one-on-one coaching. We have discovered that an important means of inducing individual and organizational change—to create tipping points where people recognize a need for change—is through vicarious learning and network contagion, the kind of peer pressure, or normalizing, effect, in which certain behaviors, or the social acceptance of certain behaviors, will be transmitted across a network of the people in the group.[3] In our work with executives, we have discovered the power of publicly stated intentions, moods, and actions and how they affect others. We know the importance of secondary gains (unconscious contrary scenarios) as deterrents to change; we have learned the power of hidden commitments (unconscious assumptions guiding behavior).[4] Taking these below-the-surface processes into consideration, our group coaching intervention technique has proved very effective in creating tipping points for changing people and organizations.

One of the reasons we are strongly advocating group intervention techniques is that one of the challenges of contemporary organizations is helping people to work together in highly complex, global, diverse, matrix-like structures. The task is made even more difficult by the need for contemporary organizations to harmonize different generations with different aspirations, motivations, and developmental needs. In these virtual, global organizations, we also need to deal with cultural differences. The dangers of silo-like behavior, turf fights, and sub-optimization are ever present. We believe that organizations willing to embrace the group coaching idea go beyond silo formation, become more boundaryless, and, most importantly, retain strategic agility. Bolstered by the group coaching process, executives are able to manage diverse, virtual teams, execute interrelated tasks, build lateral relationships, and engage in true knowledge management. Group coaching interventions build trust, constructive conflict resolution, commitment, accountability, and produce better results.

DEVELOPING PEOPLE WHO DEVELOP PEOPLE

The contributors to this book have raised issues related to the importance of the development of leadership coaches as professionals helping executives and organizations create better places to work and succeed. Not only are we trying to create authentizotic organizations, we are trying to develop people who are passionate about developing people—to help them find ways of regenerating to guide them on a journey to personal insight, by asking the right questions, and suggesting other ways of looking at knotty situations. The kind of leadership coaching we advocate helps develop leaders who are not only honest and true to others but, more importantly, are honest and true to themselves, so that they practice value-driven, authentic leadership. It is easy to see madness in others; effective coaches need to be able to recognize this madness in themselves.

Helping leaders find their true motivations and genuine beliefs—being authentic—can be a difficult and sometimes overwhelming task. It necessitates a high degree of trust. We have advocated the kind of leadership coaching that helps executives open up emotionally and share personal histories. Through these explorations—of their own and others' personal inner journeys—executives discover uncharted sides of themselves. An examination of executives' personal history provides the coach, and coachees, with a means to identify ineffective and effective patterns of behavior. At the heart of our approach is our belief in the idea of self-actualization; that people are willing to improve, evolve, grow,

248

and change continuously. This inner motivation is the raw material from which any subsequent effective intervention is fashioned.

We hope that this book will add to the development of the coaching profession, a task that is commensurate in importance with the growing role of coaching in modern HR, learning and development, and talent management practices. We want to contribute to developing coaches who can listen with the "third ear" to identify the root causes that will enable fundamental change. This implies an orientation steeped in psychodynamic theory, plus a deep understanding of systemic issues. Leadership coaches will only be truly effective if they take a holistic point of view and can extend their craft from the dyad to the triad, and beyond.

The importance to their organization of people who receive coaching support, the depth and possible sensitivity of the issues raised through coaching, and the cost of coaching, mean that coaches come in for a lot of attention (and occasionally suspicion) from the organization. To this extent, coaches are comparable to external consultants. They meet with numerous people, gather a lot of data, and have a potential impact on decision-makers. However, unlike consultants, the coaches who will have the greatest impact, we feel, will also go deep into the internal world of individual executives—and also unlike consultants, they do not share their findings, ideas, or recommendations with a wider audience. The situation is additionally complicated by the lack of conceptual clarity of the nature of relationships between the organization, the executive, and the coach. Coaches need to set boundaries and protect coachees' intimacy to increase their willingness to explore all future opportunities, remaining truthful to themselves and building trustful relationships with others.

On the one hand, the coach is a service provider, and the organization (which eventually pays the coach's bill) is its client. One major concern of people being coached at the organization's initiative is that they may be manipulated toward a development plan that is suspiciously aligned with the organization's needs. Performance-development tensions are a major obstacle to overcome for successful coaching interventions. On the other hand, the recipients of the service are specific executives. The services of the coach should help executives to be more successful in exercising their professional functions, so that ultimately the organization will be more successful at achieving its goals. Although the organization and the executives often discuss the goals of coaching interventions, some of the really important issues affecting executives' performance only become evident after the process has begun. Moreover, confidentiality principles limit the feedback a leadership coach can give the organization, making it more difficult for the organization to monitor the coach's performance, the impact of coaching on its executives, and the feasibility of spending the organization's money on the coaching process. Very often the organization has to rely on what coaches choose to communicate to evaluate the effort and effectiveness of the coach and the value of the intervention. Whatever is said, the boundaries will remain fuzzy. The leadership coach is expected to deal with quite knotty situations. Given the blurring of boundaries, despite attempts to assess coaching effectiveness, the best means of doing so is still open to debate. We predict, however, that measuring the benefits of coaching will be increasingly placed at the top of the organizational agenda.

AUTHENTIC COACHING FOR AUTHENTIZOTIC ORGANIZATIONS

For centuries people have practiced skills akin to coaching—counselors, priests, confidants, psychotherapists, psychiatrists, and psychoanalysts are all involved in helping people guide their lives and achieve their personal or professional goals. However, the leadership coach is a very new entity. While leadership coaching is still being formed and shaped as a profession, it has become a highly visible activity, not least in terms of financial turnover.[5] It is an attractive occupation that allows aspiring coaches to realign their knowledge, develop competencies, and use them in a new, creative way. However, the absence of real barriers to entry makes the profession vulnerable to abuse. We believe that the contributors to this book help set the standard for genuine and excellent coaching practice.

Development is about change: it involves learning new things and unlearning some old ones, building new networks, presenting new stories about the self to the outside world, and building a new identity.[6] Unlearning or letting go is precisely what managers do worst, because they are often unwilling to give up the things that made them successful in the past and try out new behaviors. This book has argued that when leadership coaches are engaged to help with executive development, they become change agents at an individual level (working with a particular executive), at a team level, and at an organization level.

One way in which the success of coaching interventions can be assessed is the willingness of organizational participants to participate in so-called identity laboratories. The suspension of day-to-day order and the normal work identity of the coachee means that the latter has an opportunity to think without being restricted by the norms, expectations, traditions, hierarchical rules, and other realities of the organization. In the context of teams, the challenges of engaging in such "laboratory" work are potentially bigger. But although the risks are higher, so are the potential benefits. In this context, executive coaches act as facilitators for productive discussion among top executives, dealing with the issues that the organization faces and the ways the organization's leaders handle them.[7] The aim is to improve general collaboration and the effectiveness of executive teams at seizing organizational opportunities or handling challenges. Inevitably, personal agendas, potential conflicts, misunderstandings, or mismanaged expectations need to be dealt with. Issues of trust and psychological safety are even more evident in team than in individual coaching.

Judging by the growing acceptance of coaching by individual executives and organizations, as well as the amount of new literature on the subject, leadership coaches are expected to play a powerful role in the development of executives and the creation of successful organizations. The evolution of the coaching profession, as well as practitioners' expectations, call for further exploration of this nascent field. In its early stages, leadership coaching was seen as a remedial tool to help executives deal with issues preventing them from moving forward or retaining their jobs (for example, dealing with gaps in interpersonal skills, abrasive management styles, or challenges from others). It has now become accepted as a powerful support and developmental resource for successful executives who want to move ahead in their careers and lives. Today's emphasis is on making good people even better.

Furthermore, recent views on the role of coaching in organizations suggest that it can be seen as an intervention that leads to increased organizational effectiveness, by helping leaders sharpen their focus and raise their awareness of what is happening in the organization, in the organizational culture, and within themselves, making necessary adjustments to the way they relate to and work with people.[8] Huge doses of authenticity and others' acceptance and understanding are needed to do this. Leaders struggle to "do things," while coaches ask them to inject more reflection into the highly action-oriented contexts in which they function. The ultimate goal of guiding executives in this direction is to arrive at more sensible, thought-through decisions. More often than not, reflection is the missing ingredient in leadership effectiveness and excellence, making coaching (the providers being internal or external) almost indispensable in many organizations.

Broadening the portfolio of executive development with coaching-related interventions and topics may be seen as a very positive trend—a way of building human and especially social capital. Executives who are offered coaching opportunities through their organizations will be better prepared for using the tools offered to them. Organizations, whose HR, learning and development professionals, and talent managers have an appreciation of coaching benefits, will make better decisions when buying coaching services. And despite a certain resistance toward working with an internal coach, executives and employees can still receive valuable support from people who have mastered some tools of the trade. Last but not least, coaching may be an interesting answer to the "What's next?" question for HR, learning and development professionals, and talent managers, as well as senior executives from other functions who may explore coaching as an interesting new career avenue.

Trust and psychological safety are necessary for any coaching intervention to be effective. Many executives do not perceive their working environment to be a psychologically safe place to explore their identities and behaviors, creating problems in establishing a coaching culture.[9] This may explain some of the challenges of offering internal coaching. Disclosure is difficult, or even impossible, if people feel that what is disclosed may affect their position, status, or future in the organization. However, this is not to suggest that external coaches immediately gain trust and respect from potential coachees. External coaches may not always be ready to respond to the needs of the individuals they work with, because of the specifics of the training or the coaching tradition in which they work. How the roles of internal and external coaches differ and under what circumstances one approach is preferable over the other need further attention. Those who are trained in psychodynamic/systemic approaches to coaching, for instance, may still face resistance when they bring their discovery and experimentation apparatus into coaching projects. Effective psychodynamically oriented coaches, however, may welcome the resistance, as it can provide valuable information. After all, how much do we learn from people who agree with us?

With the coaching process having transformed from a remedial to a developmental function, coaches work increasingly with successful executives assigned to challenging new roles, high-potential employees, and senior executives. From the nature of the coachees, it is easy to imagine the potential impact that these coaching professionals might have on organizations. Coaching that forms part of executive development inevitably deals with exploring executives' sense of self, the fit between their inner desires and role expectations, as well as congruence or dissonance with other important aspects of their life. Moving to a new organizational role or to a deeper understanding of how to manage and lead people, teams, and organizations more effectively, while maintaining a high level of subjective well-being (or happiness), forces executives to think about who they are, what they do, why they do what they do, the types of relationships they develop at work and beyond, the "dos" and "don'ts" that they accept unquestioningly, and the things that they should let go, stop doing and, sometimes, even stop thinking about.

With all these considerations, it is clear that there are still many unanswered questions about the impact and challenges of coaching interventions. We still do not know enough about the interaction between the science and art of coaching. Moreover, we do not know enough about the effectiveness of various types of coaching processes. We do not know enough about the coaches themselves: how they enter the profession, how they build expertise within it, and how they continue developing and growing. In this book, we have attempted to shed further light on these issues by collecting insights from the inside: learning from the experiences of the people who are involved in offering, using, buying, or studying coaching services. We wanted to address important contemporary coaching issues for coaches, coachees, and coaching clients. As a profession, coaching depends on the ability of people to learn from practice and from one another.

Kaleidoscopes are named from the Greek words, *kalos* or beautiful, *eidos* or form, and *scopos* or watcher. So a kaleidoscope is a "beautiful form watcher"—an instrument that creates reflections of reflections. In a kaleidoscope, the lines and colors of simple shapes are multiplied by mirrors into a visually stimulating vortex. The characteristics and background factors of a kaleidoscope are not stable but change with time and context. The same observation can be made about the chapters in this book. Like a kaleidoscope, this book presents a plethora of pictures, each of which allows for further scientific analysis or practical considerations.

Like kaleidoscopes, in this book, we have created pictures that address different challenges, expose various recent research findings, and share insightful reflections on the actual practice of coaching. Within this picture gallery, we present our approach for understanding effective coaching practices in both educational and organizational settings. We deal with coaching processes through the experiences of their protagonists, coaches and coachees. We delineate some very personal journeys of what becoming a coach means, commenting on the challenges and learning experiences met along the way. We balance the pictures from the coachee perspective and address how group coaching is experienced by the participants themselves. Finally, we explore how group coaching mechanisms can affect the creation and sustainability of a coaching culture at team and organizational levels.

We notice that the practice of coaching has many kaleidoscopic properties. The contributors to this book demonstrate how coaching shifts and transforms. As shape shifters, coaches help people to visualize and transform themselves. But coaches themselves do not escape this transforming experience. The practice of coaching is developing even more quickly than attempts to study the phenomenon. We are likely to see even more images from the various views and experiences of coaching. The challenge and task, however, is to stop and contemplate what we have created, so that we can learn from our experience and enjoy it. As coaches, we need to practice what we preach. Quiet reflection will contribute to even more effective action and may even lead to wisdom. As Confucius once said, "By three methods we may learn wisdom: first, by reflection, which is noblest; second, by imitation, which is easiest; and third by experience, which is the bitterest."

NOTES

1. Kets de Vries, M. F. R., Korotov, K., and Forent-Treacy, E., (2007). *Coach and Couch*. Palgrave Macmillan.
2. Kets de Vries, M. F. R. (2001). "Creating Authentizotic Organizations: Well-Functioning Individuals in Vibrant Companies." *Human Relations*, 54(1), 101–111.
3. Christakis, N. and Fowler, J. (2009). *Connected: The Surprising Power of our Social Networks and how they Shape our Lives*. Boston: Little Brown.
4. Kegan, R. and Lahey, L. (2009). *Immunity to Change: How to Overcome It and Unlock the Potential in Yourself and Your Organization*. Boston: Harvard Business School Press.
5. Coutu, D. and Kauffman, C. (2009). "What Can Coaches Do for You?" *Harvard Business Review*, 87(1), 91–97.
6. Day, D. and Lance, C. (2004). "Understanding the Development of Leadership Complexity." In D. Day, S. Zaccaro, and S. Halpin (Eds) *Leader Development for Transforming Organizations*. Mahwa, NJ: Lawrence Erlbaum Associates, pp. 41–69; Hall, D. T. (2004). "Self-Awareness, Idenity, and Leader Development." in D. Day, S. Zaccaro, and S. Halpin (Eds) *Leader Development for Transforming Organizations*. Mahwah, NJ: Lawrence Erlbaum Associates, pp. 153–176.
7. Kets de Vries, M. F. R. (2005). "Leadership Group Coaching in Action: The Zen of Creating High Performance Teams." *The Academy of Management Executive*, 19(1), 61–76; Kets de Vries, M. F. R. (2008). "Leadership Coaching and Organizational Transformation: Effectiveness in a World of Paradoxes." *INSEAD Working Paper* 2008/71/EFE.
8. Kets de Vries, M. F. R. (2010). *Reflections on Organizations*. London: Wiley.
9. Korotov, K. (2005). "Identity Laboratory." INSEAD PhD Dissertation. Fontainebleau, France: INSEAD.

INDEX

Page numbers in **bold** refer to figures, page numbers in *italic* refer to tables.